CU00704385

Derbeians of
Distinction

Derbeians of Distinction

Maxwell Craven

The Breedon Books
Publishing Company
Derby

First published in Great Britain by
The Breedon Books Publishing Company Limited
Breedon House, 44 Friar Gate, Derby, DE1 1DA.
1998

© Maxwell Craven 1998

All Rights Reserved. No part of this publication may be reproduced,
stored in a retrieval system, or transmitted in any form, or by any
means, electronic, mechanical, photocopying, recording or otherwise
without the prior permission in writing of the Copyright holders, nor
be otherwise circulated in any form or binding or cover other than in
which it is published and without a similar condition being imposed
on the subsequent publisher.

ISBN 1 85983 089 7

Printed and finished by Butler & Tanner Ltd., Selwood Printing
Works, Caxton Road, Frome, Somerset.

Colour separations by RPS Ltd, Leicester.

Cover printing by Lawrence-Allen Colour Printers,
Weston-super-Mare, Avon.

Contents

. . . .

Introduction
7

. . . .

Abbreviations
10

. . . .

Biographies A-Z
13

. . . .

Index classified by callings
229

. . . .

To:
Cornelia,
born at about the same time as
this book

Acknowledgements

Individuals whose information I have used in writing biographies in this book have been in the main acknowledged under the relevant entry; those I have omitted to mention, I take here the opportunity to record my gratitude. Also to my sister Penny, Mrs Jenny Ewers and Mrs Shirley Forman for their sterling work in typing the MS (and interpreting my writing!) Acknowledgement is also due to Anton Rippon and his colleagues, my publisher. My thanks too and appreciation go to those of my former colleagues at Derby Museum who have helped with information (especially David Fraser, Diana Peake, Anneke Bambery and Jane Wallis), to Linda Owen and the staff of the Local Studies Library and to all those others who have been so informative and helpful during the years I have been collecting personal information about Derby people I owe a great debt of thanks. Finally, to my wife Carole, for her great help and forbearance, despite the demands of motherhood, I accord my heartfelt gratitude and appreciation.

Photographic credits:

Photographs have been supplied by Derby Museum, Derby Local Studies Library, Derby Evening Telegraph, W.W.Winter, Michael Leveaux and from the author's own collection.

Introduction

NY compilation of biographies is going to be a disappointment to some and an *embarass de richesse* to others. It is difficult to know who to include, and who to leave out. Also, however conversant one thinks one is about the history of Derby, there are bound to be people who deserve inclusion in such a work who one just has not come across. In the present work, the names included are entirely a personal selection, yet one has tried to cover all walks of life, and to include the notorious as well as the glorious. The purpose of the biographies is to give the reader the basic facts, often in ruthlessly compressed form, of a large number of men and women, all now dead, but firmly connected with Derby. Unfortunately the scope of the book is such that it has largely been necessary to eschew anecdotes. Further, some people need more space than others, yet one has had to work within strict parameters, and in a way, the more famous a man or woman, the more one has had to emphasise the Derby connection over other aspects available in detail elsewhere. There are not a great many women included either. This is not because one wishes to exclude them, but is a product of a society where, over the last thousand years, women have had to be exceptional in order to escape the constraints the social framework of the time placed upon them.

A great many people are famous locally, but unknown further afield. The approximate criterion in this work is that those included have had a national (or international) dimension to their careers or notability. Other criteria have been that the subject must have been locally born; have lived for a reasonably substantial period locally; be descended from a Derby family or be associated with Derby in the main aspect of their careers. Thus: men like John Flamsteed FRS (first Astronomer Royal) were locally born, but made their careers away from Derby; men like John Whitehurst FRS (1713-1788) lived for most of their lives in the town; men like Graham Sutherland OM (1903-1980) were descended from local people and men like Sir Henry Royce Bt. (d.1933) never lived in Derby, yet had a major impact on the history not only of the City but much further afield. Where possible, I have attempted to include new insights and aspects of the subjects not generally known, although with some 300 biographies, this represents only a minority. Others have proved difficult (in the limited time I had available to produce this book) to unearth much detail about. Sportsmen in particular have presented difficulties. Yet such people are included, for readers may be able to furnish more information or may be sufficiently interested to research such people further themselves – there may be a potential university thesis subject or two lurking amongst the sketchier entries!

I have tried to write to a formula, rather based on obituary writing, of furnishing firstly, the reasons why a person's career marks them out as exceptional in some way, then providing details of birth, family, origins and early career and ending with their death and anything not covered already. Occasionally I have varied this format, but it is the usual pattern. I have also tried to provide more information, where possible, of a subject's parents, family and connections. These rarely appear in the more usual biographical dictionaries, and such aspects are often casually dismissed by today's commentators as 'gossip' or 'irrelevancies'. Yet that is to judge such people by the standards of today.

Quite apart from the reader's natural curiosity as to whether, for instance, Lord Roe was a self-made man, or that Niall Mac-Dermott MP was an Irish Prince or that Ald.

Cokayne was a scion of our ancient gentry, the family connections of these men and so many others were of crucial importance in the shaping of their careers and indeed in influencing the careers of their talented kin. Without extensive connections with other professional and gentry families, for instance, Joseph Wright (whose bicentenary was celebrated in 1997) would never have been able to establish himself so effortlessly as a portrait painter. Similarly, ties of friendship and business (which I have tried to cross reference) played a crucial role in people's careers – although nepotism and 'the old school tie' are today derided as invidious, and the promotion of friends and relatives can attract often unwarranted accusations of 'sleaze'. It is, after all, as much human nature as the hereditary principle or human competitiveness, and no amount of legislation can outlaw it. In past eras, such limitations were freely acknowledged as part of the way in which life at all levels was lived. One might add that, in 24 years working in Derby, one has been approached countless times by people researching their family history – the second most popular British pastime after gardening, we are told, if rather patronisingly frowned on as *infra dig,* by some academics and archivists – and many of the subjects of these biographies have cropped up. By trying to say more about their ancestry, siblings and offspring, one hopes that amateur genealogists might get some help and enjoyment therefrom. In many cases, I am probably in possession of far more information than appears in these pages, and no one should be deterred from enquiring further. Again, I am always pleased to receive more information, and the reader must feel free to supplement or correct my knowledge. For those of an Heraldic turn, however, there is little in the text, but where subjects of this book are known to be armigerous their details may be found in my *Derbyshire Armory,* published by the *Derbyshire Record Society* (Vol. XVII (1991) Chesterfield), which is still available.

I have tried to include not only people whose achievements are obvious, but also those who have received recognition, above a certain level. Thus I have included all Derby-descended Peers, baronets, bishops, Lord Mayors of London, knights, prelates and senior (general) officers on the basis that, however undeserving such honours may seem to people today, the sovereign or prime minister of the day rarely conferred such distinction purely vicariously. Space has prevented me from including all of Derby's MPs, but I have mentioned all those of the 20th century, most 19th century ones, and a reasonable selection of men who served in earlier times. Also, I have included MPs for constituencies other than Derby who were Derby-born, and most who were of Derby descent. I have also tried to include people of humbler extraction, like sportsmen, craftsmen and artists. The craftsmen, especially, form an unsung group of local people, yet in their time were amongst the very best, and their work can still be seen today locally and in some cases all over the country. I have also tried to include a good number of men and women who have died in the last two decades. If I have failed to do justice to anyone, however, then I apologise to those to whom it matters; the sheer quantity of material means that there are inevitably going to be errors or omissions. I have, however, generally refrained from subjective comment. On the rare occasions where I have deviated from this rule, it is because I have felt confident enough to do so.

At the end of each entry I have furnished a selection of references to sources where more information is easily available, such as the Dictionary of National Biography (DNB – of which a new and completely revised edition is shortly to be forthcoming, to which the author has contributed lives of Sir Thomas Lombe, John Lombe and Joseph Pickford) *Who's Who/Who Was Who,* Kelly's *Handbooks,* Burke's publications, etc. Where the information is new or the subject is unpublished I have tried to give some of the sources for the information, although this will be more technical and perhaps more difficult of access. Some of the more obscure secondary local sources can also be suspect, or of dubious value, too; in such cases the reader, like me, will have to use his or her own judgement in evaluating it.

Where subjects have been Mayors of Derby, or related to such, I have mentioned it. The Mayor's Officer for Derby and I have long been collecting career and family information on ex-Mayors (and, before them, ex-Bailiffs), and a file is kept on them at the Museum. Any fresh information or connections in this area would be most welcome; who knows, perhaps Derby should have a Millennium account compiled of its First Citizens?

I have been rash enough to write on a previous occasion *(Illustrated History of Derby* [Breedon Books, 1988, 2nd Impression 1990] p238) that a City's history is nothing without the story of its people; this book is a first attempt to bring together the more interesting or prominent of them throughout Derby's long history, in the hope that it will lighten dark corners, inform and, perhaps, reflect some extra credit on our city. As a companion volume, perhaps we should also have (as Birmingham has had for many years, courtesy of its local paper) a *Who's Who in Derby* to chronicle its *living* men and women of distinction!

Maxwell Craven
Derby, 1998

List of Abbreviations

This is included to help the reader make sense of the large number of official abbreviated styles which, with the recession of Empire and diminution of Honours, are much less familiar than they were. Also included are incidental abbreviations, and those appearing in the source references. If I have left any out, the reader is asked to accept the author's apology; the smallest of the Oxford Series of English Dictionaries have lists of most common abbreviations, and may be referred to with profit in the event of an omission here. Note that some of these are no longer in use.

ADC	Aide-de-Camp
Adml.	Admiral
AFC	Air Force Cross
Ald.	Alderman
AM	Master of Arts
ARA	Associate of the Royal Academy
ARCA	Associate of the Royal College of Art
ARIBA	Associate of the Royal Institute of British Architects
ARMS	Associate of the Royal Society of Miniature Painters
ASB	Alternative Service Book
ASC	Anglo-Saxon Chronicle
ATS	Auxiliary Training Service
AVM	Air Vice Marshall
b	Born
Barts	St Bartholomew's Hospital (London)
BA	Bachelor of Arts
BAOR	British Army of Occupation (Rhine)
BBCSO	BBC Symphony Orchestra
BD	Bachelor of Divinity
BEM	British Empire Medal
Bn	Battalion
Brig.	Brigadier
BRNC	Britannia Royal Naval College
BSc	Bachelor of Science
Bt	Baronet
Capt	Captain
CB	Commander of the Bath

CBE	Commander of the British Empire
Cdr	Commander (Navy)
CE	Civil Engineer
CEGB	Central Electricity Generating Board
CH	Companion of Honour
C-in-C	Commander-in-Chief
Cllr.	Councillor
CME	Chief Mechanical Engineer
CMG	Commander of Order of St Michael and St George
Col.	Colonel
CStJ	Commander of the Venerable Order of St John of Jerusalem
d	died
DA	*Derbyshire Advertiser*
DAJ	Derbyshire Archaeological Society's *Journal*
DBE	Dame of the Order of the British Empire
DCL	Doctor of Civil Laws
DCM	Distinguished Conduct Medal
DCR	*Derby & Chesterfield Reporter*
DD	Doctor of Divinity
dem	demolished
DET	*Derby Evening Telegraph*
DFC	Distinguished Flying Cross
DGStJ	Dame Grand Cross of the Order of St John of Jerusalem
Div.	Division
DL	Deputy Lieutenant
DLC	*Derbyshire Life & Countryside*
DLitt.	Doctor of Literature
DM	*Derby Mercury*
DMus	Doctor of Music
DNB	*Dictionary of National Biography*
DPh	Doctor of Philosophy
Dr	Doctor
DRI	Derbyshire Royal Infirmary
DSC	Distinguished Service Cross
DSc	Doctor of Science
DSO	Distinguished Service Order
FASS	Fellow of the Antiquaries Society of Scotland
FF	Feet of Fines (Derbyshire)

FGS	Fellow of the Geographical Society		JP	Justice of the Peace
FLS	Fellow of the Linnaean Society		KB	Knight of the Bath
F/Lt.	Flight Lieutenant		KBE	Knight Commander of the British Empire
FMG	*Familae Minorum Gentium,* Hunter, J., 3 Vols. Harl. Society 1894-6		KC	King's Counsel
FRAeS	Fellow of the Royal Aeronautical Society		KCB	Knight Commander of the Bath
FRAM	Fellow of the Royal Academy of Music		KCH	Knight Commander of the Hanoverian Guelphic Order
FRCM	Fellow of the Royal College of Music		KCIE	Knight Commander of the Order of the Indian Empire
FRCO	Fellow of the Royal College of Organists		KCMG	Knight Commander of the Order of St Michael & St George
FRCP	Fellow of the Royal College of Physicians		KCSI	Knight Commander of the Order of the Star of India
FRCS	Fellow of the Royal College of Surgeons		KCVO	Knight Commander of the Royal Victorian Order
FRGS	Fellow of the Royal Geographical Society		KG	Knight of the Garter
FRIBA	Fellow of the Royal Institute of British Architects		KH	Knight of the Hanoverian Guelphic Order
FRS	Fellow of the Royal Society		KStJ	Knight of the Venerable Order of St John of Jerusalem
FSA	Fellow of the Society of Antiquaries		LCC	London County Council
FZS	Fellow of the Zoological Society		LLB	Bachelor of Laws
GBE	Knight Grand Cross of the Order of the British Empire		LLD.	Doctor of Laws
GC	George Cross		LLM	Master of Laws
GCMG	Knight Grand Cross of the Order of St Michael & St George		LMS	London Midland & Scottish (Railway)
GCSI	Knight Grand Cross of the Order of the Star of India		LRCP	Licentiate of the Royal College of Physicians
GCVO	Knight Grand Cross of the Royal Victorian Order		LSE	London School of Economics
GEC	General Electric Company		Lt.	Lieutenant
Gen.	General		Lt. Cdr.	Lieutenant Commander
Gent.	Gentleman		Lt.Col.	Lieutenant Colonel
GHQ	General Headquarters		Lt.Gen.	Lieutenant General
GNR	Great Northern Railway		MA	Master of Arts
GOC	General Officer Commanding		Maj.	Major
GP	General Practitioner		Maj.Gen.	Major General
Gp.Capt.	Group Captain		MB	Bachelor of Medicine
GPO	General Post Office		MBE	Member of the Order of the British Empire
GSO	General Service Officer		MBIM	Member of the British Institute of Management
GWR	Great Western Railway		MC	Military Cross
HEICS	Honourable East India Company		MD	Doctor of Medicine
Hon.	The Honourable/Honourary		MFH	Master of Fox Hounds
HRH	Her/His Royal Highness		MI	Memorial Inscription
i/c	in command of		MICE	Member of the Institute of Civil Engineers
Insp.	Inspector			

MILocoE	Member of the Institute of Locomotive Engineers	RBA	Royal Society of British Artists
MIME	Member of the Institute of Mining Engineers	RCD	Royal Crown Derby
		RE	Royal Engineers
MIMechE	Member of the Institute of Mechanical Engineers	Regt.	Regiment
		Rev.	Reverend
MM	Military Medal	RFA	Royal Field Artillery
MMD	*Modern Mayors of Derby* (2 vols) 1909-1936	RHA	Royal Horse Artillery
		RMA	Royal Military Academy
Most Rev	Most Reverend	RMC	Royal Medical Corps/Royal Military College
MP	Member of Parliament	RMS	Royal Society of Miniature Painters
MR	Midland Railway	RN	Royal Navy
MS	Master of Surgery; Society of Miniaturists	RNAS	Royal Naval Air Service
		RNVR	Royal Naval Volunteer Reserve
MSLR	Manchester, Sheffield and Lincolnshire Railway	RSBA	Royal Society of British Artists
		Rt. Hon.	Right Honourable
MVD	Master of Veterinary Medicine	Rt. Rev.	Right Reverend
NEH	New English Hymnal	Sgt.	Sergeant
NS	New Style	S/Ldr.	Squadron Leader
NUR	National Union of Railwaymen	SPG	Society for the Propagation of the Gospel
OBE	Officer of the Order of the British Empire	TUC	Trades' Union Council
		TD	Territorial Decoration
OC	Officer Commanding	unm.	unmarried
OM	Order of Merit	v.	von
PC	Privy Councillor; Police Constable	V/Adml.	Vice-Admiral
PhD	Doctor of Philosophy	VC	Victoria Cross
P O	Pilot Officer	VD	Volunteer Decoration
PPS	Parliamentary Private Secretary	Ven	Venerable
PRA	President of the Royal Academy	VRD	Volunteer Reserve Decoration
PRIBA	President of the Royal Institute of British Architects	VSTOL	Vertical/Short Take-off and Landing
		W/Cdr.	Wing Commander
Prof.	Professor	WRAC	Women's Royal Army Corps
QC	Queen's Counsel	WRAF	Women's Royal Air Force
RA	Royal Academician; Royal Artillery	WRNS	Women's Royal Naval Service
R/Adml.	Rear Admiral	yeo	Yeoman
RAF	Royal Air Force	YMCA	Young Men's Christian Association
RAFVR	Royal Air Force Volunteer Reserve		

ABNEY Sir William (1843-1920)

A photographic and educational pioneer, Sir William Abney was born at The Firs, Burton Road, Derby, 24 July 1843; his father Edward was a younger son of the old gentry family of Abney of Measham Hall and of Willesley (both then in Derbyshire) and was for very many years vicar of St Alkmund and Rural Dean of Derby. His wife Katherine (1813-86) was a daughter of Jedediah Strutt of Bridgehill House, Belper, a member of the great cotton-spinning dynasty. Edward was a friend of William Fox-Talbot, the photographic pioneer who was married to one of the daughters

of William Mundy of nearby Markeaton Hall and took the new art up with some enthusiasm. He also acted as the protégé of J.A.Warwick and Richard Keene (q.v.) who began the commercial exploitation of photography in Derby and it was this acquaintanceship which influenced William in interesting himself in photography.

However, in 1861 he was commissioned into the Royal Engineers, in India until 1867 then at Chatham where, in 1871, he was appointed instructor in telegraphy (the very subject in which

Warwick specialised at the Midland Railway, q.v.) at the School of Military Engineering, adding chemistry and photography to his responsibilities shortly afterwards. In 1877, Abney, by then a captain, joined the Science and Art Dept at South Kensington as an inspector of Science Schools. Over the following 30 years, as an officer of the Board of Education (he retired from the army in 1881) he massively strengthened the teaching and provision of science in schools: a spiritual heir of Erasmus Darwin (q.v.).

Simultaneously Abney pursued his photographic work, pioneering emulsions (leading to 'instant' photographs), the development of printing-out paper and most important of all, spectro-photography and related work which led directly to the development of colour photography.

In 1882, he received the Rumford Medal of the Royal Society, having been elected FRS six years before. He was made CB in 1888 and knighted as KCB in 1900. He served four terms as President of the Royal Photographic Society and one of the Physical Society. He was also an honorary DCL and JP. In 1866 he had inherited the Measham estate, by which time he had, for two years, been married to Agnes Matilda (d.1888), daughter of Edward Smith of Tickton Hall, Yorkshire, and he remarried in 1890 Mary Louisa, daughter of Rev. Edward Mead, an Episcopal pastor of upper class Anglo-Irish descent in New York State, USA. He left a son, Lancelot (who inherited Measham Hall) and two daughters by his first marriage and another daughter by his second, on his death at Folkestone on 3 December 1920.

[DNB.11 2476; Burke, et.al Landed Gentry (1952) p.1; Birks, *Jubilee History of the Derby Photographic Society* (1934).]

AETHELFLAEDA, Queen of Mercia (d.918)

Aethelflaeda, 'Lady of the Mercians', was not, strictly speaking, a Mercian at all, having been a daughter of King Alfred (of Wessex). As part of his drive to roll back the Viking tide that had engulfed all of Mercia, East Anglia and much of his own kingdom, Alfred had married Aethelflaeda to Aethelred of Mercia, an ealdorman whom the chronicler Aethelweard calls King of Mercia, and to whom modern scholarship has once again accorded regal status. He was probably related to the house of Burghred II of Mercia, deposed as a result of the invasion of the Viking 'Great Army' in 873-4; if not, it is doubtful that he would have retained the loyalty of the Mercians as he recovered his kingdom. Unfortunately he died in 910, leaving his task barely begun. However, as his widow, Aethelflaeda (whose only child, a daughter, Aelfwyne, was too young to succeed, especially in such turbulent times) was effectively his successor, she took up where he had left off, leading the army against the Norse in a number of engagements, retaking most of the Midlands in the process.

Her crowning achievement was to defeat the Vikings at Derby in 917, where 'with the help of God, before Lammas, obtained the borough which is called Derby with all that belongs to it, and there also four of her theigns who were dear to her, were killed within the gates'.

Derby barely existed then and it is thought that the Danes had refortified the former Roman town of *Derventio*, which would explain the expression 'within the gates' as Derby itself was never walled. 'With all that belonged to it' refers to the territory surrounding Derby, thought to have been that lying to the north of the Trent, east of the Dove and west of the Erewash, an area known as Northworthy, a name which has been mistakenly associated exclusively with the Borough itself. It was a considerable and clearly hard-fought victory which also probably liberated the ancient Mercian capital of Repton.

Aethelflaeda died at Tamworth in 918 and, the security situation being critical, Edward of Wessex stepped in, deposed the hapless Aelfwyne and continued her mother's campaigns, establishing Derby on its present site as a Royal *burh* about 921. After a counter campaign by the Danes under Anlaf, defeated at the as yet unlocated Battle of *Brunanburh*, Aethelflaeda's gains were finally consolidated in 937-941 and the Saxon Kingdom of All England was at last established.

[Aethelweard, *Anglo-Saxon Chronicle* (ASC) 893; ASC sub 917; Biddle, M. & B.K. *Repton 1986 An Interim Report* (Oxford 1989),1, 16; *Medieval Archaeology* XXIX (1985)168; *DAJ.* CVI (1986) 111 f; Craven, M, *Illustrated History of Derby* (1988) 24.]

AETHELWULF, Ealdorman (d.871)

Precious little is known of Ealdorman Aethelwulf, except that he was a high Mercian nobleman who came from the Derby area. The town did not exist in his time, only the old Roman settlement of *Derventio*, the new Minster church of St Alkmund (the only thing on the present site of the city) and a vast area of land, a Royal Estate called Northworthy, stretching from the Dove to the Erewash and the Trent to the lower Peak. He was probably its lord, and St Alkmund's the spiritual centre of his lordship. His title Ealdorman was 'of Berkshire' which means that the king of Mercia had entrusted him as governor of that most southerly part of the kingdom.

It was in Berkshire that Aethelwulf died in heroic circumstances in battle against the invading Vikings, defending the southern border of Mercia from their ravages. His corpse was brought back to Northworthy – clearly his native area – and interred in St Alkmund's. The magnificent 9th-century carved millstone grit interlace pattern sarcophagus excavated from the site of the church in 1968 was almost certainly his, especially as it had been buried close to the shrine of Alkmund himself; only a person of the highest status could expect to be so placed in the chancel of an important church. The *Anglo-Saxon Chronicle* reads: 'Truly the body of the aforesaid Ealdorman was stealthily removed and taken to the Province of the Mercians to the place called Northworthy, but in the Danish tongue, Derby.' It is this passage, written in the 10th century, after the establishment of Derby as a *burh* (*q.v.* AETHELFLAEDA), which has led to the conflation of Derby and Northworthy by subsequent historians. Yet we are now certain that they were two separate entities of which the former barely co-existed before the great estate of Northworthy was dismantled by kings of England in land grants to supporters.

Aethelwulf is almost the first resident of 'Derby' whose name we know; he is certainly the first about which we have any certain facts.
[Craven (1988) 21-22; ASC *sub* 871;*DAJ* XCVI (1976) 57 & 110]

AITON, Sir John (1864-1950)

Sir John Aiton was of Scottish descent and one whose career epitomises the tradition of excellence in engineering emanating from Scotland. His father, John, was a civil engineer, for many years employed in India, where John Arthur

Aiton was born in 1864, his mother being Hannah Norah, daughter of John Clarke Marshman. Whilst in India, young John was educated privately but later went to Stanley House School, Bridge of Allan in his native Scotland; his parents later retired to Clifton.

Having been trained and apprenticed in his father's calling, John Aiton set up in Derby in 1900 as a manufacturer of steam pipes; the attraction of Derby was its communications, the presence of foundries and heavy engineering and the locomotive building at the Midland Railway's works. As time went on, the firm successfully diversified into all kinds of specialist pipework and ancillary equipment, later concentrating on shipbuilding components (with a works also in Sunderland) and pipework for power stations, distilleries and water desalination plants; although now 'taken over' it still flourishes on Stores Road in Derby, where it began. The offices, a landmark industrial Art-deco building put up in 1930-31, were designed by Aiton's daughter NORAH AITON RIBA (1904-1989) with her collaborator, Betty Scott.

Aiton, who lived at first at 109 Radbourne Street in Derby, married in 1895 Adriane Wilhelmina (Mina), daughter of Adriaan Stoop, of Dordrecht, Netherlands; their son, Wing Cdr John Marshman Aiton, was born in 1899 and they also had one other daughter. In 1914 Aiton became a member of the Derbyshire Munitions Committee (the firm having switched in part to war work) and he chaired this from 1916-18, being rewarded with a CBE when he relinquished the post. In 1934 he was President of the Derby Chamber of Commerce and he was gazetted a Knight Bachelor, 25 February 1937. From 1927 he also served as a local JP, and he moved in the 1930s to Duffield Park, former seat of the Balguys, where he died on 24 January 1950. For most of his dynamic career he held the post of 'Governing Director' of Aitons, a position which today might be described as executive chairman. Thus armed, he created, within 25 years from its establishment, one of the foremost firms of its type in the world, with worldwide operations and contracts. He had advanced ideas about employee relations and their treatment. He imported and adapted a system of works committees in which workers' representatives helped run the business. Some of his posterity still reside in the County.
[*Who's Who in Derbyshire* (1934) 6; Kelly; *Handbook, 1939*; *Who Was Who 1941-50* (1951); *Knights Bachelor 1939-46* (Leicester, 1947) 46. *Times* 16/7/1931.]

ALIBON, Robert

A medieval MP representing the Borough of Derby, Alibon was part of a dynasty of local burgesses elected to Parliament. The family first occurs at Derby in the reign of Henry III, and in the reign of Edward II and III Hugh Alibon represented Derby in the Parliaments of 1307 and 1333. Hugh was almost certainly father of Robert who served in the same capacity between 1337 and 1364. He also found time to serve as one of the two bailiffs of the Borough for the term 1352-53. He married Joan, sister of John de Holland, a chaplain. Roger Alibon, MP for Derby 1374 and 1378 and the chaplain Thomas Alibon, living 1382, were probably their sons, after which time the name fades from record. Robert died shortly before 1376 when Joan is described as a widow.

[DC. C5; FF 929; Glover, *Op.cit.* Jeayes 981, 1117.]

ALLESTREY, Elias de (living *c.* 1220-1270)

Notable as the only recorded instance known to the writer of a freed villein whose descendants still inhabit the area of his manumission, 750 years later, he was also the founder of a notable local dynasty. Elias' first certain ancestor is his grandfather, Thomas, a villein on land later given by the Touchets of Markeaton (*q.v.*) to Darley Abbey in the third quarter of the 12th century; by his wife Alice he had a son, William, Elias's father. Robert de Touchet of Markeaton, through his brother, the rector of Mackworth Church, granted to the canons of Darley 'Elias, son of William de Allestree, villein of the said church with all his brood and chattels…' Between 1248 and 1261, however, the canons liberated Elias and granted him three acres of land in Allestree at a rent of 3/6d. Elias left three sons, William, whose daughter and heiress married the very grand William de Dethick of Codinton (Cottons) before 1303; Henry and Richard, from whom all subsequent Allestrees appear to descend.

Contemporary with Elias, however, was Richard, son of Robert de Allestrey, a kinsman

and a free man holding an estate at Allestree as 'Lord' under the Abbey and land at Breadsall. It is possible that they all descend from Colle who, in 1086, held Mackworth, Allestree and part of Kniveton from Jocelyn de Touchet as under-tenant. He may be the same Colle who held a toft in 'Wall Street' in Derby, and be identifiable with Colle of Winster, Yeldersley and Harthill, himself ancestor of the Harthills and Monjoyes. If so, then Elias' ancestors may have become enslaved as impoverished (or imprudent) younger sons, whilst Richard, as the elder branch, avoided such a disaster.

[*Darley Cartulary* (ed. Darlington, R.R. (Kendal 1945) 2 vols.) 1. B33,11.K22, 24,43,46; *Domesday Book* 4.2; 6.2/10/45/76; 10.18; Jeayes, I.H., *Derbyshire Charters* (London 1906) 2092, 2739; *DAJ. XVI* (1894)159.]

ALLESTREY, James (1654-1686)

James Allestrey was of Derby descent, being grandson of another James Allestrey, a Coventry goldsmith and sixth son of William Allestrey of Alvaston (d.1598). The goldsmith's son, also James, became a citizen and stationer of London (St Faith's) notable for having lost everything in the Great Fire of London, 1666. He left, at his death *c.*1677, two daughters, Ruth and Mary, and a son, James, born in London 1654. As a student he went to Christ Church, Oxford, graduating BA in 1675 and MA 1679. Here he made a name for himself as an accomplished poet, and was later appointed Fellow of Christ Church (1680) and Reader at the University. However, he was never able to realise his full potential as a poet and man of letters, dying at Oxford, unmarried, 15th October 1686, aged only 32.

[*Alumni Oxonienses,* 18; Hunter, J. FMG.111. 1038; wills]

ALLESTREY, Richard (b.1577, living 1633)

An astrologer and publisher of almanacs, and very influential in his day. He was fourth son of William Allestrey of Alvaston, a considerable landowner of ancient family (*cf.* Elias, above), an

uncle of William (*q.v.*) and great uncle of James (*q.v.*). He lived in Derby, having been baptised at St Alkmund's Church there on 15th July 1577. He was well versed in astronomy but was of the last generation who failed to separate that science from the art of astrology, which means that all his observations were directed at the better interpretation of the future. He published almanacs for the years 1629-33, after which time we lose sight of him. John Flamsteed (*q.v.*) read his publications as a youth before he made the transition to serious astronomy; certainly the two families were well known to each other. It is not clear when Allestrey died (perhaps in the 1630s), or whether he married and had children; no record of either has yet come to light.
[Hunter, *op. cit*; Local Library Studies, Box 57A]

ALLESTREY, Rev. Prof. Richard (1619-1681)

Richard Allestrey was the only son of yet another son of William Allestrey of Alvaston; his grandfather, William, had held land at Alvaston and Turnditch, had been MP for Derby 1541-55 and five times Bailiff of the Borough (in 1541,1549,1558,1565 and 1570). Richard's father, Robert (1574-1654) was the fifth son, baptised at St Alkmund's (4 May 1578). He later occupied the family seat at Uppington, Salop, where he was steward to Mountjoy Blount, 1st Earl of Newport – a man of impeccable Derbyshire descent and a notable cavalier.

Like all the Allestreys, the young Richard, born at Uppington in March 1619, grew up a firm supporter of Church and King. As James (*q.v.*) he went up to Christ Church, Oxford in 1636, graduating BA in 1640 and MA in 1646, actually fighting for the king at Edgehill, Keinton and Oxford, despite being a student. The Civil War virtually over, the family's influence in Shropshire secured him the appointment as Chaplain to Hon Francis Newport, son and heir of 1st Lord Newport, in 1648, by which time he had taken Holy Orders and been expelled from Oxford by Parliament. Under Newport's patronage he made three delicate diplomatic missions to France and the Netherlands as emissary from the English Royalists to Charles II, only being captured in 1659 on his return, by which time the tide was about to turn in the king's favour and he was eventually set free, unharmed.

His reward, at the Restoration, was to be made a Canon of Christ Church Cathedral, Oxford and given a lectureship there; his salary for the latter post he gave entirely to the city's poor. He gained a Doctorate of Divinity in October 1660 and shortly afterwards became a Chaplain in Ordinary to the king and Regius Professor of Divinity.

In 1665 he was appointed Provost of Eton, a post he held until his death on 28th January 1681. He resigned his Professorship 18 months before, having been for some time in poor health. He was buried in Eton College Chapel; in his lifetime he published 40 sermons (2 vols,1684) and at his own expense (£1,500) extended the school. His lasting legacy at Eton, where he was regarded amongst the best of Provosts, was the efficient restoration of the institution's finances after the depredations of war. It was said that Allestrey was regarded at court as 'an uglier man than even the Earl (later Duke) of Lauderdale' and that this enabled him to stick in his monarch's mind when the Provostship of Eton became vacant. It is also said that he refused a Bishopric. He was unmarried, although his four sisters all married, the eldest, Rachel's husband, John Stanier of Biddulph, succeeding Allestrey's father as Lord Newport's steward.
[*Provosts of Eton* 24-28; Maxwell Lyte, *Eton* 258-264; DNB; *MIs at Eton and Uppington*; Hunter, *Loc.cit.*]

ALLESTREY, William (1598-1655)

Cavalier and Derby MP, William Allestrey of Derby, Uppington and Alvaston was born in Derby in 1598, eldest son and heir of Thomas Allestrey of Alvaston, eldest brother of Richard (*q.v.*). The family town house was The College, on the north side of All Saints', now the Cathedral, still extant although much rebuilt since the 17th century. He was educated at Derby School c.1609-14 and St John's, Cambridge, graduating BA in 1617 and MA in 1619. Thereafter he went to Gray's Inn (1625) and in 1636 became Recorder of Derby in succession to Timothy Levinge of Parwich.

Unlike most of his fellow townsmen, Allestrey was a zealous supporter of the Royal cause in the events leading up to the Civil War; nevertheless he was elected to the Short Parliament in 1640 as one of the Borough's two representatives, his colleague being, in contrast, the puritan fanatic Nathaniel Hallowes (q.v.) He was re-elected a few months later to the Long Parliament but refused to sign the Protestation or the Grand Remonstrance. At the outbreak of hostilities Allestrey joined the king at Oxford and effectively forfeited his seat in Parliament. By 1643, too, Sir John Gell (q.v.) had effectively deposed him from the Recordership, replacing him the following year with his brother Thomas Gell, who also eventually occupied Allestrey's seat in Parliament too.

After the Civil War, Allestrey seems to have managed to return to Derby where he died on 4 September 1655 and where he is remembered in All Saints' by a fine classical monument in black marble and local alabaster complete with timber coffin. Unfortunately some parts were lost when it was transferred from the old to the new church in 1725.

Allestrey married twice: at All Saints', 9 April 1629 to Sarah, daughter of Thomas Smith of Derby. By her (who died 2 September 1638) he had two sons and two daughters who died young and another daughter, Grace (b.1631) who died unmarried at 24. Sarah is touchingly described, on the family monument, as 'Beautiful Dust'. He remarried at Alvaston, 8th March 1640, Mary (1611-74), widow of Edward Smith, his first wife's brother and daughter of George Agard of Foston. By her he had a further three sons and three daughters, of whom only the eldest son and second daughter failed to reach maturity. However, both the other sons, Thomas (d.1706), a barrister, and Charles (1651-1708), rector of Cossington, were childless. His surviving daughter married respectively Thomas Bagshawe of

Ridge Hall, Chapel-en-le-Frith and Thomas Goodwin of Derby; the latter inherited the College, whereas the estates at Alvaston and elsewhere descended by entail to the next male heir, being irregularly dispersed on the death of Thomas Allestrey of Alvaston in 1740.

[Hunter, loc. cit.; Stone, B. Derbyshire in the Civil War (Cromford 1992) 10, 69, 76; Simpson, op. cit. III. 537-538; Craven, M., Illustrated History of Derby (Derby 1988) 37, 60]

ALLESTREY, William (1641-1699)

If the torch carried by William (q.v.) for Church and King was going to be passed on in Derby, to whom better to pass it but a member of one's own family? At the Restoration, William was dead; his sons not interested. Instead, at the Restoration, William's fourth brother Roger (1610-65) was the one to be rewarded. He was appointed to the vacant Town Clerkship of Derby in 1660 and in the following year was elected to Parliament for the Borough with the former Parliamentarian John Dalton of The Friary (q.v.) as colleague. He was an out-and-out Royalist – a proto-Tory, if you like – but like his eldest brother, his career was cut short by his death aged 54 on 1st February 1665. However, by his wife, Sarah, daughter of William Bradshaw of Derby, he had two sons and three daughters. William, the eldest, was born in 1641 being baptised at St Michael's, on 1st April that year. He proceeded to Eton and then to the 'family' college – Christ Church, Oxford – where his first cousin once removed, Richard (q.v.) was enjoying a Professorship. He graduated BA 1662 and MA 1663. On 14 October 1668, he married Frances Lorimer of St James' Clerkenwell, at Wandsworth (Surrey) and settled at Darley Hall. By this time William (again like his uncle) had qualified as a barrister at Gray's Inn (to which he had proceeded in 1659). Sometime in the early 1670s, his wife died childless and on 11 October 1676 he remarried Alice, daughter of William Booth of Wilton, Warwickshire, and before 1680 moved to Walton Old Hall, Walton-on-Trent, taking his brother, Seth, with him.

In 1685 he became High Sheriff of the County and on the death of Charles II that year, was elected MP for Derby as a Tory with John Coke for a colleague; this was James II's first Parliament and men of William's political kidney were again in the ascendant. However, the so-called Glorious Revolution came and there was no place for him in the Convention Parliament of 1689 and, by 1699, he was dead, having expired in the May. His second wife had died in 1682 and he left three sons. The eldest son, Booth Allestrey of Wilton (a seat inherited from his mother) died, aged 29, in April 1707, having married Elizabeth, a great niece of JOHN FLAMSTEED (*q.v.*) and daughter of William Flamsteed of Little Hallam Hall. Their son died, unmarried, aged 39 in 1740, ending the male line in this branch, for William's only other surviving son, Roger, had died by 1730, unmarried. Booth's elder daughter, Esther, was the only one who married, to John Hinkley of Harbourne. William's sister, Bethijah, was the only other married female in the family. She married Rev. Walter Horton (1654-1720) rector of Walton-on-Trent and vicar of All Saints', Derby. He was the second son of Walter

Horton of Catton Hall and it was he who arranged for William Allestrey to rent a suitable house at Walton, on his brother's estate. [Hunter, *loc cit.*; *Fasti Etonienses* 1500-1714. p.18; research by A.F. Fentiman Esq.; family deeds, Private Collection]

ALLPORT, Sir James Joseph (1811-1892)

General manager, later chairman of the Midland Railway; during his years in this crucial position, Sir James presided over the extension of the company's line to 1,200 miles, the augmentation of its capital to more than £50,000,000 and the increase of its income to £5,000,000 per annum. He was one of the most able and successful railway managers of this crucial era in the development of the Victorian transport infrastructure.

Sir James was born 27 February 1811, son of William Allport of Sutton Coldfield (and grandson of another William). Sometime before 1844 he became manager of the Birmingham & Derby Junction Railway but on its amalgamation (which led to the formation of the Midland) he

was made redundant and went instead to the Newcastle & Darlington Railway which he expanded to form the York, Newcastle & Berwick Railway before taking charge of the Manchester, Sheffield & Lincolnshire Railway in 1850 for three years. In 1853 he returned to the Midland again, as general manager, and held the post right through except for a break during the years 1857-60. He was knighted in 1884 and was a member of the Derby bench. He lived at Littleover House (built for him *c.*1854 by the Midland's architect John Holloway Sanders) until shortly before his death on 25 April 1892 when he moved to Duffield. By his wife Anne (1807-21/5/1886) daughter of John Gold of Birmingham, whom he married in 1832, he had three sons and three daughters, one of whom married Midland Railway engineer A.A.Langley, which gives a link to the Bowring family (*q.v.*). He was buried at Belper cemetery.

[Derby Local Studies Box 57; *Derbyshire Red Book* (1893,1898); Tachella, *op.cit.;* Williams, F.S. *The Midland Railway* 2nd Edn. (London & Derby 1877) 614-616 Marshall, J., *A Biographical Dictionary of Railway Engineers* (Newton Abbot, 1978)]

ALLSOPP, Sir Henry, Bt, 1st Lord Hindlip (1811-1887)

Pioneer of the brewing industry and creator of the brewing conglomerate Ind Coope & Allsopp, formerly Samuel Allsopp & Co, which was founded by Lord Hindlip's father, Samuel (1780-1838) but owing its inception to the latter's maternal grandfather, Benjamin Wilson of Burton upon Trent, brewer, whose daughter Ann married James Allsopp of Birlingham Hall (Worcestershire).

The Allsopps claimed descent from Colle of Parwich, Alsop-en-le-Dale, Hanson Grange and Cold Eaton in Derbyshire, ancestor among others of the Alsops of Alsop (*cf.:* ALLESTREY, Elias). This connection has never been positively established, however, although the family descends from Samuel Alsop of Derby (1651-

1729) who in 1681 benefited financially from his marriage to the widow of Edward Wast, a prosperous local tradesman and kinsman of the Protestant martyr Joan (*q.v.*). Their daughter married into the Mellors (*q.v.*), and Samuel (1688-1716) was great-great-grandfather of Lord Hindlip. The family's house in Derby – an exceptionally elegant brick residence of 1708 – is now the Wardwick Tavern.

Henry Allsopp was a third son. His eldest brother married Sarah Emma Drewry, a descendant of Derby's Samuel Drewry (*q.v.*) but Henry was the one who took the firm at Burton by the scruff of the neck. He was born in 1811 and married Elizabeth, daughter of William Tongue of Comberford Hall, (Staffordshire). Apart from his business activities, he sat as MP for East Worcestershire from 1874 to 1880, was a Deputy Lieutenant and JP for Staffordshire. He purchased a considerable estate centred on Hindlip Hall (Worcestershire) and also a certain amount of land at Alsop-en-le-Dale, before being given a baronetcy in 1880. He was raised to the peerage – the 'beerage' as one of his contemporaries quipped – as 1st Lord Hindlip of Hindlip and Alsop-en-le-Dale, in 1886. He died during the course of the following year leaving eight sons and three daughters and was succeeded by his eldest son Samuel Charles (1842-97). His representative today is Sir Charles Henry Allsopp, 6th Lord Hindlip (chairman of Christie's) who succeeded in 1993. Ind Coope & Allsopp more recently became Ansell's and is now part of Allied Domecq.

[Burke, Sir J.B. *et al, Peerage* (London 1970)1343-44; Glover, S. *History and Gazetteer of Derbyshire,* 2 vols. (Derby 1829/31) II. 28.]

ANN, Alderman Sir Edwin (1852-1913)

Retailer and entrepreneur, Edwin Thomas Ann was born in 1852 in Swansea, son of Thomas Ann of Bristol. He came to Derby in his 20s and by 1882 had acquired a haberdashery at 57-58 St Peter's Street. A combination of flair and good fortune made him a great success and in 1887 he began to expand, buying up adjacent properties and reinventing his business as a department

store – Derby's first, apart from the Co-operative Society's shop in Albert Street which is said, indeed, to have been his inspiration, although he was aiming to satisfy the purchasing aspirations of the burgeoning middle classes.

By 1892 the store, the Midland Drapery, had been replaced by a new, purpose-built edifice which sported a long and spectacular double frontage on the north side of East Street (almost as far as Exchange Street) and the east side of St Peter's Street. It was rebuilt and expanded further in 1924-29 and traded profitably until decline set in the 1960s. It closed in 1970 when the building was demolished and the site redeveloped as the lacklustre Audley Centre.

Ann himself married in 1884, Sophia, daughter of John Eastland of Margate, and became a Councillor for Becket Ward shortly afterwards. He served as Mayor of Derby twice, in 1898-99 and again in 1906-07, by which time he was also Alderman and JP. During his second Mayoralty,

Edward VII visited Derby to attend the Royal Agricultural Show and unveiled the statue to his mother Queen Victoria at The Spot, and Ann was knighted to mark the occasion, receiving a grant of arms 18 months later in 1908.

Sir Edwin and Lady Ann lived at Parkfields, Penny Long Lane, but later moved to Quarndon House where he died in 1913, leaving three sons (Harold Thomas, b.22/4/1886, later married (1924) and had issue; William Eastland (b.8/10/1887, d.12/11/1934), having married and left issue; and Edwin Francis, later of Holford, Somerset, b.1893) and a daughter, Elizabeth Eastland, later Mrs W.R.Cheshire.
[*Modern Mayors of Derby* (MMD) I.95 and II.33; Fox & Davies, A.C. *Armorial Families* (1910) 33, (1929) I.40; Tachella, B., *Derby School Records* (1902) 147, 148; *Local Directories; Kelly's Handbook*, 1911 and 1939.

ARCHDALE, Richard (1746-1824)

Richard Archdale's connection with Derby is the bizarre one that he was buried at St Alkmund's Church in Derby beside the remains of his wife. She was Anna Maria (b.1760), natural daughter of General the 5th Earl of Halifax, 'the Father of the Colonies' who died 16 September 1805; one must presume that her mother was a Derby woman, perhaps, for the Halifaxes belonged, then as now, to Yorkshire. In November 1780 she married Richard Archdale, a Dublin barrister, third son of Nicholas Montgomery of Derrygonelly (Co Fermanagh) who had assumed the surname and arms of Archdale of Castle Archdale (also Co Fermanagh) in 1728, his first wife having been the heiress of that family, which had migrated to Ireland from Stafford.

Richard was born in 1746, his mother being Nicholas Montgomery's second wife, Londoner Sarah Spurling, and he was later elected to the Irish House of Commons for Ardfert in 1790. After the Act of Union, he had a distinguished Parliamentary career at Westminster, representing Kilkenny, then Dundalk. It was probably at that period that he and his wife took a house in Spondon. He died 8 February 1824 and was interred at St Alkmund's. Of his three sons and one daughter, the second son, Rev. Dr George Archdale-Gratwicke (1787-1871) was for 36 years until his death Master of Emmanuel College, Cambridge, a college favoured, above all, by scholars from Derby School.

[Burke, J. *et.al., Burke's Irish Family Records* (1976) 853-4; Simpson, R., *History of Derby* (1826) II. 327]

ASHFIELD, Lord, see STANLEY

BABINGTON, Anthony (1561-1586)

The Roman Catholic conspirator Anthony Babington was born at the family seat, Dethick Manor (the remains of which, now a farm, is the home of the parents of the television personality and journalist Simon Groom) in October 1561. His parents were Sir Henry Babington, a considerable Derbyshire landowner, and his second wife, Hon Mary d'Arcy, a daughter of George, 1st Lord d'Arcy of Aston (Yorkshire). The Babingtons, who originated with Sir John de Babington of Over Babington, Northumberland, in the early 13th century, acquired their Derbyshire estates through the marriage of Thomas Babington of Kingston (Notts) and Isabella, daughter and heiress of Robert Dethick of Dethick, in the mid 15th century. A great uncle, Sir John Babington (d.1533) had been a Knight of Malta, serving as Bailiff of Aquila and Grand Prior of Ireland as well as being Commander of the Order's Preceptories at Stydd, Barrow on Trent, Dalby (Leics) and Rothley (Leics); the family managed to acquire the latter at the Dissolution a few years after his death.

This religious heritage was compounded by that of his mother, grandaughter of Thomas d'Arcy, KG, 1st Lord d'Arcy of Temple Newsam (Yorkshire) who was executed for his part in the Pilgrimage of Grace in 1536. Sir Henry himself was said to be 'incline'd to papistrie' and had a brother of the same religious kidney. Anthony's father died when he was ten and he was brought up by his mother, Henry Foljambe of Walton-by-Chesterfield and Philip Draycott of Painsley (Staffordshire), all covert Catholics. He ultimately married Margaret, Draycott's daughter, around 1579 (some sources name her father as John, Philip's brother).

Service at about this time as page to Mary Queen of Scots in her captivity under Lord Shrewsbury at Sheffield, led to his forming a deep devotion to the hapless Scottish monarch which, combined with a life of leisure in London, laid the seeds of sedition, encouraged by acquaintanceship with Father Edmund Campion and other Jesuits, and a visit to the continent including, it is believed, Rome. He also became a member of a secret society dedicated to a Catholic restoration.

Early in 1586 he was induced to play the leading role in a plot to assassinate Queen Elizabeth and place Mary on the throne. Having gathered a number of like-minded young men, a plan was put in hand, and written communications exchanged regularly with Mary, although Babington's leadership was marked by much 'foolish vanity' and Walsingham's spies were quickly apprised of the group's intentions, although Sir Francis played cat and mouse with them in order to better the case against them and to aid the incrimination of Queen Mary. Father John Ballard was the *eminence grise* behind the plot and the conspirators had the written blessing of King Philip II of Spain.

On 4th August, however, Walsingham's agents arrested Ballard, and Babington went on the run, being captured at the end of the month. He and his fellow conspirators were tried before a Special Commission on 13-14 September. Babington declared all with 'mild countenance, sober gesture and wonderful good grace' but put the blame squarely on Ballard. Shortly afterwards, seven more conspirators were tried and all were sentenced to be hung and quartered. Sentence was carried out at St Giles's Fields and Babington endured the most barbarous end with dignity, only exclaiming, "Parce Mihi, Domine Jesu," as the executioner used the knife on him.

Being attainted, Babington's property passed

to the Crown, much being granted to Sir Walter Raleigh, but the Dethick and Kingston estates were restored to his brothers Francis and George. His Derby town house, Babington Hall (demolished in 1822) was sold prior to his arrest, to raise funds for the plot, to the Beaumonts of Gracedieu (Leics); ironically it was there that Mary Stuart had been lodged on the night of 13 January 1585 en route to Sheffield. The failure of Babington's plot was the catalyst for the execution of the Scottish Queen not long afterwards, an event which, in turn, provoked Philip of Spain to send his celebrated Armada to defeat and destruction two years later. Babington's failed plot derives its importance from the drastic consequences of its exposure. Had it been undertaken with more discretion and professionalism, the outcome might have been very different.
[DNB; Local MS 6341; Nicols, J. *History of Leicestershire* (1806) 111.2, 964-7; Clay, J.W. *Extinct and Dormant Peerages of the Northern Counties of England* (London, 1913) 43; Craven, M. *The Derby Town House* (Derby, 1987) 37.]

BAGE, Robert (1728-1801)

An important pioneer of the English novel, Robert Bage was born in Derby in February 1728, being baptised at St Alkmund's on 26th of that month. He was the third son of George, a Quaker paper manufacturer with a mill at Darley Abbey, by his first wife, Mary (d.1729), sister of the ironsmith ROBERT BAKEWELL (*q.v.*). The business appears to have been founded by Bage's grandfather, also George (d.1747) and the latter's brother Charles. His mother died when he was barely a year old and Elizabeth Locko, whom his father married in 1731, also died within 18 months. He was thus reared under the watchful eye of his father's third wife, Mary Seal, whom his father married in 1733.

He was educated at Derby School, before being trained in his father's calling and in 1751 married Elizabeth Wooley of Mickleover, initiating a happy and lifelong union. With Elizabeth's dowry and some encouragement from his father (who died in 1766 leaving Robert's eldest brother

George in charge at Darley Abbey) he set up a paper mill at Elford, near Tamworth (Staffordshire) in 1754. This was a successful venture, enabling him to acquire Elford Hall from the heirs of Henry Howard, 4th Earl of Berkshire.

In the 1760s he became acquainted with his contemporary (then of Lichfield) ERASMUS DARWIN (*q.v.*) and through him with other members of the Lunar Society. In 1779 the failure of an iron founding business (coupled with losses incurred in a canal scheme) in which he had been involved with Darwin led him to come to terms with his £1,000-plus losses by writing. His first novel *Mount Henneth* was published in two volumes in 1781 and, like Richardson's pioneering *Clarissa* (to which it may owe something, at least in form), consists of a series of fictional letters. Bage, not anticipating much acclaim as a tyro, wrote his own criticism in a tongue-in-cheek preface.

However, its reception was favourable and further works followed until 1792 when, after a four-year pause, he produced *Man As He Is*, followed in 1796 by his finest work, *Hermsprong, or, Man As He Is Not*. Characterised by 'freshness and vigour' his works became popular and several were published on the continent in translation. These two last works were informed by a spirit of radicalism which sprang partly from his Quaker upbringing, partly from the avant-garde opinions of friends like Darwin and WILLIAM HUTTON (*q.v.*) and to an extent from the precepts which lay behind the French Revolution. Although not strong on plot, the novels are entertaining and engaging vehicles for Bage's moral and political creed. They were, a generation after Bage's death at Tamworth on 1 September 1801, given critical praise by Sir Walter Scott, much against the contemporary climate of opinion, which has ensured their place in the history of English literature. The total of novels by Bage is but six, all written between the ages of 53 and 68.

He was of an 'open, mild and sociable character', much liked by all, and two of his three sons, Charles (b.1753), Edward (b.1755) and John (1758-93) survived him.

[DNB; Tachella, *op. cit.* 15; *Gentleman's Magazine* LXXI (1801) pt.2, 862, 1202 & LXXXII (1812) pt.2, 191.]

BAGNOLD, John (1643-1698)

The local politician and dynast John Bagnold was born in 1643, his father John being the younger son of Walter Bagnold, a farmer at Marston-on-Dove. John, senior, appears to have come to Derby to make his fortune as a general trader who later became what today is called a property developer.

John junior appears to have done well in the post-Civil War boom and rebuilt his father's gabled town house in Full Street on a grandiose scale in the full Restoration style around 1680. By this time, too, he had purchased an estate at Hilton from the Shirley family and had made an advantageous match to Hannah, daughter of Joseph Parker of Derby, a kinsman of LORD MACCLESFIELD (*q.v.*)

In 1676 he was appointed Town Clerk in succession to Thomas Gery, a post he held for the remainder of his life. He was also elected to Parliament in the Convention Parliament of 1689 serving with reforming zeal until replaced on his death 1 May 1698 by George Vernon of Sudbury. He left three sons and a daughter: Joseph (b.1670) whose only daughter married German Pole of Radburne Hall; John (1672-1738) Mayor of Derby 1726 and 1737; and Walter of Burton upon Trent. His daughter, Margaret (1678-1735) married a man even wealthier than her father: the Derby-born London copper merchant Thomas Chambers (1650-1726), who acquired Bagnold's house and refronted it. Their daughter, Hannah Sophia, brought it in marriage to Brownlow Cecil, 8th Earl of Exeter, from whom it was subsequently named Exeter House, 'the largest domestic residence in Derby'.

Margaret Chambers is also noted for her splendid monument in Derby Cathedral by Roubiliac with ironwork by BAKEWELL (*q.v.*); it is topped by two flaming urns. These represent her gift to her fellow townsfolk in her will of

money to erect 80 lamps to light the streets of the Borough. These, the first street lights in Derby, were put up in 1738 and were not supplemented until 1792.

[Cox, J.C. and Hope, W.H.St J *Chronicles of All Saints', Derby* (Derby 1881) 70, 74, 80, 145-6; Local MS 8022; Craven, M., *Illustrated History of Derby* (Derby 1988) 71, 113-4; Craven (1987) 48-51, 120]

BAINBRIGGE, Gen. Sir Philip (1786-1862)

The Bainbrigge family were established at Lockington (Leics) before 1509 and several members took their part in the municipal life of Derby in the 16th and 17th centuries; William Bainbrigge, for instance, built the first house on the site of The Friary (dem 1760), was MP for the Borough 1556-57, 1562 and obtained a grant of arms in 1582. The family later had an estate at Woodseat, near Rocester (Staffordshire). Thomas Parker Bainbrigge of Mill Hill House was first postmaster at Derby, 1825-65. The latter's uncle, Col Philip Bainbrigge, was killed in action at the battle of Egmont op Zee, Netherlands, in 1799 and lived at Ashbourne. By his wife, Rachel, daughter of Peter Dobrée of Jersey, he had seven sons and five daughters.

The eldest son was Philip, born at Ashbourne on 4 February 1786. He followed his father into the army, rising to Lt Colonel at the young age of 24 when he was appointed permanent assistant Quartermaster General in 1810. He owed his rapid promotion to service with the 20th Regt (which he entered in 1800) in the Peninsular War on Wellington's staff. He received the War Medal with seven clasps and later went on to commands in Ireland and Ceylon. He was Colonel commanding 26th Foot and made a General and Knight Commander of the Bath (Military). He died at St Margaret's, Titchfield, Hants, 20 December 1862.

He had married, at Liverpool, 5 April 1816, Sarah Mary, daughter of Joseph Fletcher of that city, and left five sons and six daughters. His eldest son, Philip, (1817-81) also chose a military career, rising to become a Maj General, RE;

another son, Arthur, was Colonel, 13th Regt. and another, Lt Edward Bainbrigge, RE, was killed at Sebastopol in the Crimean War.

[Fletcher, W.G.D. *Leicestershire Pedigrees* (Leicester, 1887) 176; Nicols (*op.cit*) iii, 882-3; *Glover* (1829/31) II.552; Henstock, A. (Ed.), *A Georgian Country Town* (Ashbourne 1989) I.24-5]

BAKER, Philip John Noël, Lord NOEL-BAKER (1889-1982)

Like many of Derby's Members of Parliament, Philip NoëI-Baker never actually resided in his constituency. For this he had the precedent of another great reformer, SAMUEL PLIMSOLL (*q.v.*) as well as many grandees of the unreformed House of Commons before 1832, to which class indeed, this prominent Labour MP firmly belonged. P.J. Baker was born on 1 November 1889, son of Joseph Allen Baker, sometime Liberal MP for East Finsbury (London) by Elizabeth, daughter of Richard Moscrip of Morebattle near Kelso. The grandfather, Joseph, was a landowner from Trenton, Ontario (Canada).

He was educated at Bootham's (York), King's Cambridge and Haverford College, Pennsylvania (USA). At Cambridge he read history and economics (MA) and was president of the Union in 1912. His radical credentials were established when he became vice-principal of Ruskin College, Oxford, in 1914; during World War One he chose ambulance work on grounds of conscience, yet was much decorated for his work on the Italian Front. In 1919 he was part of the British delegation to the Peace Conference and he subsequently worked in the League of Nations secretariat until 1922.

His Parliamentary career began on his election for Coventry in the Labour interest in 1929, having failed to win Handsworth (Birmingham) five years before. However, his refusal to support Ramsay MacDonald over the National Government in 1931 resulted in his defeat and he was out of Parliament until he was elected for one of the two Derby seats, replacing the disgraced J.H.THOMAS (*q.v.*). Subsequently he held Derby South from 1950 until his retirement in 1970. He was PPS to the Foreign Secretary in the 1929-31 Labour administration and during World War Two, Parliamentary Secretary to the

Lord Noël-Baker

25

Minister of War Transport 1942-45. On the Labour victory in the latter year he became Minister of State, Foreign Office (1945-46), Secretary of State for Air (1946-47), Secretary of State for Commonwealth Relations and, in the 1950-51 government, Minister for Fuel and Power. He took no office under Harold Wilson, contenting himself as chairman of the Parliamentary Foreign Affairs group.

Noël-Baker's work in the field of international relations outside Parliament was tireless and he wrote extensively on the subject, being showered with honours, chief amongst which was the Nobel Peace Prize for 1959. He was made a Privy Councillor in 1945, an officer of the Légion d'Honneur 1976 and a Knight of the Papal Order of St Sylvester a year later. He held eight honorary degrees.

On his retirement from Parliament he was created a Life Peer in 1977 as Lord Noël-Baker of the City of Derby, (only the second peer to thus honour Derby and the first as a City). He married, in June 1915, Irene (d.1956), daughter and heiress of Frank Noël, a collateral of Lord Gainsborough's family and proprietor of a vast landed estate at Achmetaga, Euboea, Greece, on inheriting which, in 1923, Baker assumed the additional surname of Noël. The couple had one son, Hon Francis Edward Noël-Baker (b.1920) who, in his turn, has served as Labour MP 1945-69 when he resigned from the Party, later defecting to the SDP in 1981; by his Swedish wife he has four sons and a daughter.

Lord Noël-Baker died in 1982 after a most distinguished Parliamentary and international career. Derby has a school named after him; possibly his memory deserves more. [*Who's Who*, 1978, *Debrett's Distinguished People of Today* (1990) 1357.]

BAKEWELL, Robert (1682-1752)

England's most celebrated native-born wrought-iron smith was born at Uttoxeter in 1682, being baptised at the parish church there on 5 March. His father was Sampson Bakewell (d.1694) a smith, probably of Derby origin, as Sampson's brother Matthew was a carrier, as was a family of the same name at Derby, of whom Richard (1630-72) issued a ½d token there in 1666.

Robert (and his siblings, John, Thomas and Mary) lost their father in 1694, whereupon his mother, Mary, daughter of one Sale(s), a Derby blacksmith, remarried another smith, Lewis Shutt. Mary, Bakewell's sister married the father of ROBERT BAGE (*q.v.*).

Robert at 14 appears to have been sent to London to serve his apprenticeship and worked with Jean Montigny and possibly Jean Tijou who produced the iron work at Hampton Court and, later, at Chatsworth, whilst the former worked at Canons for the Duke of Bridgewater.

By 1706, Bakewell had found a patron in Rt Hon Thomas Coke of Melbourne Hall for whom he made railings for his town house in St James' Place, before taking up residence in Melbourne, where he produced his precocious *chef d'oeuvre*, the breathtaking wrought iron arbour in Coke's gardens, laid out by London and Wise, and irrigated by the skill of GEORGE SOROCOLD (*q.v.*). It was at Melbourne that Bakewell seems to have had a fling with one Elizabeth Fisher which resulted in the birth of their natural son, Bakewell Fisher, baptised at Melbourne, 26 October 1709. It is possible that this incident soured relations between the smith and Coke, for by 1711 he had set up a forge in Oakes' Yard in St Peter's Street, Derby. From there, Bakewell supplied a magnificent sequence of wrought iron gates, screens for churches – Staunton Harold and Derby Cathedral are both of the highest quality – balustrades, turret clocks, tables and screens to adorn country seats, town houses and public buildings throughout the Midlands and the Welsh borders.

Although not a virtuoso of repoussé work like Tijou, Bakewell's ironwork is both monumental and architectural, and combines the finest proportions with elegant detail. As he got older, so his work became somewhat more austere, less baroque. Among his last works, before failing eyesight forced his retirement, were staircase and balustrade at Okeover, the grilles for Gibbs' Radcliffe Camera at Oxford, and gates at Osmaston Hall, Derby.

In his declining years he handed over to his foreman, BENJAMIN YATES (*q.v.*) whose family appear to have been associated with Bakewell and the craftsmen in Montigny's circle many years before. Yates took over when Bakewell died in October 1752 and was buried in St Peter's – 'Thought to be the smith,' says the parish register coyly – on 31st. He had married Mary, a daughter of Nathaniel Cokayne and sister of FRANCIS and THOMAS COKAYNE (*q.q.v.*) by whom he had three sons and three daughters, about whom little is known. It is worth noting that the Robert Bakewell painted by Joseph Wright (*q.v.*) is the unrelated Mayor of Derby who served five times between 1739 and 1759.

[Notes on Bakewell supplied courtesy of Edward Saunders whose work on 18th century wrought-ironsmiths is forthcoming.]

BANCROFT, Thomas (*c.*1600-58)

A poet, long neglected for no good reason, Thomas Bancroft was born at Swarkestone *c.*1600 of a family long associated with neighbouring Chellaston. He completed his education at St Catherine's Hall, Cambridge, where he was a contemporary of the poet James Shirley, which implies graduation in *c.*1618/19. He was notably short of stature and was inevitably satirised as the 'small poet'!

Although he was a younger son – he speaks of his elder brother, John, dying in 1639 and dispersing the family patrimony – he seems to have had the means to live independently; it is likely he enjoyed the patronage of a local grandee, like one of the Harpurs, in whose service the family seems to have been employed. Another possibility is the Cokaynes of Ashbourne, for later in life Sir Aston Cokayne speaks of Bancroft as a 'neighbour'. He also wrote two books of epigrams and epitaphs; their dedicatees, Sir Charles Shirley, 3rd Bt. (1623-46) of Staunton Harold and William Davenport (probably of Davenport, Cheshire) might suggest themselves as possible patrons, the former especially, as he owned much land in Derbyshire, particularly near Ashbourne.

Bancroft's first published work was *The Glutton's Feaver* a narrative poem based on the story of Lazarus, which came out in 1633 and was well received. *The Epigrammes* were published in 1639 and celebrated amongst others all the most eminent figures in theatre, poetry and literature of the age, from Shakespeare downwards. They also celebrate the life of Bancroft's friend Alderman Henry Mellor, Derby's first ever Mayor, who died in office on 5th February 1638:

You seeme the prime bough of an apple tree,
Whereon if fair expected fruits we see
Whilest others' fames with ranke approaches
      meete
As mel or manna shall your name be sweete.

Bancroft made other contributions to literature in 1649 and 1658, in which later year we find him living in retirement at Bradley (not far from Ashbourne). The date of his death is not known, nor whether he was married. However, the Hearth Tax Return lists only a Jo[hn] Bancroft there in 1664, taxed on but one hearth. This suggests that Thomas died between 1658 and 1664 and John might conceivably be a son. If so, we hear no more of him, although a kinsman, John Bancroft, baker of Derby, issued a ½d token in 1666 and founded a dynasty with living posterity. [DNB; Hearth Tax Returns 1664]

BARBER, Thomas (1771-1843)

Thomas Barber was a portrait painter of more than average ability who had been a pupil of Sir Thomas Lawrence, PRA. Born at Nottingham 28 March 1771, he was the only son of Thomas Barber (1729-75) of St Mary's in that town and Ann Abbott, formerly Mrs William Tomlin. The father had been born in Castleton of a long line of Hope Valley farmers boasting an unbroken descent from John Barber of Edale, yeoman, who died 1535.

Barber set up at Parkside, Nottingham, but by 1813 was living and working in Friargate, Derby, later moving to 15 Green Lane where he was living, 1835. His first wife, Mary (born 1769), daughter of Hugh Atherstone of Nottingham, died on 28th September 1825, and Barber remarried Anne, widow of William Bateman, a Derby attorney, and relative of HUGH *(q.v.)*.

In 1819, whilst residing at Derby, he exhibited a portrait of Mrs Siddons at the Royal Academy, and he also painted in oils his fellow Derby artist Octavius Oakley, John Radford of Smalley Hall (1809), John Balguy, recorder of Derby (*c*.1828), Rev. Charles Stead HOPE, vicar of St Alkmund's *(q.v.)*, Rev. William Boultbee Sleath, headmaster of Repton and Col. Thornhill of Stanton Hall. He occasionally painted landscapes, aquatints after his 'Dovedale' and 'Matlock Bath' being in Derby Museum's collections.

Barber died at Nottingham, whence he ultimately returned in 1843, leaving, by his first wife, five sons. A daughter and his eldest son, Thomas junior (1796-1824) – also a talented artist – predeceased him. The third son, Henry (1801-78) was a gifted artist too, although he later took Holy Orders. The second son, Hugh (1799-1878) migrated to Cape Province (South Africa) in 1840 founding the distinguished South African dynasty of Hilton-Barber, of which family Miles Hilton-Barber has recently returned to live in Derby. Likewise, Thomas' youngest son, Frederick William (1813-92) also went to South Africa settling at Grahamstown, and his second son founded Barberton RSA, taking the surname of Mitford-Barberton and founding another powerful dynasty which still flourishes.
[*Derby & Chesterfield Reporter* 29/9/1825; DET 2/3/1998; Notes in Derby Museum; Burke, J., *Landed Gentry* (1965) 29-30 and (1971) 41-2.]

BARKER, Sir Henry Heaton, KBE (1898-1989)

Born 18th July 1898 at Mount Eden, New Zealand, son of John Heaton Barker, (a grandson of Alderman Thomas Henry Harrison) who was born at 9 Oriel Terrace, Gerard Street in 1867. The father emigrated to New Zealand in 1886 where he followed in the good alderman's footsteps and became a successful accountant, marrying in 1895 Martha Annie Johns.

Henry Heaton was educated at the local High

School and became a boy reporter at the age of 15 on the *New Zealand Herald*. From 1935 he was editor of the *Gisborne Herald*, but resigned 1943 to contest Gisborne for Parliament. He was also Mayor of the town nine times between 1950 and 1974, executive of the East Coast Planning Council 1972-77 and held a large number of other posts, patronages and honorifics.

In 1926 he married Anita, daughter of H.Greaves of Gisborne (hence his move to this town, named after the Derby-born New Zealand Statesman, WILLIAM *(q.v.)*.) He was a JP and made OBE (1964), CBE (1972) and knighted as KBE in 1978. His wife was also made a member of the same order in 1974. He died without leaving issue in 1989.
[Notes provided by Mrs M.M.Turley of Whiritoa Beach, NZ; Debrett, *Handbook* (1982) 100.]

BASS, Michael Thomas (1799-1884)

Michael Thomas Bass had no close familial association with Derby, nor did he ever live in the City. He was, however, from 1848 to 1883 one of the two MPs for Derby (his predecessor had been unseated for bribery) and it was to Derby, during these years that he directed much philanthropic effort and expenditure.

Son of another Michael Thomas Bass (1760-1827) of Burton upon Trent, a brewer (the firm had been started by his grandfather, William in 1777) he was born 6th July 1799; his mother Sarah was the daughter of a solicitor-turned-brewer from Stafford, Abraham Hoskins, the builder of Newton Park, Newton Solney, and of its attendant folly, Bladon Castle.

He built the vast house at Rangemoor, Tatenhill (Staffordshire) as his seat and married, on 8th December 1835, Eliza Jane, daughter of Major Samuel Arden of Longcroft (Staffordshire) whose family was one of the few in England to convincingly claim a Saxon descent.

Bass funded the open air baths and their surrounding parklands in 1867 (opened 1873) and the establishment of the free museum and library in 1878. He was also well remembered for his sense of humour: on being asked by an articulate

male line of M.T. Bass' third brother, Abraham (1804-82) is still exant.

A statue by Sir Joseph Boehm Bt. was erected to Bass' memory in Derby Market Place and was unveiled in the year of his death. After many vicissitudes it may today be seen in Museum Square. A bust of him is on display in the museum itself.

[DNB; Craven (1988) 181-3]

BASSANO, Christopher (1679-1745)

The Bassanos are one of the oldest musical families in England, descending from Jeronimo di Bassano, a Venetian sackbut virtuoso of the early 16th century. Two of his sons were recruited by Henry VIII to join the court musicians in England and another was an instrument maker and wine shipper of London from 1539. The family were originally from Bassano del Grappa (in the Trentino foothills) and are believed to have been of Jewish stock.

Arturo Bassano (1567-1624), a grandson of Jeronimo, was recruited from Venice to London by Elizabeth I and he founded the enduring English branch of the family.

The outbreak of the Civil War caused the dispersal of the King's orchestra and Richard Bassano (1605-66) fled to Stone (Staffordshire) and, with his son Richard, became vicars choral at Lichfield Cathedral. The younger Richard (1654-1729) was, by Sarah, daughter of Edward Short of Mayfield (Staffordshire) father of Francis (*q.v.*) and Christopher, the latter being his third son, born in 1679.

At first Christopher served as a vicar choral at Lichfield; he was also a composer of anthems and teacher of music. However, on 14th August 1709, he married at St Werburgh, Derby, Dorothy, daughter and co-heiress of Derby solicitor James Motteram, and the couple settled in the city. It was an advantageous match socially, especially as Dorothy's mother was Jane, a daughter and co-heiress of William Wright of Great Longstone Hall.

Here he settled again to composing and teaching until his death; he was buried at St

temperance worker what his contribution was to her crusade he replied bluffly, "My beers are allus well-wattered, madam!"

He was, throughout his long Parliamentary career, keen on improving the lot of the working man (and was himself, despite the tenfold expansion of his business under his aegis, a model employer) and took the side of the railwaymen in 1870 during their agitation for a reduction in their long hours. His initiative also led to the founding of St Christopher's Railway Orphanage at Derby in the 1870s (which re-located to Ashbourne Road in 1889). He twice refused a baronetcy (on the second occasion, one was conferred on his eldest son, Michael Arthur Bass (MP for East Staffordshire), in 1882, instead, and once a peerage. He died at Rangemoor on 29th April 1884, leaving four children, the eldest being Sir Michael Bass, 1st Bt. later (1886) created 1st Lord Burton of Rangemoor and in 1897 Lord Burton of Burton upon Trent with remainder to his only daughter, Nellie Liza and her issue male, the Baillies, who still enjoy the honour. The younger son was Hamar Bass (1842-98) whose son Sir William (1879-1952) was the second and last baronet, and there were two daughters, who became respectively Lady Plowden and Lady Chetwode (grandmother of Lady Betjeman). The

Painter'. He was born at Lichfield 17th October 1675 and spent much of his life painting funeral hatchments and other armorial embellishments for the gentry of Derbyshire, having removed there with his younger brother. His account book survives which demonstrates that he was in demand right across the Midlands and we may deduce therefrom that he was considered pre-eminent in his calling. He was also a careful anti-quary, visiting all the churches of the county and recording the arms, monuments and stained glass he saw – much of them subsequently lost.

He also painted landscapes and portraits, although little of his work can be identified today, except the portraits of Alderman and Mrs Henry Franceys, cut from his exuberantly painted ceiling of No.5 Market Place, Derby, oth-erwise destroyed in 1936. He died in Derby in 1746, unmarried.

[As previous article and: Cox, J.C. *Derbyshire Church Notes,* 4 vols. (Derby 1875-79) II.396; Derby Local Studies Library MS 3525]

Werburgh's 29th August 1745, his wife outlived him by a decade. Their surviving son, Richard (1718-93) inherited Motteram's practice and was the progenitor of a numerous family. Mary, a daughter of the younger Richard married Thomas Swanwick (1754-1814), a pioneering local schoolmaster. Of other descendants, LOUISA became an early 19th century Diva; Maria née Waterfield (wife of Richard, 1750-1815) was the model for Joseph Wright's *Maria and her Dog Silvio* and was a great beauty, and GEORGE HENRY (1840-1913) was a manufac-turing electrician who designed and perfected the Bassanophone, an early disc gramophone of extreme quality *c.*1906 and which are now extremely rare.

[Glover, S. *History and Gazetteer of Derby*, 2 vols. 1829/31 II.575 f.; Derby Local Studies Library, Deeds 6453, 16098; Nicholson, B. *Joseph Wright, Painter of Light*, 2 vols. (London 1968) I.62]

BASSANO, Francis (1675-1746)

Francis was the elder brother of Christopher *(q.v.)* and was always described as a 'Herald

BATE, Maj. Thomas (d.1643)

Maj. Thomas Bate was a typically dashing cavalier and was the fourth but eldest surviving son of Nathaniel Bate of Little Chester Manor (1604-45). The family were of Derby stock, Thomas' great grandfather – another Thomas – having made a good fortune in Derby and London as a draper. He had served as Bailiff of Derby three times (1564, 1576 and 1586) and taken a lease of the estate at Little Chester from the Corporation as well as buying up land at Church Broughton. His grandson Nathaniel – Thomas' father – was the son of Robert, of Little Chester and married Jane, daughter of Edward Turville of Newhall who bore him no less than ten children before expiring. Nathaniel later remarried Catherine, daughter of Thomas Hull of Godalming (Surrey), a widow, and went on to have a further ten children!

Thomas was probably educated at Derby School going from thence to Christ's College, Cambridge (BA 1628) before entering Gray's Inn a year later and becoming a barrister. He joined the King's colours in 1641 but was unmarried at his death in action at Shelford (Cambs.) less than three years later. It was probably as a recognition of this sacrifice that his younger half-brother Nathaniel, of Little Chester (b.1631) was nominated a Knight of the Royal Oak in 1660, although unlike most such nominees he did not receive a knight bachelorhood when it was decided not to proceed with the Order.

It was another brother, Richard of West Broughton, Sudbury, whose issue survived, his posterity settling there and at Uttoxeter (Staffordshire), Ashby de la Zouch (Leics), Essex and London.

[Lysons, S. & D., *Magna Britannia.* Vol *V Derbyshire* (1816) pp. cxvi-cxvii; Visitation of Derbyshire 1662; Local Studies Deed 2089; Nicols *op. cit.* III.2.636]

BATEMAN, Sir Alfred Edmund (1844-1929)

The Batemans are one of the most illustrious of the gentry families of Derbyshire and were settled at Hartington by 1450. The elder branch of the family later settled at Middleton by Youlgreave and produced Thomas, FSA, the noted Antiquary and archaeologist (1821-61). The younger branch were seated at Hartington Hall from the beginning of the 17th century until it was sold in the 1930s. This branch in the 17th century produced four Aldermen and a Lord Mayor of London, and enjoyed (fleetingly) a baronetcy, and became associated with Derby from the Restoration.

A descendant, Rev. John Bateman (1800-82) Rector of East and West Leake (Notts), married Emily daughter of Edward Shavell and had seven sons and four daughters, of whom the youngest son was Alfred Edmund, born 31st August 1844 at Leake vicarage. He was educated at Repton (1857-8) and Brighton before entering the Inner Temple, becoming a barrister in 1872. He became a Board of Trade official in 1865 rising to Comptroller-General of Commerce, Labour and Statistics 1897-1903 as well as Chairman of the Board's Advisory Committee on Commercial Intelligence from 1901, and he served on a num-

ber of Royal Commissions and commercial delegations. The Civil Service, always punctilious in its rewards, recommended him as CMG (1892), and he received his knighthood in the same Order (KCMG) in 1900. From 1916-19 he served as Chairman of the Enemy Export Committee before retiring to Wimbledon, although he also owned properties at Eaton Socon (Beds.) and Uttoxeter (Staffordshire)

In 1868 he married Edith Ellen (died 4th June 1909) only child of James Eland Hobson of Haverfield (Surrey) and Eaton Socon. Of their four sons and three daughters, only one son (John Keelinge Bateman, born 1872) and the daughters survived him. He died on the 7th August 1929.

[Kelly, *Handbook* (1924)147; Debrett, *Baronetage, Knightage,* etc. (1905) 712; Fox-Davies, A.C. *Armorial Families,* 2 vols. (London 1929)1. 109-110.]

BATEMAN, Edward Lewis, CB. (1834-1909)

An elder brother of Sir Alfred Bateman *(q.v.)* he was born on 10th September 1834, fourth son of Rev. John Bateman. He too was educated initially at Repton (1848-49) before going on to Marlborough. He went up to University College, Oxford where he obtained his BA 1856 and like his brother became a barrister (at the Inner Temple in this instance) qualifying in 1866. He served for many years as Assistant Secretary to the Ecclesiastical Commissioners receiving in 1898 the CB (Civil) consequent upon his retirement in June 1897.

He lived nearly all his life at the now vanished Rowditch Lodge – long a property of his family – and at 47 Duke Street, St James's (London). He died unmarried 25th January 1909.

[Kelly, *op. cit.*, 932; *Repton School Register.*]

BATEMAN, Sir Hugh, 1st Bt, (1756-1824)

Sir Hugh Bateman was of Hartington Hall, where the family had a considerable estate, and Derby, where his grandfather, another Hugh, built as a town house the elegant No.36 St Mary's Gate before 1731. This Hugh, an attorney, served as

Town Clerk of Derby 1723-40. Through his first wife, Elizabeth, daughter and coheiress of John Osborne of Derby (by Elizabeth daughter and coheiress of William Sacheverell of Morley) he ultimately inherited the large Morley Hall estate and the sumptuous Osborne Town House, St Mary's Gate House, opposite his own abode which latter he subsequently sold to Blythe Simpson whose legal firm still occupy it.

Hugh's eldest son was Richard (1718-62) whose first marriage to Anne Soresby was childless. On her death he remarried, his bride being Catherine, daughter of William FitzHerbert, MP of Tissington Hall (who had been Recorder of Derby at the same time Bateman's father had been Town Clerk). She bore him two sons, Richard (the grandfather of Sir Alfred and Edward Bateman *q.v.*) and the elder, Hugh, born 23rd September 1756.

Hugh was educated at Derby School *c.*1766 whence he proceeded to University College Oxford (BA 1774), subsequently becoming a barrister. He was a radical, although he never entered Parliament, writing numerous books and pamphlets, the best known of which was *Thoughts upon the Causes of the Present Distress of the Country, and Remedy* (Bath 1816). He inherited the family estates at Hartington and Morley on the death of his grandfather in 1777 and spent much time improving them and acting as an enlightened landlord. He also was a patron of Joseph Wright *(q.v.)* buying two lake scenes (one by day, one by night) and having himself his brother and his son (who died tragically young in 1794 at six) painted. He was a JP and QC. as well as High Sheriff of Derbyshire. He married Temperance, daughter of John Gisborne (the builder of St Helen's House, Derby) and in addition to his short-lived son, Richard Sacheverell, left two daughters; Catherine Juliana and Aurelia Anne. On 15th December 1806 he was (for no clear reason other than his political writings and distinguished connections) raised to a baronetcy with (in default of male issue) a very curious remainder to his daughters in order of birth and their issue male. On his death on 28th January 1824, the baronetcy became abeyant until 25th

February that year when Sir Francis Edward Scott of Great Barr, Sir Hugh's eldest daughter's son, was born! The Scotts became extinct in the male line in 1905, when the baronetcy passed to 1st Lord St Audries, grandson of Aurelia, Lady Hood, Sir Hugh's younger daughter. Most of the estates, however, were entailed and passed to the baronet's nephew, R.T.Bateman.

[Tachella, *op.cit* 18; Burke, A., *Family Records* (London n.d. (*c.*1904)) 49; Burke, J.B., *Peerage* (1970) 2345; Nicholson, B., *op.cit.* 1.128]

BATER, Rev. Alfred Brenchley (d. 1933)

The former teacher training college at Derby (now absorbed into the University) was notable in having three great principals in succession. The first of these was Rev. Canon A.B.Bater, appointed in 1898, nearly 50 years after the founding of the institution in 1851.

Bater took over and set out his agenda in the Autumn edition of the 1898 College magazine. He set about broadening the curriculum, expanding the students' horizons, introducing a proper library and instigated the founding of the Chapel. A building programme which ran from 1900 to 1914 included new dormitories, lecture rooms, chapel and gymnasium, all designed by P.H.Currey *(q.v.)* 'By the example of his own energy, by his power of inspiring both staff and students and by the many means he took of broadening the experience of the students, [he] succeeded in putting Derby among the foremost Training Colleges.'

Bater was also, from 1898 to 1907, domestic chaplain to the Drury-Lowes at Locko Park and in 1907-8 was Worshipful Master of the Tyrian Lodge of Freemasons at Derby. He married Lydia, daughter of H.Bloomfield Kempe of Belle Vue, Brent, Middlesex (a grandson of Admi. Kempe) and they had two sons, Kenneth and Reginald, and three daughters.

Canon Bater retired in 1927 to be succeed by Miss Helen HAWKINS *(q.v.)* and died in 1933. A window was dedicated to his memory in the chapel at the college two years later.

[Dobson, M. *The First Hundred Years of Diocesan*

Training College, Derby (London 1951) pp 23-39; Tachella, *op.cit.* 160; *Derbyshire Advertiser* 8/11/1935]

BEETHAM James Herbert (1909-1992)

J.H.Beetham was World Billiard Champion in 1960 and English Amateur Billiards Champion in 1966 and 1968. He was also a Director of White Bros. (Derby) Ltd., soft drink manufacturers, a firm started in Havelock Road in 1903 by Edwin and James White and Beetham's father, James Henry (d.1957). The Whites were two of four brothers, originally (like Beetham senior) from Bury (Lancs), later of Wolverhampton, who also founded Midland Counties Dairies, Birmingham, in 1913; they were also cousins of Beetham's mother, a Miss Birch.

James Herbert, elder of two sons, was born at Factory House, Havelock Road in 1909, joining the family firm in 1925, and taking it over prior to his father's death in the 1950s. He was a lifelong devotee of Billiards, beginning at 19 years of age and was the Derby Institute's champion by 1931; he was runner-up in the English Amateur Championships four times before winning in 1960, 1961 and 1963. He was runner-up again (at 68) in 1977. He died in April 1992, leaving, by Maude his wife, Philip J.Beetham of Littleover, who succeeded his father as Managing Director of White Bros. Of his grandchildren, one James, is a barrister, the other, Helen, an accountant.

[Consterdine, N. *et al. The Story of Normanton* (1993) 82-4; DET 26/6/1992 & 24/11/1995]

BELL, Sir John Ferguson (1856-1937)

John Bell was the son of Jonathan Bell, a Liverpool businessman and the sister of W.T.Callow, a Birkenhead gas engineer – one of the first generation of such men who helped pioneer the availability of town gas to the country. Young John began his working life with his uncle, coming to Derby in 1900 as chief engineer of the Derby Gas, Light and Coke Company. He rose to be Managing Director in 1932 and held the post

until his death in November 1937. He was a member of the Institutions of both the Civil and Mechanical Engineers, and lived at Ivy House, Mickleover.

He was elected to Derby Borough Council in 1913 as a conservative; later he became an Alderman and served as Mayor 1928-29 and again as Mayor Suffect on the death of Alderman Grant in 1930. He was also Deputy Chairman of the Derby Savings Bank and of Derby High School, a governor of Derby School and a member of the Derwent Valley Water Board. He was knighted in 1929. In 1885 he married Elizabeth, daughter of William Stroyan by whom he had a son, A.Ferguson Bell, (like his father an engineer) and two daughters. His sister, Marjorie, acted as his Mayoress during his second mayoralty.

[MMD. 11.55-57, 59; *Who's Who in Derbyshire* (1934) 14-15.]

BELL, Richard, MP (1859-1930)

Richard Bell is notable for having been Derby's first Labour MP, having been elected for the Borough in 1900, and representing it until 1910 when he was succeeded by Jimmy THOMAS *(q.v.)*.

Bell was a Welshman, born 1859, the son of Sgt. Charles Bell, Glamorganshire Constabulary, who lived at Penderryn, Glamorgan. He became a railway guard with the GWR in 1876, took a keen interest in trade union affairs and resigned from the Great Western in 1891, rising to General Secretary of the Amalgamated Society of Railway Servants in 1897, a post he retained until 1910; he was TUC president in 1904. He lived at New Southgate, London, throughout his time as Derby's MP, and on retirement became Divisional Officer to the (Central) Labour Exchange (1910), from 1912 Insurance Officer, Board of Trade Unemployment Insurance, and from 1920 Technical Officer to the Minister of Labour. He was a JP and local councillor.

He married twice, his second wife being the daughter of Swansea's Borough Engineer, Mr

Woozley, but had no children, he died in 1930. [Kelly, *Handbook* (1924)164; Debrett's *House of Commons and Judicial Bench* (1905) p.12; Gaskell, E., *Derbyshire Leaders* (n.d. c.1910).]

BELPER, Lord, see STRUTT

BEMROSE, Sir Henry Howe (1827-1911)

Sir Henry Bemrose was the eldest son of WILLIAM BEMROSE *(q.v.)* and through his mother was a great grandson of Alderman Matthew How (Mayor in 1779). He was born in the premises now occupied by Lloyd's Bank, Iron

Gate, 19th November 1827. Educated at Derby School, he entered his father's business in 1843. He later became first Chairman of Bemrose & Sons Ltd., and entered the council as a conservative in 1871 and became Mayor and an Alderman six years later. He was a freemason (Tyrian Lodge, Derby) from 1858, a JP from 1870 and a Liveryman of the Worshipful Company of Coachmakers. In 1895 he won one of the two Derby seats in Parliament, but was unseated in

1900. He was knighted 3rd August 1897 and received the Honorary Freedom of the Borough in March 1910.

Bemrose was an enthusiast for church affairs and choral music especially, acting as additional organist at All Saints'. He wrote *Systematic Lay-Work in the Church* and *A Month in Egypt* and was a distinguished bibliophile and much of his collection was bequeathed to the city on his death. His house, by T.C.Hine, was Lonsdale Hill (later Lonsdale Hall), Lonsdale Place, where he lived with his wife Charlotte (1831-1911) a daughter of Alderman William Brindley whom he married May 8th 1855. He died on 5th May 1911, leaving a son, HENRY HOWE BEMROSE *(q.v.)* and five daughters.

[Bemrose, H.H., *The House of Bemrose* (Derby 1926) 157-58.]

BEMROSE, Henry Howe Arnold FGS (1857-1939)

Only son of Sir HENRY BEMROSE *(q.v.)*, H.H.Bemrose (he adopted the additional name Arnold to distinguish himself from his like-

named father prior to the latter's knighthood) was born at Derby 13th March 1857 and was educated at Denbigh School and Clare, Cambridge (BA 1879, MA 1882). He was an enthusiastic and pioneering geologist, concentrating on Derbyshire, gaining a DSc in 1908. He wrote (with his wife) *The County Geography of Derbyshire* and the relevant chapter in the *Victoria County History of Derbyshire* (1905). He also contributed a number of periodical articles and papers on Derbyshire geology and history. He later became a Fellow of the Geographical Society. He entered the family firm in 1879 and became Deputy Chairman in 1912 and later Chairman.

He was first elected to the Derby Borough council (as a Conservative) in 1903 and joined the bench a year later. He chaired the Education, and Museums and Libraries Committees before becoming Mayor 1909-10 and an Alderman in 1910. He later served, from 1916, as Chairman of the Derwent Valley Water Board. He followed his father in being an active freemason (initiated into the Tyrian Lodge 1879). He twice refused a second mayoralty and was made an Honorary Freeman of Derby in 1935, dying four years later..

On 23rd July 1890 he married Nellie, daughter of Rev. John Hyde of Manchester (by Ellen, daughter of Alderman George Holme, Mayor of Derby in 1874). They lost their two eldest sons in World War One: Lt. Karl Bemrose, 2/5th Bn. Sherwood Foresters, killed on the first day of the Somme, and Lt. Roderick Henry Arnold Bemrose RFA, MC. who died three days before the Armistice. Two other sons were S/Ldr. Clive Esmond Bemrose OBE and SIR MAX BEMROSE *(q.v.)* with a daughter Eliza Eleanor.
[Bemrose, *op.cit.* 158; *Who Was Who* 1931-40]

BEMROSE, Sir John Maxwell (1904-1986)

Sir Max Bemrose was the fourth son of the foregoing *(q.v.)* and was born at Derby 1st July 1904 and was educated at Derby School, Brighton, where he was head boy and captain of rugger, and Clare, Cambridge, taking his MA in due course. He entered the family firm and rose to be

Chairman and Managing Director in 1952, serving as President of the British Federation of Master Printers 1967-68 and 1970-71. He was High Sheriff of Derbyshire two years later. He was much influenced by Lord Keynes, his tutor at Cambridge.

Bemrose was an active Conservative, fighting (without success) Derby in 1945 and Watford in 1950. He later became Chairman of the National Union of Conservative and Unionist Associations (1964) and was knighted 5th July 1960.

In 1933 he married Margaret, daughter of P.R. le Mare of Hertford, settling at Hazlebrow, Hazlewood Road, Duffield and had two children, Anthony, later of Melbourne, Australia and Pamela Mary, later Mrs Peter Cunningham. He died 13th July 1986.
[Kelly, *Handbook* (1976) 218; *Knights Bachelor* (1964-5) 48; WLG 11/1968 pp.31-2.]

BEMROSE, William (1792-1880)

Founder of the illustrious local printing firm of Bemrose, William came from a long line of Lincolnshire yeomen, his ancestor in the seventh generation being Thomas Bemrose of Fillingham, who died in 1602. His father, Joseph, (1760-1822) after service in the army, settled at Newark, (Notts), having married Avis, daughter of William Flower of that place, and William was born there 15th October 1792. He was, in 1807, apprenticed as a compositor to J.Mozley, printer of Gainsborough whose firm transferred to Derby with conspicuous success in 1815, Bemrose going with the company before transferring his services to a local firm. He founded his own firm 18th October 1826, transferring to the late 17th century house which now houses Lloyd's Bank a year later. He greatly expanded the firm between 1855 and 1875, pioneering lithography, colour printing and other techniques. Unlike the three generations of his posterity, he eschewed public life, never wore a watch nor an overcoat.

He married at St Peter's, Derby 29th July 1824, Elizabeth, daughter of Benjamin Ride of Lichfield; her mother had been the daughter and heiress of Alderman Matthew How, Mayor of Derby in 1779, connecting thereby a whole network of Derby municipal families of the 17th and 18th centuries, underlining the remarkable staying power of municipal oligarnies in provincial English towns, even after Municipal Reform in 1835.

William and Elizabeth Bemrose had three sons, (HENRY HOWE *(q.v.)*, WILLIAM *(q.v.)* and Edward) and two daughters. Bemrose was incapacitated by a stroke in 1875 and died in Derby 12th February 1880.
[Bemrose, *op.cit.* 157]

BEMROSE, William (1831-1908)

Second son of WILLIAM BEMROSE *(q.v.)*, William was born at the premises in Iron Gate 30th December 1831. He was educated at Bonsall and King William's, I.o.M., entering the family

business in 1847, later serving as a director to 1890; he was also an original director of Royal Crown Derby, having, as chairman of the then independent Litchurch Local Board (1876-77) been largely instrumental in the porcelain factory's establishment on Osmaston Road. He was a JP (1885), Chairman of the Derby School Board 1896-1902, Chairman of the Borough's

Art Gallery Committee, and a member of the Library and Museum, and Technical Institution Committees.

Bemrose was a notable antiquary and historian, travelling widely, reading and collecting avidly. He played a major role in rescuing historic local artefacts form oblivion and was author of *Bow, Chelsea and Derby Porcelain* (he was a notable collector of china, too) and the *Life of Joseph Wright of Derby* (1885). The latter's inspiration was undoubtedly his marriage, at Spondon 4th August 1858, to Margaret Romana, daughter of Edward Lloyd Simpson, a descendant of Joseph Wright *(q.v.)* whose daughter Anna Romana, from whom (despite the continued existence of the artist's male line) Bemrose inherited many family treasures as well as a number of pictures. By Margaret Romana he had five sons and two daughters. Of these, the eldest son, Brig. William Wright Bemrose VD, DL, JP (1859-1934) cemented the Crown Derby connection by marrying the niece of another of the firm's founders WILLIAM LITHERLAND *(q.v.)* and the third, Frederick Edward (1863-1901), married the daughter of T.C.SIMMONDS *(q.v.)*. His wife died in 1901 and on 3rd January 1903 he remarried Lilian, widow of Alderman WILLIAM HOBSON *(q.v.)* but died at his house on Osmaston Road on 6th August 1908 without further issue.

[Bemrose, *op.cit.* 158]

BENNET, Gervase MP JP (1611-1660)

Bennet's only claim to fame lies in his encounter with George Fox (1624-91), the founder of the Society of Friends. The Commonwealth, once established was, if anything, even less tolerant of religious heterodoxy than in the King's time, and Fox had been arrested in Derby for preaching in a way not sanctioned by Parliament. On 30th October 1650 he was brought before the bench in Derby, then being presided over by Alderman Gervase Bennet. 'Justice Bennet of Derby' Fox later wrote, 'was the first that called us Quakers, because I bid him "Tremble at the Word of the Lord".'

Gervase Bennet was the second son of Robert Bennet, of Littleover, a Derby lead merchant, by his wife, Anne, daughter of Michael Ward of Derby and was born in Derby on 2nd June 1611. He continued as a lead merchant but was also a Derby mercer, and was a keen supporter of the Parliamentary cause. He served as a Brother and Alderman of the Borough, becoming Mayor 1645-46 and was appointed by Sir JOHN GELL *(q.v.)* to the bench. Once the Commonwealth was established, he used his considerable fortune to acquire the sequestrated estate of Snelston Hall and served as MP for Derby, 1653-59, dying the following year.

Bennet married three times, a fact, along with the issue therefrom, he succeeded in keeping from Dugdale when he was compiling the Derbyshire Visitation after the Restoration. His first wife, Margaret (died 1639) was mother of Samuel Nathaniel (of Inner Temple in 1658) and two daughters. He then married Margaret Hope in 1641 (by whom he appears to have had no issue) and in 1655, Elizabeth, daughter and co-heiress of John Rowe of Windle Hill, by whom he had a son, Robert – who obtained and, in 1682, sold the Snelston estate – and Elizabeth. John Bennet, son of Samuel, still held land at Windle Hill in 1741.

[*Visitation of Derbyshire* 1662; Craven (1988) 60; Fox, G. *Journal… of the Life… of George Fox* (London 1694) 37-38; DAJ. LXXXVI (1966)12; Jeayes, I.H., *Records of the County Borough of Derby* (1904) III.3.68; Local Studies Library, Deed 16353; Deeds in Derby Museum]

BENNETT, Joan Sterndale (1914-1996)

Joan Sterndale Bennett was a notable actress of Derby descent, born 5th March 1914, only child of Thomas (1882-1944), composer, songwriter and entertainer, by Annie Christine, daughter of Henry Thomas Bywater of Wolverhampton. Her father was the third of six sons of Rev. James Robert Sterndale-Bennett (1848-1928), from 1889 to 1898 headmaster of Derby School. Joan's great-grandfather was Prof. Sir William Sterndale Bennett (1816-75) the Victorian composer and protégé of Mendelssohn. It is of interest to note that this was a Derbyshire family, Sir William's grandfather John having come from Ashford-in-the-Water when he married a Miss Sterndale of another old Peak District family.

Joan Sterndale-Bennett enjoyed a long and varied career, although she never achieved the heights of fame. She married (and divorced) the actor John Barron, but died 29th April 1996 without leaving issue.

[*Daily Telegraph*, *obit.* 2/5/1996; Tachella (1902) XI; DNB]

BENT, Dr Thomas (1792-1859)

Thomas Bent was one of the three inaugural physicians appointed to the Derbyshire General Infirmary. He was appointed at the remarkable age of 21 in 1813 by WILLIAM STRUTT *(q.v.)* and owed his post to Strutt's friendship with the Wedgwood family of Etruria (Staffordshire) to whom Thomas' father, Dr. James Justin Bent, was close; indeed, Bent senior had amputated Josiah Wedgwood's leg on 28th May 1768 and was acquainted with both ERASMUS DARWIN and JOHN WHITEHURST *(q.q.v.)*.

Bent's mother was Elizabeth, sister of Sir John

Edensor Heathcote of Longton Hall (a man of Derbyshire descent) and Sir John's daughter latter married Bent's elder brother Richard. Thomas was descended in the fifth generation from Laurence Bent of Bent Lanes (Lancs.) who died in 1670. Bent's wife, Mary Helen, died in 1823 along with their son, in childbirth, but he continued at the General Infirmary until his suicide in May 1859, when he bequeathed his estate at Bent Lanes and his opulent town house at 77 Friar Gate (which he had purchased in 1813 for the not inconsiderable sum of £2,205) to his nephew Arthur Rawson, son of his sister, Anne. One thing is sure; Bent did not embark on his career merely for financial reward.

[Bourke, J. *Commoners* (1833) II. 408; Reilly, R. *Josiah Wedgwood* (London 1992) 69, 111, 143; Craven, M., *The Derby Townhouse* (Derby 1987) 103.]

BENSON, Sir George (1889-1973)

Sir George Benson was that rare thing, a socialist estate agent. He was born in Manchester 3rd May 1889, the son of Thomas Duckworth Benson,

Sir George Benson

also an estate agent and socialist pamphleteer. He went to Manchester Grammar School, qualified as an Associate (later a Fellow) of the Institute of Auctioneers and Valuers and entered his father's business. He was treasurer of the Independent Labour Party 1923-24, Chairman of the Howard League for Penal Reform 1938-61 and Member of the Home Office Advisory Committee of Treatment of Offenders. In 1922 he unsuccessfully contested Altrincham (Cheshire), before trying his luck at Chesterfield in 1923 and 1924, being third time lucky in 1929. He was, however, defeated in the 1931 election, as he refused to have any truck with the National Government. In 1935 he got his seat back and sat until retirement in 1964. His only post in government was as PPS to Pethick-Lawrence, Financial Secretary to the Treasury, 1930-31. He was no slouch in his radicalism either; his credentials, including imprisonment for Conscientious Objection during World War One were impeccable. He was knighted for political services 11th February 1958.

On 25th June 1919 he married Marjorie, daughter of H.B.Lodge. After winning Chesterfield for the second time, he took up residence at 6 Constable Drive, Littleover where he died 17th August 1973. He left, with a daughter, a son, Dr George Benson of Littleover (1923-92) whose wife Barbara (daughter of Dr Henry Lavelle of Ashbourne Road) took the family in a new, political direction by being elected to the Borough Council as a Liberal in 1967. This tradition is being maintained by the present generation of his kinsmen.

[Stenton, M. & Lees, S., *Who's Who of British Members of Parliament* Vol. IV (Brighton 1981) 25; *Knights Bachelor* (1964-5) 49]

BILLINGSLEY, William (1758-1828)

William Billingsley was one of the finest china painters this country has ever produced, his flower paintings being especially accomplished; later he made several attempts to set up as a porcelain manufacturer in his own right. Billingsley was born in Derby and baptised at St Alkmund's Church 12th October 1758, his father, also William, (d.1770) being one of the first painters employed at the china factory in Nottingham Road under WILLIAM DUESBURY (*q.v.*). Billingsley *père* was also proprietor of the Sir John Falstaff Inn on Bridge Gate, and ran a button warehouse nearby. Billingsley's mother was Mary Dallison; his parents married at St Werburgh's, 9th October 1757.

Billingsley was apprenticed to the Derby China works and at 16 was taken on for five years at 5/- per week and in 1790 succeeded Edward Withers as chief floral decorator. In 1796 he left Derby to set up a new china factory at Pinxton in partnership with John Coke of Debdale Hall (Notts) who owned the site. Here he made porcelain to his own formula and worked as principal painter. However, it was never a financial success and Billingsley left in 1799 to go to Mansfield and then Torksey where he went back to decorating others' wares. The latter firm also failed in 1808. Thereafter he embarked on a series of heroic peregrinations around England with his two daughters (Lavinia b.1795 and Sarah, b.1783, later Mrs Walker) attempting to find backing for his efforts to manufacture a soft paste English porcelain fine enough to rival the best on offer on the Continent. Eventually he was able to set up at Nantgarw (Glamorgan) in 1813, but technical difficulties obliged him to work at the Swansea factory just over a year later and although he revived Nantgarw in 1817-20, it finally closed in the latter year. Thereafter, he and his partner and son-in-law, Samuel Walker, secured work at Coalport. He died 16th January 1828.

Billingsley's finest work, despite all this, was at Derby in the decade from 1780; he was friendly with Zachariah Boreman, who had arrived at Derby two years before and the latter to some extent influenced him. Billingsley was allocated the number 7 at Derby, sometimes found in red on the inside of the foot rim of his pieces with the factory mark in blue or puce.

Billingsley married at St Alkmund's, Derby 4th November 1780, Sarah Rigley (1761-1825), aunt of the china painter William Wheeldon (1790-1874) who seems to have taken over the Billingsley enterprise on Bridge Gate. Through Wheeldon,

Billingsley became related by marriage to the china painters John Yates (d.1821) and GEORGE ROBERTSON (*q.v.*), as well as JOSEPH WRIGHT (*q.v.*). Their son, James, died in infancy, and of the daughters Louisa died unmarried at Eglwysilan, Nantgarw, in 1817 and Sarah married Samuel Walker (1781-1880). After Billingsley's death he eventually emigrated to the USA where he successfully established the New Troy pottery, where his descendants flourished for many years.
[Graham, M. & Oxley, J., *English Porcelain Painters of the 18th Century* (London 1981); Jewitt, L.L., *Ceramic Art of Great Britain* II.101; Haslem, J., *The Old Derby China Factory* (London 1876) 47-61.]

BINGE, Ronald (1910-79)

Ronald Binge was born in Derby 15th July 1910 of unpretentious parentage and as a schoolboy studied organ at St Werburgh's under Norman Hibbert. The family lived at first in Westbury Street, St Lukes, later moving to 29 Wiltshire Road, Chaddesden. A talented musician, he became a good composer and better arranger, doing film scores and much work for Mantovani whose 'cascading strings' he developed and orchestrated in 1951. His compositions include the suites *Elizabethan Serenade, Sailing By* and *Spitfire,* a concerto for alto saxophone and a fine *Te Deum.*

He served in the RAF during World War Two, having early on moved to London and, with increasing prosperity, settled with his wife, Vera (whom he married in 1945) at Ringwood, Hants. He died on 6th September 1979 leaving a daughter Margaret. A plaque to his memory was unveiled in Derby Assembly Rooms in April 1998.
[*Derby Evening Telegraph* 19/8/1995, 12/10/1997, 25/4/1998; Sadie, S. *New Grove Dictionary of Music and Musicians* Vol.2 p.723]

BINGHAM, Rev. John (1607-1689)

Bingham was a one-legged puritan divine whose saintliness and pastoral gifts were widely regarded, even amongst those who, like his friend Archbishop Sheldon, were divided from him by the strictness of Conformity. He was born in Derby in 1607, the son of Thomas Bingham, rector of Stapenhill, and grandson of Nicholas, a merchant who also had interests in London. He was educated at Repton School and St John's Oxford (MA 1631). Thereafter he was obliged to undergo the amputation of a leg as a result of some accident as a child to the foot, which never recovered. The operation is said to have turned his hair white. He served as a domestic chaplain until 1640 when he was appointed assistant master of Derby School, succeeding as head two years later and serving throughout the upheavals of SIR JOHN GELL *(q.v.)* governorship until appointed by the Earl of Devonshire – thanks to his puritan outlook – to the living of Marston-on-Dove. Upon the Restoration he suffered ejection from his cure in 1662, whereupon he went to live in Brailsford, where he preached at his home on Sunday afternoons. He was nevertheless excommunicated by the conforming vicar, Barnabas Pole, despite attending church regularly. He then retired to Upper Thurvaston in Sutton-on-the-Hill parish, where he died 3rd February 1688/9. He was 'remarkably temperate, of a charitable disposition and of true unaffected piety'.

Bingham left a son, Thomas, (d.1734), a Derby mercer from whom a numerous and complex dynasty descended, although most of the family had left Derby by the mid-19th century.
[Simpson (1826) III. 561-2; Cox, *op.cit.* III. 203 & n.; Glover *op.cit.* 11.604, Walford's *County Families* (1865) 86.]

BINGHAM, Sir John Edward, Bt. (1839-1915)

John and Corless Bingham, descendants of JOHN (see above) left Derby in the late 18th century. John settled at Chesterfield where he took an interest in a foundry. His son, Edward (1809-80) moved to Sheffield and became involved in the cutlery trade, settling with his wife, Emma, daughter of Arthur Dyson of Tinsley, (Yorkshire) at Broomgrove Lodge. The eldest of their two sons (they also had two daughters) was John Edward, born 27th July 1839.

He entered the cutlery trade, developing strong links with Messrs. Walker and Hall, and much increased the family fortune. He made many munificent benefactions to Sheffield and served as Master Cutler twice, in 1881 and 1884. He also commanded the West Riding (Sheffield) divisional R.E. volunteers for 17 years, being appointed Honorary Colonel in 1900. All this was duly rewarded and he was, on 12th December 1903, raised to a baronetcy, of Sheffield.

In March 1863 he married Maria, daughter of William Fawcett of Sheffield and they settled at West Lea, Ranmoor, Yorkshire (WR). He died 18th March 1915 when the baronetcy descended on their only child Albert Edward (born 1868) but became extinct on his death 25th February 1945, leaving only a daughter Esmé Lyle, Mrs P.Elliot Inchbald of Great Baddow, Essex.
[Debrett, *Baronetcy and Knightage* (1905) 48; Burke, *Peerage* (1931) 288; *Who Was Who* 1941-50 (London 1951) 101.]

BIRCHALL, William Minshall (b.1884)

Birchall was a marine artist of considerable talent who is generally thought of as American, having been born at Cedar Rapids, Iowa, 10th September 1884, whither his father William Henry had migrated. W.H.Birchall – a self-styled 'business manager' – however, was a grandson of a Derby coal merchant Minshall Birchall of Duke Street (1792-1862). He, in his turn, was younger son of Minshall Birchall of Bridge Gate (1762-1811), a clockmaker.

Birchall, who returned to the UK at the turn of the century 'always had a brush in his hand since he can remember,' and produced a large number of marine set pieces, numbering among his clientele Gustav V of Sweden. He exhibited chiefly at the Water-colour Artists' Gallery. He married Rosetta Beauchamp and at his death left a daughter and sole heiress.
[*Who's Who in Art*, 3rd Edn. (London 1934) 38-

39; DM. 29/8/1811; Tachella (1902) 31, 36, 39, 178.]

BLOOMER, Steve (1874-1938)

Although born at Cradley Heath (Staffordshire) on 20th January 1874, Stephen Bloomer moved with his family to Derby as a child, being introduced to the delights of soccer at St James' School, later making a distinctive mark as a member of the Derby Swifts team, scoring 14 goals for them in one match! Spotted by Derby County, he joined the club in April 1892, scoring four times in his first game. He made his Football League debut that September against Stoke (when he played only because the Derby secretary forgot to register some of his team-mates in time) and soon became popular with the crowd, as he was reliable as a goalscorer. He was Derby's leading scorer in all matches for 14 seasons and won the first of 23 England caps in 1895, scoring twice in a 9-0 win over Ireland at the County Ground, Derby. He was described as 'crafty as an oriental and as slippery as an eel and is much

given to dealing out electric shocks to goalkeepers at the end of a sinuous run'.

In 1906 he was transferred to Middlesbrough, rejoining Derby to rapturous acclaim in 1910 and skippering the team to promotion. In 1914 he went to coach in Germany where World War One caught up with him and he was interned. The war over, he played with and coached Derby's reserves before ending his career at the Baseball Ground as general assistant, living at 35 Portland Street. His health failing, he embarked on a cruise (paid for by the Derby County directors) in 1938 but died shortly after his return home on 16th April at the Great Northern Inn, which his son-in-law Cyril Richards had taken over.

Bloomer's brother, Philip, also played for Derby County – once, in September 1895 having been signed the previous May. Steve Bloomer himself had four daughters of whom two died young. Of the survivors, one married a Derby County star, Alfred Quantrill (1897-1968) and their son Alan was a hockey player for Cheshire. Doris (1901-88), the other daughter, married Cyril Richards, landlord of the Great Northern Inn, Junction Street and eventually took the pub over from her husband. Their son, Stephen, a Harpenden-based journalist, was instrumental in causing the erection of a memorial to his grandfather in Lock-up Yard, Derby in 1996.
[DET. 9/11/1996; Mortimer, G., *Who's Who of Derby County* (Derby 1992) 26-27, 158.]

BLOOR, Robert (1778-1846)

Purchaser, in 1811, of the Derby Porcelain factory, from MICHAEL KEAN *(q.v.)* – which cost him £5,000 (payable in instalments) and various annuities to Kean and members of the Duesbury family – Bloor had previously been employed as a clerk and later as a salesman under his predecessors. The products of the factory under Bloor were said to have lacked the quality of those produced under Duesbury and Kean, but this reputation is largely the result of Bloor's systematic selling by auction of factory seconds in order to maximise profits to complete payment for the works to Kean. Previously

these would have been destroyed. Further, Bloor was the first proprietor not to have served in the creative side – the first businessman, in fact – and his period's quality of decoration has been criticised in the light of this, too. In fact, the quality of the best wares was probably just as high as before; one also has to bear in mind the changing taste of the clientele as England entered the High Regency age.

Bloor was born in 1778 the elder son of John Bloor, (d.1816), a Church Gresley weaver and farmer; he may have worked at a pottery in the Church Gresley area before coming to Derby. His younger brother Joseph (d.1846) worked under him at Derby, but later became a chemist and owned two inns, the Britannia (River St) and White Bear (Derwent Row). Robert had, by his first wife, a son, R.W.Bloor, who seems to have become estranged from his family, also daughters, Charlotte (d.unm.1837) and Harriet, who married in 1824 Edward Ramsbottom of Liverpool, solicitor, father-in-law of THOMAS CLARKE *(q.v.)*.

Bloor is said to have become insane through the pressures of declining business, but in fact the factory flourished in his absence (from 1828) and his affliction may have had other causes. He died at Hathern (Leics) 11th March 1846, by which time the husband of his grand-daughter and heiress, Alderman Thomas Clarke (Mayor of Derby 1862-3) had taken over by way of a Statute of Lunacy (1844) and at the end of 1848 closed it down, selling everything to a Stoke potter, Samuel Boyle. Some of the former workforce, however, left the failing Boyle and set up a new pottery on King Street, Derby, which continued the Derby factory's traditions until 1935 (see SAMPSON HANCOCK, qv).
[Haslem, *op.cit.* 27-31; Will of John (8/3/1814) and Joseph Bloor (16/4/1841); Deeds of White Bear Inn, Derby Museum; Parish records]

BLORE, Edward FRS, FSA, DCL (1787-1879)

Edward Blore was an architect who rose to official appointment to both King William IV and

Queen Victoria. He was born at Derby being baptised at All Saints', 30th September 1787; his father was of an Ashbourne family and a Derby solicitor, but later went on to become a barrister and noted antiquary and historian. His mother Dorothy (1758-1808), daughter of William Milnes of Aldercar Hall, was the widow of Philip Gell of Wirksworth. Robert Blore (d.1866), the former Derby china modeller and potter, who had been educated at Repton, was the son of a 'Mr Blore of Ashbourne' and may well have been a kinsman.

Blore developed an enthusiasm for gothic architecture as a young man at Stamford (Lincs.) whilst working as a topographical artist. His introduction to Sir Walter Scott in 1816 and his subsequent input to the design of the novelist's seat at Abbotsford (Roxburgh) made his reputation and facilitated his transition from antiquarian draughtsman to architect. A reputation for being inexpensive got him the job of finishing the extravagant Nash's Buckingham Palace in 1832 and he went on to work extensively at Windsor and Hampton Court; he was also surveyor to Westminster Abbey. He retired in 1849 but lived in London until his death 4th September 1879.

His architecture, almost all in the gothic or 'Jacobeathan' style was always a trifle pedestrian and although quite as scholarly as, say, Pugin's, it lacked his genius. Nevertheless he was responsible for 18 public buildings, work on 49 churches and cathedrals and 62 country and town houses, including Aloupka, in the Crimea for Prince Michael Woronzow (1837-40). Strangely, apart from alterations to Willersley Castle, Cromford for the Arkwrights (1843) he did no work in his native county.

Blore married, in 1819, Sarah, daughter of Rev. W.Hodges, vicar of Mattersey (Notts) and had two sons and two daughters. Of the former, one Rev. E.W.Blore was a Fellow of Trinity, Cambridge (d.1885) and the other, Rev. G.J.B.Blore, was head of King's School, Canterbury. The younger daughter, Margaret, (d.1890) married Charles Keyser of Stanmore (Middlesex) and left issue.

[Colvin, Sir H.M., *Biographical Dictionary of British Architects 1600-1840* (3rd Edn. London 1995) pp.129-135; DNB; *Derbyshire Miscellany,* 6 (6/1957) p.80; Lysons, *op.cit.* v.1-2]

BOOTT, Kirk (1790-1837)

Kirk Boott, the son of a Boston millionaire, was co-founder with Nathan Appleton and Patrick T.Jackson of the mill town of Lowell (Mass. USA) in the early 1820s. He was born, the third son of Kirk Boott (1755-1817) in September 1790 at Boston. His father was the second son of a Derby greengrocer and market gardener, Francis, whose premature death in 1776 plunged his five sons and two daughters into penury, encouraging the elder Kirk in 1781 to go to London with his life-long friend John Wright (eldest brother of JOSEPH *(q.v.)*), to seek their fortunes. Wright soon returned to Derby, but Boott was made of sterner stuff and, almost on impulse, migrated to Boston on the *Rosamund* in 1783, during which voyage he fell in love with the Captain's daughter, Mary Love, marrying her in 1785. The eldest son was christened John Wright Boott after his friend.

Maintaining contacts in Derby (which he re-

visited three times before his death in 1817) he was able to prevail on friends and family to consign materials to him to sell, including Derby Porcelain and BROWN's *(q.v.)* spar ornaments.

Kirk, the younger, was sent to England for his education, going to Rugby before returning to study at Harvard. He then joined the British Army, seeing action in the Peninsular 1811-14 before being stationed in Sheffield as a Captain in the 85th Regiment. Through all this, he made frequent visits to Derby, staying with the family of WILLIAM STRUTT *(q.v.)*, the Wrights and his aunt, Mrs John Horrocks. In 1818, he married at St Michael's, Derby on 4th November, Anne, daughter of Alderman Thomas Haden (a kinsman of Joseph Wright), by whom he had three sons and three daughters.

At Lowell (named after Francis Cabot Lowell, whose original idea it was but who died prematurely) he called on the goodwill and expertise of William Strutt for the design and equipment of his mills. As 'agent' – effectively having a free hand and all the purse strings – he was instrumental in developing and controlling almost all aspects of the town's life and layout. He even designed the church of St Anne (allegedly named after his wife) to resemble St Michael's, Derby! Numerous Derby people followed him to Lowell (including the unfortunate William Duesbury III) and his ideas there determined the character of many other industrial communities.

He died in a street accident at Lowell on 11th April 1837; his posterity is still active in America. One of the entrepreneurs he attracted to Lowell was George, the father of James Abbott MacNeil Whistler, the eminent artist, whose half-sister married Mrs Boott's nephew SIR FRANCIS SEYMOUR HADEN *(q.v.)*.

[Parker, B., *Kirk Boott and the Founding of Lowell* (Boston 1983); DNB; DM 21/6/1776, 28/8/1761, 19/11/1818, 12/12/1820; *Concise Dictionary of American Biography* (New York 1964) 90.]

BOULTBEE, John ARA (1753-1812)

John Boultbee was a talented sporting artist who was born at Osgathorpe (Leics) in 1753, twin with Thomas, who followed the same calling, if with less success. In 1776 he settled at Derby, moving to Loughborough some 20 years later and finally settling in Liverpool where he died in 1812. One of his paintings from his Derby period hangs at Calke Abbey.

[*Dictionary of Sporting Painters,* 758.8]

BOWRING, Sir (Charles) Clement, JP (1844-1907)

Clement Bowring was an opulent wine merchant whose father became a partner of the old established firm of Cox, later taking it over and vastly expanding it. Their headquarters were latterly in a well-proportioned ashlar faced new building 11-14 Iron Gate (now *P.J.Pepper's*). Bowring became a powerful figure in the local Conservative Party, becoming Chairman of the Derby Association and Vice-President of the National Union. He served 21 years as an officer in 1st Volunteer Bn. Sherwood Foresters, receiving the long service medal.

Bowring was born in Derby 25th November 1844, son of Charles Bowring (1816-89), who built the family house, Park Grange, Duffield Road to designs of G.H.Sheffield in 1868 and who was a solicitor who came to Derby at the age of two – when his father, another Charles, of Wellington (Salop) died – to live with his grandmother. His mother was Maria (d.1885), widow of B.Langley of Tutbury (Staffordshire), a surgeon. Bowring was educated at Derby School and articled to his father, before entering the firm of Messrs. Cox. He was knighted for political services in 1900 and died in 1907. In 1872 he married Violet Camilla, daughter of Samuel Ball of Wallasey (Cheshire) and they had two sons, Charles Stuart Bowring (1880-1964) and Col. Edward Langley Bowring OBE, DSO (1882-1956). A grandson, Derek Bowring Esq. was the last solicitor of the firm, retiring in 1995.

Bowring's half brother was the Midland Railway engineer A.A.Langley, who married a daughter of SIR JAMES ALLPORT *(q.v.)* which

connection placed him at the hub of a powerful group of local businessmen.

[Briscoe, *op.cit.* 358; Debrett, *Knightage* etc. (1905) 721; Tachella, *op.cit.* ix 45, 126, 131, 164.]

BRADSHAW, Anthony (living 1633)

A citizen and goldsmith of London, Bradshaw was born 1585, probably the third son of William Bradshaw, a third generation Derby butcher and one of the Brethren of the Corporation, by Anne Whinyates of Chellaston whom he married there, 8th May 1581. Thomas Bradshaw, who had been MP for the Borough in 1450, was probably a close kinsman.

Bradshaw appears to have amassed a considerable fortune in London and married before 1609 Judith, daughter of Walter Audley of Lincolnshire. In that year their son German was baptised at St Alkmund's on 22nd February, suggesting that Bradshaw's business activities encompassed Derby as well as London. Another son, William, was born in 1619 and was living in 1633, also a goldsmith.

[Visitation of London, 1633; *Reliquary,* vii (1867) 22.]

BREGAZZI, Samuel(e) (1782-1841)

Andrea Bregazzi was a poor resident of Stazzona, great grandson of another Andrea, living there in 1676. The former married twice, having two sons, (Domenico and Samuele) by his first wife and three more (Giovanni, Innocente and Pietro) by his second. Of these all but Giovanni, a priest who died, much lamented, at Nesso in 1877, went to the English Midlands. Andrea also had a brother, Domenico, and a daughter, who married Giacomo Crosta, later a barometer maker of Bridlesmith Gate, Nottingham. Conceivably it was this event which precipitated the positive stampede of Bregazzis which followed.

The elder sons of Andrea were certainly in Derby by 1808, and probably some years earlier, Samuele (born in 1782) setting up in Willow Row – then rather a run-down area – as a carver and gilder but very shortly thereafter also describing himself as a barometer maker in partnership with William Rutherford. Domenico moved on to Hull, where he set up as an artist, his son marrying Guiliana, daughter of the Liverpool barometer maker Pietro Gobbi.

In 1810 Samuel (as he now spelt his name) married at All Saints', Derby – now the Cathedral – Mary Renn of Weston-on-Trent and they had three sons and five daughters between 1811 and 1829. In the meantime, Samuel's half-brothers Innocente and Pietro (Peter) came to Nottingham, where they seem to have joined their uncle-by-marriage, Giacomo Crosta. Innocente further cemented the Italian connection by marrying Maria, daughter of Giovanni Cetta, a London maker and produced a son who married the daughter of Bercini, Cetta's partner and successor, before the entire family went back to Stazzona in 1835.

Pietro married his niece of the half-blood, Samuel's daughter Guiliana (b.1813) in St Michael's, Derby; their son, William, became a London art dealer in the 1860s. Finally

Sebastiano and Carlo Bregazzi, sons of Andrea's brother Domenico, left Stazzona in 1820 and were apprenticed to Samuel in Derby where Carlo married (at St Alkmund's Church in 1831) Marianne Cox before leaving to set up as a barometer maker in Dublin. Sebastiano worked for a while in Nottingham before settling in the Isle of Man in 1838.

The barometers of Samuel Bregazzi are surprisingly numerous and vary from modest wheel instruments to large opulent ones like Derby Museum's best example which incorporates a clock by JOHN WHITEHURST II *(q.v.)*; nor were stick barometers absent from his repertoire.

Bregazzi also made thermometers for domestic and industrial use, exhibiting one of the latter at the Derby Mechanics' Institute in 1839. In his wheel barometers this element was nearly always incorporated into the lower half of the main dial. Even small instruments with 6" dials had this refinement – if refinement it was for, with a smallish dial, the thermometer was too short to be read easily. Invariably the casework is very similar. The partnership with Rutherford ended in 1817.

Samuel Bregazzi, who early in his career moved to Queen Street, Derby (close to the Whitehursts' old works) finally worked from 2 Cheapside, in St Werburgh's Churchyard, where he died in 1841. He was succeeded by his son, John Baptist Bregazzi, later of 27 Cornmarket (1820-63). In 1847 he married Eliza, daughter of Edwin Court Wilcox Day, an eminent Derby gunsmith.

Descendants still live in Derby, whereas John Baptist's next brother Charles Lorenzo, also a barometer maker, emigrated to Australia after being widowed in 1857, whilst his offspring by his first wife remained in Derby (their posterity are there still), but he remarried in Australia, leaving descendants there as well. It is not known whether he made barometers there, however. The third brother, Domenic (sic) (1829-80) was an artist, whose sister Louisa married in Derby (1855) to John Siddall of London who pursued the same calling. Siddall's brother Mathew later married Louise's sister, Martha.

[Goodison, Sir N., *English Barometers* (1969); research by family members; local Directories and parish registers; DM.14/4/1808, 15/2/1810, 22/8/1810, 19/3/1812., 5/6/1817, 7/8/1817, 9/5/1821 and 19/12/1827.]

BROWN, Richard (1736-1816)

Richard Brown was, apart from Matthew Boulton, the finest spar turner and manufacturer of *objets de vertu* in England in the last quarter of the 18th century. After Boulton's withdrawal from the trade he was pre-eminent.

The family go back to Richard Brown (d.1684), all three of whose younger sons, Henry, Joseph and Solomon, were stonemasons and from them descended a dynasty of masons, builders and architects. However, the eldest son, Richard, was father of another Richard (1700-56) who was not only a stone carver of considerable talent, but was also in the happy position of being parish clerk at All Saints' 1727-56. His first wife, Sarah Ford, died in 1729 without surviving issue, so he married secondly (at All Saints' 15th April 1734) Ann Twigg (1703-38) whose eldest child was Richard Brown, baptised 25th July 1736. He had a sister, Mary, but his mother died giving birth to another boy, William.

In 1756 aged barely 20, young Richard succeeded his father as Parish Clerk to All Saints' parish and three years later he married Ann, (d.1787), a relative of the Halls of Castleton, who had a lease of the Blue John Mine there. By 1761 he had obtained control over the black marble works at Ashford-in-the-Water and had rented a redundant portion of the Old Silk Mill at Derby (the Old Shop) as a workshop. Here he turned out not just church memorials, but also a series of first rate urns, tazzas, candelabra, obelisks, fireplaces etc. of Blue John, Black Marble, various fluor spars and the distinctive Chellaston Alabaster. Later he bought in ormolu fittings to mount his products.

In 1793 he took over the lease of Old St Helen's House from JOSEPH WRIGHT *(q.v.)* and here in 1802 he installed a steam engine and specialist lathes perfected by his friend JAMES

FOX *(q.v.)*. He was an associate of JOHN WHITEHURST *(q.v.)* and acquainted with ERASMUS DARWIN *(q.v.)* to whom he supplied mineral specimens. He also designed a mechanical saw for cutting his marbles.

In the 1790s he took into partnership the future geologist JOHN MAWE *(q.v.)* who in 1794 married Brown's daughter, Sarah. On his death on 22nd August 1816, his operations in Matlock and Ashford were taken over by his son, Richard (b.1765) and those in King Street, Derby, by Joseph Hall, a relation of his mother and a London 'mineralist' who in the same year married Brown's granddaughter Ann, daughter of Joseph Walter Pitman by Ann Brown (1761-1814). Hall pulled down Old St Helen's and built a purpose-built marble works on the site, most of which survives to this day. The firm was taken over from the Halls by R.G.Lomas and closed in the early 1930s. It was the mechanisation of his works in collaboration with Fox which ushered in the trend towards heavy engineering in Derby. [Craven, M. *John Whitehurst* (Mayfield 1996) *passim;* will of J.W.Pitman; local records and MIS; Cox and Hope, *op.cit.* 39, 41, 43, 44, 198.]

BROWNE, Sir George Buckston (1850-1945)

Dr Harold Buckston Browne, physician to the Manchester Royal Infirmary was grandson of George Buckston Browne (1756-1811), a Derby surgeon himself, second son of Theophilus of Derby apothecary (1715-86). Another son of the latter was the celebrated chemist, Harold Browne FSA (1760-1831) Mayor of Derby in 1799. The family were descended from Rev. John Browne (d.1623), rector of Loughborough. Dr. Browne married Anne, daughter of George Hadfield MP for Sheffield and also a man of Derbyshire ancestry.

They had a daughter, Anne Hadfield who married James, the son of Sir James Watts of Upper Hall, Kinder, and a son, George Buckston, born 13th April 1850. He was educated at Reading, Manchester and University College,

London, graduating as a multiple medallist and developing a career as a brilliant surgeon as well as a prolific medical writer. Most importantly he was donor and, for the remainder of his life, Honorary Curator of Downe House (Kent), Charles Darwin's home for 40 years. He also gave the Royal College of Surgeons (of which he was a member) a research farm nearby. He was, too, a great collector and inveterate traveller. He was knighted in 1932 and died aged 94 on 19th January 1945.

He married in 1874 Helen Elizabeth, daughter of George Vaine of Sparsholt, Hants. and had a daughter and a son, the family's fourth George Buckston, who was killed in action in World War One. However, a fifth George Buckston Browne had been born to the latter in 1903.
[*Who Was Who* 1941-50 (London 1951) 151; Yeatman, J.P. *Feudal History of Derbyshire* 6 Vols. (1886-1907) 4.VII.15; *Reliquary* V (1865) 229; *Knights Bachelor* (1939-46) 383.]

BULLOCK, Noah (1644-1687)

Noah Bullock was a counterfeiter of coin in Derby whose fame (or notoriety) rests upon the circumstance that he resided upon a vessel moored in the Derwent 'above St Mary's Bridge' – inevitably dubbed The Ark – whereupon he pursued his dubious calling, and upon the leniency of his treatment when eventually arraigned before SIR SIMON DEGGE *(q.v.)*.

He was the son of William Bullock (about whom nothing is known) and Joan, his wife and was baptised at St Peter's 19th May 1644. On 21st April 1667 he married (also at St Peter's) one Anna Clarke (d.1703) whose father may have been Isaac Clarke. A Moses Bullock, who paid hearth tax in St Peter's parish in 1670, may have been a brother.

We are told he had three sons called, with crushing logic, Shem, Ham and Japhet. He became a joke throughout Derby; Hutton records 'if they publicly ridiculed him, he privately laughed at them for he knew Justice could not easily overtake him; and if it should, the deep was ready to hide his crimes and utensils'.

How he was able to operate a small furnace on his 'ark' is difficult to say. Perhaps it was his undoing for, in 1676, he was sent for by Justice Degge whom, we are informed, 'he personally knew'. Degge said that he had heard that Bullock had taken up a new occupation and disingenuously asked to see a sample of his work. Against an assurance that he would be immune from prosecution if he should relinquish his trade – a capital offence in those days – Bullock produced a specimen, a silver sixpenny piece. As a result of a stern warning by Degge he 'broke up his ark and escaped the halter'.

This tale does, however, exhibit points of divergence from the record. That he had a son called Japhet is not in doubt, although he was born in 1681, five years after the confrontation with Degge. In 1679 there was but one son, Samuel (b.1670) and two daughters Anna (1668-81) and Rebecca (b.1675). The other sons were Joseph and Benjamin (1682-1738); the latter's son Robert (1727-86) became a wealthy skinner. Probably it was a good yarn, embroidered with Shem and Ham before even Hutton heard it. Another historical problem is that if the 'ark' was indeed moored 'above St Mary's Bridge' it would have been in St Alkmund's parish not St Peter's, where the family are all recorded. Probably the vessel was moored in the Morledge or by Cockpit Hill; the former thoroughfare has supported an inn named after Bullock's floating abode since about the time of the publication of Hutton's story – perhaps before.

The unlikely and lenient treatment of the counterfeiter might suggest that Bullock, who 'knew Degge personally', was well-connected – perhaps a scion of the decayed house of Bullock of Darley Hall and Norton. He died in 1687.
[Hutton, W. *History of Derby* (Derby 1791) 236-38; Craven (1988) 105-106; Parish records.]

BURDETT, Peter Perez (1734-1793)

Burdett's greatest achievement was to survey, draw and publish the first English county map to the scale of 1":1 mile, a task he commenced with a £100 grant from the Society of Arts and pub-

lished in 1767. A decade later he also published similar maps of Cheshire and Lancashire and he was also a highly gifted draughtsman, as his drawings (engraved by Edward Rooker for William Enfield's *Essay towards the History of Liverpool* (1773)) attest. He also pioneered the development of aquatinting, and a process for printing views onto ceramic bodies.

Burdett's early life is shrouded in uncertainty. He was the son of William Burdett by Elizabeth, younger daughter and co-heiress of Rev. Peter Perez, vicar of Eastwood, Essex (d.1750). He was born in 1734 or '35 (probably the former) but where and of his education and training we know nothing. Although he moved effortlessly in the highest circles, there is no evidence that he was a member of the Burdetts of Foremarke Hall, despite his posing on an obscure part of that family's estate for the magnificent double portrait painted by his friend JOSEPH WRIGHT *(q.v.)* in 1765. Possibly his family had a connection via a natural son.

He first settled, and married a lady called Elizabeth, in Manchester, where three sons were born (Peter, Thomas and William) in 1753, 1756 and 1759 respectively. Yet we hear no more of any of them, and he next turns up lodging with EARL FERRERS *(q.v.)* at Staunton Harold (Leics) where he appears to have assisted Ferrers in his observations of the Transit of Venus, in which the mathematician James Ferguson, FRS also seems to have had a hand and which was published by the latter, as well as in the Royal Society's *Journal Book* (10/12/1761 p.221).

Having begun his map, Burdett moved to Derby, to a house in Full Street rebuilt for him in Gothick by his friend JOSEPH PICKFORD *(q.v.)*, payment for which was advanced by Lord Ferrers against the purchase price of Wright's painting *A Philosopher Lecturing Upon an Orrery* (1765) commissioned by Ferrers and depicting Burdett taking notes. Burdett was also an accomplished 'cellist and played regularly with Wright and other friends. He was notoriously feckless with money, however, and owed Wright the balance of the price of the painting for years, which Wright later fruitlessly tried to get back from Ferrers. Nevertheless, such considerations never affected Burdett's friendship with Wright who consulted him frequently on compositions and other matters. He was also on friendly terms with JOHN WHITEHURST *(q.v.)* who seems to have supplied him with a waywiser and compass to aid his survey.

In January 1761 he married again, at St Mary's, Leicester, to Hannah Wansell, daughter of a local merchant and older than he; presumably Elizabeth had died, unless the match was bigamous, which might indeed accord with his nature. In 1768, his map published but, seriously in debt, Burdett left to live in Liverpool, where he surveyed Cheshire and taught perspective at the Warrington Academy (although this may possibly have been during his Manchester years). He was first president of the Liverpool Society of Artists and made a tour of the continent where he seems to have made powerful connections and have become a Strict Observance Freemason. It was through his influence that Catherine the Great was encouraged to purchase Wright's *Iron Forge* in 1774. He was made a Fellow of the Society of Arts in 1771 but debt continued to dog his steps. He sold his aquatinting process to Paul Sandby (who later took the credit for it) for a mere £40 and unsuccessfully attempted to interest Josiah Wedgwood (on Whitehurst's recommendation, one suspects) in his ceramic printing process.

In 1774 he fled Liverpool to escape his creditors, leaving his wife and her companion in penury, and once again went on the Continent, taking service with Markgraf Karl Friederich of Baden in the December.

Here at last he found his métier. He was commissioned into the Prince's army (becoming a Major in 1788) and undertook a topographical survey of the state. In June 1787 he married a third time, to Friedericke Kottewska – conceivably his former wife's companion, whom Wright called 'Miss Fredried'. Burdett died at Baden 9th September 1793, leaving a daughter who later married Count Franz Anton v. Nostitz, a Bohemian nobleman whose family built the Prague Opera House (later the Stavovska Divadlo) in 1783.

[Craven, M. *John Whitehurst* (1996) 59-61, 62-3, 68-70, 221-222; will of Rev. P.Perez 16/4/1748; Nicholson, B. *Joseph Wright* 2 vols. (London 1968); Harley, J.P. & Laxton, P. *A Survey of …Chester* (Liverpool 1974) 1-11; Meteyard, E., Life of *Josiah Wedgwood* (2 vols. London 1866) 11.233; Mayer, J. *History of the Art of Pottery in Liverpool* (Liverpool 1855).]

BUTTER, Dr William (1726-1805)

Butter was a native of the Orkneys, but studied medicine at Edinburgh where he became acquainted with ERASMUS DARWIN *(q.v.)* and whence he graduated MD in 1761. Thereafter he practised for many years in Derby, writing various medical theses there including *An account of puerperal fevers, as they appear in Derbyshire and some counties adjacent* (1775) and a *Treatise on the Infantile Remittent Fever commonly called Worm Fever* (1782). He later moved to London where he was described as 'too much under the influence of very favourite hypotheses'.

On 19th September 1777 Dr Johnson and James Boswell (whilst staying in Ashbourne with Dr Taylor) went to Derby where Butter was their host and they dined at his house. Boswell was a cousin once removed of Mrs Butter, a daughter of Sir John Douglas 3rd Bt. of Kelhead. Mrs Butter took Boswell to see the silk mill whilst her husband chatted to the good doctor. Butter died in London 23rd March 1805.

[DNB; Boswell, J. *The Life of Johnson* (London 1905) II.120-121; DM. 23/3//1805; Burke, *Peerage* (1970) 2190.]

CANTRELL, Rev. Henry (1685-1773)

Henry Cantrell was a long-serving vicar of St Alkmund's who was the high priest of pro-Jacobite sympathies in Derby from the time of the 'Fifteen until the eclipse of PRINCE CHARLES EDWARD *(q.v.)* after 1746. When the news of the Old Pretender's uprising reached Derby, three clergymen declared their support for him; only Cantrell, who is said to have 'drunk the Pretender's health upon his knees' had sufficient spirit (and powerful connections) to survive the experience. He also made a valuable record of the 'Forty-Five in Derby' in a (lost) journal.

Cantrell was the eldest of three sons of Simon Cantrell (d.1744) and Mary, daughter of that

J.Reeve who, as builder of the County Hall in 1659 'drank away the profits'. Simon's father, Henry, was a minor gentleman at Cloughead (Staffordshire). Tachella makes him the son of Rev. Thomas Cantrell, head of Derby School 1684-97 but this is not borne out by the records. He was born at his father's house on Nuns' Green (Friar Gate) in 1685 and attended Derby School until 1700, later going up to Emmanuel, Cambridge (BA 1704, MA 1710), then being inducted to the vicarage of St Alkmund's in 1711 through the influence of Samuel Goodwin of The College who, on his death a year later, greatly increased the endowment of the vicarage. After some opposition he also received support from LORD MACCLESFIELD *(q.v.)*. Early on, Cantrell took up cudgels against Dissent, publishing *Invalidity of Lay Baptism* (1714), *Dissenting Teachers* (1714) and *The Royal Martyr* (1716). He was a competent antiquary and regularly is said to have drunk from St Alkmund's well for his health, reviving a pre-Reformation practice.

He married Constance, daughter of William Cobb from Lincolnshire (by whom he had three sons and three daughters) She died *c.*1730 and he remarried at St Alkmund's 2nd August 1732 Jane, daughter of Rev. Joseph Cradock, vicar of Quorn, of an old Loughborough family; they had two more sons and two further daughters. Cantrell died in 1773 being survived only by his eldest son, Rev. William Cantrell (1715-87) – vicar of Normanton (Rutland) whose son became a Derby bookseller, leaving a numerous Posterity – and by his youngest, Joseph Cradock Cantrell (b.1737).

[Cox (1879) IV.114 & n. 115; Craven (1988) 22-23, 75,78; Hutton, *op.cit.* 243; Tachella, *op.cit.*]

CARTER, Horatio Stratton (1913-1994)

A footballer at national and international level of truly legendary talents, Horatio ('Raich') Carter was born in Sunderland 21st December 1913, son of the engagingly named Toddler Carter, himself a former professional footballer who had played for Burslem (Staffordshire) FC, later Port Vale.

Raich Carter began, after an elementary schooling, with Sunderland FC, at first as an amateur but from 1931 to 1945 as a professional, although through the war years this was nominal as he served with the RAF. In December 1945 he transferred to Derby County (where he had 'guested' during the war while stationed in Loughborough and when his wife was living with her parents in Derby), playing in the legendary 1946 FA Cup winning side and staying until March 1948 when he went to be player-manager for Hull City. Further moves were, as a player for Cork Athletic 1952-53; Leeds United as manager, 1953-58; Mansfield Town, 1960-63 and Middlesbrough from 1963 until his retirement at the age of 52 in February 1966. He died early in October 1994.

[*Derby Evening Telegraph* 10/10/1994; Mortimer, *op.cit.* 43-45.]

CAVENDISH, Gen. Hon. Henry Frederick Compton, MP (1789-1873)

Henry Cavendish was the last of a succession of Derby MPs who belonged to the family of the Borough's heredity High Stewards, the Dukes of Devonshire. He was born 5th November 1789, third son of Lord George Augustus Cavendish, later (1831) created 1st Earl of Burlington, who also sat as MP for Derby (1780-97) before transferring to Derbyshire, sitting, in all, in nine Parliaments. Lord Burlington was second son of William, 4th Duke of Devonshire KG, patron of

JOSEPH PICKFORD (*q.v.*). Henry Cavendish's mother was Lady Elizabeth Compton, a daughter of Charles, 7th Marquess of Northampton.

Lord Burlington's Parliamentary seat in Derby was taken over by Hon George Walpole – a carpet-bagger with an illustrious Whig name – but in 1806, Henry Cavendish's elder brother William became MP until his premature death in 1812. Typically, in a Parliamentary seat supported by such patronage, Henry, his brother succeeded to it, remaining as one of the Borough's MPs until 1835 when it was taken over by an Irish cousin, J.G.B.Ponsonby.

Cavendish's career in Parliament was a fairly low-key affair, as the Whigs were out of power for much of the period. However, he had also entered the army, seeing action in the later stages of the Napoleonic Wars, becoming Colonel, 2nd Dragoon Guards, and later a General. In 1837 he became chief equerry and clerk marshal to Queen Victoria. When in Derby he lived first at Devonshire House, Cornmarket and later utilised the Judges' Lodgings when they were available.

He married three times; firstly 24th October 1811 to Sarah (who died in 1817), daughter of W.A.Fawkener by whom he had a son (Col. W.H.F.Cavendish, ancestor of Maj. Gen. Peter Cavendish, High Sheriff of Derbyshire, 1986-87), and two daughters. On 16th June 1819 he remarried Frances Susan, Mrs Frederick Howard and sister of 'Radical Jack' Lambton, 1st Earl of Durham, and had another four sons and a daughter. Frances Susan died in November 1840 and he married yet again – much later, in January 1873 – to Susannah Emma Byerlie (who died in 1910) and died just four months later, 5th April 1873.

[Burke, *Peerage* (1970) 796-797.]

CHADDESDEN, Ralph de (d.1266)

The Chaddesdens, who took their name from the village of which they were, for more than 200 years, Lords, were a gentry family founded by Erneis and William, probably sons of Robert fitz Robert of Chaddesden, living *c.*1150. They were also notable for the large number of clerics, the most illustrious of whom was Ralph, Chancellor of the Diocese of Lichfield 1259-1266.

He was probably born about 1210, younger son of Gilbert de Chaddesden; his elder brother, Sir William was Lord of Chaddesden. He rose within the church becoming, by 1259, Chancellor of Lichfield and in that year a prebend of the Diocesan living of Sawley where he founded a chantry dedicated to the Blessed Virgin Mary in honour of the Prebends and other officials of Lichfield diocese. He died, leaving his building work at Sawley incomplete, in 1266; his rather mutilated effigy survives.

His two close kin, Thomas de Chaddesden and his brother John, lived in Derby; the latter served as MP for the Borough 1306/7. William, possibly the latter's son, was also MP in 1347, holding 1/8 of the Manor of Chaddesden. A nephew of Ralph was Ven Henry de Chaddesden (brother of another Sir William) who also had a glittering ecclesiastical career rising to become Canon of Lichfield and Archdeacon of Leicester before dying 8th May 1354 and being buried in St Paul's Cathedral. He bequeathed a chantry at Chaddesden by 1346, completed and re-endowed by his nephews, Nicholas and Geoffrey, respectively rector of Bishop's Bourne (Kent) and Long Whatton (Leics). It is now Chaddesden parish church, still largely dating from Henry's time.

[Cox, *op.cit.* III.304-6, IV.381-5; *Darley Cartulary F73*; *Burton Cartulary* 103, 168, 184, 201; *Feet of Fines, Derbys* 853 (1355), 912 (1372); Jeayes (1906) 309, 609, 1957.]

CHAMBERS, Thomas (1660-1726)

Thomas Chambers was a multi-millionaire mining entrepreneur who was born in 1660, the younger of three sons of Derby barrister, John Chambers, being baptised at All Saints' 28th December. Whilst his elder brothers were content to be lawyers, he seems to have opted for trade, much helped by his grandfather, Thomas Hammond, a London merchant whose business connections Chambers built competently upon, his mother Hannah (1617-99) acting as the conduit for her father's encouragement and patronage.

Chambers moved to London, becoming proprietor of a network of copper mines and having a hand too in several of the processes by which the raw materials was turned into products, like the sheathing for ships' bottoms, a mill for rolling which was set up by his associates at Derby less than a decade after his death.

He married Margaret, daughter of JOHN BAGNOLD MP *(q.v.)* by Hannah Parker, a kinswoman of LORD MACCLESFIELD *(q.v.)* an invaluable connection for Thomas especially in

CHARLES, Alexis Léon (1851-1929)

Alexis Charles was a most distinguished Secretary to the Midland Railway – its last – from 1899 virtually until amalgamation in 1923. He was also President of the Chartered Institute of Secretaries 1905-06.

Charles was the elder son of Emmanuel Nicholas Charles (d.1864) a former Belgian army officer who had come to Nottingham c.1850 (where Alexis was born) before setting up in Midland Road, Derby as a toy dealer. By the end of the 1850s he had also become a professional photographer, but he died in 1864 leaving two sons, Alexis and Armand Charles (1854-74). His widow, Sarah Ruddle, remarried Charles' photographic assistant, W.W. Winter, ensuring the survival of the business which continues to the present day.

Alexis was educated at Derby School and entered the service of the MR in 1865 in the accounts dept, transferring to the Secretary's office a year later. He became an assistant in 1883 and Assistant Secretary in 1891. He was also Secretary of the Somerset & Dorset Joint

those days. By this marriage, Chambers also inherited Exeter House which he re-fronted in Queen Anne style c.1712. On 26th July 1723 he obtained a grant of arms, the shield bearing three copper cakes (ingots) and a cannon barrel (Chamber piece), the crest a copper miner in a mine, all redolent of the manner of his fortune! He died at Derby 9th January 1725/6 and was buried in All Saints' under a splendid baroque marble monument by Roubiliac with an iron-work surround by ROBERT BAKEWELL *(q.v.)*, which includes portrait busts of himself and his wife, who died late in April 1735. Her legacy was money to pay for and endow the town's first street lighting, 80 lamps in all.

Their son, Thomas, and a daughter died young; of the two surviving daughters, Arabella became Mrs William Bate of Foston Hall and Hannah Sophia, the wife of Brownlow Cecil, 8th Earl of Exeter (hence the later name of Chambers' grand Derby house).
[BL. Add. MS. 24460; *Reliquary* XIV (1874) 126; Lysons, *op.cit.* 118; Cox and Hope, *op.cit.* 145; *Notes and Queries* 63.]

Railway, a director of the Derbyshire Building Society, Chairman of the Liversage Trust, the Railway Servants' Orphanage and numerous other bodies. He was also a JP and a churchwarden of St Andrew's Church. He married, at St George's (later Holy Trinity) London Road, Sophia, second daughter of Gilbert Dallison of Osmaston Villa, Osmaston Road, 9th September 1872 and they lived in a villa at 198 Osmaston Road. Charles died 22nd February 1929, 31 years after his wife.

[Briscoe, *op.cit.* 379; *Derbyshire Red Book* (1899); Tachella, *op.cit.* 61, 66.]

CHATTERTON, John (1742-1800)

John Chatterton lived in Amen Alley, Derby (probably in the house now occupied by the solicitors Powell & Co.) and gave practical expression to many of the developments in domestic economy adumbrated by JOHN WHITEHURST *(q.v.)* and ERASMUS DARWIN *(q.v.)*, with both of whom he was on intimate terms, and he was later to subscribe to Whitehurst's *Inquiry*. When Whitehurst undertook to design plumbing, ranges, boilers, hot water and heating systems for the 2nd Duke of Newcastle at Clumber, it was Chatterton who installed it all and no doubt ironed out any difficulties. He was also the inventor of Chatterton's Compo, a substance which, little altered, is still in use today.

Chatterton was the elder son of John Chatterton (1700-74) a whittawer apprenticed to George Wallis, grandfather of the man who established numerous stage coach services from Derby, and John was apprenticed to that trade before specialising as a plumber and glazier. His brother Richard was admitted a Derby Freemason in 1793 in the local Tyrian lodge of which John had been a founder member, admitted on 5th April 1785.

He married twice, at St Peter's 8th February 1765 to Mary Abbott, by whom he had no issue; she died about 1769 and he married secondly to Elizabeth (1729-84) by whom he had one surviving son, John, *(q.v.)* and a daughter, Elizabeth.

Quite apart from his plumbing specialisms, Chatterton was a prosperous lead merchant (one of the materials of his trade, after all) and may have been involved with ANTHONY TISSINGTON FRS *(q.v.)* an opulent mine owner and mineralist who was also close to both Whitehurst and Darwin. He died on 3rd March 1800 and was buried at All Saints'. The daughter of one of his apprentices, John Holmes, was later mother of HERBERT SPENCER *(q.v.)*

[Craven, (1996) 81, 100, 156, 223, 234, 243; Nottingham University Library Newcastle MSS; Grand Lodge Roll 468 p.369.]

CHATTERTON, John (1771-1857)

Only son of the foregoing, John Chatterton was a continuator of his father's business, not only in plumbing but as a lead merchant. More importantly, he was a minor protégé of ERASMUS DARWIN, his father's friend, joining his revived Derby Philosophical Society in about 1790 as a young man. He later succeeded his mentor as its next but one Chairman in 1824, replacing William Strutt *(q.v.)* a post which he held until the early 1850s. He was also an officer in the Derby Militia, rising to Adjutant in 1832.

By his first marriage (of 1799) to Miss Fletcher he had four daughters; Emma, Mrs John Donington, Mary, Mrs G.J.Green of Edgbaston, Penelope, who married Charles Borough (a surgeon who lived next door to Chatterton in Amen Alley) and Elizabeth, Mrs John Scott of Edgbaston, a relation of Sir HUGH BATEMAN *(q.v.)*. By a second marriage he had a son John (1810-91) who relinquished plumbing for dealing in lead, at first with the Cox family on the Morledge, Derby, later in London, whose own son G.J.Chatterton of Islington became an LCC councillor on the formation of that body.

Chatterton was a councillor and later an Alderman of the Borough, serving as Mayor in 1832 and retiring in 1835. He died 22nd April 1857 and was buried at All Saints'.

[Glover, *op.cit.* II.609; Q & A. 153; Tachella *op.cit.* 24, 40; Craven, *op.cit.* 223, 231.]

CHAUNCEY, Dr William (d.1736)

Derby has never been a spa town, but Dr William Chauncey's enterprise was a brave attempt to establish it as one. Derby and its surrounding area has ever boasted a number of Chalybeate Springs, the mineral enriched waters of which have long been deemed beneficial to the health. Miniature spas were opened up at Quarndon and Kedleston in the 18th century, but despite a stylish classical building and a nearby inn at the latter, neither was of more than local significance. Dr Chauncey, a physician, founded a spa on the former New Lands of the Abbey of Darley, SW of Derby, providing accommodation and baths for treatment in 1733. Lack of records have, however, rather told against any assessment of its initial success. However, his death three years later appears to have taken much of the enterprise out of the scheme, although it seems to have survived until at least 1764.

William Chauncey was born c.1685, son of Charles Chauncey, an Ashbourne surgeon who was churchwarden at St Oswald's Church there in 1706 and who died 16th August 1707. For some years, Chauncey practised in Derby. His wife, who died at Melbourne 1st October 1755, was mother to their only son, Rev. Charles Chauncey (b.1720), later rector of Ayot St Peter (Herts) and four daughters, of whom the second, Frances, married Dr. Johnson's friend Thomas Lawrence (1711-83), great nephew of Henry Lawrence MP, one of Cromwell's peers.

Although the site of the spa (first recorded in 1611 as 'a watering place at the Nether End of Abbie Barne') continued to be marked on local maps as late as 1819, it was then the residence of William Boothby who sold it in 1823. Certainly, by 1852 only a portion of the accommodation building remained, turned into an inn in 1832, which, as the Old Spa, it remains to this day.
[Craven, (1988) 103-104; Simpson, *op.cit.* II.531-2; DAJ.XXXVI (1914) 93; White's *Directory* (1857) 310; Lysons, *op.cit.* 123; Harris, J. and Jackson-Stops, G., *Robert Adam at Kedleston* (London 1987) 8, 92; Cox, T., *Magna Britannia et Hibernia Antiqua et Nova* (London 1720-31) 445; DM 22/8/1821; 14/3/1823.]

CHESTER, Simon de, MP (living 1317/1348)

A long-serving Member of Parliament and a member of a prominent local family deriving its name from Little Chester, Simon de Chester was probably the son of one William, surnamed variously as 'de Chester' and 'de Parva Castra'. Simon first appears as a witness to a local deed in 1308 and in 1331 is described as 'now bailiff of Derby'. Yet he had been sent to Parliament by the Borough even before that, in 1319, and again in 1328, 1335, 1337 and 1342. He witnessed a land grant as late as 1348 and was probably father of William de Chester, attested as an attorney in 1366 'to the bailiffs of Derby' – i.e. a sort of proto-town clerk – and who himself represented the Borough in Parliament in 1353, 1357, 1365 and 1372.

This family was, in the late 17th century, claimed as ancestors by the Chesters of Bush Hall (Herts). A kinsman in Derby sealed with a griffin passant which creature features on a chief on the arms of the Bush Hall family.
[*Darley Cartulary* D2, D3, D31(b), H41, P7; *Derbyshire Feet of Fines* 618; Jeayes, *op.cit.* 973, 976; Simpson, *op.cit.* III.757-758; Burke, J., *Landed Gentry* (1846) I.212.]

CLARKE, Alderman Thomas (1814-1877)

Clarke's chief claim to fame is that he was the last owner (by inheritance) of the old Derby Porcelain Factory, which he effectively closed down within two years of its acquisition by selling the moulds, stock-in-trade and so on to Boyle, of Stoke (*q.v.* BLOOR, R.) in 1848. Having asset-stripped the site he sold part of it to the Catholic Church (on which was erected Pugin's splendid but short-lived Convent of St Vincent de Paul) and retained the remainder to facilitate the expansion of his malting business.

Clarke's father and mother were Thomas and Mary, of Nottingham Road, and he was born in

CLAYTON, Thomas Gething (b.1830)

Thomas Gething Clayton was a talented engineer whose organisational skills and flair made possible the development of the Midland Railway's new carriage and wagon building facility from 1873, the year in which he was appointed by SIR JAMES ALLPORT *(q.v.)* at a salary of £700 p.a. He also developed American ideas on passenger comfort acquired on a visit to the USA in the previous year to transform the coaching stock of the Railway into some of the best in the country. One of his 12-wheeled composite carriages with 'soft' third class accommodation won the Grand Prix at the Paris International Exhibition in 1889, and his American-style Pullman cars were the first in the UK.

Clayton was born into a farming family from Madeley (Salop) in 1830, a younger son who chose a career in railway engineering. On appointment to Derby he lived at Normanton Grange, and married Mrs Gough, a widow, who was the daughter of James Byrt-Jordan of Cricklade Manor, and had two sons, Thomas George Clayton (b.1879) and Charles Stanley Jordan Clayton (b.1881), both of whom were educated at Derby School. He resigned his post in 1902 and died at Normanton some years later. [Radford, J.B. *Derby Works and Midland Locomotives* (London 1971) 60, 700, 126; Tachella, *op.cit.* 128, 136.]

1814 and married Sarah Elizabeth, daughter and heiress of Edward Ramsbottom, the Liverpool solicitor who had married Bloor's daughter. Clarke was originally a maltster in a small way, but in 1871 bought out L.W.Raynold's brewery (late David Paine, who was taken over in his turn by Henry Hunt of Nottingham Road, established early in the century). Clarke was also a cornfactor, a concern he had taken over from his father *c.*1840.

Clarke was elected for Derwent Ward *c.*1850, becoming Mayor in 1862-63, an Alderman in 1865 and a JP, resigning both in 1877. He lived at The Elms, Five Lamps, where he died in 1877. He was a churchwarden, Poor Law Guardian and a man of 'singular firmness of purpose and energy'. He left five sons, of whom the second, Robert, ran the firm's maltings at Bedford and the eldest, Thomas, obtained a grant of arms in 1890 and lived at Masson House, Cromford, leaving five sons and seven daughters.
[MMD I. 19-20; Tachella, *op.cit.* 57, 67, 68, 116, 161; Fox-Davies, A.C. *Armorial Families* (1910) 322 and (1929) I.376-7, Briscoe, *op.cit.* 360.]

COFFEE, William John (1773-*c.*1846)

Coffee was a talented china modeller and sculptor who resided in Derby between 1793 and 1814. He came to Derby as a figure modeller for WILLIAM DUESBURY II *(q.v.)* from a spell working in London for Mrs Coade, with his father William (d.1840). However, in early summer 1795 he worked briefly at Church Gresley Pottery before returning to Derby until 1798; 'Coffee was never surpassed in pastoral and grotesque subjects' wrote Haslem in 1857. In 1798 Coffee followed WILLIAM BILLINGSLEY *(q.v.)* to Pinxton where he remained until 1803 when he returned to Derby under the patronage of WILLIAM STRUTT *(q.v.)* for whom he undertook his most celebrated creation: the giant terracotta statue of Aesculapius placed on the dome of the new General Infirmary in 1810 (which had to be re-made, supported by public subscription, after the first model burst in the kiln) and the marble Florentine Boar which JOSEPH STRUTT *(q.v.)* transferred to the Arboretum in 1840. Neither, unfortunately, have survived. He also sculpted many local and national figures; of the former may be mentioned ERASMUS DARWIN *(q.v.)*, d'Ewes Coke, Hannah More, Sir Richard Arkwright and EDWARD FOSTER *(q.v.)*.

Coffee was born in September 1773, being baptised at St Clement Danes on 12th, son of William and Catherine. He had two brothers: John Thomas, later of South Carolina (USA) and James (1788-1818) who also worked at Coade's works. Coffee married first in London, May 1792, Patty, who died soon after, and on 21st May 1793 at Derby, Martha Dudley, by whom he had Henry (1793-1871), a modeller and sculptor of London, and Catherine.

In 1814 or 1815 a lack of commissions led him to leave Derby and in 1816 he went to New York (USA). Later, whilst in Virginia, he modelled busts for Jefferson and James Madison as well as President Monroe. He did other members of Jefferson's family who were, effectively, his first patrons in America and it was through them that he was commissioned to make the series of neo-classical reliefs for Jefferson's pavilions at the University of Virginia. He died in retirement at Albany, N.Y. around 1850, after a spell in Lowell (Mass.).
[Gunnis, R., *Dictionary of British Sculptors* (London 1953) 109-110; Bricknell, B.R., unpublished MS 2 vols (1993-4).]

COKAYNE, Alderman Francis (1688-1767)

Cokayne was born in 1688, third son of Nathaniel Cokayne (d.1704) of Derby by Elizabeth, daughter of John Nixon of Sandiacre, although some sources make him the son of

Nathaniel's brother Francis (1652-1739) four times Mayor of Derby and a successful mercer. The family was a branch of the Cokaynes of Chaddesden, descended from George Cokayne of Ballidon, second son of Sir Edward Cokayne of Ashbourne who died in 1606.

Francis was educated at Derby School and certainly worked for his uncle, Francis, before moving to London, where he served as Lord Mayor 1750-51. He died in 1767.
[DAJ. III (1881) 109-111; Tachella, *op.cit.* 9.]

COKAYNE, Col. Thomas (1697-1749)

Youngest of the four sons of Nathaniel Cokayne of Derby and presumably *(q.v.)* a brother of Alderman FRANCIS COKAYNE. He obtained a commission in the army after an education at Derby School, rising to Lt. Col. of the 13th Regiment at Gibraltar and Deputy Judge Advocate of the forces in Flanders. He also commanded his regiment with some distinction at the battle of Culloden in April 1746. He married a Miss Mildmay and at his death in 1749 left a son Thomas Mildmay Cokayne of Hertfordshire, whose son Thomas was later rector of Stapleton, Bristol. Col. Cokayne's eldest sister Elizabeth was the wife of ROBERT BAKEWELL *(q.v.)*.
[Tachella, *loc.cit.*; DAJ, *ibid.*]

COKAYNE, Rev. William MA, BD (1717-1798)

Brother of Col. THOMAS COKAYNE *(q.v.)* the Rev. George Cokayne (1684-1730) was, from 1707 until his death, vicar of Doveridge. He was father of Rev. William Cokayne, who followed in the tradition of JOHN FLAMSTEED *(q.v.)* by becoming a notable astronomer.

He was born at Doveridge in 1717 and educated at Oxford where he gainecd a BD and MA. He was chaplain to his uncle, Lord Mayor COKAYNE *(q.v.)* later being appointed Professor of Astronomy at Gresham College, Oxford where he died unmarried in 1798.
[Sources as previous; Cox, *op.cit.* III.117.]

COKE, Daniel Parker, MP (1745-1825)

A radical Tory MP was a rare thing in the later 18th century, especially one whose 'views were decidedIy untraditional'. Daniel Parker Coke was the elder son of Thomas Coke of Derby (1700-76) by Matilda, daughter and heiress of Thomas Goodwin of The College, born there 17th July 1745. The grandfather, Rev. Thomas Coke of Allestree was third of five sons of Richard, of Trusley Hall, and in 1716, Thomas junior had become the senior male representative of his family, although the estate passed via an heiress to the Wilmots.

Coke went to Derby School, proceeding to Queen's College, Oxford whence he migrated to All Souls (BA 1769, MA 1772) and thereafter to Lincoln's Inn, followed by Middle Temple in 1776, the year he was elected in the Tory interest for Derby. In 1780 he went to Nottingham to aid the candidate, Sir Edward Every, 8th Bt. of Egginton, but so successful were his efforts that it was Coke, rather than Every, who was elected, with Robert Smith (later 1st Lord Carrington). He held the seat until 1812 with an interruption in 1802 when violence forced his withdrawal from the town during polling, resulting in the election of his Whig rival, although this result was later overturned after an enquiry. Nevertheless, Coke then sponsored a Bill giving a County's magistrates the right to act against disorder during elections in a chartered town (to obviate a repetition of his own experience) which became law, but was seen by most municipal dignitaries as a serious diminution of their influence.

He practised at the Bar on the Midland Circuit and was Chairman of the Derby Quarter Sessions until 1818; socially, he enjoyed friendships with such unlikely people as ERASMUS DARWIN (q.v.), and appears in the spectacular conversation piece by Joseph WrIght, with his distant cousins D'Ewes and Hannah Coke of Brookhill Hall, contemplating what may well be plans by WILLIAM EMES (q.v.) to landscape their parkland. W.J.COFFEE (q.v.) also made a bust of him. He was also a Commissioner for settling America's claims following Independence,

despite having been a close ally of Prime Minister Lord North during the Revolutionary War.

He was also the prosecutor of the ringleaders of the 'Church and King' mob who had rioted in Birmingham in 1791, burning Joseph Priestley's house. He led with 'Had I been in Birmingham when his (Priestley's) property was attacked, I would have lost my life in his defence, and this sentiment I hold all the more strongly because I do differ from him'. He was also a Protectionist and his career was marked by 'independence, moderation and sobriety'. He died 6th December 1825, unmarried. He left a brother, John, – who appears to have inherited little; John's son Edward and grandson John both appear to have worked in the burgeoning field of telegraphy – and three daughters, the eldest of whom was married to Thomas Heathcote of Derby.
[DNB; Blackner, *History of Nottingham* (1815) 395-7; Tachella, *op.cit.* 16; will dated 23/8/1823; Craven (1987) 42-45.]

COLLINS, Sir William Job, MP, KCVO (1859-1946)

Sir William Collins had a long and distinguished career as an ophthalmic surgeon, anatomist, diplomat and Liberal politician; his place in Derby's history is that he sat for the Borough in Parliament from 1917 – when he succeeded LORD ROE *(q.v.)* at a by-election – to 1918. He had previously sat for West St Pancras 1906-10 and was a London County Councillor 1892-1906, serving as Chairman 1897-98.

Collins was the eldest son of Dr William Job Collins, an Oxford GP who later practised in the Regent's Park area of London, and Mary Anne Francisca, daughter of Edward Treacher (of an old Huguenot family). He was educated at University College School, London, and Bart's, eventually gaining a DPh, MD, MS, BSc and Fellowship of the Royal College of Surgeons. He sat on many Royal Commissions and represented the Government on a number of international medical conventions. He was knighted in 1902 and made KCVO 12 years later. He was a JP and DL for London and from 1925-45 a Vice-Lieutenant of the County of London.

He married Jean, daughter of a fellow Liberal MP, John Wilson of Hillhead House, Glasgow (who sat for Govan) on 2nd August 1898; she died without issue in 1936. He died in London 12th December 1946.

[*Who Was Who* 1941-50 (1951) 238-9.]

COOPER, Sir William Mansfield LLB (1903-1992)

Sir W.M.Cooper was Vice-Chancellor of the University of Manchester from 1956 to 1970, having spent his entire professional life there, as assistant lecturer and lecturer (1938-49), registrar (1945-52), Professor of Industrial Law (1949-70) and Emeritus Professor from 1970, when he retired. It was at Manchester University, too, that he gained his own first degree (LLB, 1936); he was also called to the bar (Gray's Inn) in 1940 and held six honorary doctorates.

William Mansfield Cooper was the son of William Ellis Cooper of Newton Heath, Manchester where he was born 20th February 1903; his mother was Georgina Caroline. He was great grandson of William Mansfield Cooper of

Derby (1808-62) architect of the original Mechanics' Institute and the man who encouraged a group of his employees to form England's second Co-operative Society. W.M.Cooper's father Joseph (1778-1835) was also an architect and builder of some distinction in Derby, who had married Elizabeth, daughter of William Mansfield. Joseph was a great grandson of Thomas, a joiner, who married one of the Fox family.

Sir William was knighted in 1963, made C.St.J. in 1970 and in 1936 had married Edna Mabel, daughter of Herbert Baker of Manchester; latterly they lived at Royston (Herts). At his death 18th November 1992 he left a son, Christopher.

[Debrett's *Distinguished People of Today* (London, 1990) 1217; *Who's Who* (1978) I.615]

COTTON, Rev. John (1584-1652)

John Cotton was the archetype Pilgrim father, one of the pioneers of those who left England for America, making the crossing in 1633 with John Winthrop. They landed on the Massachusetts coast, and it was thanks to Cotton – one of Derby's precious links with the United States (cf. BOOTT, KIRK, q.v.) – that Boston, once established, was so named, for he had been lately vicar of St Botolph's, Boston (Lincs.) until he was ejected for non-conformity.

Cotton was born on 4th December 1584, eldest of three sons of Rowland Cotton, a Derby lawyer, then of Bridge Gate, later of Full Street who died in 1604. In August 1582 Rowland had married Mary Herbert; he was of a gentry family, being grandson of Clement Cotton of Cotton Hall (Cambs.) John was educated at Derby School (one of the earliest pupils of whom we have a record) 1593-97. Thence he proceeded to Trinity, Cambridge (BA *c.*1600) later going to Emmanuel College (MA, BD, 1613) where, after ordination in 1610, he had a brilliant academic career, being senior lecturer, dean, catechist and a fellow of his college. He was also in 1612 appointed to Boston where, from about 1615, his increasing Puritanism got him into bad odium.

He married, at Boston (Lincs.), Elizabeth, sister of a fellow local cleric, Rev. James Horrocks, but his subsequent re-marriage to Sarah, daughter of Anthony Hawkridge (cf. DOUGLAS HAWKRIDGE, *q.v.*), widow of William Storey, decided him to leave for America, especially as he had been summoned to appear before the Court of High Commission. He resigned in May 1633.

Once in America he swiftly became the leading spirit of the church in New England and he published more than seven works of theology (all in London) between 1641 and 1658. Nevertheless, as he grew older, his religious views became more extreme, his secular ones more reactionary: he lacked faith in his fellow men and supported oligarchical rule. He died 23rd December 1652, his wife re-marrying Richard Mather (whose son by his first marriage, Increase, married one of the Cotton's daughters). He also left a son, named from the place of his birth in August 1633 *en route* to New England, Seaton. The present Edwin William Cotton (b.1932) is his senior descendant in the 9th generation.

[Burke, *American Families* (1939) 2.633; FMG I.173-4; *Dictionary of American Biography* (1964) 194-5, Tachella, *op.cit.* 1.]

COX, Sir Christopher William Machell, GCMG (1899-1982)

Sir Christopher Cox was a most distinguished civil servant who specialised in education, as well as being an eminent academic and archaeologist. He was a scion of an important Derby family, being a grandson of Rev. J.C.COX (*q.v.*); his father Arthur Henry Machell Cox was of Plymouth and later of St Audries, Somerset, Christopher, the eldest son, being born 17 November 1899.

He was educated at Clifton before proceeding to Balliol, Oxford, his studies being interrupted by service as a subaltern (RE) in World War One. He went on to obtain a double first in 1923 and was appointed to a Craven Fellowship 1924-26. In 1924 he made the first of a number of archae-ological explorations in Turkey (the last was in 1931), an interest fired in youth by his grandfather. He was appointed a Fellow of New College in 1926, retiring as an honorary Fellow in 1970.

From 1937 to 1939 he was Director of Education, College Principal, and a member of the Governor's Council in the Sudan, moving, from 1940-61, to be advisor on education to the Secretary for the Colonies, from thence until 1964 to the Secretary of State for Technical Co-operation and finally to the Ministry for Overseas Development. He had five honorary doctorates and co-wrote *Monumenta Asiae Minoris Antiqua* (Vol.V, 1937). He was made CMG in 1944, KCMG in 1950 and GCMG in 1970 on retirement. He died unmarried 6th July 1982.

[*Who's Who* (1978) 545-46; Debrett's *Handbook* (1982) 400; Cox, W., *Pedigree of Cox of Derbyshire* (Derby 1889).]

COX, Rev. John Charles, LLD, FSA (1843-1919)

Dr Cox was one of Derbyshire's greatest antiquarians and historians, even in an age of leisured antiquarianism – he wrote a total of 37 books in all; in later life he also turned to writing works of national scope, too. He was a scion of the prolific house of Cox founded by William Cox of Derby, vintner, innkeeper and lead merchant (1762-1827), himself grandson of William Cox of Brailsford, tutor to EARL FERRERS (*q.v.*). John Charles Cox was born 29th March 1843, second son of Rev. Edward Cox (1802-1869), rector of Luccombe (Som.), later of Toddington, and Anna, daughter of Charles Horsfall of Liverpool, whose brother married Edward Cox's cousin Charlotte. He had two brothers, Edward and Henry and four sisters.

Cox was educated at Repton, Bath and then Queen's College Oxford where he obtained an LLD. He was appointed vicar of Barton-le-Street (WR Yorkshire). He was the author of *Notes on the Churches of Derbyshire*, 4 Vols. (Derby and London 1873-79); *Chronicles of the Collegiate*

Church of All Saints', Derby (with his kinsman and protégé Sir W.H. St JOHN HOPE *(q.v.)* 1881); *How to write the History of a Parish* (1880); *Three Centuries of Derbyshire Annals,* 3 vols. (London 1890) and *Memorials of Old Derbyshire.* His *Little Guide to Derbyshire* (1902) ran into many editions extending well into the period subsequent to its author's death.

Cox was a founder member of the Derbyshire Archaeological Society and for a time editor of its Journal, as well as *The Reliquary,* its predecessor, and *The Antiquary*; he was a member of the British Archaeological Association, the Royal Archaeological Institute, the British Numismatic Society and a Fellow of the Society of Antiquaries. He married 23rd October 1867 Marion, elder daughter of Edward William Smith of Gainsborough (Lincs.); her mother Matilda Machell was the representative of one of the most distinguished Huguenot families. His wife was the sister of Agnes, who, three years before, had married (Sir) WILLIAM ABNEY *(q.v.).* Cox had seven sons and three daughters, of whom the second son, Arthur (b.1870) was the father of SIR CHRISTOPHER COX *(q.v.).* A great great grandson (descended from Cox's third son Charles Neville Machell Cox, b.1871) is Professor T.M.Cox of the University of Cambridge School of Medicine at Addenbrooke's Hospital.

Cox converted to Roman Catholicism in 1917 and died 23rd February 1919 at St Albans, his house at Sydenham (Kent).

[Cox, W., *ibid.*]

CRAVEN, Hugh Bertie, MA (1862-1944)

Hugh Craven was one of the many distinguished hunting men of the County, but about the only one to have lived within the present city's boundary. He settled at Moor House, Chaddesden on his marriage 12th June 1899 to Mildred Louisa Lucy (1868-1931) sister of Sir Francis Whitmore 1st Bt. In 1912 he moved to Fairfield House, Quarndon and after World War One to Wheathills House, on the edge of what later became the Mackworth estate.

Craven's father, John Albert, had from 1869 to 1872 been MFH of The Pytchley and the family then lived at Whilton Lodge, near Daventry, Northants.; it was from his father that Hugh developed a passion for riding to hounds. Once in Derbyshire, he became a leading member of The Meynell, his attendance at the meets of which only slightly diminished with the onset of years. His grandfather, Hiram Craven of West Wickham (Kent), had made a fortune in London, thus enabling his son to enjoy a county life and marry Hugh's mother, Ellen Majendie, a member of a noted gentry family. Craven junior was educated at Radley and Christ Church, Oxford (BA 1887; MA 1891) and rode regularly with The Pytchley before coming to Derby.

He and his wife had an only child, Muriel Ethel Frances who, in April 1928 married Capt. Arthur Beauclerk Coventry RN OBE of Monkton Park Chippenham (whose grandmother had been an – unrelated – member of the house of Craven); they had two daughters. Mrs Craven died in 1931 and Hugh on 26th March 1944 at Wheathills.

[Gaskell, E., *op.cit.*; Burke, *Peerage* (1920) 666 & 2818.]

CROMPTON, Abraham (1648-1725)

Abraham Crompton started, in 1685, Derby's first bank, also one of the earliest provincial banking houses. He was the son of Rev. John Crompton (1611-69), a member of the old Lancashire family of Crompton of Brightmet, and was vicar of Brailsford until 1662 when, Like JOHN BINGHAM *(q.v.),* he was ejected for nonconformity. Born two years before his father was appointed to Brailsford, in 1648, Crompton was educated at Derby School before being apprenticed in Nottingham to a mercer, setting up in Derby in that capacity about 1670. His enterprise was undoubtedly given a boost by his choice of wife, for she was Elizabeth (1652-90) daughter and heiress of Derby alderman Luke Whittington, also a mercer.

Such was the success of Crompton's Market Place business, that he embarked on money lending almost accidentally, but within a decade had transformed himself into a banker; by the time of his death in 1725 he was very rich indeed, and his services much in demand. The bank later became Crompton & Evans Union Bank, later absorbed by the NatWest. Crompton left three sons and two daughters, of whom his eldest son, Samuel (1680-1757) remained in Derby as proprietor of the bank, building The Friary in 1731. The two younger sons, Abraham and John (d.1750) retired to the ancestral estate at Chorley, Lancs. John Crompton of Chorley Hall, son of the younger, was ancestor through the female line of Sir Adrian Boult and Beatrix Potter. Three descendants of Samuel are noted below.

[Burke, J., *Landed Gentry* (1898) II.1261n, (1937) 2122; Glover, *op.cit.* II.593-5, DNB.]

CROMPTON, George (1823-1897)

George Crompton, a member of the family banking firm, was the founder of a company which pioneered the manufacture of electrical equipment, both domestic and industrial. His seat, Stanton Hall, Stanton-by-Dale, was the first in Derbyshire to have been lit by electricity in 1891-92; the firm later became well-known as Crompton Parkinson Ltd., and the original works were in Derby where the firm still had a presence until 1998. This diversification came about when his bank took over the struggling iron foundry of B. and J.Smith at Dale Abbey (originally established in 1788), effectively founding the Stanton Iron Works (1877).

George Crompton was great-great-grandson of ABRAHAM CROMPTON *(q.v.)*, his father being Gilbert Crompton (b.1786) of Durant Hall, Chesterfield, by his second wife, Deborah Catherine, daughter of Rev. George Bossley, vicar of Chesterfield; George's grandfather, John, (1753-1834), Mayor of Derby 1792, 1800, 1810, 1817 and 1826, was younger son of SAMUEL CROMPTON *(q.v.)*. The second son of the marriage, George, was born in 1823, and died 14th November 1897, leaving four sons and two daughters. The elder two sons, George William

(1863-1946) and Charles Robert (1869-1952) were responsible for further developing and expanding the family firm.

[Burke, *Landed Gentry* (1952) 1342-3; Glover, *loc.cit*; Briscoe, *op.cit.* 287; Nixon, F., *Industrial Archaeology of Derbyshire* (Newton Abbott 1969) 56.]

CROMPTON, Rebecca, see SOAR

CROMPTON, Samuel, DL (*c.*1712-1782)

Samuel Crompton was the most eminent banker of his day in Derby, his capital backing many of the great enterprises of the time, including those of JEDEDIAH STRUTT *(q.v.)* and Sir Richard Arkwright. His rivals were THOMAS EVANS *(q.v.)* with whom his sons and successors ultimately teamed up (by amalgamation) and the HEATHS *(q.v.)* whose bankruptcy in 1779 gave both the others an unrivalled opportunity to expand their businesses.

Crompton was the eldest son and heir of Samuel Crompton (1680-1757), builder of The Friary and the Piazzas at Derby (1708) and himself son of ABRAHAM CROMPTON *(q.v.)*. He was born about 1712, probably at Long Laughton (Yorkshire) where his mother's father William

Rodes had his seat. He became a Brother of the Corporation about 1745 and succeeded his father (with his brothers John and Joshua) in 1757, and he became Mayor of Derby for the first time a year later, serving again in 1767. A decade later he served a third-term on the premature death of Robert Hope. Crompton was the first of his branch of the family to hold the high shrievalty (in 1768) subsequently becoming a Deputy Lieutenant and on 8th May 1744 married Elizabeth, a daughter of Samuel Fox, a fellow member of the municipal oligarchy. At his death in 1782 he left a daughter and four sons: Samuel (1750-1810) and John (1753-1834) succeeded him at Derby, Joshua (1754-1832) married Anna Maria Rookes, a Yorkshire heiress and settled at York and Gilbert (1755-1837) was of Chesterfield, where he was Mayor in 1823-4, and Nun Monckton, Yorkshire.

[Glover, *op.cit.* II.578.]

CROMPTON, Sir Samuel, 1st Bt MP (1785-1848)

Sir Samuel Crompton was the only son of Alderman Samuel Crompton (1750-1810) and grandson of SAMUEL CROMPTON *(q.v.)*, and was born in Derby in 1785. His mother, Sarah, was the daughter of his grandmother's brother, Samuel Fox of Derby, the younger. Crompton inherited his father's estates of Burton Blount (which he sold) and Woodend, near Thirsk (Yorkshire NR) where he settled, marrying in 1829 Isabella Sophia, daughter of Rev. Archibald Hamilton Cathcart, niece of 1st Earl Cathcart. He sat in Parliament for Retford (Notts) from 1818 until 1826; for Derby from 1826 to 1830 and for Thirsk from 1834 to 1841, all in the Whig interest. Although not particularly notable, Crompton's Parliamentary career spanned both reformed and unreformed houses, and his support during the Reform Crisis (when he was out of Parliament) was much valued by premier Lord Grey who created him a baronet in 1838. He died 29th December 1848 leaving four daughters and the baronetcy became extinct. Only the eldest

daughter, Elizabeth Mary married, her husband of 1850 being her cousin, Alan, 3rd Earl Cathcart.

[Brown, Sir Richard, *Baronetage* (1844) 207.]

CROOKS, Samuel Dickinson (1908-1981)

Sammy Crooks, despite a frail appearance, was a footballer of pace, dexterity and intelligence, playing for Derby County for 20 years and turning out for his country as outside-right 26 times between the Wars. He scored more than 100 goals for Derby. He was also the Players' Union secretary for 14 years. Once his playing career at Derby was over he spent three years as the Rams' chief scout before managing Retford Town (1949-50), Shrewsbury Town (1950-54), Burton Albion in 1957 and Heanor Town (1959-1960). He ended his career back at Derby, again as chief scout, from 1960 to May 1967. By a bitter irony he was unable to play in Derby's epic FA Cup victory in 1946 due to an injury sustained in an earlier round, he nevertheless paid a fulsome and unselfish tribute to his replacement, Reg Harrison, saying, 'Reg didn't let me down'.

Crooks was born a miner's son at Bearpark, Co. Durham 16th January 1908 and after an elementary education found himself turning out for the local colliery side before moving in quick

succession (as his talent flowered) to Brandon Juniors, Tow Law Town and Durham City, where he started in May 1926. He was 'head-hunted' by GEORGE JOBEY *(q.v.)* less than a year later.

He married Freda and they lived in Blagreaves Lane between the Wars, although they had retired to Belper when he died 3rd February 1981. His son, Stuart, was a commercial manager at Derby County in the 1980s. One of Sammy Crooks's nephews served as a Derby Councillor; his son, Howard, is a distinguished surgeon at Cheltenham, specialising in radiography and is founder of the Cobalt Unit's appeal fund; he has two daughters.
[Mortimer, *op.cit.* 59-61; DET. 28/7/1995.]

CROWSHAW, Richard (1561-1631)

Born 1561 at Mackworth, son of a blacksmith of Markeaton, this opulent London silversmith became free of Goldsmiths' Company, deputy of Broadstreet Ward and sometime Master of the Worshipful Company. He died 2nd June 1631

leaving benefactions to various charities of nearly £5,000 as well as extensive legacies to various kinsmen, by his will dated 26/4/1631. He was buried at St Bartholomew, by the Royal Exchange (demolished) and a large monument to him was erected in All Saints', Derby. Chief heirs: Sir Thomas Metham and John Crowshaw.
[Cox, J.C. & Hope, W.H. St J. Chronicles of *All Saints', Derby* (Derby 1881) pp.144-5.]

CRUMP, Thomas (c.1800-1870)

Thomas Crump was the inventor of an efficient and modern flushing lavatory system in 1846, but the Patent was registered just months after that of the Londoner, Thomas Crapper, by which happenstance the latter's surname entered colloquial English and not the former's. Nevertheless, the business founded by Crump at 106 Friar Gate was an important one and flourished for over a century.

Crump was not a Derby man, but he had set up by 1838 as an 'engineer, plumber and gas fitter' having originally arrived as the first superintendent of the Derby Gas Works. He swiftly became a freeholder and a burgess, his first big contract being the lighting by gas of the new Derby Trijunct Railway station of 1839, providing 747 lamps and over 1000 yards of four inch piping. As well as leading his company to prosperity he also returned to the Derby Gas Light & Coke Co. as General Manager, in which role he oversaw the design and commissioning of the Litchurch Gas Works. He was succeeded by William Duesbury V (1828-93), great-grandson of the first WILLIAM DUESBURY *(q.v.)*.

At his death in 1870 he left three sons, of whom Thomas ran the firm in Friar Gate, James became a cabinet maker and Francis (b.1843) became a director of the ironfounders J. & G.Hayward. He and James married sisters, daughters of Robert Brookhouse, plaster manufacturer. In all, four generations of Crumps ran the firm, and Alice, one of Thomas Crump's great-granddaughters ran the Midland Hotel, Heysham (Lancs.) keeping alive a link first forged at the Trijunct Station five years before the Midland Company was even formed.

[Craven (1988) 121, 151, 174; Glover, S. *History and Directory of Derby* (Derby 1843) 86-87; *British Architect* (30/6/1882) 309.]

CUMMINGS, Maria (c.1898)

Maria Cummings was a most celebrated and distinguished actress of the late Victorian and Edwardian era. She was born in Derby in the 1850s daughter of Henry Cummings of The Chestnuts, Normanton Road, first master of the National School, Curzon Street from 1846 to 1871, when he died. He also served as Chairman of the Litchurch Local Board to 1869. Maria's brother, another Henry, was a solicitor who bankrupted himself developing the expansion of New Normanton in 1890. He later became a government official in South Africa.

[*Derby Express* 28/7/1996.]

CURGENVEN, Dr William Grafton (1841-1910)

Curgenven was a member of a very ancient Cornish family who came to Derby as a surgeon at the General Infirmary, and found fame as a cricketer for the county during the stirring years 1872 to 1878.

Third son of John Curgenven, a Plymouth solicitor, he was born 3rd November 1841 and during his time in Derby he lived from 1879 at 41 Friar Gate, the house built for himself by JOSEPH PICKFORD (*q.v.*). In 1874 he married Pamela Barrett, daughter of Henry Philip Harman. After a very distinguished career as Medical Officer to the Infirmary and as a consultant, he retired in 1908 to Fareham, Hants, where he died 18th March 1910.

His eldest son, Herbert (1875-1959), remained in Derby and followed his father in the ranks of the elect, being selected to play for Derbyshire County Cricket Club 1896 and 1897. The next brother Gilbert (1882-1934) also played for Derbyshire 1901 to 1927, but the youngest

son, Capt. William Charles Curgenven was killed in action on Trafalgar Day, 1914, serving with the South Wales Borderers. He also left three daughters.

[Information by courtesy Mr C.I.Curgenven.]

CURREY, Percy Heylin, FRIBA (1864-1942)

One of the East Midlands' most talented Arts and Crafts architects, P.H.Currey was born in 1864, the third son of Derby solicitor Benjamin Scott Currey of Eaton Hill (1830-1910) a member of the family which for generations acted as the lawyers for the Dukes of Devonshire. B.S.Currey's cousin was the London architect Henry Currey. Percy, educated at Derby School 1875-82, was articled to FREDERICK JOSIAS ROBINSON (*q.v.*) 1882-86 and afterwards became assistant to Sir Arthur Blomfield (1886-87) later acting as clerk of works at Repton School Buildings (November 1887-May 1888). In August 1888 he set up in practice at 3 Market Place, Derby, his first commission being St Stephen, Borrowash, although he had built three houses on the corner of Peet Street/Uttoxeter New Road Derby for his father the same year. He was elected Fellow of the RIBA 14 June 1907, his sponsor being Thomas Harrison Thorpe. He wrote numerous learned articles for the Derbyshire Archaeology Society's *Journal* and other publications. At St Anne's 4th October 1897 he married Augusta Mary Anne Emily Fredericka Leacroft (of an old Derbyshire family) and at his death in March 1942 left three children: John Heylin Currey (1901-86) an eminent railway signalling engineer; Charlotte Maisie (1900-86) and Joyce, later Mrs Drew. His maternal grandfather had been Dr James Heygate of The College, Derby (1801-72) whose kinsman Samuel Unwin was a forebear of RAYMOND UNWIN (*q.v.*).

Currey's earlier work was much in the mould of F. J.Robinson, but he quickly evolved an Arts-and-Crafts style which, in developed form, marks him out as one of the most accomplished provincial architects of this type. He later developed a neo-classical mode perhaps influenced by Sir Edwin Lutyens, and which is epitomised at The Provost's House, Highfield Road, Derby (1928). He undertook a variety of churches, his finest being St Osmund, Derby (for his brother, Lancelot, its patron and first incumbent) with its vicarage and ancillary buildings in austere form of his Arts and Crafts style. From 1903 until 1926 Currey was in joint practice with Charles Clayton Thompson and they clearly worked jointly on some works but by no means on all. Currey was appointed Diocesan surveyor in 1895.

[Tachella, B., *Derby School Register* (Derby 1902) 91, RIBA fellowship application 13/3/1907; *Bulmer's Directory* (1895) 573.]

DALTON, John MP (1610-1679)

John Dalton was a puritan draper, Mayor and MP for Derby, the high point in whose career was the period of the Civil War and the Commonwealth. Born in 1610 in Nottingham, where his father and grandfather, both called John, were vintners, he moved with his father to Derby. His mother was Isabel (d.1652), daughter of Henry Wallis of Nottingham who, on his father's death 26th March 1651, remarried Henry Wandell of Derby, who had been Mayor in 1641-43.

Dalton was apprenticed to a Nottingham draper, a calling which he followed with success in Derby. On 17th September 1633 at St Michael's, he married Margaret, daughter of John Parker of Derby, and had two daughters, one of whom, Mary, later married Thomas Houghton, a member of another mayoral family.

Under the new dispensation of SIR JOHN GELL *(q.v.)*, his municipal career burgeoned. He was elected Alderman in 1645 and served his first term as Mayor in 1647-49 and a second in 1652-53. In 1659 he and GERVASE BENNET *(q.v.)* were elected to Parliament in place of Gell and THOMAS SANDERS *(q.v.)* and he managed, by adroit change of allegiance, to secure re-election to the first Royalist Parliament of 1661, serving

the following year as well, along with the Royalist Roger Allestrey. He even managed a third Mayoralty in the changed political climate, serving in 1668-69, and he kept his place on the Aldermanic bench until 1670.

After the death of his first wife, he remarried Anne (d.October 1673), daughter of Richard Pyott of Streethay Hall (Staffordshire) and had three sons, Samuel, Richard and James and a daughter who, by her marriage with Hugh Bateman of Hartington (1616-82) became kin to SIR HUGH BATEMAN *(q.v.)*. On his father's death in 1651, he inherited The Friary, Derby, where he died 30th August 1697, being succeeded by Samuel, a barrister at the Inner Temple, who married Elizabeth (d.June 1696) a daughter of George Harpur of Twyford. It was Samuel's son Samuel (d.1743) who sold The Friary to the CROMPTONS *(q.v.)*.

[Visitation of Derbyshire 1662; Parish Registers; Jeayes (1904) III.1.3.80; Craven (1987) 56-59.]

DARWIN, Dr Erasmus, FRS (1731-1802)

Erasmus Darwin lived in Derby for just two decades, yet many of the most important achievements of his life stem from these years. He was born at Elston (Notts) 12th December 1731, fourth son of a country gentleman, Robert Darwin, himself a great grandson of William, of Cleatham, Lincs. (d.1664). He qualified as a physician at Edinburgh and took up practice at Lichfield from 1756, where he quickly made the acquaintance of Matthew Boulton, Benjamin Franklin and James Ferguson. Within 18 months he had added JOHN WHITEHURST *(q.v.)* to his acquaintanceship and within a decade these men, with other, later, friends such as Josiah Wedgwood, James Keir and James Watt, had formed that epoch-making informal scientific grouping, the Lunar Society.

Darwin was probably the most notable and visionary polymath of his age; his grasp of fundamental principles and his fertile imagination led to his propounding or actually inventing a huge variety of concepts covering almost all scientific disciplines, amongst which were: air

travel, artesian wells, canal lifts, copying machines, educational improvements, evolutionary theory – presaging by many years the work of his more famous grandson, Charles – microscopy, oil drilling, rocket motors, speaking machines, steam carriages, submarines, water closets (with Whitehurst, with whom he also shared research into vulcanology), ventilation and women's rights. Many appear in his commonplace book, along with numerous important medical matters; others were expressed in his series of didactic poems – *The Botanic Garden* (1789/1792) *Zoönomia* (1794-96), *Phytologia*

(1800) and *The Temple of Nature* (1803) – written in heroic couplets and which made him the most famous poet of his age as well as influencing the Romantic school which followed him. The unlikely power of this form is aptly illustrated by:

Soon shall they arm, Unconquerd steam! afar
Drag the slow barge, or drive the rapid car;
Or on wide-waving wings expanded bear
The flying chariot through the fields of air.

Many of his ideas were shared unselfishly with friends and protégés – in Derby, WILLIAM STRUTT *(q.v.)* – who often developed them. Wedgwood built Darwin's horizontal windmill at

Etruria, a prototype of which was built for him in 1767 by JOSEPH PICKFORD *(q.v.)*. He was twice painted by JOSEPH WRIGHT *(q.v.)* whose physician he was.

He married first at Lichfield, Mary Howard, by whom he had three surviving sons, including Robert, Charles's father, by a daughter of his friend Josiah Wedgwood. He later had two natural daughters – the Misses Parker, whom he installed in charge of a school at Ashbourne run along his own principles – after the death of Mary, before re-marrying, to Elizabeth, the widow of Col. E.S.Pole of Radburne Hall in 1781. They set up at 3 Full Street, Derby a year later where they lived until about a month before his death when they moved to Breadsall Priory, a house purchased by his eldest son (a local solicitor who died tragically at 40 in 1799). They had a further seven children, all of whom received their primary education in Derby at the hands of HERBERT SPENCER's *(q.v.)* grandfather, whose academy was also run along Darwinian lines.

Being in Derby, rather more distant from Boulton and the Lunar Society, he then formed (or re-formed) the Derby Philosophical Society as a rather more formal offshoot which lasted well into the next century. With Whitehurst, and later William Strutt, he began to agitate for the founding of an Infirmary and began a free dispensary for those in the town who were least able to afford medicines or medical advice. At his house he sank an artesian well (1785) and constructed a hand-operated private ferry across the Derwent.

His last years were clouded by a reaction against his radicalism (he had espoused the cause of the American Revolution) and by an emphatic passage in *Zoönomia* (I.503):

> The final cause of this contest among the males seems to be, that the strongest and most active animal should propagate the species, which should thence become improved.

This outraged orthodox Christian belief and provoked a series of attacks on him, although it clearly sets out his grandson, Charles's, agenda on evolution.

He died in his study at Breadsall Priory on 1st April 1802 and was buried at the parish church there. Coleridge ('Dr Darwin is everything but the Christian' he reported after their first meeting) said of him that he had 'a greater range of knowledge than any other man in Europe'. This, added to his charm and ease of manner, encapsulates much of his unique character.

[King-Hele, D., *Doctor of Revolution* (London, 1977); Darwin, C., *Life of Erasmus Darwin* (1879); Schofield, R.E., *Lunar Society of Birmingham* (1963); Glover, *op.cit.* II.154-56.]

DAVIS, John (1810-1873)

One of the most distinguished domestic and industrial scientific instrument makers, John Davis was born at Thame (Oxon.) into a family of Jewish instrument makers based in Leeds but operating largely peripatetically in the later 18th century. In that period the family already had contacts in Derby, possibly including DR ERASMUS DARWIN *(q.v.)*, the academy of whose protégé, Matthew Spencer (1762-1827) having educated John, David, William and a Miss Davis of this family between 1788 and 1799. Of these it is thought that John was John's father; we only know for certain that he had a brother called Edward, and an uncle Gabriel, back in Leeds,whose own instrument making firm in Boar Lane survived at least into the time of his grandson.

It is assumed that John Davis served an apprenticeship with one of the family – probably Gabriel – before setting up permanently in Derby about 1832 in 24 Iron Gate, lately vacated by JOHN WHITEHURST II *(q.v.)* whose rival he swiftly became. His first instruments were domestic barometers and thermometers but he had begun to concentrate on industrial instruments, especially for mining: anemomers, compasses, safety lamps etc. and later still made surveying instruments, too. Around 1871 the firm – by now John Davis and Son – had moved to the corner of Amen Alley and Full Street, where it flourished until about a century later when it moved again. In spite of several take-overs it is still flourishing.

Davis died in 1873 and by his London-born

wife Angela left six sons and two daughters. Henry (1852-1917), the fifth son, took on the firm in Derby, his younger brother Herbert going to the USA. Frederick, (1843-1900) the eldest son, trained as an engineer, but became a notable antiquary, publishing *Derbyshire Place Names* and two books about the archaeology of Silchester (Berks), in the excavation of which Roman City he took a prominent part. Alfred, the second brother, ran the firm's London office and the fourth, Francis, became a merchant in Brussels. The family's connection with the firm was not severed until the time of Bruce Davis, John's only grandson, in more recent years.

[Tachella (1902) 43, 62, 76, 105, 146; Census returns; Directories; Spencer's *School Register,* MS in Derby Museum (1785-1807) and assistance from Mr Colin Barnes.]

DEACON, Augustus Oakley (1819-1899)

Deacon was an artist of some merit, and with T.SIMMONDS *(q.v.)*, a co-founder of the Derby School of Art, initially in St Peter's Street, in 1857, and from the same year was visiting art master at Derby School, to 1871.

He was a grandson of John Deacon and his father married a daughter of George Oakley, probably brother to Octavius Oakley, a highly gifted Derby artist and theatrical scene painter whose influence probably brought Deacon to the town, where he took a house in Burton Road, later moving to Ockbrook (where he befriended J.A.WARWICK *(q.v.)*.) He was certainly living in Derby by 1851 (as was his sister Frances) and was painting fairly prolifically from that time. He died 31st December 1899 having married twice. By his first wife Anne (whom he had married before coming to Derby) he had five sons and a daughter and by his second, another son Arthur. His third son was Maurice Deacon MICE, FGS, JP, a Derby School educated engineer who became managing director of the Sheepbridge Iron Company; one of latter's daughters, Hilda, married Alfred FitzHerbert Melville Wright, a member of a numerous, distinguished and opulent local family.

[Tachella, *op.cit.* 49, 53, 64, 90, 178; Derby Museum Art Dept. *Index;* Charles Wright Esq.]

DEELEY Richard Mountford (1855-1944)

The Midland Railway produced a number of fine engineers, and R.M.Deeley was one of the few to hold the post of Locomotive Superintendent, being only the third holder of that post. Deeley was a member of a very ancient gentry family who first came to notice at Halesowen (Worcestershire) in the late 16th century; their name is a corruption of d'Oyly. Edwin Deeley of The Lye (Worcestershire), whose mother was sister and heiress of Richard Mountford of Park House, Shifnal (Salop), was the father of Richard Mountford Deeley of The Lye (1825-1909) an accountant who had business connections with the Midland Railway. He married a cousin, Eliza While of Ebbw Vale (Glam.) and R.M.Deeley was the eldest of their eight sons. The youngest, Douglas, worked for a time on the *Derby Daily Express* as a journalist. The eldest (b.1855) was R.M.Deeley the younger, subject of this memoir.

Young Richard was educated at Chester Grammar School and later was a pupil of the engineer, E.B.Ellington at a Chester foundry. In 1876 he transferred to S.W.JOHNSON *(q.v.)* at Derby under whom he rose swiftly to Head of Testing (1890) and Chief Assistant, succeeding him in 1903. His main achievement was to perfect and multiply Johnson's 4-4-0 compound locomotives. He also pioneered the electrification of the Morecambe and Heysham (Lancs) line. Unfortunately, in 1907, (Sir) Cecil Paget was made general superintendent, and the two failed completely to get on. Paget imposed an experimental locomotive design on Deeley (busy with one of his own). When it proved less than a success, Deeley took the blame, and on 13th August 1909 he resigned in disgust, although he continued to reside in his ebulliently gothic residence on Osmaston Road, Melbourne House.

He was a member of both the Institutes of Mechanical and Civil Engineers, and a Fellow of both the Geographical Society and the Royal Meteorological Society and one or two other

bodies which underlined the talent he displayed as an engineer. He later retired to Isleworth (Middlesex) where he died, unmarried, on 19th June 1944. A nephew, Horace (1888-1931) was latterly proprietor of Darley Abbey Mills.
[Hamilton Ellis, C. *The Midland Railway* (London 1953) 116-134; Redford, *op.cit.* 80 f; Burke, *Landed Gentry* (1937) 595-6.]

DEGGE, Sir Simon (1612-1703)

Degge was the longest serving of all the Recorders of Derby, having been appointed at the Restoration in 1661 and serving until his death in 1703. He was noted for the equability of the justice he dispensed – as with the strange case of NOAH BULLOCK *(q.v.)* – and for the general affability of his character. He held the Recordership in plurality with the post of Justice of North Wales and the Marches and the High Shrievalty of Derbyshire for 1673-74.

Degge was born in 1612, younger son of Thomas Degge of Stramshall (Staffordshire), near Uttoxeter, by Dorothy Critchlow of Wolscot (Staffordshire); Thomas was the seventh in descent from Hugh, of Stramshall, living in the late 14th century. During the Civil War Degge emerged as a fervent Royalist, suffering imprisonment under the Long Parliament. On his release in 1649 he went to the Inner Temple, being called to the bar in 1653. At the Restoration he was on the roll of those Cavaliers nominated for Charles II's projected Order of the Royal Oak and the same year (1660) was appointed Judge in West Wales. However he returned to be Recorder of Derby a year later and was made Knight Bachelor 2nd March 1669/70; he had already received a grant of arms (1661). He was author of *The Parson's Counsellor and the Law of Tithes* which ran into seven editions between 1676 and 1820.

Degge lived at Derby and Stramshall, his Derby residence being the so called 'Old Mayor's Parlour' in Tenant Street. His first wife (who died in 1652) was Jane, daughter of Thomas Orrell of Slaugham, Sussex, by whom he had a surviving son, Whitehall Degge, whose grandson was a Derby doctor. He remarried Alice, daughter of

Anthony Oldfield of Lincolnshire (whose niece Alice married Whitehall's son S.B.Degge) and had another son, Simon (1655-76) and three daughters. He died at Derby in 1703, and his wife remarried James Trollope of Thoraldby (Lincs). [DNB.; Thoroton R. (Ed. Throsby, J.) *History of Nottinghamshire* (1790) I.319; Parish registers; Hutton, *loc.cit.*]

DEGGE, Simon, MD, FRS, FSA (1694-1729)

Simon Degge was one of Derbyshire's first scientific archaeologists, and was the man whose excavations at Repton in the 1720s inspired those of Drs M. and B.Biddle in the 1970s and 1980s. He was a careful antiquary and a noted Derby physician for whom Abbott's Hill House was built, on Babington Lane.

Degge was the only son of William (d.1695) elder son of Simon, the younger son of SIR SIMON DEGGE *(q.v.)*; he was born in 1694 at the Old Mayor's Parlour, Derby, and was brought up in his grandfather's household there. His mother was Elizabeth How, a Londoner. Young Degge may have had his interest in antiquarianism fostered by Sir Simon, and he probably inherited his library. He was educated at Heydon (Cambs.) and proceeded to St John's, Cambridge on 1st December 1710 aged 16. He graduated, and by about 1724 had been a Fellow of the Society of Antiquaries for at least a year, and on 8th February 1727 was elected its director; he was a regular attender at the Society's meetings and frequently exhibited coins, medals, manuscripts and other objects there. Two months after he was elected FSA he also became a Fellow of the Royal Society, proposed by William Stukeley – no mean feat for a man in his 20s. In *Philosophical Transactions* in 1727 he published his important paper on his excavations at Repton; he was also (from 1726) a member of the Spalding Gentlemen's Society.

He married on 31st January 1711 Elizabeth (1683-1753) daughter of George Ne(e)dham of Wymondley (Herts), a descendant of a notable Tudor architect, James Needham, of Derbyshire ancestry. They had an only daughter, Elizabeth born the following year, later Mrs Hay (who died in 1738).

He probably lived for part of each year at Graveley (Herts), his father-in-law's seat, and certainly excavated a Roman site there in 1722-23. He died in his prime on 8th November 1729 at 35 and was buried in Graveley church.
[Clutterbuck, R. *History and Antiquities of the County of Hertford* (London 1821) II.5501; DNB.; Le Neve, P., *Pedigrees of the Knights,* Ed. Marshall, G.W., Harleian Society VIII (London 1873) 231-2.]

DENBY, Charles (*c*.1735-1793)

Derby has produced very few composers; Denby and C.BASSANO (*q.v.*) are the only ones representing the 18th century. He wrote much church music, anthems and voluntaries as well as minor orchestral works, solo pieces for keyboard and trio sonatas. One of several published works was a set of *Three Duetts for the piano forte and german flute or violin with a favourite Air with Variations and a sonata for the piano forte,* dedicated to 1st Lord Scarsdale's daughter Hon. Juliana Curzon, Opus 3, which came out posthumously in 1794. His Op. I and 2 were harpsichord sonatas (1775 and 1778) and in 1792 he was attempting to collect subscriptions towards a piano concerto. In 1784 he was one of the provincial musicians who played at the great Handel Commemoration in London. He pioneered local music festivals including the use of a church – All Saints' – in which to perform an oratorio, a move which led to some opposition in Derby. He promoted a larger event there in 1792 which was the first of a cycle of such festivals for which Derby became famous for more than two decades.

Denby, born *c*.1735, was the son of William, who on 31st January 1743 had been appointed organist of All Saints' at a salary of £30 per annum (paid out of pew rents) which he augmented by teaching privately. By the 1760s Charles was playing with JOSEPH WRIGHT (*q.v.*) (flute), P.D.BURDETT (*q.v.*) (cello), Rev. Thomas Blackwall (rector of Mugginton) and William Denby (violins) and Rev. C.S.HOPE (*q.v.*) on continuo, mainly at his own house but

also, as a leading light of the Derby Society of Musicians, at the Tiger, Cornmarket, newly completed (1764) by JOSEPH PICKFORD (*q.v.*).

On his father's death in 1771, Charles was appointed (10th October) to succeed him at the same salary. His contract added, 'and that he shall give his best assistance towards introducing any person (who will offer themselves) in singing once a week, to wit, Sunday after evening service'. Whilst his social circle appears to have been firmly rooted amongst his contemporaries Wright and Burdett, the subscribers to his Op.3 included HUGH BATEMAN (*q.v.*), Juliana Curzon, D.P.COKE (*q.v.*), ERASMUS DARWIN (*q.v.*), REV. THOMAS GISBORNE (*q.v.*), Alderman Haden, SAMUEL HARRISON (*q.v.*), the wife of the poet William Hayley, Wright's friend John Holland of Ford, Kirkman, the London harpsichord maker, F.N.C.MUNDY (*q.v.*), WILLIAM STRUTT (*q.v.*) and others, all suggesting that he was widely known and appreciated, although his music has less spontaneity and sparkle to it than contemporaries such as Charles Avison; he was certainly no John Stanley.

He died in 1793, one son, Charles Calamy Denby (1752-1792) having predeceased him. His eldest son, Col. William Denby (1750-1830) was long in the employ of the East India Company; of his second, John (b.1763) we know little. His daughter Mary Ann married Joseph Wright's friend, the draper Thomas Sale, in 1779. He also had kin in Virginia (USA), and he was succeeded at All Saints' by GEORGE CHRISTOPHER FRITCHE (*q.v.*).
[Cox and Hope, *op.cit.* 47; Nicholson, *op.cit.* 1. 194; Tachella, *op.cit.* 21; Sturgess, R.P., in *Music Review* (39) 3/4 (August-November 1978) 179-82, John Rooks, Esq.]

DENSTONE, James (1724-1780)

Second son of Abraham Denstone, *stuccadore* of Derby (1687-1753) who worked on Derby All Saints' and the 1731 Guildhall; his grandfather came to Derby from Burton-upon-Trent in 1651, and his mother was Elizabeth Mosley of Derby whom he married at Duffield 30th December

1708. James was apprenticed to Solomon Brown as a mason and bricklayer, gaining his freedom 26 April 1748, being described later as a builder and architect. By 1753/4 he appears to have been building for Wrightson Mundy at Markeaton Hall and virtually acting as his agent in numerous estate transactions. He married at Chaddesden 15th May 1755 Elizabeth Ordish, but appears to have had no children. His building business appears to have been run jointly with his elder brother Abraham (1723-79) also a *stuccadore* and an associate of JOSEPH PICKFORD *(q.v.)*. Their business seems to have passed to Abraham junior's sons-in-law, John and Seth Bridgart, for Abraham's sons had set up as bakers on his death in 1780.

Much circumstantial evidence points to Denstone as being architect of Markeaton Hall, and he later succeeded Samuel Wyatt as Clerk of Works under Adam at Kedleston until Lord Scarsdale dismissed him in 1775 for 'promoting his Whiggish views'. He was succeeded by Joseph Pickford. It is also reasonable to propose him as architect of The Cedars, Ashbourne Road, built at about this period for Lord Scarsdale as a town house; it has affinities to Markeaton in its detailing. He also built 51-55 Wardwick, Derby for F.N.C.Mundy 1768-71. Denstone was also proprietor of the Mitre, Amen Alley.
[Craven (1988) 93, 133; Saunders, E.J., *Joseph Pickford of Derby* (Stroud 1993) 32, 67, 173; Local Studies Library: Mundy Papers, Parcel 225; Deed 1051; Poll Book (Derby) 1769; Will of Abraham Denstone DRO 9090/CT8 & CT17-13.]

DENNIS, Denny, see POUNTAIN
DERBY, Bishop of, see Pearce
DERBY, Earl of, see FERRERS

DERBY, Hugh de (d. by 1179)

Hugh, dean of Derby was a powerful local magnate and a pivotal figure in the mid- to late 12th century in the town. Although we do not know the names of his parents, the Norse name of his brother Anghemund – a burgess in 1156-57 – suggests that the family were of Viking stock. His title of dean may refer to his being (rural) dean of Derby, for by this time the Dean of the combined College of All Saints and St Alkmund was the Dean of Lincoln.

His most important act was in about 1146 when he gave land from his patrimony at Little Darley (Darley Abbey) to the canons of St Helen, founded in the town a decade or so earlier. This gift marked the establishment of the Augustinian house of St Mary, Darley, the largest monastic foundation in Derbyshire. It was later taken under the protection of ROBERT DE FERRERS, EARL OF DERBY *(q.v.)*. He was also the patron and proprietor (by hereditary right) of St Peter's Church in Derby.

Hugh's wife was the sister of Henry de Touchet the younger, Lord of Markeaton and Mackworth and grandson of the Domesday tenant of those estates, Joscelin son of Anketil de Touchet, a Norman in the service of Hugh d'Avranches, Earl of Chester. John, a descendant, succeeded as 5th Lord Audley of Heleigh (Cheshire) in 1405. By her, Hugh had three sons as well as a daughter, who married Stephen de Derby; the eldest, Henry, succeeded to Hugh's wealth and property and became Dean in his place, as well as perpetual vicar of St Peter's, the family church.

Hugh was a very powerful figure and the strict control he, his kin and his descendants held over the affairs both sacred and secular in medieval Derby was only broken in the 14th century, probably due to the depredations of the Black Death.
[Darlington, R.R. (Ed.), *The Cartulary of Darley Abbey* (Kendal 1945) iii-v, xxxv-xxxvi, A13, 18, 28-29, 54, K35, 02, 08; *Domesday Book* 4.1; Craven (1988) 24, 33, 36-7.]

DERBY, Walkelin de (living 1135/1161)

Derby had been constituted a Saxon burh by Edward the Elder in the 920s, and this had included a mint, which outshone that of

Nottingham in importance, and continued until closed by Henry II in c.1154/55. The last mint-master was Walkelin de Derby, a relation by marriage of HUGH de DERBY, the Dean, *(q.v.)* and was, with his wife Goda, an opulent bene-factor to both the town and to the new Abbey of St Mary, Darley. Amongst these benefactions was the hall of their house 'which shall be used for a school for clerks and the chambers shall serve as a hostel for the master and clerks in per-petuity'. This benefaction has been taken by many as the origin of Derby School, actually founded under the provisions of a Charter of Queen Mary I in 1554; however, later charters clearly imply that the provisions of this particu-lar benefaction were never carried into effect, although the Abbey certainly had a school by the 16th century. That said, the 18-year gap between dissolution in 1536 and the possible establish-ment of Derby School under Mary's settlement – not necessarily an immediate consequence of the latter – represents a massive discontinuity impossible to gloss over.

Walkelin's parentage is not known for certain, but he must have been born c.1100. His wife, Goda, appears to have been the daughter of (Sir) Ralph Hanselin of Haverholme (Lincs.) and Derby and who is probably to be identified with the Azelin who held Egginton and Alvaston under Geoffrey Alselin (Hanselin) – probably his uncle – in the Domesday Book. Walkelin's daughter Hawise later married Ralf son of Geremund (son of Azelin) her putative first cousin. Goda's sister Iolenta married Roger son of Ralph, a junior grandson of Joscelin de Touchet of Markeaton. On Walkelin's death, c.1161-2, Goda remarried Master Robert de Derby, youngest son of HUGH the dean *(q.v.)*. By Walkelin, however, she had three daughters, of whom Quenilda married Ingeram de Wardwick, their son Peter marrying Eustacia 'Lady of Derby' a granddaughter of Hugh. Goda had two more daughters and two sons, probably by Master Robert.

Thus, by sheer opulence – he was able to play a fine of £100 to Henry II in 1159, a huge sum, probably incurred for coining irregularly during Stephen's reign – and careful inter-marriage, Walkelin and Goda bore a central role in the expansion of Hugh the Dean's powerful dynasty. [Darlington, *op.cit.* xi-xiv; DAJ LII (1925) 164-65; Craven, *loc.cit.;* Derbyshire *Feet of Fines* 12 of 1202.]

DEXTER, John (1926-1990)

John Dexter was one of the major British theatre directors of the latter part of the 20th century, for almost 30 years directing the National Theatre, The Royal Court (1957-1972) and crowning his career as Director of Production at the Metropolitan Opera, New York. The essential Dexter was caught by his friend Arnold Wesker in his 1998 volume *The Birth of Shylock and the Death of Zero Mostel*, in which the director fea-tures as the anti-hero in the staging of Wesker's *Shylock* as 'A fevered camp neurotic, who is at once Wesker's oldest friend and a manipulative near-sadist who plays "Get-the-guest" with everyone in sight.' Dexter's treatment of the cast gives the playwright great anxiety, yet he feels a real affection for the 'egotistical monster', who declares of the play: "You'll love it when you see it on stage, but you'll hate it when I talk about it." In fact, Dexter had directed all of Wesker's first five plays – his own first work in the theatre. Indeed, the Weskers had befriended Dexter after he was released from prison, convicted of attempting to seduce a young man, something that was then still an indictable offence.

John Dexter was the son of Henry (Harry) Dexter, a plumbing engineer with the local gas undertaking, and Rose née Smith, being born in 1926. He was educated at Friar Gate House School and thereafter at Derby School. During the later stages of World War Two he joined ENSA, and on return, decided to make his way as an actor, appearing initially at the Little Theatre, Derby (later the Derby Playhouse), where his tal-ent and temperament swiftly got him noticed, and he departed for London as soon as the opportunity arose.

He played in repertory and in between times on the wireless, where he appeared on *The Archers* as P.C. Bridon. He also obtained parts in TV

of his ward, much assisted by his intelligence, tact and affability.

A Sikh, born in 1933, Dhindsa trained in India as a teacher before coming to Britain on 27th June 1962 from Beaspind, Punjab, with his wife Jasbir Kaur and their two elder sons Hardyal and Balbir. He came to Derby and found work as a toolsetter at Messrs. Parker Hannifin, Wetherby Road, where he was employed for many years. Latterly the family lived in Empress Road, Nirmal Dhindsa serving as Mayor of Derby 1994-95. He died on 19th March 1996 leaving two sons and two daughters, the latter having been born in Derby. He seems to have founded – following a long Derby tradition – a new political dynasty, for his elder son, Hardyal Singh Dhindsa (b.1959) was elected to the County Council in the early 1990s transferring to the City Council in 1996. A senior probation officer, he has three sons of his own. Mayor Dhindsa's other son is a communications firm manager, and his daughters Ranjit and Manjit Kaur are respectively a solicitor and a dentist.

[*Derby Evening Telegraph* 12/5/94, 19/5/94, 18/6/94 and 1/4/1996.]

plays, too, before taking with verve to directing in 1957. From that year he directed 15 plays for the Royal Court Theatre followed from 1963 by a further 15 for the National. His only film direction was *Virgin Soldiers*, two years after he had made his debut as an opera director with *Benvenuto Cellini* at Covent Garden in 1966. His *Who's Who* entry listed his recreation solely as 'work'. From 1974 until his death he was in New York with The Met. He died unmarried in March 1990.

[*Who's Who* (1978) 656; Wesker, *op.cit.*; Information courtesy family members.]

DHINDSA, Nirmal Singh (1933-1996)

Councillor Nirmal Dhindsa was the first Asian Mayor of Derby and as such marked a watershed in the long history of the office. He was a councillor from 1973, having been elected for Sinfin Ward in the Labour interest, and during his long service as politician and community leader did much credit to his community and to the electors

DOCKER, Norah, Lady (1905-1983)

Sydney Royce Turner was a native of Shaftesbury Crescent and inter-related with a whole group of families resident there from the late 19th century and most of whom worked for SIR FRANCIS LEY *(q.v.)*. He himself, however, set up as a shop fitter, with premises at 4 London Road, Derby, and one of his most prestigious contracts was the fitting out of Boot's new store on the corner of East Street and St Peter's Street in 1912. He later moved to Birmingham, with his young daughter, Norah Royce, who was born in 1905. It was she who much later became a celebrated socialite as the second wife of the financier Sir Bernard Docker (1896-1978), whose grandfather Ralph was a Birmingham man.

Norah Docker was glamourous, even in late middle age, had a powerful but winning personality, and an irrepressible flair for publicity. Somehow, any announcement she made about such envy-inducing domestic accoutrements as gold (plated) taps or personalised accessories merely served to endear her and – let it be admitted – her sheer vulgarity to most readers of the tabloid press. Her ability to make an entrance was legendary.

Her first husband was Clement Callingham; her second, whom she married in 1946, Sir William Harry Collins (d.1947), was chairman of Fortnum & Mason's. It was her third, however, who gave her talents full reign: Sir Bernard Dudley Frank Docker of Coleshill House, Amersham (Bucks) and Davies Street, Mayfair. Two of his uncles, Ralph (1855-1910) and Ludford (1860-1940) had been cricketers for Derbyshire – in 1874 and 1881-86 respectively – and had lived in Derby for a time. He himself was head of two railway rolling stock building firms, adding considerably to an inherited fortune. His first wife was nearly as memorable as Norah, for in 1934 he had married the actress Jeannie Stewart, but divorced shortly before he was made KBE in 1939. Norah Docker's star waned after Sir

Bernard's death in 1978, although she continued to live in great style and with her customary *élan* until her death in 1983.
[Burke, *Landed Gentry* (1937) 624; *Who's Who* (1947) 560; and (1978) 673; information courtesy Mrs B. Richardson.]

DOUGHTY, Alderman Samuel (1626-1710)

Alderman Doughty's claim to fame was his period during the Commonwealth as Treasurer to the Army, a crucial role in keeping the forces of puritan repression in the field. The victories of Worcester and Dunbar are probably testimony to his efficacy in this role. He also served as a captain in the Parliament's Army, and staked out a favourable future by going over to Col. Charles White during the 1659 insurrection.

Doughty was baptised at All Saints' Derby 10th March 1626/7, eldest son of Samuel (1586-1639) a mercer who served as an alderman bailiff in 1632-33, and as churchwarden of All Saints' 1621-22, and was himself the third son of Robert Doughty of Derby. The business had been built up by the latter, passing to the elder Samuel's brother Richard who died in 1623 leaving it to young Samuel's father.

Samuel was an alderman of the Borough; in 1666 he issued a copper ½d token and was a member of the Worshipful Company of Mercers, as well as the Derby Mercers' Company of which he was warden from 17th April 1677 and again in 1683, retiring to 'dwell in the country' – a house he had acquired in Mickleover in 1660 – the following year. He was a churchwarden of All Saints' 1668-69. He married Ann and at his death, probably in 1710, had three sons, Samuel, George and Charles, and two daughters. Samuel, although the eldest son, became a clockmaker, the younger sons maintaining the business in Derby. The clockmaker's elder son, John (1682-1717), entered the church serving as curate of Mickleover; the younger son Samuel (d.1757) was also a clockmaker.
[Derby Local Studies Library.]

DOWNES, Prof. Ralph William, CBE (1904-1993)

Ralph Downes was an organist and choral conductor who also designed the organ installed at the Royal Festival Hall in 1951. The latter was controversial, but Downes was a reformer in organ building, resorting to French techniques to produce Baroque concepts.

Downes was born at North Parade, Derby, son of James William Downes, a Midland Railway engineer and Constance Edith, his wife. As a child, he was inspired by the sound of the organ and had piano and organ lessons from an early age. He entered the Royal College of Music at 18 (later FRCM) and became assistant organist at Southwark Cathedral in 1923 going on to become organ scholar at Keble College, Oxford two years later (MA) where he developed a taste for contemporary composers. He was studying and teaching in the USA until 1936 when he became organist at Brompton Oratory, a post he only relinquished in 1977, and under him the services there attained an almost legendary majesty and inspiration.

Apart from the Festival Hall organ, he designed several others, all very distinctive, and from 1954 to 1975 taught at the Royal College of Music where he became Professor of Organ Music. He married in 1929 Agnes Mary Rix, after whose death in the following year he converted to Roman Catholicism. He died 29th December

1993, leaving an only son, Prof. (John) Kerry Downes, Professor of Architecture at Reading University and the biographer of Vanburgh, Hawksmoor and Wren.
[*Daily Telegraph*, 30/12/1993; *Who's Who* (1978) 689; Debrett, *Distinguished People* (1990) 578.]

DRAGE, Lt. Cdr. Geoffrey, MA, RNVR (1860-1955)

Geoffrey Drage was, with Sir Henry Bemrose, one of the surprise Conservative winners at Derby in the 1895 election. As the Borough had not sent a Conservative to Westminster since

W.T.Cox in 1865, both, unsurprisingly, lost their seats in the 1900 election. However, he effectively ended the Parliamentary career of the Liberal Home Secretary Sir William Vernon Harcourt and Bemrose's victory was the only hiatus in the 30-year career of LORD ROE *(q.v.)*. Most of Drage's work was as an inveterate committee man and author: he was an expert on labour and labour relations, international affairs, welfare and sea training.

Drage was the son of a doctor, Charles Drage, and was born in 1860, being educated at Eton and Christ Church (Oxon) where he took an MA before going to the Middle Temple and Lincoln's Inn, although he never practised as a barrister. He also studied at a number of continental universities. He was Secretary to the Royal Commission on Labour 1891-94 and Vice-President of the International Congress on Accidents at Milan (1894). His career was further boosted by his marriage in 1896 to Ethel Sealby (d.1952), daughter of T.H.Ismay of Dawpool, founder of the White Star Line; his brother-in-law was on the *Titanic* in 1912.

He was a leading light in sea training for cadets, serving several stints as Chairman of T.S. *Exmouth* 1901-22, being commissioned into the RNVR in 1914. In 1916 he transferred to Military Intelligence. He was a Director of several companies (including Cunard-White Star) and a London County Council Alderman 1910-19. He wrote novels, treatises on sea training, labour relations and Russian history and died at his house, 39 Hyde Park Gate in Mayfair, 7th March 1955. [*Who Was Who* 1945-61.]

DREWRY, Samuel (d.1769)

Samuel Drewry was the founder of Derby's first enduring local newspaper, the *Derby Mercury* first issued on 2nd March 1732, putting out of business the *British Spy* or *Derby Postman* of 1726. It was published for almost 200 years, closing in 1930, a staid, Tory-inclined newspaper issued at first weekly but later as a daily journal.

The paper's founder, Samuel Drewry, set up in Derby Market Place in around 1723 as a printer, having come from Stafford where the family printing firm remained in the hands of his brother Joshua. Their father may have been one William Drewry (b.1660). Samuel died without issue in August 1769, leaving the firm (and the *Mercury*) to his nephew John (d.1794), elder son of Joshua, by which time the firm had moved to Irongate. John's younger brother Joshua (II) died less than two years later, having previously been editor and proprietor of the *Stafford Mercury*, a sister paper. His son John (II) (d.1834) succeeded and, unlike his predecessors, concentrated his business in Derby, which he served as Mayor in 1806, 1814 and 1823. His brother-in-law, Alderman Samuel Rowland, held the same office in 1809 and 1818. The last member of the family to run the *Mercury* was John II's son, John III who married Alderman Rowland's daughter, but dying, again childless, in 1840, sold the business to WILLIAM BEMROSE *(q.v.)* on 27th March 1839. He sold the newspaper on, but developed the printing side. Drewry's brothers were James, a Burton upon Trent solicitor (first of a line of Drewrys to follow this calling there) and Edward, a Derby surgeon. [Glover, (1829/31)11.601; Parish registers; DM

3/6/1840, 3/5/1842; Bemrose, *op.cit.* 42; Rippon, A., *The Book of Derby* (Buckingham, 1980) 98; Craven (1988) 104.]

DUESBURY, Henry FRIBA (1806-1872)

A grandson of WILLIAM DUESBURY the younger *(q.v.)*, proprietor of the Derby Porcelain Factory, Henry's father was Frederick Duesbury, a London physician who was born in Derby. He was born in 1806, trained in London as an architect and was in partnership there later as Duesbury and Lee, the latter being associated in his first local commission, the rebuilding of the Guildhall (Matthew Habershon, 1828) after a destructive fire in 1841-42. He followed this with the restoration of Boylestone church, with the addition of a tower and a school (1844-45). In 1848 his partnership became Duesbury and Patterson, and in the year following he built Mickleover Manor for the Newtons and the Derbyshire County Lunatic Asylum nearby, both in Jacobethan style (1849-51). In 1850 he designed the attractive classical Lodge in Arboretum Square and provided a Grand Stand for the newly established Derby Racecourse in 1852 (demolished 1911) at a cost of £2,400. He also designed Newark Corn Exchange. He died in London in retirement in 1872. [DM. 28/7/1847; *Derbyshire Life* 2/1995; White's *Directory of Derbyshire* (1857) 80, 84; Haslem, *op.cit.* 42-43.]

DUESBURY, William (1725-1786)

William Duesbury was the founder of the famous Derby Porcelain Factory which he established in premises on Nottingham Road around 1751, at first (and until a little after 1756) with the Huguenot refugee ANDREW PLANCHÉ *(q.v.)* and from 1756 to 1779 with financial backing from JOHN HEATH *(q.v.)*. The firm was quick to flourish and gain a reputation for its fine porcelain; Duesbury's aim was to rival the best that continental Europe could offer and, in this, he can be said to have succeeded brilliantly, aided by his determination to employ the finest craftsmen and artists available. No wonder Dr Johnson grumbled (on a visit to the works in 1777) that 'it was too dear; for that he could have vessels of silver as cheap as were here made of porcelain'.

William Duesbury was the son of William Duesbury (1704-68), a Cannock currier, later of Longton (Staffordshire) and grandson of another William. He was born at Longton 7th September 1725 and trained as an enameller in London. He married Sarah James of Shrewsbury (d.1780) at about the time of the founding of the firm. In his fervour to obtain the best men, he took over both the Bow (1775) and Chelsea (1770) china factories, closing the first and continuing the second for some 12 years before transferring it, too, to Derby. His clients included members of the nobility, George III and Queen Charlotte, aided by the opening of a London showroom in 1773. His house, built 1768 on the site of a cottage occupied by his father in his declining years, appears to have been by JOSEPH PICKFORD *(q.v.)* although, apart from a weighbridge house in Pickford's hand, the works were earlier and extant drawings are in another hand.

Duesbury died in November 1786, leaving two (possibly more) sons and four daughters. It is clear that the factory was never sufficiently profitable to keep this brood in idleness, for apart from the eldest son WILLIAM *(q.v.)* who succeeded to the business and a possible third, John, who was a china painter there (before going to Pinxton with BILLINGSLEY *(q.v.)*), the others (if they were not cousins) were apprenticed to trades (Edward, (fourth), shoemaker, Samuel, (fifth), clockmaker). The ne'er-do-well second son, James, may have migrated to America. Of the daughters, Anna married the London china dealer Richard Egan and Dorothea married Rev. Charles Chawner of Church Broughton, a member of the London goldsmithing dynasty from that place. Samuel's descendants declined into poverty; of Edward's, one branch emigrated to Australia (where they still flourish), another flourished as Derby business people, producing Alderman Frank Duesbury

(1854-1905), Mayor of Derby in 1897-98. Both branches boast numerous descendants.

[Haslem, *op.cit.* 15-25; DNB; Rice, D.G., *Derby Porcelain, The Golden Years 1750-1770* (London 1983) 9-37; information courtesy of Andrew Ledger.]

DUESBURY, William (1751-1796)

Successor of his father and continuator of the porcelain manufacturing company he had built up, the second William Duesbury embraced the neoclassical style and continued the policy of hiring the best craftsmen he could get. He also placed more emphasis on aggressively marketing his products and his letters to his London agent, John Lygo, bear this out. He also shared his London showrooms with RICHARD BROWN *(q.v.)*, presumably to their mutual advantage, as the arrangement lasted some time.

The younger William was born 18th December 1751 and married within two months of succeeding his father, at St Alkmund's 4th January 1787, his bride being Elizabeth (d.1840), daughter of Alderman William Edwards, the family's Derby attorney. Duesbury seems to have been made of less stern stuff than his father, for the

strain of running the business affected his health, to which end he took on MICHAEL KEAN *(q.v.)* as partner, but died in October 1796, leaving Kean in charge and six children of whom the eldest, William III (1787-1845) eventually disposed of his interest in the china factory and set up a firm at Bonsall developing new methods of making paints and dyes, including the substitution of Barytes instead of white lead; on its undeserved failure in 1826 he migrated to Lowell (Mass.) where he espoused Universalist principles, designed and built a church there in which to pursue them, worked as an industrial chemist, married bigamously a local widow (siring three children) and died by his own hand 12th December 1845. A second son died young (Nathaniel 1791-1809) and the third was father to HENRY DUESBURY *(q.v.)*. One of the daughters married Alderman Francis Jessopp, who lived at Jacobean House, Wardwick.

[Haslem, *loc.cit.;* DNB; members of the family; local deeds.]

EASTWOOD, Reuben (1833-1877)

Reuben Eastwood was one of Derby's most successful ironmasters, who took over Eastwood and Swingler's foundry from his father James (its co-founder) in 1874. The firm, the Victoria and Railway Iron Works, was one of a group situated in Cotton Lane and thrived on contracts for components from the Midland Railway.

Eastwood was born at Liverpool in 1833, second son of James Eastwood (1808-74), of a Derbyshire family; James, known as 'Handsome Jim' had married Ellen Caroline at Mugginton in August 1828. The foundry had been started in 1852, the original partner being Thomas Frost, who died in October 1853; his son J.W.Frost left Eastwood and joined Thomas Swingler in Cotton Lane. In 1864 Eastwood moved his foundry from the crowded Morledge to a site adjacent to Frost and Swingler and the two amalgamated, Swingler's son, Henry, marrying Eastwood's daughter, Sarah Elizabeth.

Reuben at first acted as works manager, being the driving spirit behind the expansion of the works and the business conducted therein; the workforce was very large and well looked after. He lived in a villa on Osmaston Road and was an active member of the Litchurch Local Board, a director of the Derby Commercial Bank, a trustee of the Liversage Charity and a leading freemason in the local Tyrian Lodge. In 1860 he married Sarah, sister of LORD ROE *(q.v.)* and at his premature death aged 44 on St Valentine's Day 1877 he left two sons and five daughters. The second son, Thomas Carline Eastwood (1866-1930) of Littleover Grange later took over the running of the foundry and left numerous descendants.

[DM. 6/10/1853; Craven (1988), 165-66.]

EATON, George Morley, PRIBA (d.1940)

G.M.Eaton was the last of a dynasty which produced three architects, separated by two centuries. Son of Arthur Eaton (1857-1940), to whom he served his articles, he joined his father in practice prior to World War One. After that conflict, he opened an office in Ashbourne and from 1938 until his death in 1940 he served as President of the Royal Institute of British Architects and acted as Ecclesiastical Surveyor of the Diocese of Derby. His only new church, however, was St Edmund's, Allenton (1939), although he designed a number of felicitous village halls, e.g Flagg (1931), Newton Solney (1932) and Osmaston-by-Ashbourne (1937). In Derby he also designed offices for Rolls Royce, the Midland Drapery Arcade, the Christian Science Chapel, Friary Street (recently listed) and much work for the Derby Corporation Electricity undertaking, extending the Power Station and building showrooms, offices, boiler house and other refinements. For himself he built Brailsford Green, an Arts and Crafts timber-framed house of considerable size.

His father married in 1886 Mary Elizabeth, daughter of Robert Morley and, in addition to George, had two daughters, Kathleen, Mrs Edward Rickard and Doris, Mrs G.H.Lake. Arthur was seventh in descent from George Eaton (1611-89), the architect/builder responsible for Derby's fine Shire Hall of 1659 and the elegant chapel at Locko. All the intervening gen-

to develop theories about the assassination of President Kennedy and other *causes célèbres.*

He was born at Friarfield, Duffield Road, Derby on 8th October 1903, youngest of three sons of Charles Randolph Beaumont Eddowes (1865-1951), a solicitor whose father, C.K.Eddowes, had established the firm. Previously the family had been surgeons in Loughborough, although they traced their ancestry back to John Eddowes, a late 17th-century freeholder of Dilhorne (Staffordshire). After going to Uppingham he served his articles, eventually leaving his father's firm in Derby (which still exists) and moving to London where he set up in Berkeley Square. He sold the practice in 1956, starting the incomparable Bistro Vino restaurant in Manson Mews, Kensington (and, later, elsewhere) as well as designing a sports car, dealing in property and fighting causes. He had also been very sportive as a young man, playing in the Wimbledon Doubles and minor counties cricket for Derbyshire – his whole life resembled that of an adventurer from an earlier era. He was thrice married and left, at his death, 30th December 1993, two sons.

[*Daily Telegraph*, 1/1/1994; Fletcher, W.G.D. *Leicestershire Pedigrees and Royal Descents* (Leicester, 1887) 190-191; *Who's Who in Derbys.* (1934) 56-57.]

erations had been farmers at Sutton-on-the-Hill or Etwall where the family can be traced back to 1560. With the death of George Morley Eaton on 2nd April 1940 then, this remarkable dynasty came to an end, leaving Derby's built environment considerably the richer.

[Craven (1988) 69; Tachella, *op.cit.* 52, 54.]

EDDOWES, Michael, LLB (1903-1993)

Michael Eddowes was at various times a lawyer, author, restauranteur and ardent conspiracy theorist, the latter distinction growing effortlessly out of his interest in the case of Timothy Evans, executed in 1950 for the murder of his child, but in reality framed by the mass murderer Reginald Christie; it was Eddowes' tenacity and his 1955 book on the affair *The Man on Your Conscience* which led ultimately to the clearing of Evans' name. Later, in 1962-63 he met Stephen Ward, Christine Keeler and Eugene Ivanov as the Profumo affair was unfolding and he later claimed to have been convinced about the facts long before they became public. He later went on

EDWARDS, William (b.1796)

Unexpected changes of profession are not so uncommon, although they become remarkable if the change is between two quite unrelated callings. Such was the case of William Edwards, a Derby attorney, of the fourth generation of his family to follow this profession. Yet in 1832 at the age of 36, he sold his practice and started Hay's Pottery, near Burton upon Trent, purchasing Butt House, Woodville, from Earl Ferrers.

This sudden change of direction is perhaps less surprising when it is noted that Edwards' aunt, Elizabeth (1767-1828), had married, successively, WILLIAM DUESBURY the younger *(q.v.)* and MICHAEL REAN *(q.v.)*. By 1832 the Duesbury (and hence Edwards) connection with the Derby factory had long ended and to a man fascinated by seeking perfection in new wares, such an opportunity was not one to let slip.

Edwards was the eldest son of Nathaniel Edwards of Derby (1768-1844) by Salona, daughter of Alexander Cuthbertson (later Mrs Flack), born 1796. He himself had married 22nd September 1818 Marianne, daughter of Emmanuel Allen of Westminster, and all of their six sons and a daughter had been born by the time the family moved to Woodville. The eldest son, Nathaniel (b.1821) later emigrated to Auckland (NZ) where his descendants still flourish.

In the event Edwards' venture was not successful in the long term, having been sold by 1846.

[Jewitt, L.L. *Ceramic Art of Great Britain* (1878) II.328; Glover (1829/31) II.589.]

EMES, John (1763-1808)

John Emes was one of a number of outstanding Regency goldsmiths working in London but of West Derbyshire origin: others included Chawners, Eleys and Fearns. Emes was born at Bowbridge Fields (now Bowbridge House) on the Markeaton estate in 1763, third son of WILLIAM EMES *(q.v.)* and Mary, daughter of John Innocent. His maternal grandfather may also have been a member of a family of silversmiths, for a John Innocent of St Anne's, Soho, Goldsmith, was father of an eponymous goldsmith born about 1780 and conceivably a younger brother of Mary.

John Emes was apprenticed to William Woollett of Queen Street, London from 7th October 1778 and became free of the Worshipful Company of Goldsmiths on 5th July 1786. He worked for a decade before setting up in partnership with Henry Chawner (1764-1851), whose cousin, Rev. Charles Chawner had, a decade earlier, married Dorothea, 6th daughter of WILLIAM DUESBURY I *(q.v.)*, entering a joint mark that year. Two years later he was working alone and so continued until his death in June 1808. His widow, Rebecca, thereupon entered into partnership with John's elder brother William (b.1760) who himself

may have died by 1812, when she took as partner her husband's former apprentice Edward Bernard, this arrangement lasting until *c.*1815, when Rebecca may have retired. They had three daughters, one of whom was Mary, who married James Clay, (1764-1828), a London merchant of Derbyshire extraction whose son became MP for Hull and whose grandson, Cecil (1847-1920), composed 'Songs of Araby' and wrote plays.

Emes, who was described, like his father, as 'of Bowbridge Fields and Elvetham Park' made some fine neo-classical pieces of the very highest quality, including a boat-shaped silver cruet for Lord Nelson, apart from the large quantities of flatware which constituted the contemporary silversmith's 'bread and butter'.

[Jackson, *Goldsmiths and their Marks* (1948); Fallon, J.P. *Marks of London Goldsmiths and Silversmiths* (Newton Abbott, 2nd Edn. 1988) 70,122-124; and see next entry.]

EMES, William (1729-1803)

A landscape gardener and architect who was a close follower of Lancelot (Capability) Brown – although they never seem to have met – Emes' origins are shrouded in mystery. His father's name and his place of birth are unknown, although circumstantial evidence suggests the Church Broughton area, west of Derby.

By 1756, Emes was employed as a gardener at Kedleston, but where he trained is not known; subsequent favour shown to him by F.N.C.MUNDY *(q.v.)* might suggest at Markeaton, where he was granted by 1760 a lease of 51 acres at Bowbridge Fields on the estate, on which he subsequently re-built a good brick house. That year he resigned at Kedleston in order to work for himself, his first commission being to create the landscape at Foremark Hall then being completed by JOSEPH PICKFORD *(q.v.)* with whom he subsequently worked at Etruria (Staffordshire), Sandon (Staffordshire), Markeaton, Calke Abbey, Darley and quite possibly at Longford, St Helen's House (Derby), Shipley and Locko Park too. He also continued freelance at Kedleston, realising the landscape Adam was creating around the

house. He also worked with JOHN WHITE-HURST *(q.v.)* there as well as at Oulton Park (Cheshire) installing hydraulic works.

At Kedleston, he worked with Samuel Wyatt (clerk of works under Adam) and after Pickford's death continued to collaborate with him, as well as with Benjamin and James Wyatt, in Derbyshire probably at Egginton Hall (c.1781). In 1781, too, he was involved at Bowood (Wilts) for Lord Shelburne, a Lunar Society patron who had nurtured Joseph Priestley's career. Another probable project, linked to his earlier work at Foremark, was the romantic landscape at the Burdetts' secondary seat at Knowle Hill nearby, rebuilt as a gothick folly by Pickford c.1767; if true, it places Emes in the forefront of the new movement. He was also one of the rare friends of the younger WILLIAM DUESBURY.

In 1790, he took a lease of Elvetham Park, Hants. although he retained Bowbridge Fields (both being named tombstone) and shifted the centre of gravity of his commissions from the Midlands to the South. and West. His last known datable work was at Chippenham (Cambs.) in 1795. He may have retired thereafter, leaving his business in the hands of his protégé, John Webb.

Whilst at Kedleston, Emes married, at Mackworth, Mary, daughter of John Innocent whose son may be identifiable with a man of that name who was apprenticed as a London gold-smith 20th December 1754 (free 1763). This suggestion gains in stature when it is noted that of Emes' three surviving sons, two, JOHN EMES *(q.v.)* and William (b.1760) were also London goldsmiths, linked by partnerships to the dynasties of Chawner, Eley and Fearn, all from West Derbyshire.

William Emes, son of Emes' son Philip, lived at Ashby de la Zouch (Leics) and became brother-in-law to Anna Maria, sister of JOHN WHITEHURST III *(q.v.)*. The Holywood actresses, Joan and Constance Bennett were related by marriage to John Emes's posterity.

Emes died at the house in London of his son-in-law Rev. William Holmes, vicar of St Giles', Cripplegate in March 1803 and was buried there, where his tombstone was found amongst the bombed out wreckage after World War Two. [Craven (1996) 65-7, 78-82, 216-18; Jacques, D., *Georgian Gardens* (London 1983) Ch.3-5; Derby Local Studies Library, Mundy MSS. 9352-3, parcel 225 and DL 82 1/540; *Country Life* 4/1/1990, p.50 f.]

EVANS, Thomas (1723-1814)

Thomas Evans was the founder of a banking and cotton manufacturing dynasty in Derby which wielded much influence from the later 18th century in alliance with the Strutts. Evans founded a bank in 1771, using the fortune built up by his father, Edmund Evans, of Upper Bonsall (1690-1746) and his father-in-law, the unrelated William Evans (d.1773) who, by 1734, had established rolling and slitting mills for the processing of copper plate on The Holmes at Derby and whose operation was almost certainly a continuation of the enterprise of THOMAS CHAMBERS *(q.v.)*. Thomas Evans, like his father-in-law, was an Alderman of the Borough (by 1769) although he refused the Mayoralty.

On the failure of the bank of JOHN HEATH *(q.v.)* in March 1779, Evans was appointed receiver in bankruptcy and brought himself and Heath's creditors some benefit by buying some of the failed bank's assets, no doubt trading on his position. One of these assets was a flint mill at Darley Abbey, the site of which he developed with help and advice from his friend JEDEDIAH STRUTT *(q.v.)*, as a cotton mill, 1782-83; JOSEPH PICKFORD *(q.v.)* may have been involved in the design and building of the mill, which burnt down in 1788 but was immediately replaced. Evans was also a prime mover in the creation of the Derby Canal, completed in 1796, which used the Derwent to gain access to the mills at Darley Abbey. The weir, which harnessed the river there, was also used to canalise the Derwent for the purpose. With two of his sons, William (1755-96) and Walter (1764-1839) he established a new village at Darley which, with the mills (closed 1960s), survives almost intact, a most remarkable monument to the industrial history of the UK. He also built a seat, Darley House (c.1796), since demolished, a church, St Matthew's (1819) and a fine school (1825), the latter two to designs by Moses Wood.

Evans' family stemmed from Anthony Evans of Winster, yeoman and lead entrepreneur whose marriage to Hannah, heiress of the similarly employed but gentrified Fernes of Bonsall transformed his fortunes. His son, Edmund, married into the established gentry, taking Rebecca, daughter of Thomas Gell of Middleton, to wife. There were four sons and three daughters, and the three younger sons all married advantageously, George (1726-1808), the third son, marrying into the equally lead- and cotton-rich Nightingales of Lea. Thomas himself married twice: first in 1750 to Sarah, daughter of Alderman William Evans (by whom he had two sons, Edmund and William and a daughter, Sarah, Mrs Charles Upton) and later to Barbara Stubbs of Ranton Abbey (Staffordshire), by whom he had Walter, Henry and Barbara who married WILLIAM STRUTT (q.v.); the latter's sister, Elizabeth, married the second son, William, thus cementing what had previously been purely a business relationship. He died in March, 1814. [Glover, op.cit. II.18-19; Burke, Landed Gentry (1937) 358-9; Craven (1988) 88-9; Nixon, F. Industrial Archaeology of Derbyshire (Newton Abbott 1969) 98, 190; MI at Ashbourne to Frances Anne Walker.]

EVANS, Alderman Sir Thomas William, 1st Bt. MP (1821-1892)

A descendant of THOMAS EVANS (q.v.), Thomas William Evans was born in Darley House 15th April 1821, elder son of William Evans MP of Allestree Hall (1788-1856), himself eldest son of Thomas' second son William and Elizabeth Strutt. His mother was Mary, a daughter of REV. THOMAS GISBORNE (q.v.) and his younger brother William (who married another Gisborne) became agent in Russia for the mills at Darley Abbey, by then in the hands of his cousin, Walter Evans (1826-1903). He was educated privately and at Trinity, Cambridge (BA, 1842; MA, 1844).

Evans' father had been MP (latterly for Derbyshire, in the Liberal interest) from 1837 to 1853 and on his death (1856), Evans was adopted for the new seat of South Derbyshire for which he was returned to Parliament from 1857 to 1868 when he was defeated over his support for Irish disestablishment. He regained the seat however, and finally retired in 1885. He served as High Sheriff in 1872 as well as being JP (1847) and DL. He was also elected to Derby Corporation for Bridge Ward in 1857, becoming an Alderman almost immediately, serving until his death, and as Mayor in 1869-70, bestowing various benefactions on the town and even more on his estates: Allestree school and new churches there and at Parwich, for instance. He was a great promoter of the Derby Art School and a distinguished linguist

and traveller. He was also Chairman of the Derbyshire Quarter Sessions 1859-92, a County Councillor for Brailsford from 1888 and first Chairman of the County Council from 1888.

In later life he travelled ceaselessly, even going abroad (for his wife's health) during his mayoralty. He served for 21 years in the Derbyshire Imperial Yeomanry, becoming Colonel commanding in succession to Sir Charles Colville in 1877, retiring in 1885. He was a close friend and political ally of SIR HENRY WILMOT, VC (q.v.).

He was created a baronet (as Evans of Allestree Hall) in the Jubilee honours, 18th July 1887, but the title became extinct on his death without issue in 1892. His widow was his mother's niece, Mary Gisborne, whom Evans married at the Governor's Palace, Corfu (when the island was under British suzerainty and governed by his father-in-law) in 1846; his heir was Rev. Edmund Carr of Holbrooke Hall (1826-1916), nephew of his aunt, Ellen, to whose family he was related twice over.
[Burke, *loccit.;* MMD. I.28-31; Craven, *op.cit.* 63, 136, 183.]

FERRERS, Robert de, 1st Earl of Derby (d.1139)

Robert de Ferrers was the third son of Henry de Ferrers who, according to Wace, was one of the Conqueror's companions. Certainly, by 1086 Henry held 210 Lordships including the Honour of Tutbury which itself consisted of 112 manors in Derbyshire as well as the Lordship of Derby. Robert's grandfather was Walchelin de Ferrers, lord of Ferrières-St-Hilaire, Chambrais and Longueville (dept. of Eure, Normandy); his mother was Bertha. Henry was a Domesday book commissioner and the founder of Tutbury Priory.

Robert succeeded his father, because his eldest brother, Engenulf, had died before Henry and the second brother, William, went on the first Crusade, his son returning to be Lord of Ferrières in France. Robert himself built Duffield Castle (on a deserted Roman and Saxon site) as his chief

seat, with Horsley Castle nearby to control the middle Derwent. Duffield was, in fact, the third largest castle in England after London and Dover. In 1130 he leased the lead mines of Wirksworth, probably as a result of the requirements of his building works at Duffield. Eight years later he was one of the leaders of the army which was victorious at the Battle of the Standard, as a result of which he was created by Charter, 1st Earl of Derby. He died the following year.

By his wife, Hawise de Vitry, Ferrers had three sons and three daughters, of whom the eldest, William (said by some to have been created Earl of Tutbury) was killed in London, before his father's death, in 1138 unmarried, for he was a Knight Templar.

The second son, Robert (d.1162) succeeded as 2nd Earl of Derby and in 1144 married the heiress of the disgraced William de Peveril, inheriting yet more lands, including the Honour of Tickhill (Yorks). He also was co-founder (with HUGH DE DERBY, *q.v.*) of Darley Abbey. Walkelin, the third son, was also a crusader who left a son, Hugh. The second Earl's great-great-grandson, Robert, 6th Earl, was attainted as a result of the Barons' war against Henry III, but his son Sir John Ferrers of Breadsall was summoned to Parliament in 1299 as 1st Lord Ferrers of Chartley. He was an ancestor of EARL FERRERS *(q.v.)*.
[DAJ. LV (1934); Complete Peerage, Vol. III DNB.]

FERRERS, Washington, 5th Lord, see SHIRLEY

FINNEY, John (1729-1804)

Up until the mid 19th century, there was little distinction between builders and architects; the one was perfectly capable of operating as the other. They also undertook surveying, teaching, property dealing, auctioneering and valuing. One dynasty of such men was the Finneys, of which John was baptised at St Michael's, Derby on 26 July 1729, son of Charles Finney, joiner, and grandson of Richard (1650-1727). The family yard was in Bridge Gate. Richard was a younger son of William Finney of Finney Lane (Cheddleton, Staffordshire) of a minor gentry family of some antiquity. His mother was Mary, daughter of Richard Bateman of Hartington Hall, whose relative position enabled him to be trained as a surveyor and find a position in Derby.

John worked with his father and seems to have attracted the attention of WILLIAM STRUTT (q.v.) for he appointed him surveyor to the Improvement Commission in 1794 and he did much architectural work and building for that body, including pitching Bridge Street and building the more elegant houses (eg: Nos. 18-20), building St Mary's Bridge (to designs by Thomas Harrison of Chester) and he also built St Michael's Workhouse 1792-93. Numerous notices in the *Derby Mercury* show him at work as a property auctioneer, too.

By his wife, Anna, (1743-1820) he had two sons, Charles (1773-1828) who took over the firm on his death in July 1804 but became bankrupt *c*.1819 and John, who became a cabinet maker.

[Simpson, *op.cit.* II.456; Improvement Commission Papers, PRO; Poll Books; Parish Records; Information from late Mrs O.A.Dale and from Mr R.L.Platts.]

FIREBRACE, Sir Henry, Kt. (1619-1691)

Sir Henry Firebrace was a noted cavalier, civil servant and landowner, sixth son of Robert Firebrace of Derby, saddler, where he was born in 1619. His great-grandfather was Henry Firebrace of Duffield, living 1543. Although a saddler, Henry's father probably plied his trade at the highest level and almost certainly had business connections in London, for he married Susannah, daughter of Thomas Jerome, a London merchant who came from Keyworth (Notts).

It was probably through Jerome's influence that the young Henry was brought to the Earl of Denbigh's notice, and obtained a place at Court

as page to Charles I. He later rose to become Yeoman of the Robes and Clerk to the Kitchen, and when the civil war broke out he was rarely away from Charles, becoming a trusted advisor. When Charles was captured and incarcerated in Carisbrooke Castle, Firebrace managed to smuggle letters to and from him and contrived two escape attempts, neither of which were, ultimately, successful. The first required the king (a small man) to squeeze between the bars of his cell window; in the event he became stuck and the complex arrangements for his escape had to be cancelled. After Charles's execution, Firebrace appears to have gone into exile but returned at the Restoration and was re-appointed to the Court, rising to Clerk of the Green Cloth under James II. For his loyalty to Charles I, his son knighted him.

Firebrace married thrice: his first wife, Elizabeth, daughter of Daniel Darell (or Dowell) of Stoke Golding (Leics) brought him a modest estate there, where he settled. They had four sons and a daughter, of whom the second son, Basil (d.1724) a merchant and government spy, was Sheriff of London in 1687 and was created a Baronet 28th July 1698. The title became extinct on the death of Basil's grandson, Sir Cordell Firebrace 3rd Bt., MP, of Melford Hall (Suffolk) in 1759. His aunt and heiress married Basil Feilding, Earl of Denbigh and Desmond. Sir Henry himself married, secondly, Alice, daughter of Richard Bagnall of Reading and thirdly, Mary, daughter of Richard Dalton, Charles II's serjeant of the wine cellar, and a man anciently of Derbyshire ancestry. Sir Henry Firebrace died in 1691.

[Burke, J., *Extinct Baronetcies* 1st Edn. (London 1838) 196-97; DNB; Local Studies Library, Deeds 6744W (1598) 10084W (1594) and 15416 (of 1616).]

FISHER, Most Rev. & Rt. Hon Geoffrey Francis Fisher PC, GCVO, Lord Fisher of Lambeth (1887-1972)

The only archbishop of Canterbury with a direct link to a Derby descent is Lord Fisher of

Lambeth, probably the most distinguished and notable holder of that ancient office of the twentieth century. Archbishop Fisher was born 5th May 1887, fifth son (by Kathleen Richmond) of Rev. H.Fisher, rector of Higham-on the-Hill (Leics), the third successive member of the family to hold that incumbency. He was sixth in descent from Alderman Thomas Fisher (d.1719), Mayor of Derby in 1709 and 1714, whose second wife Ann was a cousin of FRANCIS COKAYNE *(q.v.)* and thus of ROBERT BAKEWELL *(q.v.)*. The Alderman's father, a Derby attorney, was of an old Foremark family whose ancestors are traceable at Repton into the Middle Ages. Geoffrey Fisher's wife's connections were also with Repton – with the School (where, incidentally, Alderman Fisher had been a scholar in 1677) rather than the town. Rosamund Chevallier was the daughter of Rev. Aemilius Forman (also of a Derby family) a notable master of the school, by the daughter of Dr S.A.Pears, a celebrated Victorian headmaster there, and they married in 1917.

Geoffrey Fisher was educated at Marlborough and Exeter College, Oxford (where he was made an Hon Fellow in 1939). He was ordained in 1913 whilst serving as an assistant master at his old school. In 1914, he was appointed – appropriately enough – headmaster of Repton, which he left to become Bishop of Chester in 1932, being translated to London shortly before the outbreak of World War Two, at the close of which he became Archbishop of Canterbury. In his 16 years as archbishop, his ministry epitomised almost all the qualities for which one looks so hard in today's Anglican church: scholarship, spirituality, firmness of purpose and humanity.

In 1947 he became Bailiff Grand Cross of the Venerable Order of St John and the year before had been appointed President of the World Council of Churches, a post he held for eight years. He was a freeman of several cities and the holder of over 20 honorary degrees. He was also Knight Grand Cross of the (Greek) Order of the Redeemer (1947), of St Olav (Norway, 1947); and held the second class of the Czech Order of the White Lion. He was sworn onto the Privy

Council on his appointment to London, given the Royal Victorian Chain (1947) and became a Knight Grand Cross of the Royal Victorian Order at the coronation of the Queen, which ceremony he performed with dignity and aplomb. On his retirement in 1961 he was made a life peer as Lord Fisher of Lambeth and became rector of Trent (Dorset), dying in 1972.

Fisher left six sons; his eldest, Sir Henry Fisher is a barrister, scholar and a Judge; the second, Hon Francis Forman Fisher was a housemaster at Repton before becoming Master of Wellington College in 1966; all men of great talent and ability. [Burke, *Landed Gentry* (1952) 863-64; *Peerage* (1970) 1011-12; *Who's Who* (1971) 1053-54.]

FISHER, Phyllis Anne, BA (1913-1994)

Anne Fisher was a redoubtable schoolmistress and literally a commanding figure, being over six feet tall. She was the niece of ARCHBISHOP FISHER *(q.v.)*, her father being his brother Rev. L.A.Fisher, fourth successive member of the family to be rector of Higham; her mother was Beatrice Eustace and she was born at her father's rectory, 8th March 1913; her brother, James, later became canon in residence at Windsor. She was educated at Abbot's Bromley (Staffordshire) and gained a BA in history at Bristol. After a brief spell teaching in England she went in 1941 to South Africa, to St Anne's, Natal, later being appointed head of St Winifred's at George, Cape Province. After almost three years back in Britain she was appointed to a school in Kenya, where she guided her pupils through the Mau Mau insurgency, with a revolver strapped to her waist; numerous tales of her experiences she would regale subsequent charges at Wycombe Abbey (Bucks) where she was a strikingly successful head for 12 years from 1962-74.

Her physical presence, deep voice and two decades of African experience had led to her being considered to have had an eccentric streak. But at Wycombe Abbey she 'inspired a mixture of awe and affection and had a profound influence on her pupils'. She re-inforced these qualities with a phenomenal memory. It was Anne Fisher who coined the classical piece of advice for young women, that socially, the best companions were homosexual men. 'They will take you out to dinner and won't ask for anything afterwards'! She died, unmarried 5th May 1994.

[*Daily Telegraph, obit.* 6 May 1994, Burke, *loc.cit.*]

FITZHERBERT, Alleyne, 1st Lord St Helen's (1753-1839)

Lord St Helen's was one of the most accomplished diplomats in the crucial period leading up to the Napoleonic Wars, and a valued courtier of George III in his declining years. His father, William FitzHerbert of Tissington (1712-72) was Recorder of Derby from 1768 until his suicide in 1772, the second of three eponymous holders of that office; in 1762 he had been returned to Parliament for Derby in succession to George Vernon of Sudbury who had been elevated to the peerage as 1st Lord Vernon that year, and he held his seat in the Whig interest until his death. The

necessity to be in Derby meant that he spent much more of the year at his town house there, Old St Helen's House, King Street, and it was there that Alleyne FitzHerbert was born in 1753, although in 1772 the house was let to JOSEPH WRIGHT *(q.v.).* His mother was Mary, daughter of Littleton Poyntz Meynell of Bradley Hall (and sister of that notable sportsman, Hugo) by Judith, daughter of the recently repatriated Barbados magnate Thomas Alleyne – hence the boy's name. His elder brother was William FitzHerbert, who succeeded his father as Recorder of Derby, before becoming a courtier like his brother and being created a baronet 22 January 1784.

Alleyne FitzHerbert went to Derby School, to Eton and thence to St John's, Cambridge (BA 1774; MA 1777). In 1777 he was appointed Minister at Brussels and thereafter served as Plenipotentiary to the Court of Paris (1782), a peace negotiator at the close of the American War of Independence (1783), Envoy Extra-ordinary to Catherine II (The Great) of Russia and from 1787 Chief Secretary to the Lord Lieutenant of Ireland, sitting in the Irish House of Commons as MP for Carysfort from the following year. In 1784 he was Envoy to The Hague, being raised to the Irish Peerage as Lord St Helen's (taking his title from his Derby birth-place) on his appointment as Ambassador to the Court of Madrid 26th January 1791. In 1801, he was Ambassador to St Petersburg but retired to London in 1803, becoming Lord of the Bedchamber to George III in 1804. He was also given a UK peerage on the abolition of the Irish Parliament in 1801, becoming Lord St Helen's of the Isle of Wight on 31st July that year. He died, unmarried, at his house in Grafton Street, Mayfair, 19th February 1839.

As a diplomat, he was exceptionally gifted but became much more 'laid back' as he grew older, drawing criticism from time to time from his political masters at St James's. However, faced with a crisis or matters of importance he would act 'with promptness and energy' and with unerring judgement.

[DNB; Burke, J. *Extinct and Dormant Peerage* (1884) 608-09; Tachella, *op.cit.*]

FLAMSTEED, Rev. John, FRS (1646-1719)

The position of Astronomer Royal was sponsored in 1675 by Charles II with hard-headed economics in mind: the necessity to improve and make safer maritime trade through the discovery of a method of determining longitude. In the 17th century, the clocks available did not have the necessary accuracy at sea; Harrison's marine chronometer was still a century away. Thus it was thought that the solution lay in astronomy, and King Charles accepted the recommendation of Sir Jonas Moore that his protégé John Flamsteed be appointed 'Astronomical Observer' (later Astronomer Royal) at an annual salary of £100. Sir Christopher Wren designed and built an observatory in Greenwich Park and Flamsteed's friend, the eminent horologist Thomas

Tompion, provided the necessary timepieces. Using astronomical instruments, largely made by himself or for him to his own designs, Flamsteed set about first principles: mapping the heavens.

The first Astronomer Royal was son of Stephen Flamsteed, ironmonger, maltster and lead merchant of Derby (1618-88), who built a grand house on Queen Street. He was third son of William Flamsteed of Little Hallam Hall, near Ilkeston, claiming descent from William Flamsteed 'who came out of the North and died 1514'. In fact, the family probably originated in Northamptonshire. He was born, however, on 19th August 1646 at Denby, wither his father had taken the family during the upheavals of the Civil War, at a house later called Crowtrees, a family property connected with a coal mine nearby. His mother, Mary, daughter of the Parliamentary Alderman John Spateman, died when he was barely three, and in 1652 his father remarried, at West Hallam, Elizabeth, daughter of Nathaniel Bate of Little Chester, a fervid Royalist – no wonder the family felt obliged to withdraw from Derby during those difficult years, with close relations supporting both sides in the conflict!

Flamsteed was educated at Derby School, but ill health interrupted his studies and he was kept at home, where he studied first astrology, then, finding the subject unrewarding, changed to astronomy, encouraged by Immanuel Halton of Wingfield Manor, algebraist and astronomer, and two Derby men.

In 1670, he not only managed to obtain an introduction to the Royal Society but also was able to proceed to Jesus College, Cambridge where he obtained his degree and accepted ordination. As early as 1669 he had drawn up a set of Equation of Time Tables (published in 1673), constructed a 3 foot quadrant, made tidal calculations, modified Halton's 'Improved Sundial', published a set of solar tables and had made notes *On Some Eclipses of the Fixed Stars by the Moon*. He also made five barometers (one of which he presented to Sir Jonas Moore) and made notes and co-ordinates for a projected map of Derby in 1673.

Once installed at Greenwich, Flamsteed started systematic observations; between September 1689 and 1703 he had made more than 30,000 to an enormously improved standard of accuracy. He was slow to publish however, resulting (with other matters) in his falling out with the powerful Sir Isaac Newton, once his friend. He also fell out with Edmund Halley, the man destined to be his successor. In 1703, Newton became President of the Royal Society and decided to publish Flamsteed's star catalogue over its author's head, edited by Halley; it was published in 1712 as *Historia Coelestis*, many copies of which Flamsteed called in and burned (as insufficiently accurate) when Newton's star began to wane after Queen Anne's death.

At first, Flamsteed, who on 23rd October 1692 had married Margaret, daughter of Ralph Cooke of London, had to struggle financially but his induction to the living of Burstow (Surrey) and his wealthy father's death in March 1688 removed the fiscal pressure. He died on the last day of 1719 (N.S.) but it was not until 1735 that his *Atlas Coelestis* appeared with two companion volumes, edited by his former assistants, Joseph Crosthwait and Abraham Sharp. The accuracy and thoroughness of these volumes brought him great, albeit posthumous, credit.

He had no children, his heir being the son of his half-sister, Katherine, James Hodgson. The elder branch of the family expired with the death of John Flamsteed of Little Hallam in 1745, the descendants of his sister, Mrs Alvery Dodsley, taking the name in addition to their own and inheriting the estate.

[DNB; Baily, F., *An Account of Rev. John Flamsteed FRS* (London 1835); Royal Greenwich Observatory MSS RGO 1; Tachella, *op.cit.* 4; Thoroton, *op.cit.* 11.85; Craven, M., *John Whitehurst* (Mayfield 1996) 12-14.]

FLETCHER, Constance, see SPRY

FLETCHER, Percy Eastman (1879-1932)

Composer of musicals (such as *Cairo*, sequel to *Chu Chin Chow*) and arranger of many others, Fletcher was an extremely gifted and versatile musician. He arranged music for the infant BBC, for Novello's and Curwen's; indeed, he was one of the first living composers to have his work performed regularly on the wireless. His repertoire was extensive: songs (solo and part), anthems, orchestral and operatic works. He wrote the suite *Woodland Pictures* (written for brass band for the Crystal Palace Festival) and on 7th July 1931, conducted a concert in his native Derby with the band of the 1st Bn. Sherwood Foresters, including one of his own works.

Percy Eastman Fletcher was born in Derby in 1879, only son of Alfred William Fletcher (b.1855) of 92 Curzon Street, himself a music teacher, composer, organist and choirmaster at the Victoria Street Congregational church. John Walter Fletcher, the father's younger brother, was a businessman with offices in St James' Street in succession to Percy Fletcher's grandfather, W.Fletcher of Kedleston Street, who had started out in a very modest way, ending up with premises in Market Place.

Unlike his father, Percy did not go to Derby School (probably through lack of funds) and was taught keyboard and violin by his father with whom he founded the Band of Hope Festivals. An early patron was F.J.Bonas (1861-1938), an opulent Derby tape manufacturer and amateur organist at the Ashbourne Road Wesleyan chapel, who first encouraged Fletcher to conduct and to whom the latter dedicated an Anthem *The New Born King*. He conducted his cantata *Harvest Praise* in Bonas' chapel in 1902 before proceeding to the Royal College of Music where he studied violin under Emile Sauret, then principal violin at Her Majesty's Theatre – hence Percy's introduction to the world of theatre music which he really made his own. He died at Farnborough (Hants) September 1932.
[Tachella, *op.cit.* 69; *Derbyshire Advertiser* 16/9/1932; *Derby Daily Telegraph* 13/9/1932; *Derby Evening Telegraph* 11/1/1974; *Derbyshire Life,* 6/79, p.45.]

FLETCHER, Richard (d.1607)

Until the Cavendish family obtained a stranglehold on the nomination of candidates for the Borough of Derby's seats in Parliament, this duty was one which fell to the municipal oligarchy of the town, mainly rich tradesmen. Richard Fletcher was a typical example, being returned to Parliament in 1584. He also served three times as bailiff of Derby (an office held by two men each year, replaced by a single mayor in 1637) in 1578, 1588 and 1597 and as church-warden of All Saints' in 1572. He had been instrumental in the Corporation's belated construction of the Free Grammar School in St Peter's Churchyard. He was a rich mercer with (inevitably) commercial connections in the capital and, if we are correct in identifying his father as Richard Fletcher, butcher of All Saints', he was upwardly mobile, for Richard, the butcher (d.1589) held the bailiffate but once, in 1585 (seven years after his son's first term) and was churchwarden at All Saints' after Richard the mercer in 1577; nevertheless, the evidence points to their being father and son and the fact that the butcher's ancestry is lost might imply that he was the first of his family to acquire the economic leverage to enjoy a municipal career, conceivably, indeed, on the shirt-tails of his son, who, as a mercer, was in a far more profitable trade. If we knew the family name of his mother, Eleanor, we might be able to see an explanation, for she might have been the heiress of another mercer.

Richard Fletcher, like his father, married twice. His first wife was a widow, Emmot, whose previous husband was Thomas Draper of London – conceivably another element in Richard's swift rise. They married at All Saints' 9th October 1564, but she died in June 1569, her two children by him dying at about the same time, perhaps from one of those periodic outbreaks of plague which troubled Derby (as elsewhere) in those times. Fletcher, however, remarried – the same year – Rachel (d.1602) and had by her, Richard (b.September 1576), Mary, Mrs Massey, Elizabeth and Jane. The younger Richard succeeded his father on the latter's death in January 1606/7 and a deed of 1623 establishes that their premises were on Iron Gate; young Richard later married Alice and died October 1624, leaving a son, Edward and two daughters.

[MI at All Saints'; Parish Registers; Simpson, *op.cit.* II.356; Local Studies Library, Catton Deed 6603.]

FLINT, Abraham John MP, DL (1903-1971)

A County Court Judge and National Labour MP for Ilkeston, A.J.Flint belonged to an old Derby family, his ancestors representing six generations of attorneys, four in Derby – from Abram Flint, the MP's great great-grandfather – and two in Stafford in the 18th century. A relative was Thomas Flint (d.1787), the Lichfield attorney who was an acquaintance of Dr Johnson during his visits to Dr Taylor at Ashbourne. Abraham Flint broke the family mould insofar as he was a barrister (Inner Temple 1929), rising to become a judge of circuit 18 (Nottingham) in 1957.

He was born in 1903, only son of Alderman Abram *(sic)* Reginald Flint of Derby (1876-1954) who refused the Derby Mayoralty in order to continue to appear in the Borough Courts. A.R.Flint was elected to the Borough Council as a Liberal in 1905 but switched to Labour in the 1920s, a move which influenced his son's political direction. Oundle-educated, A.J.Flint followed the lead of Ramsay MacDonald in 1931, however, securing election for Ilkeston by a (then) record of two votes – a record only equalled by the contest at Winchester on 1st May 1997. He was defeated in 1935. In World War Two he served as a Major in the Artillery. He had an office at his father's firm, 42 Full Street, Derby but lived at Little Aston (Warwickshire) and later at Newton (Notts). He died 23rd January 1971, having married in 1930 Eleanor Mary, daughter of J.J.Jones of Loughborough, leaving two daughters.
[*Who's Who* (1971) 1071; Stenton & Lees, *op.cit.* III.117-118; DET 28/9/1954.]

FOSTER, Edward (1762-1864)

Edward Foster was a locally celebrated centenarian and a nationally renowned silhouettist who enjoyed a long and varied life. He executed silhouettes of many national figures including members of the Royal Family at Windsor and in addition taught painting and lectured locally on educational topics.

Foster's father had been agent to Sir Robert Burdett Bt. at Foremark, his great-grandfather Anthony having owned a small estate at Dunleer (Co. Louth), although the family was originally from Cumberland. His second cousin, J.T.Foster, a womanising gambler, was the first husband of Lady Elizabeth Harvey, mistress and later second wife of 5th Duke of Devonshire. His mother was a relation of the Duke of Norfolk, daughter of Robert Howard. Foster was baptised at All Saints', Derby 8th November 1762 and at the age of 18 was serving in the American War of Independence as Lieutenant in the 20th Regiment of Foot, later transferring to the 95th, seeing service at Alexandria (1801) and retiring in 1805. He, for many, years, practised from a shop in the Cornmarket, Derby, retiring at 100.

He married five times during his long life, siring 17 children. By his first wife, Elizabeth Ward, he had Edward Ward Foster, himself a notable artist; his second wife (whom he married in 1817) was Mrs Anne Staley and by his fifth wife (who outlived him by less than a year) he had his

last child, Phyllis Howard Foster in 1852, when he was 90! He died aged 102 years and 124 days on 12th March 1864.

[Burke, *Peerage* (1970) 1772; Robinson, J.B. *Derbyshire Gatherings* (London 1866) 81.]

FOWLER, Sir Henry, KBE (1870-1938)

Henry Fowler was a Midland Railway engineer, the first and last Chief Mechanical Engineer on that line, and Chief Mechanical Engineer from 1925 on the London Midland and Scottish Railway, responsible for the design of such locomotive types as the 'Royal Scots' and 'Patriots' which, although initially slightly flawed, in the long run proved their worth both in utility and in also generating good publicity.

Henry Fowler was the son of Henry Fowler of Abbey Gate, Evesham (Worcestershire.) in which town he was born in 1870 and educated before moving on to the Mason Science College, Birmingham, thereafter entering railway service. He moved from the Lancashire and Yorkshire Railway to the Midland in 1900. In January 1910, he was appointed as Chief Mechanical Engineer of the Midland Railway at Derby in succession to R.M.DEELEY *(q.v.)*, having previously been works manager, and when war broke out he was recruited as Director of Production, Ministry of Munitions (1915) before taking control of the Royal Aircraft Factory the following year, and went on to serve in a variety of senior posts in the Munitions Ministry until 1919, when he returned to his post at Derby. Here one of his first tasks was to introduce electrical power into the works, which he was wont to tour on a bicycle.

At the 1923 amalgamation of the railway companies to form the 'Big Four', the Lancashire and Yorkshire's George Hughes became Chief Mechanical Engineer of the newly formed LMS into which the Midland became absorbed, Sir Henry merely being his deputy. In 1925, Hughes retired and Fowler slid effortlessly into his chair, retiring in December 1930. He was a great committee man, attaining the presidency of the University of Birmingham Engineering Society (1912-14), the Locomotive

Engineers' Institution (1912-14), the Institution of Automobile Engineers (1919-21), the Institution of Locomotive Inspectors and Foremen (1921-23), the Engineering Section of the British Association for the Advancement of Science (1923) and the Institution of Mechanical Engineers (1926). He was also a co-opted member of the Derby Borough Education Committee and a member of the Council of the British Association. He was a considerable sportsman, a goalkeeper on the soccer field, an able wicketkeeper at cricket and he also played hockey for Derbyshire and the Midland Counties. A numismatist, a strict teetotaller and a great enthusiast for the Scout movement, he was made CBE (1913) and knighted in January 1918.

Fowler married in 1895 Emmie Needham, daughter of Philip Smith of Horwich (Lancs.) who died in 1934, and they had two sons and a daughter: Harry, (b.1897), George Eric (b.1911, DFC (1941) and a barrister) and Dorothea, JP, Mrs Joseph Peat. The family lived at Saxelby House, Osmaston Road and later at Spondon Hall (sold 1946) where Sir Henry died in 1938.

[Hamilton Ellis, C., *The Midland Railway* (London 1966) 134, 172-73; *Who's Who in Derbyshire* (1934) 69-70; Kelly's *Handbook* (1924) 597; Radford, *op.cit.* 146-161, 183.]

FOX, Sir Charles (1810-1874)

Sir Charles Fox is notable as the engineer who realised Sir Joseph Paxton's designs for the Crystal Palace built at Hyde Park in 1851 to house the Great Exhibition. He was a civil engineer of real distinction who was responsible for a number of large-scale projects in an age when such undertakings were becoming commonplace. He worked 18 hours a day for seven weeks with Paxton and Sir Thomas Cubitt on the Exhibition, all three being knighted at the project's successful conclusion. He also oversaw its re-erection at Sydenham. He went on to construct the first narrow gauge railway in India, the Medway Bridge at Rochester, Barnes, Richmond and Staines bridges over the Thames, the roofs at Paddington and Waterloo stations and numerous other projects worldwide.

Fox was born in Derby, on 11th March 1810, fifth and youngest son of Dr Francis Fox of The Wardwick (d.1833) by Charlotte, daughter of Archibald Douglas of Sandybrook Hall, by which marriage he became brother-in-law to WILLIAM and JOSEPH STRUTT (q.v.). His grandfather, Francis (1724-89) was the scion of an old gentry family from Youlgreave and his marriage to Dorothy (1733-93), daughter of Edward Ward, made him a cousin of EDWARD FOSTER (q.v.). Three of Fox's brothers followed their father into the medical profession; one, Douglas (1798-1885) marrying his cousin, Marianne, daughter of the younger Jedediah Strutt. He was himself intended for the profession of medicine, but his taste for mechanics caused him to apprentice himself to Capt. Ericsson, then building the 'Novelty' engine for the Liverpool and Manchester Railway, which brought him to the attention of Robert Stephenson, whom he helped with the construction of the London and Birmingham Railway. He and pioneered the design of skewed arches for bridges and later improved the design of railway wheels and invented a switch for pointwork. From 1857, he practised in London as a civil and consulting engineer with his two eldest sons SIR CHARLES and SIR FRANCIS FOX (q.q.v.). He was a founding life member of the British Association and a fellow of the Society of Arts, the Royal Asiastic Society and the Royal Geographical Society.

In 1830, Fox married Mary, a daughter of the Derby plaster manufacturer Joseph Brookhouse, and had three sons (the third was Henry Fox of Putney Hill 1846-1926) and a daughter. He died at his home at Blackheath (Kent) 14th June 1874. [DNB; Glover (1829/31) II.593; DM. 10/12/1789.]

FOX, Sir Charles Douglas (1840-1921)

Sir Douglas Fox was the elder son of SIR CHARLES FOX (q.v.) and was born in London in 1840, being articled as a civil engineer to his father and working with him until his retirement when he took control of the firm with his brother FRANCIS (q.v.). He was a Fellow and President of the Institution of Civil Engineers. Educated at King's College, London, he was one of the engineers of the Mersey Tunnel (1886) and of numerous other prestigious projects, receiving the honour of knighthood the same year. He was a County Councillor and Alderman of Surrey (and a JP) and a member of the Institutes of Civil, Mechanical and Electrical Engineers.

He maintained his connections with Derbyshire by his marriage in 1863 with Mary, daughter of Francis Wright of Osmaston Manor, by whom he had a son and four daughters. The son, Francis Douglas Fox (b.1868) continued the family firm of Sir Charles Fox & Sons; the youngest daughter married her cousin E.B.FitzHerbert Wright. He obtained a new grant of the family arms in 1903 and died in 1921.
[Debrett, *Knightage* (1905) 702; Fox-Davies, A.C., *Armorial Families* (London 1910) 602.]

FOX Sir Francis (1844-1927)

Younger brother of the preceding, Francis Fox was perhaps by far the more eminent as an engineer. Born in London 29th June 1844, he was educated in Nottinghamshire before starting with his father in 1861 and undertook a large number of prestigious engineering projects including, with his brother, the Mersey Tunnel. He was also engineer to the Manchester Sheffield and Lincolnshire Railway from 1882 and from 1893 built the Liverpool Overhead Railway, both highly innovatory and difficult projects. From 1894 he oversaw construction of the Great Central Railway's line to London. His later career was marked by the construction or conservation of major buildings, notably the underpinning of Winchester and restoration of Lincoln cathedrals, amongst several similar undertakings. In 1894 he was a member of a commission of three to report on the plans for the Simplon Tunnel under the Alps (opened 1906) and did much to develop railways in Southern and Eastern Africa. He was knighted in 1912 and was elected Hon ARIBA.

In 1869 he married Selina Wright, his brother's sister-in-law, who died in 1900. In 1901 he remarried, his bride being Agnés, younger daughter of Henry King Home of Guerres, Normandy. By his first wife he had two sons and three daughters, of whom latter the eldest, Selina, a doctor, founded the Bermondsey Hospital in 1904. He died at his home in Wimbledon 7th January 1927.

[DNB, and as previous articles.]

FOX, James (1760-1835)

James Fox was the man who began the transformation of Derby's industry from high quality craftsman-made consumer goods – clocks, silk etc. – to precision engineering, a change which culminated in the establishment of Rolls Royce in 1907. Born in Staffordshire in 1760, he started life as a footman in the employ of REV. THOMAS GISBORNE *(q.v.)* who, being the enlightened radical that he was, when Fox seemed less than diligent in his duties, discovered that he had an over-riding talent for mechanics. In due course, therefore, he set him up on part of his St Helen's House estate at Derby – on City Road, Little Chester – in a works which spe-

cialised in the manufacture of lathes and precision engineering machinery.

He also made lace machinery, and supplied both lathes and, in 1802, steam engines of Boulton and Watt's design to RICHARD BROWN *(q.v.)* to mechanise his new works at Old St Helen's and to Agard's cornmill (with a 22" cylinder). His products were exported as far afield as Russia, France and Mauritius. He also designed and built the first planing machine and manufactured Brown's marble sawing device. By his wife, Ann, Fox had a son and successor, John (b.1800) who married at St Alkmund's, Derby 29th January 1822 Ann Tatlow, a relation of John Tatlow, an associate of ANTHONY TISSINGTON *(q.v.)* and JOHN WHITEHURST *(q.v.)*. Their two sons, James (1831-97) and Joseph continued the firm until it was taken over by the neighbouring concern of SIR ALFRED HASLAM *(q.v.)* in 1858 by which time they had diversified into domestic and architectural ironfounding. James Fox died in 1835.

[Smiles, S., *Industrial Biography* (London 1863) 258-59; Forward, E.A. in *Transactions of the Newcomen Society* XVIII (1938); Tachella, *op.cit.* 63; Measom, G., *The Official Illustrated Guide to the Great Northern and Midland Railways* (London 1866) 208-10; Glover, (1829/31) I.202; DM. 29/7/1802.]

FRANCEYS, Ald Henry (1692-1747)

Henry Franceys is known to most Derby people as the only Derby tradesman to be allowed to attend the county's assembly rooms, an exception which has been variously ascribed to his claimed (but inauthentic) gentle birth, his marriage to Anne, daughter of John Harpur of Twyford Hall (of a distinguished local family) or to his intimate knowledge, through his calling, of his aristocratic clients' medical intimacies.

His family can be traced back, not to the gently-born Franceys's of Coxbench, Foremark or Ticknall, but to William, son of Ralph Franceys, a grazier on the Markeaton estate who died about 1558. It was claimed that William's wife, Margaret, was a relation of RICHARD CROW-

SHAWE *(q.v.)*. Their son, also, William, was a grazier and butcher who farmed Bower Ground and held a shop from the Corporation in Breadleaps (Market Place). The next three generations, Ralph (d.1612), William (1583-49), and William (1611-83) followed in his footsteps except that the burgeoning prosperity enabled the last William to build a fine new house in the SW corner of the Market Place in 1648. On his death without issue, this passed to his brother, John, also a butcher, of whose two sons, one, John, (1651-1720) followed the trade of butcher and William (1650-1724) became an apothecary, acquiring the family house in 1683 and rebuilding it in a spectacularly up-to-date style in 1695. He was successively Registrar, Warden and Steward of the Derby Guild of Mercers, an Alderman and thrice Mayor of Derby, in 1697, 1699 and 1700. By his wife, Sarah, he was Henry's father, their son being born in 1692.

Henry was educated at Derby School (1700-06) whence he proceeded to Emmanuel College, Cambridge (BA 1709; MA 1713) and entered his father's business in 1710, becoming a Brother of the Corporation and in 1733 an Alderman. He

succeeded to the business in 1724 and 'the place he occupied in the estimation of his fellow citizens was as high as or even higher than his father's'.

He beautified the saloon on the first floor of his house with a frescoed ceiling (almost certainly by FRANCIS BASSANO *q.v.*) of the Gods on Parnassus, which, amusingly, included portraits of himself and his wife Anne. Here, after the assizes in 1733, he entertained the Borough's High Steward, the Duke of Devonshire and Lord James Cavendish 'until four in the morning', a contemporary report adding that Franceys was 'a great favourite with the neighbouring gentry'. It is in fact likely that he was the Duke's agent in Derby responsible for the promotion of his Grace's Whiggish hold over the Corporation. Certainly the scale of his Civic Hospitality 'outshone that of his contemporaries'.

During the 'Forty-Five he left Derby along with most of his fellow Aldermen but *in absentia* was host to Lady Ogilvy and Mrs Murray of Broughton, but he died in 1747 during his Mayoralty. His elder son George sold the business in 1751, the younger, Henry, was incumbent of Trowell (Notts) and Dorothy, his daughter, married (1736) Francis Ashby of Tean (Staffordshire) who moved to Derby.
[*Derbyshire Advertiser* 14/6/1935; Tachella, *op.cit.* 5, 9, 21; Jeayes (1904) III.3.132, III.3.73/126/144/ 195; DAJ. XI (1889) 5-6; Parish Registers.]

FRANCIS, Percy Ollivant (d.1947)

Although a Derby solicitor, Francis's chief claim to fame was that he was a footballer for Derby County FC 1893-96, going on to be a director of the club and a committee member of the Derbyshire County Cricket Club. His football career, during which he played as an amateur, included appearances in the team which finished runners-up in the First Division for the first time 1895-96; he was considered a talented player.

Percy Francis was the eldest son of Dr Alfred Ollivant Francis (d.1900), a doctor who occupied Mundy House, Wardwick, with his wife Emily. His sister married Alderman Arthur Frederick

Longden JP (1860-1938) whose father had been Mayor in 1865-66. At the time of his birth his father was practising at Birmingham but on qualifying as a solicitor he joined his family in Derby about 1888. His partner was J.T.Wykes and the firm still exists in Derby. He lived with his wife at 352 Burton Road and at his death 21st June 1947 left a son, Percy.

[Mortimer, *op.cit.* 79; Deeds to Mundy House.]

FRITCHE, George Christopher (1769-1835)

The Fritche family was a remarkable musical dynasty which began with George Christopher who was baptised at All Saints', 21st February 1769, only son of George Fritche (1726-99) – landlord of the George and Dragon, Cornmarket, later (1767) moving to run the Green Man, St Peter's Church Yard – and his wife, Elizabeth.

Instead of following his father's convivial trade, George Christopher showed musical talent, becoming a member of the Derby Society of Musicians and a protégé of CHARLES DENBY *(q.v.)* on whose recommendation he succeeded him as organist of All Saints' in 1793, a post he retained until his death in 1835. He wrote a great deal of music, much of it undeservedly forgotten, and helped promote and played continuo in the continuing series of grand concerts and music festivals initiated under his predecessor. It is interesting to note that his sister Charlotte (b.1778) married JAMES WARD RA (1769-1859) *(q.v.)*, the painter who was a pupil of JOHN RAPHAEL SMITH *(q.v.)* of Derby, where the couple lived from 1827.

Fritche married twice. By his first wife, Jane (d.1860), daughter of Thomas Hope of Derby he had a son and successor George Christopher Fritche (1800-90) who was as distinguished as his father as organist of All Saints' and who retired to Leamington Spa. Of his younger sons, John Francis, was also a professor of music, although the elder, Rev. George Cheslyn Fritche, married a daughter of the distinguished Derby lawyer William Whiston and became curate of Littleover and Chaplain to the County Lunatic Asylum. By his second marriage Fritche became father of Christopher Froude Fritche who succeeded his brother as organist of All Saints', although his three sons deserted music in favour of surveying, business and dentistry. G.C.Fritche died in 1835.

[Tachella, *op.cit.* 29, 33, 44, 48; Cox & Hope, *op.cit.* 47, 196; DAJ LXVII (1947) 1-54.]

FRYER, Edward (1852-1883)

It is remarkable how late in the 19th century the intertwined trades of building and architecture remained united in the English provinces, despite the increasing professionalisation of architecture. One of the last Derby men to combine the two trades was Edward Fryer whose wife, Louisa Jane, was the heiress of a building firm and a notable contractor, a fact that did wonders for the career of her husband, the son of Joseph Fryer (d.1872), a successful, if small, builder.

Fryer was the third son, born 28th July 1852; because his elder brothers Joseph and W.J. were sufficient for the successful conduct of their father's business, he was educated at Derby School and then articled to architect George Thompson, setting up on his own account in 1874 in Albert Street. He began by designing villas for his brother to build in Leopold Street and elsewhere, as well as his own house in Mill Hill Lane (*c.*1875). He designed seven houses in Pear Tree Road (1878), The Cedars, Mickleover, and Laurel Cottage, Kedleston Road, for his cousin George. With A.A.Langley he designed and built the demolished St Christopher's Railway Servants' Orphanage, Ashbourne Road (1882) in French château style and the Surrey Street Wesleyan Chapel (dem.) was also by him.

In 1877, he married Louisa, daughter of Alderman John Harpur, a major building contractor and brick manufacturer, by his wife, daughter of John Tomlinson of Allestree, also a notable builder and civil engineering contractor. This match considerably widened the scope of his concerns, and the building and contracting firm his father founded, and his own alliances so enhanced, continued until the 1980s. That of his wife's grandfather, Tomlinson's, later refounded by a cousin of Louisa's, still flourishes in a national context.

Fryer, who was Borough Councillor, died 31st March aged 31, leaving three children. His elder son, Edward Harpur Fryer, became an architect and joined T.H.Thorpe, whose firm also still exists. The younger son, John Harold (d.1959) developed the building and contracting firm, leaving numerous posterity to maintain the momentum. Mrs Fryer remarried (as his second wife) Rev. Thomas Edwin Bradbury (first vicar of St Chad, Derby) who also died relatively young in 1885.
[Derbyshire *Red Book* (1887) 146; DM. 13/3/1872; DET. 27/10/1995; Local Studies Library, Tilley/F; Tachella, *op.cit.* 55, 76.]

GADSBY, William Hippon RBA (1845-1925)

Gadsby was a most accomplished painter of portraits and of flowers whose genius has had difficulty in outliving him due to his refusal to sign his work, believing that 'a picture should speak for itself' and not be judged by the artist's name. His subjects also included children, particularly,and he was also a good copyist, reluctantly working in this capacity for Queen Victoria.

He was the third son of Alderman John Gadsby (1818-83) of the Old Mayor's Parlour, Derby, solicitor and Mayor of Derby 1858-59, by Sarah, daughter of William Lindley. His middle name derived from George Hippon of Featherstone (Yorkshire) whose daughter Lindley had married. The Mayor was great-grandson of John Gadsby of Ford Street. W.H.Gadsby's next brother, Harry Freckleton Gadsby (1852-1902) was also a solicitor and served as Town Clerk of Derby from 1879 until his death. Gadsby's father had hoped that he would enter the church, but after leaving Derby School he tried farming and working in his father's office before going to Hatherley's School, London and in April 1865 entering the Royal Academy Schools, where he became a protégé of Sir John Everett Millais, with whom he remained on friendly terms for many years. In 1870 he went to Rome and Venice to further his studies

and was elected a member of the Royal Society of British Artists. He won a silver medal at the International Art Exhibition at Crystal Palace in 1884 for his painting *Girl with Grapes*. His favourite model was the future music hall star (and later Countess of Orkney) Connie Gilchrist whose favours he is alleged to have shared both with Millais and Lord Orkney.

Gadsby lived at Tufnel Park latterly and married Kate Adsetts, but there were no children, which led to his adoption of his niece Beatrice, youngest of six daughters of his elder brother Edward Paget Gadsby, who became his heir after he died in a street accident in a London 'pea-souper', 15th October 1924.
[Tachella, *op.cit.* 35,44,45,50; MMD.I.17; information courtesy of Mrs S.Cannicott.]

GAMBLE, John Curzon

J.C.Gamble was that rare thing, a painter of pictures born to a painter of houses: he had a successful but unremarkable career as an artist, specialising in portraiture in oils as well as some landscapes. He was the eldest son of John Gamble; his grandmother, Elizabeth How was the niece of Alderman Matthew How, making him a cousin of WILLIAM BEMROSE (*q.v.*). He was born about 1771 and educated with his three brothers at Mr Spencer's school (*q.v.* HERBERT SPENCER). His younger brother, Stephen, became a successful furniture dealer in Iron Gate and was Mayor of Derby 1841-42. He married in 1808 Fanny Harrison and six years later, having been widowed, he remarried Mary Wibberley. His eldest son (by Fanny) was Alderman John Gamble, also a painter (1808-71); his youngest son, Edward (by Mary) was a solicitor and his son William was sometime partner of P.O.FRANCIS (*q.v.*).
[MMD.I.7; Art Section notes file, Derby Museum.]

GAWLOR, Col. George (1795-1869)

Col. Gawlor was a memorable governor of South Australia from 1838 to 1841, colonial administrator and controversial soldier. He was the son of Capt. Samuel Gawlor, 73rd Regt., of Great Marlow (Bucks) and was born 21st July 1795. He was educated at Great Marlow Military College and joined the army in 1810 seeing action with 52nd Light Infantry through the Peninsular Campaign from November 1811 until its end, sustaining wounds at Badajoz and San Muños. At Waterloo, he led the right company of his regiment, later attaining the rank of Colonel. In later life he spilled much ink contending that his regiment, supported by the rest of Adams' brigade (and not the Guards) had defeated Napoleon's final attack. Right or wrong, the climate of the time was not one conducive to obtaining a concession from the Guards on such a contention!

He continued in the army, being sent as governor to South Australia to restore morale, but despite embarking on ambitious public works and doing much to improve the city of Adelaide, was recalled in 1841 for exceeding his budget. He spent the remainder of his life in religious and philanthropic pursuits, dying at Southsea 1st May 1869.

His connection with Derby was his residence in the Borough from about 1816 until the 1840s, during which time he married Maria (1796-1870), daughter of John Cox, a Derby wine merchant, and relative of J.C.COX (q.v.). He is also memorable for having discovered the horticultural talents of JOSEPH WHITAKER (q.v.) who accompanied him to Australia. He left two sons (three others died young) and two surviving daughters. The eldest son, Col. John Cox Gawlor (1830-82) became keeper of the Regalia at the Tower in 1872; his brother, Henry, (1827-94) went back to Adelaide and practised there as a barrister, leaving a son and two daughters. [Cox, W. *Pedigree of Cox* (Derby 1889); DNB; information from N.Moyes, Esq.]

GELL, Col. Sir John, Bt. (1593-1671)

Not so long after the outbreak the Civil War, on 31st October 1642, a body of troops from the army of Parliamentary General, the Earl of Essex, entered Derby. At its head was the newly enno-

bled Sir John Gell, Bt. of Hopton Hall, who therewith seized control of the Borough for Parliament, a control which was not subsequently relinquished, over a four year period of garrison, despite the fact that the remainder of Derbyshire was then still in Royalist hands. Having seized power and finding the elected Corporation too unreliable, Gell appointed a committee of his relatives and personal supporters (and no townsmen) which supervised the collection of taxes and dues, directing the proceeds towards the payment and provision of his troops. He arranged for the town to be defended by bridgeworks and earthworks on main roads.

Such was Gell's high-handed conduct of affairs as the war proceeded, opposition arose, especially with the rolling back of the Royalist threat, led by Maj. THOMAS SANDERS (q.v.) whom Lord Essex eventually obliged Gell to include in his Committee. Despite constant turmoil in Derby, Gell used the town as a base from which he could pick off Royalist strong points in the County. Parliament's victory and the formation of the New Model Army ultimately led to the disbandment of Gell's regiment. Gell himself slowly became disillusioned and was ultimately summoned to London and charged with treason. This got him out of Derby and, despite the eventual withdrawal of the charges, he was effectively neutralised. By the Restoration, Gell was for the King and was thereby able to retain his patrimony intact.

John Gell was born at Hopton Hall 22nd June 1593, eIder son of Thomas Gell (d.1594) by Millicent, daughter of Sir Ralph Sacheverell of Stanton, and seventh in descent from Ralph Gell of Hopton (d.1327). A half-brother of Gell's father's, John Gell of Shottle, was ancestor of the younger branch of the family who sold Hopton Hall not so long ago. John went to Magdalen College, Oxford in 1610, having already married a year earlier (aged 16), Elizabeth, daughter of Sir Percival Willoughby of Wollaton (Notts) and aunt of PERCIVAL WILLOUGHBY (q.v.).

Gell never took his degree but was subsequently High Sheriff of Derbyshire 1635 and shortly afterwards was made a collector of the hated 'Ship Money' for Derbyshire to which, in contrast to his actions during the Civil War, he assiduously applied himself, in the process seriously harassing Sir John Stanhope of Elvaston who refused to contribute to the £3,500 Gell was charged with raising. Despite much reported animosity, Gell subsequently married Stanhope's widow, Mary, daughter of Sir Francis Radcliffe of Ordsall (Lancs.) as his second wife.

On 29th January 1642, Gell was created a

baronet by Charles I – either to acknowledge his efforts in collecting ship money or in an effort to keep him in the Royalist camp. After the war, during which he and his brother Thomas (1594-1657) – MP for Derby and later for Derbyshire during the upheaval – built a fine brick house in Derby (16 Friar Gate) which remained in the family until at least 1850, he lived quietly, dying at his London home in St Martin's Lane on 26th October 1671 and was buried at Wirksworth. He was succeeded by his elder son, John, (1613-89) upon the death of whose son, Sir Philip Gell (1710) the baronetcy became extinct and the estates passed to one of the latter's sisters, Catherine, Mrs William Eyre of Highlow, whose posterity assumed the Gell name and arms.

[DNB; Visit. Derbys. 1662; Craven, M. (1988) 60-62; Burke, *Landed Gentry* III (1972) 368.]

GERY, Col. Philip

A scion of a distinguished municipal family, Philip Gery was noted for his breeding of prime bloodstock and his patronage of the turf. He had an estate in Leicestershire, a house on Brookside, at Derby and was a prominent figure at Derby Races, then (*c*.1730/40) held on Sinfin Moor. At his death, he left a daughter and heiress, Philadelphia (b.1733).

Gery was the son of William, of Derby, (1663-1731); his great uncle Thomas (1631-83) and the latter's son Thomas (d.1723) were rich apothecaries, the latter serving as Mayor in 1717-18. They were descended from Peter Gery, Bailiff of the Borough in 1605, 1613 and 1619 although the name appears in the town's records as far back as the 13th century.
[Nichols, J. *History and Antiquities of the County of Leicester* 4 Vols. (London 1795-1807) III.1041; Parish Records; Darley Cartulary A32,37; Jeayes (1904) III.3.103.]

GISBORNE, Thomas MD, FRS (*c*.1733-1806)

Gisborne was a notable doctor, having been Physician in Ordinary to George III and President of the Royal College of Physicians 1791, 1794 and 1796-1803; he had been a Fellow since 1759, delivered the Gulstonian lectures the year following and was Censor of the College six times.

He was born in 1733 or '34, the second of the three sons of Rev. James Gisborne, rector of Staveley (d.1759) by Anne, daughter of Dr George Jacson of Derby, himself fourth son of John Gisborne the younger of Jacobean House, Wardwick, Derby. Dr Gisborne's elder brother Francis (1732-1821) succeeded their father as rector of Staveley; his younger, General John Gisborne MP (d.1778), was a distinguished soldier who was Governor of Charlemont and set-

tled in Ireland. Thomas went to St John's, Cambridge, where he was later a Fellow and gained his BA in 1747, MA in 1751 and MD in 1758. Early in 1757 he was appointed physician to St George's Hospital (London) where he continued until 1781. He was also associated with the establishment of the Birmingham Infirmary where he became peripherally involved and friendly with members of the Lunar Society and was later elected Fellow of the Royal Society. He rebuilt Romiley Hall (Clowne) in villa style probably to designs by William Lindley of Doncaster and had Rev. Christopher Alderson landscape the grounds. He died there, unmarried, 24th February 1806.
[DNB; Glover (1829/31) II.246.]

GISBORNE, John (1770-1851)

John Gisborne was a minor Romantic poet, friend of Wordsworth and a man who did much for the prosperity of his adopted town, Blackpool (Lancs.). He had a keen eye for nature but modesty caused him to destroy many of the written compliments he received for his books *The Vale of Wever* (1797) and *Reflections* (Darley Dale, 1835). He was also an exceedingly religious man, his devotion reflected in his diary, extracts from which were also published.

He was the second son of John Gisborne for whom JOSEPH PICKFORD (*q.v.*) built St Helen's House, Derby, being born there 26th August, 1770. He was educated at Harrow and St John's, Cambridge (BA 1792). In 1792 at All Saints', he married Millicent, daughter of Col. Edward Sacheverel Pole of Radburne Hall (stepdaughter of ERASMUS DARWIN (*q.v.*)) and they lived until 1815 at Wootton Lodge (Staffordshire). Thereafter they resided at Blackpool, on account of his wife's frail health where 'he exerted himself actively for the welfare of the inhabitants and did much for the prosperity (of the town)'. He was universally popular for his 'geniality, humility and sympathy'. He lived at Hackney Lane House, Darley Dale from the later 1820s for some 20 years. He died at Pentrich 17th June 1851, leaving four surviving sons and five

daughters. The eldest son, John, (1793-1871) remained at Hackney Lane, whilst his next brother Hartley Packer Gisborne (1800-82) became a Manchester merchant. Henry Franceys (1807-87) and Edward Sacheverel (1812-91) both lived in Full Street, Derby, respectively a surgeon and a surveyor; the former served as Mayor of Derby 1856-57.
[DNB; Glover, *op.cit.* 392; E.N., *A Brief Memoir of John Gisborne, Esq. to Which are Added Extracts From his Diary* (Derby, 1852).]

GISBORNE, Rev. Thomas (1758-1846)

Thomas Gisborne is best known locally for his close friendship with JOSEPH WRIGHT (*q.v.*), especially during the artist's later years. They painted and drew together in the park at Yoxall Lodge (Staffordshire), Gisborne's seat, and had earlier played music in Darley Grove (behind St Helen's, Derby, his town house) together with Alderman Thomas Haden; here, Wright, a flautist, 'loved to hear echoes'. Gisborne was also the intimate friend of anti-slavery campaigner William Wilberforce, whom he had met at St John's, Cambridge (where he gained his BA in 1780). Wilberforce was a frequent visitor at Yoxall, where Gisborne, whom many expected to enter politics, chose to spend almost all his life. Indeed, the sequestered calm of Needwood forest exerted a powerful spell upon him and he expressed it through a number of poems in the style of Cowper. He also wrote several campaigning and ethical works: *Principles of Moral Philosophy* (1789), *Remarks respecting the Abolition of the Slave Trade* (1792), *An Inquiry into the Duties of Men in the Higher Ranks of the Middle Classes* (1794), *Inquiry into the Duties of the Female Sex* (1797) and *Essays on Recollection of Friends in a Future State* (1822). These, added to his collected poems (*Walks in a Forest* (1794) and *Poems, Sacred and Moral* (1798)), various evangelical works and collected sermons, amounted to a considerable output.

Thomas Gisborne was born at 11-16 Bridge Gate Derby 31 October 1758, brother of JOHN (*q.v.*) and son of John Gisborne (1716-79) and

Anne, daughter of William Bateman of Derby. He was at first 'given a liberal and scientific education' under REV. JOHN PICKERING *(q.v.)* mathematician and vicar of Mackworth, before going to Harrow in 1773 and entering St John's Cambridge (BA 1780) in 1776. He married on 1st March 1784 Mary, daughter of Thomas Babington of Temple Rothley (Leics) and a kinsman of ANTHONY BABINGTON *(q.v.)* He was perpetual curate of Barton-under-Needwood (Staffordshire) and Prebendary of Durham, where his close friend, Shute

Barrington was Bishop. After the death of Wright in 1797 he withdrew from Derby (having also inherited Yoxall from his father in 1779) and sold St Helen's to WILLIAM STRUTT *(q.v.)* in 1803. He died at Yoxall 24th March 1846 leaving six surviving sons and three daughters. His eldest son, Thomas John Gisborne, MP (1794-1852) was a politician who fought hard for the Reform Bill as MP for N. Derbyshire (1832-37) and was a free trade enthusiast. His daughter Sophia married JOHN

GISBORNE'S son H.F.Gisborne; her sister Mary (1786-1859) was the mother of SIR WILLIAM EVANS *(q.v.)*.
[DNB; Glover, *op.cit.* 246; Nicholson, *op.cit.* 133-37, 281-82.]

GISBORNE, Hon William MP (1825-1898)

William Gisborne was a colonial pioneer, politician and administrator who served New Zealand as Colonial Secretary, Minister of Public Works and of Mines (1879), a Privy Councillor, MP and the city of Gisborne, North Island, was named after him. After a long and distinguished career he ultimately returned to England where he lived for a while at Lingen (Herefs.) and Allestree Halls.

He was the third son of Thomas John Gisborne of Corfu and Holme Hall (Bakewell) (d.1862), by Sarah, daughter of Antony Krechmer of Courland (Germany) and the grandson of REV. THOMAS GISBORNE *(q.v.)*. The family are a distinguished one, having come from Hartington in the 16th century to Derby where members of the family were regularly mayors between 1659 and 1856. William was born in 1825 and married Caroline Gertrude, daughter of Commissary-General Charles Bridgen. Their son, Lionel Guy Gisborne (1866-1928) of Allestree Hall left descendants now in Zimbabwe and there were three daughters. He died at Allestree in 1898.
[Kelly, *Handbook* (1890) 472 and (1924) 639; Burke, J. *Colonial Gentry*.]

GODBER, Sir Frederick, 1st Lord Godber (1888-1976)

Lord Godber was striking evidence of the social mobility which marks British Society from that of some of its continental neighbours. The son of a man who started as a labourer, he rose to become Chairman of Shell, a senior figure in the oil industry, a financier and advisor to successive governments. With LORDS ST HELENS, WAKEFIELD, BELPER, ASHFIELD and ROE *(q.v.)* he is one of only six hereditary peers of new creation born in Derby, and also like all but Lord Belper, the honour became extinct on his death.

Godber was the son of Edward Godber (1851-1938) who in 1872 was a labourer in the West End. His grandfather, Edward, was also a labourer. Lord Godber's father married firstly at St Werbugh's 7th April 1872, Elizabeth, daughter of William Holmes, by whom he had no children. He married secondly 2nd September 1878 Marion Louise (d.1932), daughter of George Peach, by whom he had three sons and two daughters. Frederick, born 5th November 1888, was the youngest son. After an elementary education he went to the USA in 1919 and became involved with the oil industry, gaining much experience, acquiring excellent contacts and a good grounding in the workings of that booming commodity. In 1922 he became President of the Rhoxana Corporation and a director of Shell, rising to

become Chairman in 1940. During World War Two he was Chairman of the Overseas Supply Committee of the Petroleum Board and served on a number of crucial government missions, being knighted for his efforts in 1942. He retired in 1961, having been created 1st Lord Godber of Mayfield (Sussex) in the New Year's Honours of 1956. He took his title from Cranesden, Mayfield, Sussex, his home for many years, the house's name inspiring the cranes which supported his arms. Shell being a Dutch company, he was also made a Grand Officer of the Order of Orange Nassau in 1947 and was later an honorary Bencher of the Middle Temple (1954), Liveryman of the Worshipful Company of Leathersellers (1962), Fellow of the Institute of Petroleum (1965) and a Trustee of Churchill College, Cambridge.

He married 29th August 1914, Violet Ethel Beatrice, daughter of George Albert Lovesey of Cheltenham (Glos.) and had two daughters, Joyce, Mrs Andrew Agnew and Daphne, Mrs Archibald Debenham. On his death in 1976, the Barony became extinct.

[Burke, *Peerage* (1970) 1114; *Who's Who* (1971) 1205.]

GREEN, Alderman Albert JP MP (1874-1941)

The Green family owned a large silk and narrow tapes mill in Derby, established by Joseph Green of King Street in 1878 and still flourishing under his great grandson Nicholas Green today. The family were long resident in Derby, and Joseph's son Albert was born at King Street 3rd November 1874. He was educated at St James's Board School, later going to Derby Technical School before entering the family's firm which he took over on his father's death in 1902.

He was elected a Borough Councillor in August 1911 for Dale Ward by a majority of four. He served as Mayor of Derby 1915-16 and became an Alderman in 1917. He was elected Coalition Conservative member for Derby in succession to Sir William Collins at the Coupon Election in

1918 but was defeated by Charles Roberts when the coalition collapsed in 1922. He lived at The Knoll, Normanton-by-Derby (since demolished) with his wife, Mary (1877-1955), daughter of Godfrey Turner of Derby, whom he married in 1900. Green's business expanded from two mills employing 40 hands in 1900 to a nationwide concern with a thousand strong workforce by his death on 25th September 1941. He left two sons, Joseph Godfrey Green of The Pastures, Duffield and Wilfred Herbert Green of Green Bank, Turnditch to continue his business.

[*Modern Mayors of Derby*, Vol.II (1937) 36-37; Local Studies Library, Tilley/G.]

GRESLEY, Cuthbert (1876-1963),
GRESLEY, Frank (1855-1936),
GRESLEY, Harold ARA DCM (1892-1969),
GRESLEY, James Stephen (1829-1908)

The Gresley family in three generations managed to produce four highly competent artists, of whom, one, Harold, might be considered outstanding as a topographical watercolourist. The family originated with Thomas Greasley (later spelt Gresley) of Sandiacre, a lace manufacturer and freeholder of some standing in the first three decades of the 19th century. The family name originates from Greasley (Notts) nearby, there being no connection (despite the similarity of name) with the Gresleys of Drakelow.

By his wife, Mary, Thomas had a younger son, James Stephen, born at Sandiacre in 1829. In 1854 he married Mary Smith at Sneinton (Notts) and earned his living painting landscapes in oils: competent, often striking, but much in the general run of topographical painting of the Victorian era. The couple ultimately moved to Chellaston, where J.S.Gresley died in 1908, leaving a son, Francis (Frank), born in 1855.

Frank also lived and worked in Chellaston, painting numerous Trent Valley landscapes in both oil and (more commonly) water-colour. At St Peter's, Derby, 13th May 1876 he married Harriet (b.1856), daughter of George Fearn of Derby, then landlord of the Corporation Hotel at the Cattle Market, where he was installed when the building (by H.I.STEVENS *q.v.*) was completed in 1861, having previously run the Bull's Head (Queen St). Gresley's father-in-law's brother and four sons were also pub landlords, running between them a total of at least 16 inns! Frank and Harriet Gresley had three sons and a daughter, Sybil, Mrs Francis. Only Horace seems to have been other than an artist: Sybil's husband was a gilder at Royal Crown Derby; Cuthbert (the eldest, born 1876) and Harold (the youngest son) both followed in the tradition of their father and grandfather. Frank Gresley died at Chellaston in 1936.

Cuthbert Gresley lived at Derby and was known as a fine painter for Royal Crown Derby and King Street Works on porcelain. He died at Ockbrook in 1963. Harold was born in Derby 9th March 1892, was educated at Chellaston Board School and Derby and Nottingham Schools of Art and, later still, at the RCA where he won both bronze and silver medals. He exhibited widely, including at the Royal Academy, of which he later became an Associate. During World War One he served as an NCO in the Sherwood Foresters, winning the DCM in 1917. He painted landscapes and figures in both oil and water-colours; his topographical water-colours of Derby commissioned by the philanthropist A.E.Goodey are particularly accomplished. For many years he was assistant art master at Repton School and a good deal of his work was published. He married Clara Hitchen and died at Crow Tree House, Chellaston, the family home, in 1969, leaving a niece and a nephew.

[*Who's Who in Art* (1934) 175; Pamphlet published by Derby Museum; Local records.]

GRETTON, Very Rev. Dr George (c.1755-1820)

Gretton was a distinguished Churchman, Dean of Hereford from 1809 and a chaplain to George III. He was a nephew of JOHN WHITEHURST FRS *(q.v.)* who married his aunt; his father was Rev. George Gretton, rector of Blore in 1752 and later of Norton (Salop.) Gretton was born, the eldest of three brothers, about 1755 at his aunt's house in Derby and was educated at Repton and proceeded to Trinity, Cambridge (BA 1776, MA 1779, DD 1791). He was thereafter successively rector of Hedsor (Bucks) and St Saviour, Dartmouth (Devons.) before being appointed to Hereford. He died unmarried in 1820.

The family descends from Rev. Anthony Gretton, 'incumbent' of Boylestone 1650-61: both his sons weaolbury and Trusley. His sister was the wife of Robert Wright and mother of Whitehurst's ne'er-do-well cousin and self-proclaimed heir, James Wright. Mrs Wright's sister, Anne was mother of THOMAS RIVETT MP *(q.v.)*.

[Repton School register; will of John Whitehurst 1788; MI's at Blore (Staffordshire); Derby Local Studies Library, Tilley/G.]

HADEN, Sir Francis Seymour (1818-1910)

Sir Francis Seymour Haden achieved great eminence in two contrasting fields: as a surgeon and as an artist. In the former he advanced the science of obstetrics, championing ovariotomy and becoming Vice-President of the Obstetrical Society. He was also one of the principal movers in the foundation of the Royal Hospital for Incurables in 1850 and served on a number of commissions and public bodies as well as on the jury of the Great Exhibition of 1851. It was more for his medical work (from which he retired in 1887) as for his art that he was knighted in 1894, although he won numerous medals and awards for his etchings, the artistic medium in which he excelled. He was also a notable writer on art and a critic. His early work included a number of family portraits influenced by JOSEPH WRIGHT *(q.v.)* and landscapes after the manner of J.M.W.Turner, but later on his style was remarkable for its originality. Amazingly, his most prolific period was at a time when he was at his busiest professionally. From 1858 he enjoyed a close relationship with his half brother-in-law J.A.McN. Whistler, whose half sister, Dasha Delanoy he married on 16th October 1847. Their art for a while demonstrated a vigorous cross-fertilisation of ideas and style, but later they fell out rather badly – a hazard of any relationship enjoyed with the volatile Anglo-American Impressionist.

Haden was born in Sloane Street, London, 16th September 1818, son of Dr Charles Thomas Haden (1786-1824) first surgeon at the Derbyshire General Infirmary and Emma, daughter of SAMUEL HARRISON *(q.v.)*, the Belper-born tenor. His grandfather was Alderman Thomas Haden, a relation by marriage of Joseph Wright's, whose brother's medical practice he joined and to which he ultimately succeeded. Thomas was also a friend of WILLIAM STRUTT and ERASMUS DARWIN. Sir Francis' aunt, Ann, (1788-1869) married KIRK BOOTT *(q.v.)* of Lowell two months after he was born, and it was Boott who persuaded Francis' future father-in-law Maj. George Washington Whistler to set up a locomotive manufacturing plant at Lowell.

Haden was educated at Derby School, Christ's Hospital and University College, London, going on to extend his medical studies at the Sorbonne and Grenoble where later he lectured on surgical anatomy at the military hospital. From 1857 he was a Fellow of the Royal College of Surgeons. In 1888 he retired to Woodcote Manor near Alresford (Hants) where his wife died in 1908 and he died 1st June 1910. They had three sons and a daughter, Hon Mrs Charles Thynne (1848-1937): Francis Seymour (1850-1918), the eldest son, was made CMG after a distinguished career in the Colonial Service in South Africa. His cousin Charles Sydenham Haden married Mary Love Boott, a granddaughter of Kirk. The family ultimately originated from Dudley, near Birmingham.

[DNB; DAJ. LXVI (1946) 59f.; Glover, *op.cit.* II.601; information from Dr R.Spencer.]

HALLOWES, Nathaniel (1582-*c.*1672)

Hallowes was a revolutionary, dedicated puritan and creature of SIR JOHN GELL *(q.v.)*, who did much during the Civil War to make life in Derby unbearable for the increasing number of citizens who did not see eye to eye with him. Nor was he without power to do so, being appointed Sequestrator for Derbyshire and a member of the Committee for Derby for raising and maintaining the New Model Army, as well as upon that on the Ordinance of Plundered Ministries. He sat as one of the MPs for Derby in 1639, 1640 and during the Long Parliament to 1653. During the course of his Civil War career, he swiftly fell out with Gell and was probably instrumental in having the charge of treason laid against him during the Commonwealth, making him an ally of THOMAS SANDERS*(q.v.)*.

Hallowes was the son of Thomas Hallowes, a Youlgreave-born man who set up in Derby as a woollen draper and died in 1622. His mother was Catherine Carpenter (d.1603) and he was the eldest of two brothers, being baptised at St Werburgh's on 25th November 1582. His sister Isabel married Stephen Sleigh, a relation of JOHN FLAMSTEED *(q.v.)*. He was probably educated at Derby School and was apprenticed to his father, whose business he took over in 1622.

He was also an Alderman of the Borough and served as Mayor in 1657-58. He was a signatory to the Protestation and Grand Remonstrance early in his Parliamentary career. During the Civil War itself he led a company under Gell's command with no little success.

Hallowes made some rich pickings during the Civil War, acquiring Mugginton Hall from the bankrupt Cavalier Sir Andrew Kniveton, Dethick Manor, Newbold Hall and in 1647 Dowell Farm, Hartington. However, his career went into eclipse after the Restoration and he had to leave Derby, dying shortly afterwards (about 1672) on one of his country properties. He married twice. His first wife, Margery Potter, he wed at St Werburgh's 3rd October 1608 by whom he had a son, Thomas, (1610-37) and two daughters. She died in 1618, whereupon he remarried, at St Peter's, Nottingham, Eleanor, daughter of Robert Sherwin of that town (who died 1673) and had seven sons and eight daughters. Of them, the third, Samuel was of Norton, whose second son, Samuel, settled on his grandfather's property at Dethick, which the family continued to own until earlier in the 20th century although they actually resided on another estate at Glapwell Hall, acquired by marriage with the heiress of Woolhouse of that place. Geoffrey Hallowes, a descendant, was the third husband of the late Odette Hallowes, GC, the French Resistance and SOE heroine.

[Stone, B., *Derbyshire in the Civil War* (Cromford 1992) 10-11, 24, 49-50, 74, 87; Craven, M. & Stanley, M., *The Derbyshire Country House* (2 vols. Matlock 1982/4) I.30, 36; *Derbyshire Family History Society, Branch News* X (1/1983) 1f.; *Daily Telegraph* 14/3/1995.]

HAM, Very Rev. Herbert, FRCO, MA (1869-1965)

Herbert Ham was the first Provost of Derby Cathedral, having been appointed when the Diocese of Derby was created in 1927, retiring 11 years later in 1938. He was able to slip into the new post relatively effortlessly, having been appointed vicar of All Saints', Derby, two years earlier. He was a considerable musician as well as a formidable churchman, having gained a Fellowship of the Royal College of Organists in 1898. The late Dr Heath-Gracie, appointed organist at Derby Cathedral by Ham, detested him, probably because two equally gifted organists in one cathedral was not necessarily going to make for harmony, especially as Heath-Gracie was as demanding a man as the Provost. Further, Ham faced a daunting task in creating a fresh, human, spiritual and diocesan centre of excellence at his cathedral which previously had been a staid parish church; it was inevitable that some sparks would fly. Nevertheless, Derby had what was unmistakably a cathedral when Ham retired in 1938, which was certainly far from the case in 1927.

Herbert Ham was the elder son of the appropriately named Robert Dillon Ham, a Bath butcher, although the family later removed to Ilminster, and was born 29th October 1869 at the former place. His younger brother, Dr Albert Ham also became an organist at Bristol (St Mary Reddliffe), Ilminster and St John, Taunton. Herbert went up to Worcester College, Oxford (BA 1899, MA 1916) and after ordination became curate of Wormley, Herts. (1900-03) and of Chelmsford, Essex (1903-10) before being appointed vicar of St James the Greater, Litchurch, Derby in 1910 moving to Wirksworth in 1917, adding Carsington and Alderwasley to his cure in 1920 and 1922. He was an honorary Canon of Southwell 1924-28 and of Derby 1928-38. After retirement he spent the war years as priest-in-charge of Dethick, Lea and Holloway. He died aged 95 in October 1965 at Morley Hall. His wife was Hilda Annie (1878-1958) daughter of SIR ALFRED HASLAM (q.v.) and they married in 1910, a union that was instrumental in bringing him to Derbyshire. They had two sons: the elder, Michael Gervase, was a RAFVR officer, killed in action in November 1940; the younger was Christopher Haslam Dillon Ham (1915-94) of Morley Hall and later of Saffron Walden, who left three sons and two daughters.

[Heath-Gracie, G., *Organist, Why?* (unpublished MS, 1980, 2 vols.) II.236-38; *Who's Who* (1961) 1296-7.]

HAMPSHIRE, Frederick William (1863-1941)

F.W.Hampshire was a name famous in Derby as that of a successful firm of manufacturing chemists ultimately absorbed by Messrs. Reckitt & Coleman. Its founder was a largely self-taught but highly competent chemist who started the firm at around the turn of the century, moving to the Old Silk Mill in 1908, only to lose everything when the venerable edifice was largely destroyed by fire in 1910. However, the company was revived and in 1927 moved to Sinfin Lane. Frederick Hampshire was a Fellow of the Chemical Society, Vice-President and life governor of University College and Cromer Hospitals and Vice-President of Derby YMCA. He was also a trustee of Derby Women's Hospital and the Derbyshire Children's Seaside Home. During World War One he founded and edited *Le Courier Belge* which gave news for Belgian refugees and played a major part in the re-uniting of families from that country scattered by the German invasion. He was also founder and President of the Union of Commonwealth.

Frederick William Hampshire was born on 13th April 1863, son of Matthew William Hampshire and his wife Esther Moody. His father was a successful railway contractor and the family was well-to-do, despite which he received only a Board School Education. In 1903 he married Elizabeth Katie Walters by whom he had two daughters and a son. In 1927, he married again, to Jessie Deakin. He died 20th July 1941, control of the business having already passed to his son David Alan Hampshire (1918-90). David was better known for his successful career as a motor racing driver which he took up as a 19-year-old in 1938 and resumed after World War Two, retiring in 1954. He lived variously at Monte Carlo, Minorca and Derby but died in August 1990 at

Newton Solney. He left two sons, Robin and Jeremy, – the latter also a racing driver for a time – and a daughter Carole.

[*Who Was Who* (1941-50) 494; *Derbyshire Advertiser* 20/7/1941; DET 21/7/1941; 12/9/1962, 12/8/1990.]

HANCOCK, Sampson (1817-1895)

When Alderman THOMAS CLARKE *(q.v.)* closed the Derby Porcelain factory in 1848 five former apprentices and Samuel Hancock – all former workers there – set up a new porcelain manufactory at Derby which flourished until 1935 when it was absorbed by Royal Crown Derby. The premises were adjacent to and on part of the land of the spar works founded by RICHARD BROWN *(q.v.)*, then in the hands of Joseph and Thomas Hall. Hancock had been a painter and gilder at the old works; his co-founders were William Locker, Samuel Fearn, John Henson, Samuel Sharpe and James Hill. After Locker's death in 1859, Hancock gradually consolidated his hold on the business, being sole proprietor by 1875.

At first the wares produced were much similar to those of the old Derby factory and King Street reacted to a revival of interest in many of the 18th century figures and patterns. Later, under Hancock's guidance, the works developed its own particular style and he always kept quality at a premium. Although the King Street factory was always a small one, its wares remained sought after right up until closure and are much collected today.

Sampson Hancock was the elder son of James Hancock (1791-1865) of Stoke-on-Trent (later Worcester), colour maker and ground layer. He himself was third of the four sons of John Hancock (1757-1847), a gilder who had been apprenticed to WILLIAM DUESBURY *(q.v.)* 29th September 1769. James' grandfather George (d.1774) was a Nottingham man who had come to Derby by 1769. Nearly all John's descendants worked in the pottery trade. By his wife, Margaret Best, whom he married at Claines (Worcestershire.) 21/11/1814, he had James (b.1824) and Sampson, born at

Worcester in 1817, before moving to Derby. He died at Derby still in control of the King Street factory, 15th November 1895. By his wife, Elizabeth, (1817-95), daughter of John Jefford of Burton upon Trent, he had two sons and four daughters. John (1839-1911), the elder son, became an employee at the Midland Railway's locomotive works, but left numerous descendants. The second son, William Henry (b.1844) also eschewed the pottery trade. The business, therefore, devolved on the son of the youngest daughter, Frances (b.1841), who had married at St Alkmund 23rd July 1862 George Jabez Robinson, a son of John, a hatter. The son, James, ran the firm for most of the rest of its existence, continuing to employ excellent artists and to insist on high standards. The recession of the early '30s really sounded the death knell of the company.

[Jewitt, L.L., *Ceramic Art of Great Britain* II.109-110; Derbyshire *Red Book* (1896) 191; Twitchett, J. *Royal Crown Derby* (London 1976) 16; Haslem, J. *The Old Derby China Factory* (London 1876) 125-33, 237; information from Mrs K.A.Head (a descendant).]

HANDYSIDE, Andrew (1805-1887)

An ironfounder and heavy engineering works proprietor of international reputation, Andrew Handyside's Britannia foundry was taken over from Messrs. Marshall, Baker and Wright in 1848. It had been founded in 1818 by Weatherhead, Glover on land behind St Helen's made available by WILLIAM STRUTT *(q.v.)*, and at first produced ornamental and architectural ironwork, later adding railway and rolling stock components. Handyside dramatically increased its scope by casting major bridges and components for buildings like market halls, barracks, palaces etc. Several eminent architects and engineers like Sir Gilbert Scott and SIR CHARLES FOX *(q.v.)* commissioned material from the firm as, in later days did Rolls-Royce. A particular gem was a Moghul style pavilion designed by Owen Jones for use in Bombay in the 1860s.

Andrew Handyside was a Scot, born in Edinburgh 25th July 1805, youngest of the three sons and one daughter of Hugh Handyside, a local merchant, and Margaret Baird, his wife. The latter's brother, Charles, was an engineer based in St Petersburg (Russia) where ultimately all three sons of Hugh and Margaret joined him, first as apprentices, later as assistants and colleagues. One of his brothers, the eldest, William (1793-1850), became a major designer and builder of bridges, steam vessels and structures in Russia; in later years Andrew supplied the components from Derby. Dr James Ronaldson Handyside (1796-1872) the next brother migrated to St Petersburg and his son, Henry, also an engineer, eventually went from Russia to New Zealand where his son James Ronaldson Handyside (II) settled.

Andrew returned from Russia with a bride from Balanka, Ukraine, called Anastasia; they were a devoted couple but had no children. They settled at The Cedars, Ashbourne Road which they leased from Lord Scarsdale and Handyside began his régime at Britannia Foundry in 1848. In due course (1873) his manager and heir designate was Alexander Buchanan (1829-1912), son of his sister by Rev. Robert Buchanan of Glasgow. Handyside was a Councillor for Bridge Ward 1855-58, and a churchwarden of St John's, Bridge Street (built with much Weatherhead & Glover ironwork by Francis Goodwin in 1827). He was also a director of the Derby and Derbyshire Bank, dying at The Cedars 9th June 1887.

The firm ultimately, and for complex reasons, failed in 1910, although it was revived in both 1915 and 1924, going into final liquidation in 1931.
[*Derbyshire Miscellany* XII.4 (Autumn 1990) 112-22; information from Janet Jenkins; *Red Book* (1888).]

HARCOURT, Rt. Hon. Sir William Vernon, PC, MP (1823-1904)

Sir William Vernon Harcourt was, from 1880 to 1895 one of Derby's MPs, and its most distin- guished politically, serving as Gladstone's deputy from 1886, only missing Prime Ministerial office on the Grand Old Man's resignation when the Queen sent for Lord Rosebery instead, Gladstone's advice being wanting due to his absence through ill-health. Harcourt was a distinguished, if unpopular, Home Secretary and will no doubt go down in the annals of infamy as the man who, as Chancellor of the Exchequer, introduced death duty, raised income tax from 6d to 7d in the pound and passed legislation to allow the control of public houses at local level. His support for Irish Home Rule was unswerving yet only served to increase his unpopularity, especially in Derby.

William George Granville Vernon Harcourt was born at the Old Residence, York on 14th October 1823, his father, Rev. William Harcourt being then a canon of York, where the latter's grandfather, Most Rev. & Hon. Edward Venables Vernon (a younger son of Lord Vernon) had been a long-serving Archbishop, dying in 1847. William's mother was Matilda Mary, daughter of Col. William Gooch. He had an elder brother, Edward, a Conservative MP who inherited the family estates of Nuneham Courtnay and Stanton Harcourt (Oxon), which he himself came into in the last months of his life following the death without issue of Edward's son Aubrey on 22nd March 1904. He was educated privately at Preston, where the Bread Riots of 1842 made an indelible impression on him, inclining him to radicalism. He went to Trinity, Cambridge (where he was later Professor of International Law (his 'passion') 1869-1887) and thereafter to the Inner Temple, whence he was called to the bar in 1854, taking silk in 1866. He was elected MP for the city of Oxford in 1868, but on losing his seat in 1880, he was returned for Derby through the good offices of SAMUEL PLIM-SOLL *(q.v.)* who moved aside for him. After the Liberal defeat of 1895 he and LORD ROE *(q.v.)* were replaced by the Tories GEOFFREY DRAGE and H.H.BEMROSE *(q.q.v.)* but he was able quickly to find another seat at Monmouth Boroughs.

He was Solicitor General 1873-74, Home

Harcourt was also involved in sending Gen. Gordon to his death at Khartoum in January 1885, and indeed, the Government did not long survive the humiliation, despite being in part bailed out by the despatch of Sir Garnet Wolseley. Nevertheless, he was characterised as 'One of the last and one of the greatest of the Old School Parliamentarians who preserved into the Twentieth Century the grand manner of the Whig orators of the Eighteenth.' He lived for most of his career at Malwood Park, Hants, but died at Stanton Harcourt on 1st October 1904. [DNB; Burke, *Peerage* (1970) 1240.]

HARRISON, Thomas Cuthbert (1906-1980)

Although an older contemporary of David, son of F.W.HAMPSHIRE *(q.v.)*, T.C.Harrison also enjoyed a hectic career in motor racing, and the two did overlap in the years immediately preceding World War Two. Harrison, however, was more a specialist in rallying and sports car racing rather than grands prix and he enjoyed a consid-

Secretary 1880-1885, Chancellor 1886 and 1892-95, being knighted 12th December 1873 and being made Privy Counsellor 29th April 1880. His first wife was Marie Thérèse (d.1863) daughter of Thomas Henry Lister of Armytage Park (Staffs), by whom he had two sons, Julian and Lewis, the latter also having a distinguished political career, serving as his father's Private Secretary 1884-95 and as Colonial Secretary under Asquith from 1910 to 1915, being created 1st Viscount Harcourt in 1917, a title which became extinct in 1977. William's second wife was Elizabeth Cabot (d.1928), Mrs T.P.Ives,. daughter of Hon. John L.Motley, sometime US Minister in London, by whom he had a further son, Robert (1878-1962).

erable share of success. He was also the founder of a thriving motor dealership at Derby which grew substantially and has today been for many years the main Ford dealership in the area.

Harrison was born in 1906 and lived in Derby before acquiring Baslow Hall from his rival, Sir George Kenning. He sold it in 1957. On his death in 1980 he left two sons of whom the elder, Edward, lives at Bradbourne Hall and has two daughters. James Harrison, son of the younger son, was manager of the commercial vehicles section at T.C.Harrison's in 1989, for T.C.Harrison is yet a family firm.
[DET. 22/12/1961; Craven & Stanley (1982) p.17, No.14.]

HARVEY-BAILEY, Alec (1920-1997)

The coming of Alec Harvey-Bailey to Rolls-Royce at the beginning of World War Two turned a phenomenon into a dynasty, for he was the second generation of his family to work at Rolls-Royce (to Derbeians, always 'Royce's') and the second in a line of outstanding engineers.

Alec Harvey-Bailey was born in 1920, son of Robert W.Harvey-Bailey MBE (d.1986) who himself joined Rolls-Royce as a motor engineer and rose to be Chief Engineer. He lived at 36 Ashbourne Road and had also two daughters, Olive Harvey-Bailey BEM (d.1983) and Margaret, of Hunstanton (Norfolk). Young Alec was educated at Derby School and Loughborough College (now University) and studied automotive engineering with the aim of joining Rolls-Royce. When he did so, it was not cars which were to concern him but aero engines; he was swiftly put in charge of the Merlin engine accident and failure investigation team based at 23 Agard Street, becoming the 'crucial cornerstone' in the development of the Merlin throughout the war years.

From 1952-55 he was manager and chief engineer with Rolls-Royce Australia, supervising the building of a new facility near Sydney. In 1955 he returned to Derby as Chief Quality Engineer, aero-engines, becoming a director in 1967. He was the support team leader for the

RB211, eventually retiring to write about the company.

By his wife, Joan Heath (d.1996), whom he married in 1942, he had a son Rhoderick (b.1946), also an engineer, and he died 3rd March 1997 at Mickeover. He and his wife had latterly lived at Hilton.
[DET. 12/4/1996, 6/3/1997 and 7/4/1997.]

HASLAM, Sir Alfred Seale, MP (1844-1927)

Sir Alfred Haslam was the founder of the Union Foundry in City Road, Little Chester – so-called because it included the former concern of JAMES FOX (q.v.) – which specialised in refrigeration machinery, the use of which in ships he pioneered. The business was established in 1868 and the Haslam Refrigerator was not only a welcome refinement on the great liners and capital warships but was also the one piece of equipment which facilitated the expansion of the meat trade with Australia, New Zealand and South America. The firm became a limited liability company in 1876.

Sir Alfred also became a councillor for Derwent Ward (in which his business was situated) becoming Mayor 1890-91, a JP in 1906 and an Alderman in 1902. His international reputation was recognised on 21st May 1891 when he was knighted by Queen Victoria on Derby station; he was also her official host for that day for her state visit to Derby to lay the foundation stone for the new Derbyshire Royal Infirmary. The celebrations were lavish and largely funded by Haslam himself.

Haslam's booming engineering works largely created the suburb of Little Chester, previously a mainly agrarian outlier of the parish of St Alkmund, and he enlarged the church of St Paul (1897), donated stained glass windows to the new church of St Werburgh as well as other Borough churches. He also gave £1,000 to the DRI building fund. He also served as President of the Children's Hospital and of the Royal Deaf and Dumb Institution. He was President of the Chamber of Commerce 1891-94 and received the Freedom of the City of London in 1888, as well as being a liveryman of the Merchant Taylors' and Coachmakers' Companies, being master of the latter in 1904-05.

In 1900 he was elected Unionist MP for Newcastle-under-Lyme and in 1902-05 was Mayor there (although not a member of the Corporation). He presented Newcastle with a bronze statue of Queen Victoria in 1903, having previously given a similar one to the City of London, erected on the Thames Embankment at the approach to Blackfriars Bridge. He lost his Parliamentary seat in 1906 but received the Freedom of Newcastle for his efforts on the town's behalf.

Haslam was born in 1844, fourth son of Alderman William Haslam (1805-78), ironsmith and bell-founder of Derby who, with his third son, EDWIN *(q.v.)* revived the art of decorative wrought iron making in the tradition of BAKEWELL and YATES *(q.v.)*. His mother was Ann, daughter of Joseph Smith. The family came from a long line of Duffield yeomen and William was co-partner with Alfred in the Union foundry, managed by Alfred's fifth brother

William Gilbert Haslam (1855-1935).

Haslam was educated at Derby and then became an apprentice engineer with the Midland Railway going on to work with Sir William Armstrong, before acquiring Fox's Union Foundry with the backing and encouragement of his father. He lived at North Lees, Duffield Road, before retiring to Breadsall Priory, but died in London in January 1927, leaving over £1,000,000. However, a complex will and death duties forced his firm to merge with C.A.Newton

Ltd. although the Derby Pure Ice and Cold Storage Ltd. (the 'Ice Factory' on The Morledge) remained in family control.

By his wife, Annie, daughter of Thomas Tatum of Long Eaton he had three sons and three daughters, although two of his sons, Alfred Victor and William Kenneth pre-deceased him; the former of typhoid in 1907, the latter killed in action in 1917. The second son, Eric Seale Haslam (1886-1967) died at Breadsall Priory without issue. The eldest daughter, Hilda (1878-1958) married Very Rev. HERBERT HAM *(q.v.)*. [MS family history, courtesy Mrs P.Haslam; MMD. I 73-79; Lodge, *Peerage* (1911) 2896; Fox-Davies, A.C., *Armorial Families* (London 1910) 640, (1929) I.897.]

HASLAM, Edwin (1843-1913)

Edwin Haslam, with his father, Alderman William Haslam, was responsible for the revival of the art of decorative wrought iron manufacturing in Derby. Edwin's contribution was to bring an Arts-and-Crafts flair to the work where his father had worked much more in the 18th century tradition. He was born in 1843, educated locally and served an apprenticeship with his father, for his eldest brother, John, had become a Baptist minister and the next brother, William, died young; on the fourth brother, ALFRED, see preceding article.

He diversified the firm, moving into gas equipment and fitting and later into electrical equipment. In the field of wrought iron he opened a new showroom in Iron Gate (previously occupied by JOHN DAVIS) in which to display 'Articles of *vertu*, fancy goods, bronze hanging lamps, chandeliers, candelabras, gas brackets, gas globes ...burners... Sugg's crank bells, gongs, table and dinner bells, wrought-iron gates and altar rails'. He refurbished Bakewell's screen at All Saints', adding to it in 1873. Some of his wrought ironwork was exported as far afield as New Zealand.

He married Mary Ann Jackson and died at Derby in 1913; he lived in a large semi-detached house on Duffield Road, the other side of which

was inhabited by his brother W.G.Haslam; Alfred lived opposite in an altogether grander residence. He was succeeded by his only son, William Harcourt Haslam (b.1879) who sold the electrical and gas side of the firm (based beside the spar works in St Helen's Street) to W.T.Furze & Co. Ltd. who were later taken over by Batterby and Hefford. In 1986 the concern was sold to Smith's Clocks. The firm of Taylor, Whiting and Taylor ultimately continued the wrought iron business. [As previous article.]

HAWKINS, Helen (1888-1985)

'The appointment in 1927 of Miss H.K.Hawkins as principal of the Derby Training College' Margaret Dobson avers, in her history of the Institution, 'marked an epoch in the history of the College. For the first time a woman enjoyed full authority as head of this College for women'. Helen Hawkins' aims included the development and expansion of the College; as a first stage she sought separate bedrooms for students, a good library and an enlargement of the Chapel. In the long term, the 'Geddes Axe' of 1931, the intervention of the war (with the consequent transfer of the College to Elvaston Castle for the duration) and the following secularisation of society were to frustrate these somewhat, but she achieved much of the remainder. She also 'liberalised' the regime for the students a little and did much to integrate the College into the community. Sport and drama were for the first time given prominence and a new library (dedicated to her predecessor Canon BATER *(q.v.)*) was opened.

Helen Hawkins was the daughter of an Indian colonial family, being born in the Peninsular in 1888 to W.Hawkins, who held the Imperial Service Order and the Volunteers' Decoration. She grew up and was educated in India and the UK, took an MA and entered the teaching profession in an age when a full career in education precluded marriage. She was a determined and resourceful woman with highly tuned diplomatic skills. By the time she retired in 1952 the College had been expanded to some extent (achieved by buying up villas nearby in Uttoxeter New Road) and numerically much strengthened. Her full expansionist aims and a later one of admitting men were achieved under her equally notable successor Miss A.E.G.Sephton. It was the combined skills over a remarkable 72 years of Canon Bater, Helen Hawkins and Amy Sephton which made Derby's college the prime mover in an amalgamation with the Derby Technical College in the 1970s to provide the essential nucleus which, although never a polytechnic, was able to form the core of the new University of Derby in 1992.

Helen Hawkins was made OBE in 1951 for services to education and she retired in 1952 to become a government advisor where her work took her to the Caribbean, especially Trinidad. She died unmarried aged 96 in 1985.

[Dobson, M. *The First Hundred Years of the Diocesan Training College* (London 1951) 40f.; *Who's Who in Derbyshire* (1934) 81-82.]

HAWKRIDGE, Douglas FRCO FRAM (1907-1983)

Douglas Hawkridge was a distinguished and notable organist of St Paul's cathedral from 1936 and Organ Professor at the Royal Academy of Music from 1945. He was a veteran of the BBC with a 37-year broadcasting career behind him. In wartime London he formed an *ad hoc* choir from the Metropolitan Police, the standard of which earned them performances on radio with the BBC SO under Sir Adrian Boult.

Hawkridge was a member of an old Derby family, being 9th in descent from Robert Hawkridge, whose son, Henry, was baptised at All Saints' in 1665. Douglas' father, George Hawkridge, of 23 Curzon Street was a master tailor and the 7th such in succession in the family. Douglas' great uncle, Percy Hawkridge (1863-97) was the first education advisor to the newly formed Derbyshire County Council. The future musician was born at Curzon Street in 1907 and was educated at Derby School; even then he was picked to broadcast piano solos from the BBC in Nottingham. He studied organ under T.Herbert Bennett, Organist of All Saints', whose school of music was at 99 Friar Gate. He received gold medals for the highest marks in England at Grade 6 and Grade 8.

In 1922 he was appointed organist of St Michael, Kirk Langley, entering the Royal Academy of Music in 1926 studying under Claud Pollard and Sir Stanley Marchant. His professional career began in 1930. Apart from his post at St Paul's, he was also organist at St Philip's, Kensington. At Derby he gave the opening recitals at the new Victoria Street Congregational Church in 1964 and the new St Alkmund in 1972. He became a freeman of the Borough in 1922, the 8th generation of his family to be so. In 1940 he married Miss G.M.Dudden and he died without leaving issue in 1983.

[DLC 4/1982, p.43; Parish records and Poll Books.]

HEATH, Alderman John (1705-1782)

Heath's name is memorable as a 'badhat' banker whose financial house went broke in Derby in March 1779 leaving many of his fellow citizens destitute and seriously inconveniencing even some of the richer members of society, like Robert Holden. Holden had purchased Darley Hall and estate from Heath around 1777 and had hired PICKFORD *(q.v.)* to improve the house. On Heath's bankruptcy it emerged that Darley was not his to sell, he having assigned it previously to his merchant bankers, Boldero & Co., London, as collateral. Holden had to buy it a second time, on this occasion at a premium because of the improvements to the house he had himself made (and paid for)!

John, Christopher (1718-1815) and Isaac Heath were the three sons of John Heath (d.1765), a Makeney copyholder and farmer. John was baptised at Duffield 14th August 1705 and the three brothers proceeded to Derby where they entered into business in Full Street with Joshua Bradshaw, a scion of a Duffield gentry family who had married their sister. By 1745 they were money lending and the bank was instrumental in providing 'venture capital' for both the Cockpit Hill pot works and DUESBURY'S porcelain factory in the 1750s. It is a measure of the success of the two factories that only the latter survived Heath's collapse. Joseph Pickford certainly performed agency tasks for the Heaths who may have backed his acquisition of property in Friar Gate 1768-72, and John and Christopher were both painted by WRIGHT *(q.v.)*, who captured their corpulent insincerity in masterly style.

John Heath was elected Alderman 15th December 1762 and served as Mayor 1763-64. After the bankruptcy he retired to Fenny Bentley. He married twice, his second wife, whom he married at Duffield in 1769, was Hannah, Mrs White of Duffield. He left no issue at his death in 1782; he had only a natural son, Christopher, who predeceased him.

Christopher, his brother, was Mayor and Alderman 1774-75 and married Elizabeth Alsop

of Loughborough (d.1804) who also had no issue. He retired to Duffield. Another sister was the mistress of Rev. Francis Revell of Carnfield Hall by whom he had two natural children, Col. Tristam Revell *alias* Heath and Charlotte.

It is difficult to be certain if the Heaths were honest financiers who had overstretched themselves or (as their contemporaries perhaps understandably thought) were merely crooks. Despite ending in disaster, several schemes backed by them prospered, like Crown Derby. Yet, out of four failed Derby banks in the period 1770-1820, only the Heaths suffered real opprobrium, which inclines one to suspect (with Mr Holden) that they had always played fast and loose.

[DM. *passim*; Local Studies Box 57/H; Poll Books; Saunders, *op.cit.* 33-34, 36, 170; information from Philip Heath Esq.]

HEWITT, Henry Richardson (d.1912)

H.R.Hewitt was a mining engineer and HM Inspector of Mines who was killed in heroic circumstances rescuing men at Cadeby Main Colliery, Rotherham, (Yorks, WR) trapped after an explosion, 9th July 1912. He had previously been assistant manager of Whitfield Colliery, Stoke-on-Trent (Staffordshire) and Principal Assistant to the family firm, Messrs. Hewitt and Bobart, before receiving his official appointment.

Hewitt was born about 1870 in Uttoxeter Road, Derby, second son of John Richardson Hewitt CE, M.l.C.E. His elder brother was Charles E.R.Hewitt, a mine proprietor of Charnwood Street, and his younger brother was Arthur Bernard Hewitt (b.1881), also a mining engineer. The family later moved to The Poplars, Alvaston and ultimately to Swanwick. Henry was educated with his brothers at Derby School before being taught his trade by his father. He married at St Chad, Derby 28th October 1904 Eleanor Elizabeth, daughter of William Hollingworth of Dean Hall, Caunton, Notts., and his death in circumstances of selfless personal sacrifice left his children to be brought up by their mother with help from their uncle, C.E.R.Hewitt.

[Tachella, *op.cit.* 107; Tilley/H.]

HEYWORTH, Lawrence MP (1786-1872)

The Heyworths were a powerfully emergent manufacturing dynasty in Lancashire,and Lawrence was born at Rochdale in 1786, youngest son of Peter Heyworth of Rochdale and Greensnook (Lancs.) by Elizabeth, daughter and heiress of Lawrence Ormerod of Greensnook, after whom he was named. He was educated at the local grammar school before entering his father's firm of Ormerod, Heyworth & Co. of Liverpool, of which he later became a partner. In 1820 he married Betsy Aked of Bacup (Lancs.) and they had four sons and two daughters.

In 1848 he became Whig MP for Derby with MICHAEL THOMAS BASS *(q.v.)* on the unseating of EDWARD STRUTT (later 1st LORD BELPER, *q.v.*) and Frederick Leveson-Gower (elected the previous year) for electoral irregularities. He was defeated in 1852 but returned again in 1853 serving until 1857 when Samuel Beale replaced him. He lived, ironically, at Yewtree, West Derby, (Lancs.) and died in 1872.

His eldest son Peter's grandson, was Dr George Alexander Frederick Heyworth of The Hollies, Belper (1881-1934), first of a dynasty of three local GPs; the latter's younger grandson is Malcolm Heyworth, the creator of TV's *Treasure Hunt* and other entertainments. Lawrence Heyworth's second son migrated to the USA where he was instrumental in co-founding Chicago.

[Walford's, *County Families* (1865) 496-7; *Who's Who in Derbyshire* (1934) 85; DLC 7/1967, 19.]

HINDLIPP, Lord, see Allsopp

HIVES, Ernest Walter, 1st Lord, CH, CBE, CStJ (1886-1965)

Lord Hives was the man who helped sustain Rolls-Royce after the death of SIR HENRY ROYCE *(q.v.)* and led the firm through the war years, continually inspiring its workforce to meet seemingly impossible production targets in the most difficult possible circumstances, and facilitating the developments of new, more powerful, aero-engines at a breakneck pace of new technology, forced by the competition of conflict. Throughout, he ensured that the firm maintained its commitment to quality and reliability and in 1945, was behind the take-over (viewed by some as ruthless in the extreme) of Sir Frank Whittle's Power Jets Ltd., thus ensuring Rolls-Royce's paramountcy into the jet age. It was Hives who, like Hon C.S.Rolls *(q.v.)*, foresaw that the firm's future lay with aero-engines rather than with quality motor cars, whilst ensuring that the reputation of the car rubbed off on the engine. He also rapidly ended car production at Derby when World War Two broke out (concentrating it at the firm's Crewe plant) and was influential in 'bringing on' promising young engineers such as Sir Stanley Hooker and Jack Warwick, (*q.v.* J.R.WARWICK *sub* J.A.WARWICK).

Ernest Walter Hives was the son of John William Hives and was born at Reading (Berks.)

HOBSON, Prof. Alfred Dennis FRS, FZS (1901-1974)

The fertile and talented Hobson dynasty was founded by Robert (1751-1821) master of Bonsall Free School and his son John, an Ashbourne bookseller, publisher, auctioneer and valuer. Alfred Dennis Hobson was Professor of Botanical Science at the University of Newcastle-upon-Tyne and Professor of Zoology at King's College, Durham. From 1932 he was Director of Dove Marshe Laboratory, Cullercoats. He was the author of many scientific papers, chiefly on cytology and parasitology.

Hobson was born 25th July 1901, only son of Alfred Edward Hobson (1865-1912), a Derby solicitor and his wife (whom he married at Eccles (Lancs.) on 3rd March 1893), Marie Anne Magdalen, elder daughter of Henry Kershaw of Eccles. He was educated at Highgate and Christ's College, Cambridge, (MA), going on to University College, London, as assistant in the Dept of Zoology. From 1925-32 he lectured at Edinburgh University and was Ray Lankester Investigator at the Marine Laboratory, Plymouth 1928-29. He was later elected FRS, FRS (Edinburgh) and FZS. He married in 1924, Mary Gladys Petra Paula, only daughter of John Woods of Walton-le-Dale but retired in 1966 and died without issue 11th July 1974.
[Henstock, A., *Ashbourne* (1978) 27; information courtesy of late E.G.B.Atkinson; *Who's Who* (1961) 1445.]

on 21st April 1886 and was educated at Redlands School there, joining Rolls-Royce in 1908, the year it opened in Derby, and rising to become Chairman, from which post he retired in 1957. He was made MBE in 1920, later became CBE and Companion of Honour in 1943. He was also CStJ. and in 1950 was raised to the peerage as 1st Lord Hives of Duffield, where he lived at Hazeldene. He died 24th April 1965 leaving by his wife, Gertrude Ethel (1891-1961), daughter of John A.Warwick of Ockbrook (see JOHN ALFRED WARWICK *q.v.*) whom he married in February 1913, five sons and two daughters. He was succeeded as 2nd Lord Hives by his eldest son, the noted agriculturalist, John Warwick Hives CBE (1913-1997). His second son, P/O Edward Hives RAF (b.1915) was killed in action in the Battle of Britain in 1940, unmarried. The youngest son Gp. Capt. D.B.Hives (b.1931) was also an RAF officer, whilst the third son, Peter, (b.1921) served in the RNVR. The latter's son, Matthew, succeeded as 3rd Lord Hives in December 1997.
[Burke, *Peerage*, (1970) 1345; *Who's Who* (1961) 1442; *The Derbeian* passim; DET 9/5/1994; Tilley/H.]

HOBSON, Prof. Ernest William, FRS (1856-1933)

E.W.Hobson was Sadlerian Professor of Pure Mathematics at Cambridge from 1910 and a Fellow of Christ's College Cambridge – a mathematician and philosopher of great eminence. He was the eldest of the four sons of Alderman WILLIAM HOBSON *(q.v.)* and Josephine, sister of Dr J.G.Atkinson of The Grange, Rotherham (Yorkshire). He was born 27th October 1856 and

was educated at Derby School 1865-73, winning an open scholarship to Christ's in 1873, becoming Senior Wrangler and Fellow in 1878 and MA in 1881. In 1890 he became Senior Deputy Lowndean Professor of Astronomy, DSc (1892) and FRS in 1893. He wrote *A Treatise on Plane Trigonometry* (1891) and various articles in learned journals, but his most influential work was his *Theory of Functions of a Real Variable* (1907). He was a governor of Derby School and President of the School in 1896 and, unlike most mathematicians, did his best work later in life.

He died at Cambridge on 18th April 1933, having married in 1882, Serina Rose, daughter of Rudolph Knüsli of Glarus, Switzerland and had four sons (one of whom predeceased him), the eldest of whom was SIR OSCAR HOBSON (*q.v.*). [Tachella, *op.cit.* 66; Kelly's *Handbook* (1924) 783; DNB; Obit, DA.21/4/1933.]

HOBSON, Harold CBE (1891-1973)

Harold Hobson (no relation of the distinguished critic Sir Harold Hobson, a contemporary) was a highly distinguished consulting engineer who ended his career as Chairman of the Central Electricity Generating Board, being made CBE in recognition of his services. He had formerly been a Director of GEC, the Calcutta Electric Supply Corporation and Calcutta Tramways.

He was the only son of John Atkinson Hobson of Hampstead (1858-1940), the writer and economist, next brother of PROF. E.W.HOBSON (*q.v.*), and Florence, daughter of Jonathan Edgar, a New Jersey (USA) attorney. He was educated privately in England and the USA before going up to King's College, London. He was consulting engineer with Merz and McLellan, London 1914-25, working for CEGB and its predecessors from the latter year. His Chairmanship was 1944-47. He lived at 44 Montagu Square, London WI and married twice: in 1914 to Coralie Jeye (d.1946), daughter of A. von Wernher of Chatham, by whom he had a son and a daughter, Mabel who, was the daughter-in-law of C.P.Scott, the famous editor of the *Manchester Guardian*. In 1948 he remarried Margaret Busvine, Mrs Hand. They lived at The Pastures, Hilton, Hunts. He died 12th June 1973. [*Who's Who* (1961) 1446; as previous article.]

HOBSON, Sir Oscar Rudolph (1886-1961)

Sir Oscar Hobson was one of the most famous and perceptive City journalists, becoming Financial Editor of the *Manchester Guardian* 1920-29, Editor-in-Chief of the *Financial News* 1929-34 and City Editor of the *News Chronicle* 1935-59. He was also Chairman of the Association of Unit Trust Managers, a governor of the LSE and a council member of the Royal Economic Society. He was knighted in 1955.

Oscar Rudolph Hobson (who took his names from his mother's family, the Swiss Knüslis) was born 15th March 1886 at Cambridge, son of PROF. E.W.HOBSON (*q.v.*) and was educated at Aldenham and King's, Cambridge. In 1910 he entered on a career in merchant banking by joining the staff of the London Joint Bank before discovering a talent for journalism which he astutely combined with his expertise in the markets.

He lived at Chafont St Giles (Bucks) with his wife (and doubly his cousin) Frances Josephine (Queenie), daughter of Charles Milner Atkinson JP of Leeds. Her mother, Mary Josephine, was a daughter of Alderman W.HOBSON *(q.v.)* and her father a nephew of A.W.Hobson's wife. Her own nephew, E.G.B.Atkinson, was the last editor of the *Derbyshire Advertiser*. They had two daughters and Sir Oscar died in 1961.
[Burke, Peerage (1956) 2.516; *Who's Who* (1961)1446.]

HOBSON, Alderman William JP (1825-1897)

William Hobson was the co-founder in 1846 (with his father) and proprietor of the *Derbyshire Advertiser* which he also edited for most of his life. He used it to campaign for a number of radical causes, including the revival of the Derby School of Art. He was also a supporter of the Derby School of Science, was a governor of both, a member of the School Board (1871) and the Board of Guardians (1859). All this led him into local politics and he was elected for Derwent Ward as a Liberal in 1869, becoming an Alderman in 1879 and in 1880 the first JP who was also a member of the press. He was Mayor of Derby in 1883. He was a great promoter of the idea of a Free Library and Museum, accepting MICHAEL BASS's offer of £5,000 towards the cost of a new one with alacrity during his mayoralty of 1883-84. He later chaired its committee until 1894. He was also a founding governor of the Derbyshire Deaf and Dumb Institution. In 1886 he became a Liberal Unionist as a consequence of Gladstone's embracing Irish Home Rule. On 19th August 1885 the ironmaster Alderman Henry Fowkes, who had succeeded him as Mayor, died and Hobson served the term out. He himself resigned in 1894 due to failing health, dying in 1897.

Hobson was born in 1825, eldest of the two

sons and a daughter of John Hobson of 12 Market Place, Ashbourne, bookseller, publisher and co-founder of the *Advertiser*, by a sister of Adam Smedley of Bonsall. In 1854 he married Josephine, sister of Dr J.G.Atkinson of Rotherham and had four sons (including E.W.HOBSON *(q.v.)*), and two daughters. The third son, Henry Mortimer Hobson (1861-1921) was also Mayor of Derby and succeeded his father, on his death at his home, 39 Charnwood Street, as Editor and proprietor of the *Advertiser*. In turn, Henry's son Charles (1892-1964) took it on before it passed to the late E.G.B.Atkinson, his cousin.
[Modern Mayors of Derby 1 (1909) 58-61, 63; Tachella, *loc.cit.;* Atkinson, *op.cit.*]

HODGSON, Very Rev. Francis (1781-1852)

Francis Hodgson was Archdeacon of Derby from 1836 to 1852, holding the post with the Provostship of Eton to which he was appointed in 1840. He was a poet of note, an intimate friend of Byron, author, critic and man of letters.

Hodgson was born 16th November 1781 at Croydon (Surrey), second son of Rev. James Hodgson (d.1810) rector of Humber (Herefordshire) by James Coke of the Herefordshire branch of the Derbyshire Cokes. He was educated at Eton (1794), going up to King's, (Cambridge)in 1799 (BA 1804, MA 1807, BD 1810) to which he was ultimately elected a Fellow, and where he made the acquaintanceship of Lord Byron, with whom he went to stay at Newstead in 1808. After teaching briefly at Eton he turned to writing, his historical verse being somewhat influenced by Byron's style.

In 1814 he married a Miss Taylor (who died without issue in 1833) being appointed vicar of Bakewell in 1816, to which cure the Duke of Devonshire added the incumbency of Edensor in 1838, in which year, on 3rd May, he remarried Hon Elizabeth Denman, daughter of his Derbyshire-born and life-long friend Thomas, 1st Lord Denman, by whom he had a son and three daughters. His son, John Thomas Hodgson, MA, married Marie Blanche Verelst and in turn had two sons and three daughters. He died 29th December 1852 at Eton; Derby never had a more distinguished man of letters as its archdeacon.

[Foster, J. *Peerage* (1881) 206; DNB.]

HOLMES, Brig. Kenneth Soar, CBE, CB (1912-1995)

Kenneth Holmes was a telephone engineer of great distinction which he applied in an army career which culminated in his appointment as Director of the Army Postal Services, War Office, with the rank of Brigadier 1950-59. He thereafter retired from the forces, becoming Director of Postal Services, GPO, and in 1971-72 Managing Director, Posts.

Kenneth Soar Holmes was born at Derby in 1912, son of William Joseph Holmes, later of 19 Chaddesden Park Road, and educated at Bemrose School and Derby Technical College. He entered the GPO and was in 1930 appointed assistant traffic superintendent (telephones)

before beginning his military career with the outbreak of war as O.C. 43rd Div. Postal Unit, and Assistant Director, posts, BAOR. He was appointed CBE (1954) and CB (1963). In 1936 he married Ann, daughter of C.Chapman of Leicester and at his death in February 1995 left a son. He lived at Banstead (Surrey).

[DET. 14/2/1995; *Who's Who* (1971) 1509-10.]

HOLZENDORFF, Georg, 6th Count von. (b.1838)

It is strange to think that a descendant of Otto Holtzendorpe, a Brandenburg *Reichsritter* of 1297 should turn out to be a direct ancestor of one of the best 19th century artists working at the then newly established Royal Crown Derby factory. Yet, such was the case, for v. Holzendorff was 'headhunted' from the Dresden factory in 1878 when the Derby factory was set up and lived and worked in Derby for just over a decade before returning to Saxony to take up his responsibilities as heir apparent to a *Reichsgraf* created in June 1746.

Count Georg v. Holzendorff was born in Dresden, son of Count Hans v. Holzendorff, 31st July 1838. He was educated at the military academy and later at the University where he became an enthusiastic artist. Although of a junior branch of the family, he had no real need to work and, indeed, was expected to enter the Saxon Army, but he seems instead to have tried living as an artist before offering his services as a china painter to the Dresden porcelain factory. He specialised in topographical views, as at Derby, and one of his plates made by the latter factory in the Derby Museum collection bears a delightful vignette of a view down Beckett Street.

After leaving Derby, he inherited as 6th Graf von Holzendorff on the death of his uncle Bernhard, 5th Count, on 9th April 1905, leaving only a daughter, Sophie. Georg had married, 2nd May 1872, at Dresden, Thérèse (from whom he was divorced in 1877, a major spur to his exile at Derby), daughter of Abrecht v. Jordan; they had two children, a daughter, Thérèse, and a son, Hans (b.1873), later 7th Graf von Holzendorff, who, in 1909, married Maria, daughter of Glauchau v. Herder. Their son, Hans, (later 8th Count) was head of the family in 1973. Unfortunately it has not been possible to establish when Georg died. The family's townhouse in 1914 was 32, Bischofsweg, Dresden.

[Ruvigny et Raineval, Marquis de, *The Titled Nobility of Europe* (London 1914) 794; *International List of Nobility* (Geneva 1973) 65.]

HOPE, Rev. Charles Stead, AM (1762-1841)

Apart from JOHN WHITEHURST (*q.v.*), Tories were rare beings in the glittering musical, literary and scientific circles of late 18th century Derby, as much as amongst the ranks of the Aldermen, dominated as they were by the Borough's Whig High Steward, the Duke of Devonshire. Yet Charles Stead Hope was just that. Thomas Mozley wrote of him that he 'was in all respects a big man, with a sonorous voice, a commanding manner and a quick temper'. He was vicar of St Alkmund and of All Saints', an alderman, and served as Mayor of Derby in 1797, 1805, 1817 and 1825, and was a founding member, as a 21-year-old, of the Derby Philosophical Society, from which he was forced unceremoniously to resign by its chairman, ERASMUS DARWIN (*q.v.*) for his opposition to the French Revolution. He was in his third Mayoralty when the Pentrich rising occurred, with the precepts of which many of the poorer artisans of the town 'heartily agreed'. This was not lost on Hope, who took very swift and proper measures for the occasion, calling up the Yeomanry and Militia, swearing in constables and manning the approaches. After the arrest, incarceration and execution of the ringleaders, Hope conducted the funeral at All Saints' and preached a sermon remarkable (given his Establishment views and stance as Mayor) for its moderation and unifying sentiments to a packed congregation, eager for scandal. He seemed to know almost all his fellow townsmen and they him, and his stature grew from his handling of the 1817 crisis. Later, with full Masonic rites, he was invited to lay the foundation stone of St John's Church, Bridge Street in 1826.

Charles Stead Hope was the eldest of four sons and two daughters of Rev. Charles Hope (1732-98), vicar of St Werburgh's and All Saints' and once a member of the musical coterie that played in The Tiger and which included WRIGHT and BURDETT (*q.v.*). The father was fifth in descent from Charles Hope of Trusley living 1561, whose descendants furnished numerous Mayors and Bailiffs of Derby. Charles' niece, Jane, married GEORGE FRITCHE (*q.v.*) and by marriage C.S.Hope was related to Gen. BAINBRIGGE (*q.v.*) and D.P.COKE (*q.v.*). His mother was Susannah, daughter and heiress of Benjamin Stead of Bradfield (Yorkshire). Charles Stead Hope was educated at Derby School and Harrow before going up to St John's, Cambridge (BA 1784). He was ordained 24th December 1786 and succeeded his father at All Saints' in 1797 and as curate at St Werburgh's 1785, a cure he resigned in 1797 being additionally appointed by the Corporation to St Alkmund in 1802. He was also vicar of Youlgreave 1797-1802.

He married at St Werburgh 6th April 1793 Ellen, daughter and co-heiress of Robert Mellor of Alsop and they lived at St Alkmund's vicarage, rebuilt for them by CHARLES FINNEY (*q.v.*) before going to Duffield where he died in January 1841, leaving two sons (both Derbyshire parsons) and six daughters.

[Hunter, J., FMG. 1.333; Glover, *op.cit.* II.585; *Alumni Cantabrigenses* (1752-1900) 404; Mozley, J., *Reminiscences* 2 vols. (Derby 1885) ii.188-194.]

HOPE, Sir William Henry St John, K.StJ, FSA (1854-1919)

Sir W.H. St John Hope was one of the greatest antiquaries, historians and archaeologists of his day and was a celebrated and prolific author and Director of the Royal Archaeological Institute. His chief interest was ecclesiastical architecture but he was a considerable expert on Roman Britain, heraldry, alabaster and stained glass as well. From 1885 to 1910, he was Fellow and Secretary of the Society of Antiquaries, his authority in antiquarian circles being unique and he was notable for his keen powers of observation and retentive memory. His monograph on Windsor Castle (by Royal command) of 1913 is still a standard work and he was rewarded in 1914 with a Knighthood. He was also in that year made a Knight of the Venerable Order of St John of Jerusalem.

Hope was born 23rd June 1856, eldest of three sons of Rev. William Hope (1823-89), vicar of St Peter's, Derby (1847-89) and notable as being the only pupil, for a short time, of Derby School under Dr Bligh. William, senior, was second son of Robert Hope of Derby, brother of CHARLES STEAD HOPE *(q.v.)*, making W.H.StJohn Hope a great nephew of the Tory parson. His mother was Hester, daughter of Rev. John Brown Williams, rector of Llantrisant (Glam.), although his father married twice more, having another son by his third wife Geraldine O'Connor. He went to Derby School (by this time much revived), Hurstpierpont and Peterhouse, Cambridge in 1877, (BA 1881, MA 1884, DLitt 1912) and conducted his first excavation at Dale Abbey as an undergraduate. He married twice, in 1885 to Myrrha, daughter of Maj. Gen. Edward Norman Perkins, by whom he had an only son. In 1910, he married Mary Jefferies (d.1952), daughter of John Robert Jefferies of Ipswich, who was made a Dame Grand Cross of the Venerable Order of St John when her husband received his Knighthood. They lived at Great Shelford, Cambs. where he died 18th August 1919. His brother, Gerard Llewellyn Hope, later of the USA, married a cousin of LORD ROE *(q.v.)* and another brother, Robert Charles (1855-1926) was also an author and antiquary. W.H.St John Hope published prolifically all his life, his output almost matching his contemporary J.C.COX *(q.v.)* with whom he shared much in common. [DNB; *Alumni Cantabrigenses* 1752-1900 ii.436.]

HOWE, Sir Robert George GBE, KCMG (1893-1981)

After Lord St Helen's, Sir Robert Howe was the most distinguished diplomat to have come out of

Derby, retiring after eight difficult years as HM Governor General of the Sudan (1947-55). He was no stranger to difficult postings, however, having served as Assistant Counsellor at Peking 1934-40, during the Chinese Civil War and the Japanese invasion. In 1940 he was posted to HM Embassy in Riga, leaving when the Soviets invaded Latvia in 1941, and being transferred to yet another trouble spot, Addis Ababa, at a time when the Italians were the dominant power in Ethiopia (then called Abyssinia). Only from 1945-47 did he see a quiet period, being appointed Assistant Under-secretary of State at the Foreign Office by Ernest Bevin.

All this was a far cry from 6 Carrington Street, Derby, where Robert George Howe was born 19th September 1893, son of Harold Howe, a locomotive driver with the Midland Railway. There is some evidence to suggest that his father was son of Henry Merry How(e), great-great-grandson of Thomas Howe, baker, son of John (1701-57), hatter, and brother of Alderman

Matthew Howe, the great grandfather of Mrs WILLIAM BEMROSE (q.v.). It neatly illustrates the switchback of social mobility in Derby life, as with the extended kin of LORD ROE (q.v.). Howe won a scholarship to Derby School, where he was a pupil from 1907-12, going on to St Catherine's College, Cambridge (BA 1915).

He entered the Foreign Office and his first posting was as Third Secretary at Copenhagen in 1920, swiftly followed by promotion to Second Secretary. Thereafter he served in rapid succession in Belgrade, Rio de Janeiro and Bucharest before returning to a desk at the Foreign Office in 1930. He was made CMG in 1937, KCMG in 1947 and GBE in 1949, and in 1955 retired to Cowbridge, Lostwithiel, Cornwall where he served as JP and enjoyed equestrianism. He died 22nd June 1981 leaving, by his wife Loveday Mary (d.1970), daughter of G.Hext, JP of Cowbridge – hence his choice of residence – a son.
[Who's Who (1978) 1201; Derbeian.]

HOWELL, Charles Alfred, OBE, MP (1905-1974)

Charles Howell was MP for Perry Barr (Birmingham) from 1955 until he was defeated in 1964. A Labour member, he was an opposition whip 1959-64 but for most of his career was an official of the National Union of Railwaymen, having been – as so many Derbeians of his era – a railway employee. He sat on the NUR executive 1951-53, was Secretary of the Derby Trades Council 1945-55 and NUR branch secretary 1939-55.

Charles Alfred Howell was born at Derby 22nd October 1905, son of Charles Howell, a miller at Stretton's Brewery who later moved to Burton upon Trent and lived at Winshill. After an elementary education there, he became a railway guard on the Midland Railway (later the LMSR) and his appointment as Union Branch Secretary in 1939 was the first step on the ladder. He was also elected a Derby Councillor in 1943, remaining on the Council until 1954 when he was selected to fight Perry Barr. He was Chairman of

Derby Labour Party, President of the Midland District NUR Council the same year and a member of the LMS sectional council No.3, 1945-55. In Derby he was a member of the No.2 Hospital Management Committee and Chairman of Derwent Hospital, 1948. He was made OBE in 1965.

He lived on the Cowsley estate at 36 Cardigan Street with his wife Ivy Jeanette, daughter of Arthur Silvester, whom he married on Christmas Eve 1927 and by whom he left, at his death 26th October 1974, a daughter.
[Who's Who (1971) 1544; Stenton & Lees, op.cit. IV.176.]

HUDSON, Brig. Charles Edward, VC, CB, DSO, MC, DL (1892-1959)

Col. Hudson is one of Derby's four VC winners, which distinction he won during World War One, on 15th June 1918. He was serving as acting lieutenant, 11th Bn. Sherwood Foresters on the Asiago Plateau, Italy. He led a desperate counterattack with a motley crew of 'B' echelon personnel after the enemy had unexpectedly penetrated the British front line, killing all the other officers. With six men, he carried out a flank attack on 200 enemy and, despite being seriously wounded in a foot by a bomb, managed to direct the continuing counter-attack taking 100 prisoners and six machine gums. For this, he also received the Italian Valore Militare medal.

Charles Edward Hudson was born at Fern Bank, Trowells Lane, Derby 29th May 1892, son of Col. Herbert Edward Hudson, a Sherwood Foresters officer, and was educated at Sherborne and RMC, Sandhurst. From 1912-13 he ran a tea plantation in Ceylon (Sri Lanka) but returned to join up on the outbreak of the war, being commissioned into the Sherwood Foresters. He was a good and efficient officer and earned rapid promotion, as well as showing outstanding bravery winning also an MC, DSO and bar, a French Croix-de-Guerre and was mentioned in despatches four times. He was mentioned twice more in 1919-20 when he served as Brigade

Major in the force which intervened in the Russian Civil War.

After the war he was chief instructor at Sandhurst before going on to command 2nd Bn, King's Own Scottish Borderers and later 2nd Infantry Brigade. He was appointed CB after Dunkirk and retired in 1946 after two years as ADC to King George VI.

Hudson married in 1920, Gladys Elizabeth, daughter of Matthew Lee of Allendale, Northumberland and they had two sons, the elder of whom was tragically killed in action during World War Two. They lived at Kerswell House, Chudleigh (Devon) and he was a Deputy Lieutenant of that County before his death 4th April 1959.

[*Who's Who* (1947) 1368; McCrery, N. *For Conspicuous Gallantry* (Derby 1990) 68-69.]

HUMPSTONE, Robert, VC (1832-1884)

Chronologically, Humpstone was the first of Derby's four VCs to be awarded. He won it on 22nd April 1855 as a rifleman in 2nd Bn. the Rifle Brigade when he and two others (who also received the VC) beat back a number of Russian snipers who had dug into pits commanding the Regiment's only water supply. The award was gazetted 24th February 1857 and he also received the *Légion d'Honneur*. He attended the first ever VC investiture to receive his award from Queen Victoria in Hyde Park 26th June 1857. He later served in India during the Mutiny being involved in heavy fighting around Lucknow.

Robert Humpstone was born in Derby in 1832, third and youngest son of Samuel Humpstone, tobacconist, who had married Robert's mother, Mary Hill, on 27th May, 1824. Samuel (b.1799) was probably the youngest son of Dr Randall Humpstone of Duffield (d.1822) and Elizabeth Spaulton of Mackworth. James Humpstone (b.1794), brother of Samuel, was a Derby tobacconist as well; both may have been involved in the same business. Frederick Samuel, Robert's eldest brother succeeded to the tobacconist's business, marrying Mary Ludlam of Greenwich (Ripley) at Ironville on 4th February 1856.

William, the next brother was a Derby petrifactioner who married Elizabeth Allsop at St Werburgh's on 6th June 1870. Their sister was Mary Anne, wife of Henry Watkinson, a surveyor. Little is known of Robert's subsequent life; the only photograph (a *carte-de-visite* of the 1870s) suggests that he was in comfortable circumstances; possibly he had an interest in the family tobacconist's, or perhaps a position at the lead merchants run by his cousin Samuel Poyser (grandson of his elder brother, Thomas); both the Poysers and the Humpstones originally came from Weston Underwood. Robert Humpstone died in 1884.

(McCrery *op.cit.* 10; Derby Local Studies Library, QA 340, BA 365 and MS4620 3.651.]

HUTTON, William, FASS (1723-1815)

William Hutton was called 'The Celebrated Historian' by Simpson within a decade of his death, and wrote the first published history of Derby (1791, 2nd edn. 1819) and a fine history of Birmingham (1780). He also published numerous other historical and topographical works and a number of collections of poetry.

Hutton was born in Bridge Gate, Derby, 30th September 1723 of a family which migrated from Northallerton (Yorkshire) to Derby during the Civil War. His father, William Hutton (1691-1758) was a woolcomber and had married, as his first wife, 8th February 1718, Anne, daughter of Matthew Ward of Mountsorrel (Leics), grocer. At seven William was sent to work in the Silk Mill and remained there until 1737. After an unhappy apprenticeship to his uncle in Nottingham, a stockiner, he became a bookbinder, settling in Birmingham in 1750. In 1755 he married Sarah Cock of Aston-on-Trent. In 1772 he was appointed Commissioner of the Court of Requests and a year later Commissioner of the Lamp and Street Act. He was elected a Fellow of the Antiquarian Society of Scotland in 1782.

Being a Dissenter and a radical he suffered greatly during the 1791 riots in Brimingham, los-

The Greatest Gift of All four years later. In all she wrote – also under the *noms de plume* Elizabeth Arthur and Nancy Bell – 21 books. She was widowed on 6th July 1986 and she herself died 7th June 1992.

Her output seemed to increase as she got older but in no way affected the elegance and power of her writing.

[*Derby Trader* 8/4/1987; DET 12/7/1986; 10/6/1992.]

ing his house, library and possessions to the value of £8,000 or more. He was the first to open a circulating library in Birmingham and in the same year a pauper warehouse. He died 20th September 1815, leaving a son, Thomas (1757-1845) and daughter Catherine (1756-1846), an author in her own right. Hutton's brother Samuel (1733-1801) lived in Nottingham and his descendants are very numerous.

[Hutton, W., *Life of William Hutton* (Birmingham 1816), *passim*; Simpson, *op.cit.* III.695-723.]

IRISH, Elizabeth May (d.1992)

Betty Irish was a Derby housewife, married to businessman, Eric Arthur Irish MBE of Allestree, who concentrated on bringing up her three children: Neville, Stephen and Vivienne (for many years now the highly stylish editor of *Derbyshire Life*) before turning to literature. Her first novel was published in the late 1950s, her second *From Dawn to Dusk* in 1960 and she followed this with

JAMES, Eric John Francis FRIBA, Lord James of Rusholme (1909-1992)

Lord James of Rusholme was the former High Master of Manchester Grammar School and first Vice-Chancellor of York University who 'stood out unflinchingly for academic standards… against the meretricious educational nostrums peddled with such disastrous results in the post war years.' His devotion to intellectual excellence had little appeal to the educational theorists of the 1960s. A Fabian Socialist who believed fervently in equality of opportunity, he advocated a pure meritocracy. His contribution to the expansion of the University of York and his avoidance of strident turbulence during his period in office 1962-73, was a considerable achievement. He is also remembered as the Chairman of an enquiry, instigated by Lady Thatcher in 1970, into Teacher Training. His report (1972) envisaged teacher training Colleges as mini Universities where two years of purely intellectual effort (ending in a Dip. H.E.) would be followed by a further two years' intensive practical and theoretical training. He also proposed, very sensibly, that teachers should attend at least one in-service training course every seven years. The report was ferociously opposed by those, such as the NUT, who felt most threatened by a sharp rise in standards, but it was accepted by the Government, and James and Lady Thatcher developed a lively admiration for one another.

Eric John Francis James was born at 57, Breedon Hill Road 13th April 1909, the younger son of a commercial traveller, Francis William James (1865-1945) who later retired to Parkstone (Dorset) and his wife Lilian (d.1961) daughter of Robert Taylor of Whitehaven (Cumbria), whom he married in 1895; the family were of dissenting stock. He was educated at Brighton and Taunton's School, Southampton, from whence he won an exhibition to Queen's College Oxford where he took a first in Chemistry (BA & BSc. 1931, MA 1933, D.Phil 1933, Hon Fellow 1963), although family impecuniousness prevented him from adopting a medical career as he had intended. He went instead into teaching. He consequently taught chemistry at Winchester 1933-45 before going to Manchester. He was a member, too, of the Standing Commission on Museums and Art Galleries and of the Press Council. He also appeared on the *Brains Trust* and wrote two books adumbrating his educational beliefs, and a chemistry textbook.

James married in 1939 Cordelia May, daughter of Maj. Gen. Fitzgerald Wintour, CB, CBE, whose brother Charles became a notable Fleet Street editor (and whose daughter, Anna's, fame has since eclipsed that of her father in journalism). Their only child is Prof. Hon. Oliver Francis Wintour James, professor of medicine at Newcastle University. Lord James was also FRIBA, and was knighted in 1956. He was raised to the Peerage for Life 19th February 1959 as Lord James of Rusholme, of Fallowfield, Lancs, but unusually, failed to obtain a grant of arms to accompany it. He died 17th May 1992.

[Burke, *Peerage* (1970) 1439; *Daily Telegraph* 18/5/92.]

JARVIS, Ronald (1911-1994)

Ronald Jarvis was one of the last of the old style locomotive designers, a role since usurped by computers. He was latterly locomotive design engineer at the then newly-opened Derby Railway Technical Centre, from which the Inter City 125 multiple unit later emerged, in 1967. In 1973 he created the power car for the High Speed Train (HST) which in 1973 reached 143 mph. winning the world speed record for Diesel rail traction. The Inter City 125s, developed from the HST, are outstanding and still regularly clock up 350,000 miles per year; in one trial run a unit covered the 268 miles from Newcastle to London in 2 hours 9 minutes, an *average* speed of 115mph! In the realm of steam traction he was also responsible for the complete re-design of the ex-Southern Railway 'Spam Can' pacifics (the 'Merchant Navy' and 'West Country' 4-6-2s) in the 1950s which proved an outstanding success.

Jarvis was born the son of a builder in Middlesex in 1911 and educated at St George's School, Harpenden, winning an engineering apprenticeship at the LMS Works, Derby. He simultaneously studied at Derby Technical College and obtained a London University external degree. He then joined the Derby locomotive drawing office, later the research department. In 1936 he was made assistant to Sir W.A.Stanier FRS, the CME, and helped in the development of a streamlined articulated Diesel multiple unit, a project killed by the outbreak of war.

After a spell in India he was, in 1950, appointed chief technical assistant to the Southern Region CME at Brighton, returning to Derby a decade later. He was a modest man and a keen railway modeller and photographer as well as a dedicated preservationist, putting much work into the restoration of the Ffestiniog Railway, near which he lived after he left Derby at Llanbedr (Caerns). He mar-

ried May Baldock in 1942 and at his death on 27th November 1994 left a daughter.
[*Daily Telegraph* 28/11/94.]

JEFFS, Gp. Capt. George James Horatio, CVO, OBE (1900-1996)

Jimmy Jeffs was the mainspring behind the development of modern air traffic control techniques, and was long looked to by the international aviation community for advice and assistance. From 1957 to 1960 he was Airport Commandant at Heathrow; thereafter he became a consultant.

George James Horatio Jeffs was born at Derby 27th January 1900, son of James Thomas Jeffs. He was educated at Kedleston Road School, leaving to join the colours as a pilot in the RNAS, transferring to the RAF in 1918. In 1919 he transferred to the Air Ministry until 1923, when he was appointed first commandant at Croydon (Surrey) Airport, later serving at Heston (Middlesex) and after the war at Prestwick (Scotland). During the war he was variously involved with Fighter, Ferry and Transport Commands. He retired with the rank of Group Captain.

He was made OBE in 1946 and CVO in 1961, as well as receiving the US Legion of Merit. He married Phyllis Rosina Bell in 1921 and they lived at Pixham Firs Cottage, Dorking (Surrey). He died 20th May 1996 leaving two sons end a daughter. His son, Cyril Jeffs OBE, is an aviation insurance expert.
[*Who's Who* (1978) 1277; *Daily Telegraph* 21/5/96.]

JERRAM, Jane E., Mrs William (living c.1810-1873)

Mrs Jerram was a notable Victorian children's author and friend of Mary Howitt, amongst whose titles were *The Pale Star*, *My Father's House*, *Hare Bell and Other Stories*, *Mamma's Stories*, *The Pearly Gates* and The *Children's Story Book*. She

was the daughter of John Brookes Holmes of Mickleover, a farrier, was born about 1809/1810 and received an elementary education. She later married William Jerram of Derby and they moved to Bannells Farm on the Radbourne estate near Mickleover where she produced the majority of her vastly popular, but today rather dated, *oeuvre*, described in their day as 'graphic, lively, entertaining and morally instructive.' She died in 1873, leaving issue.
[Derby Local Studies Library; Hall, Spencer T., *Days in Derbyshire* (Derby 1863) 219-20.]

JOBEY, George (1886-1962)

After Brian Clough and Dave Mackay, George Jobey, who was in charge from 1925 to 1941, was the most successful manager in Derby County

FC's history. It was, indeed, the club's a most consistently successful period in Division One. Jobey was extremely shrewd in the transfer market, although ironically, three of his finest players, Jack Barker, Jack Bowers and SAMMY CROOKS *(q.v.)* cost him next to nothing. Although a martinet at times he had a 'laid-back' management style; nevertheless his players stood in some considerable awe of him.

George Jobey was born on Tyneside in 1886 and played half-back for Newcastle, Arsenal and Leicester. In 1922 he became coach/manager at Wolverhampton Wanderers, helping them to the 3rd Division North Championship in 1924 before going into the hotel business from whence the chance to manage Derby recalled him.

He lived with his wife at 102 Kedleston Road (later Bangor St, Chaddesden) but was sacked in 1941 for paying illegal bonuses and inducements. He was banned from all football for ever, although, inevitably, his directors got off a lot more lightly. His ban was lifted in 1945, but he did not work in soccer again until he managed Mansfield briefly in 1952. He died in May 1962 in Chaddesden, leaving two daughters; one married the late Ald. Jack Bussell, the other to G.W.Collett-Jobey.
[Mortimer, *op.cit.* 215.]

JOHNSON, Samuel Waite (1831-1912)

S.W.Johnson was the Midland Railway's longest-serving Locomotive Superintendent, working from taking over from MATTHEW KIRTLEY *(q.v.)* in 1873 to retirement in 1903 when he was succeeded by R.M. DEELEY *(q.v.)*. He adopted a policy of smallish well-designed locomotives, rather than build fewer, large, locomotives for exceptionally heavy trains, for he believed in double-heading. Hence, he designed some superb 4-2-2 singles and 4-4-0s, including the first of the Midland Compounds, greatly multiplied by his successor. He was also a keen amateur photographer, and a close friend of RICHARD KEENE *(q.v.)* whom he brought in to take official photographs until Keene's pupil Thomas Scotton was appointed

permanently. Johnson was a genteel character, meticulous, and a fervent christian.

He was born at Bramley, near Leeds in 1831 and educated at Leeds Grammar School. From there he went to Wilson's Railway Foundry as a pupil of James Fenton; his first independent job was manager of the GNR's loco repair workshops. Thereafter he was works manager at Gorton (MSLR), then locomotive and carriage and wagon superintendent on the Edinburgh & Glasgow Railway – all this before he was 30! He remained at the latter under North British Railway management as Locomotive Superintendent, Western Division. Thereafter, he was with the Great Eastern Railway 1866-73 before coming to Derby.

'During his long and active life,' writes J.B.Radford, 'he had bought a certain poetic beauty into his locomotive designs' – none more so perhaps than the elegant but instantly obsolescent *Princess of Wales* 4-2-2s of 1900. He retired to Nottingham in 1903 and was tragically killed in a street accident there 14th January 1912.
[Radford, *op.cit.* 63-4, 80, 1119; Hamilton Ellis, *op.cit.* 61-120.]

KEAN, Michael (c.1760-1823)

Michael Kean was recruited to help manage the Derby Porcelain Factory in 1790 by WILLIAM DUESBURY the younger, when the latter began to suffer from indifferent health. Kean later became a partner in the works, and was a fine designer and miniature painter. After Duesbury's death, Kean took over the business and on 29th October 1798, at Quarndon, married Elizabeth, Duesbury's widow, a considerable beauty and mother of three sons and two daughters. Kean continued the business until 1811 when it was sold to ROBERT BLOOR (q.v.) for £5,000. Kean himself had separated from his wife and left Derby for London where he remained for the remainder of his life. Whilst in Derby, Kean was Captain of 6th Company of the Derby Volunteers, whom he supplied with china clay for pipe-claying their accoutrements.

Michael Kean was born in Dublin about 1759 or 1760 son of Michael Kean, later (1765/7) listed as a drawing master of Red Lion Square, London. He was awarded the Society of Arts medal at Dublin in 1779, where he was apprenticed to sculptor Edward Smith. He seems to have returned to London in about 1780 and set up as a miniaturist, living at 20, Southhampton Street., W1, and later at 1190 Picadilly. He exhibited at the Royal Academy 1786-90. He died on 11th November 1823, leaving by his wife a son (b.1800) who was a notable merchant marine Captain who may have been the Michael Kean who, by his wife, Grace, had a child, William, baptised at Bonsall 18th June 1828, but there is no confimation of this. It is notable, however, that Bonsall is where the younger William Duesbury (III) had his unsuccessful colour works at that time; the latter had, as a youth, been Kean's nominal partner in the Derby factory. Kean himself was noted for a mercurial temperament allied to a warm hearted and generous nature.
[Haslem, *op.cit.* 26-28, 145-46; DCR 13/1/1823.]

KEENE, Richard (1825-1894)

Many provincial English towns and cities pro-

duced outstanding topographical photographers in the Victorian age, but Derby's Richard Keene was an exceptional figure not only because his career began early, but because of the quality of his work and his connection with W.H.Fox-Talbot, the original pioneer of English photography. Between 1853 and his death, Keene made an incomparable record of the changing topography of Derby and Derbyshire to the highest technical and compositional standards. He also marketed and sold his work, adding almost all of the UK Counties to his portfolio in time.

Richard Keene was the only son and eldest child of Richard Keene (1794-1863) of Beaconsfield, Bucks, and Bethnal Green (where the younger Richard was born 15th May 1825), the family being of solid yeoman stock from Amersham (Bucks). His mother was Priscilla Kimpton of Hackney, a master weaver's daughter. Keene *père* was a book-keeper who managed a series of fabric mills. In 1828 he came to Derby as manager of Peet & Frost's silk mill (where the Silk Trades' Lock-out later began).

Young Keene was educated in Derby at Thomas Swanwick's academy, then run by his widow, the daughter of RICHARD BASSANO (q.v.), moving to Spencer's academy c.1836, where he met and was befriended by the young HERBERT SPENCER (q.v.).

In 1841 he was apprenticed to Thomas Richardson & Son of Ashbourne, printers, moving to their London offices. In 1844 he began working for Simpkin, Marshall & Co. there to learn publishing and bookselling. He set up as a printer, publisher and bookseller at 24 Iron Gate, Derby (the former residence of JOHN WHITE-HURST, FRS, (q.v.)) in 1851. He broadened the scope of his business, too, running a circulating library, undertaking picture dealing, framing and publishing an almanac.

Here he met J.A.WARWICK (q.v.) and the two of them were befriended by Canon Edward Abney (1811-92), father of SIR WILLIAM ABNEY (q.v.) an enthusiastic amateur photographic pioneer who was a friend of Fox-Talbot, whose wife was a Mundy of Markeaton Hall, close neighbours of the Abneys and sharing the

same sort of background. As the friends' enthusiasm for photography developed from 1852, they travelled much and took early wet plate collodion views of Derby and Derbyshire, which by 1861 Keene was selling at his business as prints or stereoscopic views from an ever-increasing catalogue. In time, this side of the business dominated all else, and Richard Keene & Co. became nationally known for high quality topographical views. He also produced private commissions for firms, estates and families, as well as running a portrait studio. Nevertheless, their chief rival W.W.Winter always had the edge in portraiture. With this friend JOHN DAVIS (q.v.) he also sold photographic equipment and accessories. He acted from time to time as official photographer to the Midland Railway until his protégé Thomas Scotton was appointed in 1882. Another protégé was Abney's son William.

In 1851 Keene married Mary Eleanor Barrow (1825-68) and died at his house in Radbourne Street, Derby on14th December 1894 of a 'paralytic seizure'. They left five sons and three surviving daughters. The business passed to the eldest son Richard (1852-99, also of Burton, where he was succeeded by J.S.Simnett) and the third, Charles Barrow (1859-1937), the latter being eventually sole proprietor and a gifted photographer in whis own right. The second son, William Caxton Keene (1855-1910) was a talented London-based illustrator, and Alfred (1863-1930) was a notable Derby artist, as was his wife, Annie Brailsford (1864-1931). C.B.Keene closed the firm on his retirement, and was grandfather of Cllr. Richard Keene who served as Mayor of Derby 1986-87.

Keene was a founder of the Derby photographic Society (1884) – William Abney was a frequent guest and several times addressed them – and a member of the Photographic Convention of the UK, of which he was president elect at the time of his death. He was noted for his charm and modesty and was greatly liked. His many thousand surviving photographs stand testimony to his ability with the awkward and cumbersome cameras of his day.
[Craven, M., *Richard Keene's Derby* (Derby 1993) 8-32; Birks, J., *Jubilee History of the Derby Photographic Society* (Derby 1934) 1-24; DAJ. VI (1884) 109-56; DM, *obit.*, 19/12/1894.]

KIRTLEY, Matthew (1813-1873)

Matthew Kirtley was the Midland Railway's first locomotive superintendent and had the unenviable task, on appointment in 1844 with the creation of the company, of welding the disparate stock of the three constituent Companies into a coherent whole. He also prevailed upon the Board (and SIR JAMES ALLPORT, q.v.) to move away from buying locomotives and stock from independent producers and build them from scratch at Derby. Justly in this respect, Kirtley can be regarded as the creator of the locomotive building industry in Derby which itself led to the creation of other local foundries, supplying components; it was a notable achievement. Kirtley had also driven, in 1830, the first train on the Liverpool and Manchester Railway (whether he

was responsible for killing poor Mr Huskisson on that occasion is not recorded) and as a driver on the London and Birmingham Railway drove the first train that entered London on that line, in 1839. Hamilton Ellis calls him a 'Rough, jovial, homespun sort of engineer,' which seems to have endeared him to his workforce in Derby, where he lived at 2, Temple Grove, Burton Road.

Matthew Kirtley was born in 1813 the second of three sons of William Kirtley, a coal mine proprietor of Tanfield, Co. Durham, the cradle of railway development. His elder brother Thomas (1810-47) also became an engineer, latterly working on the London, Brighton and South Coast Railway. Thomas' three sons were educated at Derby School which might suggest that after his early death they were brought up by Matthew and trained at Derby; certainly Edwin, the second son was, but he died aged only 19 in 1863. His elder brother Frederick (1842-85) later became senior manager on the Neath and Brecon Railway.

At only 13 Matthew, already a devotee of railways, left home to join the Stockton and Darlington Railway as a driver for over three years. After periods on the Liverpool and Manchester and the London and Birmingham he was, in May 1839, appointed locomotive foreman on the Birmingham and Derby Junction Railway at Hampton-in-Arden becoming the Company's locomotive superintendent in June 1842, enabling him to slip easily into the same position with the Midland on its creation from the B&DJR, Midland Counties and North Midland Railways in 1844.

He continued *en post*, conservatively but consistently improving the stock of the Company until his death in harness 24th May 1873, by which time he was resident at Litchurch Grange. Just before leaving the L&BR he had married Ann (b.1812) daughter of Mr Pelham of Walworth (Surrey) and they had two sons and two daughters. The eldest son was William (1840-1919) of Clapham, Surrey; the younger, Matthew, was apprenticed to his father at Derby 6th November 1857. The daughter Elizabeth was unmarried, but Emily (1845-1909), the younger, married LORD ROE *(q.v.)*.
[Radford, *op.cit.* 45f; Hamilton Ellis, *op.cit.* 8, 40-60; Williamson, *op.cit.* 286-87.]

KNATTRIESS, Albert Henry, see STANLEY, Sir Albert

LEAPER, Ald Richard JP, (1759-1838)

The distinguished amateur architect Richard Leaper was the 3rd son of Alderman William Leaper, (1713-80) born 21st May 1759, and at an early age went into the family bank. He also built up a tanning business and was appointed chief distributor of Government Stamps for Derby. He was elected to the Corporation, becoming an Alderman *c.*1791, and served four times as Mayor of Derby: in 1794, 1807, 1815 and 1824. In 1829 Glover wrote of him: 'He is the oldest magistrate of the Borough, and for his impartiality in the exercise of his magisterial duties, is universally respected by his townsmen.' The same author adds: '(Thornhill) was built by Richard Leaper, Esq. and is now the property of

Mrs Trowell'. Usually when Glover says 'built by' he names the client, but it is clear from a deed in the local collections that the client was the eccentric Col. John Trowell. This is confirmed when Glover adds, later, 'This villa (Highfields) was built under the direction of Richard Leaper, Esquire, a gentleman who has had great taste and much experience in building family mansions, having erected besides this the Pastures House (Littleover) and Thornhill (Derby)'. To this brief *oeuvre* can confidently added by attribution The Leylands, Mill Hill House, Derwent Bank, The Firs (Burton Road), Temple House, Field House (Osmaston Road) and Parkfield (Duffield Road) all built between 1810 and 1827. It is likely that his executant architect was Joseph Cooper for their work shares details in common, including wonderfully *passé* cornice mouldings, and both patronized the iron founders Weatherhead, Glover & Co., Duke Street, Derby for iron decoration. Leaper also designed Wheathills House in 1809 for F.N.C.Mundy of Markeaton.

Leaper left no children, and his heirs were the issue of his eldest brother, John Leaper Newton of Mickleover Manor (1754-1849). He died 18th September 1838, unmarried.
[Glover (1829) II. 602, *603-4; Derby Mercury 19/9/38;* Local Studies Library, Mundy Papers, Parcel 225.]

LEGGE, Phyllis Mary, ARCA, ARMS

Miss Legge is a largely unsung hero of the world of art, for she was a most innovative and accomplished etcher, enameller and water colourist whose work was remarkably popular during the inter-war period and was much reproduced. She worked as art mistress at West Ham School of Art (London) and exhibited frequently at the Royal Academy and much further afield including Detroit (USA) and France.

She was a daughter of Arthur Legge RSBA, also an artist of repute, a watercolour by whom of Breadsall has recently been donated to Derby Museum. He was born in 1860 at Derby, younger son of surgeon William Legge of 45, Friar Gate and educated at Derby School. He later resided at Buckhurst Hill, Essex, where Phyllis grew up, being trained at West Ham Art School (where she later taught) and the Royal College of Art, of which she became an Associate in 1917. She was also elected ARMS, too. She was a notable amateur violinist and lived at 146 Romford Road, Stratford, E15.
[Tachella, *op.cit.,* 84; *Who's Who in Art* (1934) 252.]

LEY, Sir Francis, 1st Bt, KGStJ (1846-1916)

Sir Francis Ley was not only the proprietor of the largest foundry in Derby (and later controller of a nationwide empire of similar concerns) but also the man who introduced (ultimately unsuccessfully, it has to be said) baseball into this country. Both were the result of his foresightedness in travelling to the USA in the late 1870s to study founding there. He brought back the rights to manufacture in the UK the Ewart Chain Belt, which revolutionised some aspects of coal mining, and also an enduring love of baseball. His foundry, Ley's Malleable Castings, set up between the Osmaston Road and the Derby-Birmingham main line in Litchurch in 1874, quickly prospered mightily, boosted by the impetus of the Ewart tie-up. An adjoining 12 acre space he devoted to the recreation of his numerous employees, and part of this he dedicated to his baseball team founded in 1888. A league had come into existence by 1890 and a national association by 1894. By the end of the century, however, enthusiasm had dimmed and the league collapsed, many of its teams concentrating on soccer, including Preston North End. In 1895, however, the Derby County Football Club had migrated to Ley's facility from the Cricket Ground and such lights as STEVE BLOOMER (*q.v.*) also turned out for the Derby baseball team when they won the Association's Cup for the second time in 1897. However, with baseball gone, football continued on the Baseball Ground until

the club moved to Pride Park in August 1997.

Francis Ley, although self-made insofar as he made his own fortune, was of gentry stock having been born in 1846, only son of George Phillips Ley of Winshill (1821-86) by Sarah, daughter of John Potts, a gentleman farmer of Yoxall (Staffordshire). G.P.Ley was ninth in descent from William Ley of Mayfield (Staffordshire), d.1550, at which place the younger branch of the family lived at the Old Hall until 1766, the heiress transmitting the estate to William Greaves. This branch were related to WILLIAM STRUTT *(q.v.)* through the Douglases and to JOSEPH WRIGHT *(q.v.)* through the Brookes family. At the age of 15, young Francis became apprenticed to ANDREW HANDYSIDE *(q.v.)* as a draughtsman, leaving in 1874 to set up his own foundry with family money, his father becoming a partner. After the death of his first wife, Georgina Townsend, daughter of George Willis of Aislaby Hall (Yorks) in December 1886 (they were married in 1870), he consolidated his position in the world of Derby ironfounding by marrying (in 1888) Alison Catherine, one of the daughters of John

Jobson JP, another important foundry proprietor.

Ley's empire was growing so fast that he delegated much of the day-to-day running of his works and lived in Nottinghamshire at Epperstone Manor, where he was JP, DL and High Sheriff in 1905, the year he was raised to a baronetcy as Sir Francis Ley of Epperstone. He was also a Knight Grand Cross of the Venerable Order of St John and died in 1916. By his first wife he had a son and successor Maj. Sir Henry Gordon Ley 2nd Bt. (1874-1944) – whose contemporary successor is Sir Ian Ley, 5th Bt. of Fauld Hall (Staffordshire) – and two daughters, of whom the younger, Ethel Boyd-Carpenter MBE (1873-1953), became aunt of the former Tory minister Lord Boyd-Carpenter. He had two more sons by his second marriage, both tragically killed in action in World War One, unmarried.

[Burke, *Peerage* (1970) 1603; Derby Local Studies Library, *Pocket Book* of R.C.Greaves, Box 57/9; Briscoe, *op.cit.* 93.]

LILLY, Lt. Col. Harold Hutchinson OBE, TD (1888-1954)

Col. Lilly was commanding officer of 1st/5th Bn, Sherwood Foresters from February 1934 to May 1935 and again from May 1939 until November 1945. His long second tenure arose from the unit's capture by the Japanese at Singapore on 29th January 1942. His conduct during the terrible 3½ years during which he and his diminishing number of officers and men worked virtually as slaves on the construction of the Thailand Burma Railway at Wampo (and previously in Changi gaol) was exemplary in the extreme. He had charge of 1,500 PoWs and during the period 450 officers and men died from brutality, starvation and disease, and his own health was irreparably compromised. He continuously looked to the welfare of those under him, often risking the wrath of their Japanese guards. He intervened more than once to save the life of a PoW about to be executed and he was assiduous in the welfare of members of other units as he was of his own men. On his liberation he stayed in command until November 1945 receiving the OBE in recognition of his services.

Harold Hutchinson Lilly was born at Spondon in 1888, son of Maj. Oliver Morgan Lilly of The Croft, Church Street, a Derby manufacturer. He had a brother, Charles, who died in his twenties. He was commissioned into the army on 27th February 1915 and saw action on The Somme the following year. He busied himself after the war in the family business and died unmarried at Spondon in October 1954, having been made TD for his services in the Territorials during the preceding period.

[Derby Museum, regimental notes.]

LINACRE, Rev. Dr Thomas (c. 1460-1524)

Thomas Linacre was perhaps the most eminent physician of the early Tudor period, qualifying at Oxford before travelling on the continent, studying the latest techniques and spending some time in Florence and Rome. The Duke of Tuscany was a prominent patron, terming him 'the politest scholar of the Age'. He was also a friend of John Collet and Erasmus, which, Hutton perhaps rashly observes, 'proves him to have been a theologist'.

He eventually returned to England, residing in Knight Rider Street, later erecting the first College of Physicians in his grounds there, a building unfortunately destroyed in the Great Fire. He became physician-in-ordinary to Henry VII, Henry VIII and the future Edward VI and Mary I; he was also physician and tutor to the unfortunate Prince Arthur. This, and his fashionable practise, made him very wealthy, but it was wealth he put to good philanthropic use, also founding two public lectureships at Oxford and one at Cambridge. He also established a charity at Derby. Hutton adds, 'This ornament of human nature, out of mere love for his species, rescued the Medical Art from the bold empiric and the illiterate monk.'

Linacre was born in Derby c.1460, the younger son of John Linacre of Brampton and Derby, himself a younger son of John Linacre of

Linacre Hall in Brampton, 11th in descent from Edmund Linacre of Linacre, living c.1100. His elder brother, John, continued the life of a Squire on the small family estate. Late in life Dr Linacre was ordained a priest, and attempted to heal souls after a lifetime of healing bodies. He died in 1524 unmarried, and was buried in St Paul's.

[Hutton, op.cit. 179-80; Lysons, op.cit. V. 110-111; Jeayes (1906) 2564.]

LIGHTBOWN, Sir David, MP (1932-1995)

Sir David Lightbown was Conservative MP for Staffordshire SE from 1983 to 1995, assistant government Chief Whip from 1986 and Lord Commissioner of HM Treasury from the year following. He had very properly relinquished the post of engineering director of West Midlands PLC on being elected, and was an extremely well-liked and hardworking member.

David Lincoln Lightbown was born at Normanton-by-Derby 30th November 1932, only son of L.Lincoln Lightbown of 15, Offerton Avenue, Normanton. The family were not at all well off and after a local education he made his way in engineering by his own efforts. He also had two sisters, Mrs George Green and Mrs John Jones, and a number of other relatives in Derby.

He was elected a Councillor on the District Council at Lichfield (where he lived) in 1987 and was a Staffordshire County Councillor 1976-84. He was knighted in 1994 and died in December 1995, unmarried.

[Debrett's *Distinguished People of Today* (1990) 1107; *Times Guide To The House of Commons* (1984) 210; *Daily Telegraph* 13/3/1996.]

LITHERLAND, William (1803-1883)

William Litherland was born at Leicester in 1803 of Lancastrian stock and after many years as a china retailer in Liverpool he co-founded the Royal Crown Derby Porcelain Factory at Derby in 1875 with EDWARD PHILLIPS (q.v.).

Also involved were the younger WILLIAM BEMROSE (q.v.), a great connoisseur of china, John MacInnes and Litherland's able nephew

Henry (1851-1925), son of William's brother Thomas, an Ashby (Leics) china retailer who became a shareholder as well as an important outlet for the new factory's products. Litherland's business ability, combined with his understanding of the china trade helped make the firm the success it has been ever since. He served as Chairman of the Company 1878-83, but died in April 1883 without issue; his heir was Henry, a director from 1880, who became joint managing director with MacInnes' son, Edward, a post they shared with significant success until their retirement in August 1924. Henry died 9th September 1925 at Fairfield, Burton Road, leaving a son, Capt. William Bradshaw Litherland, an RCD director and two daughters. Henry's sister, Mary Elizabeth, further cemented the Derby Company's founding alliance by marrying Bemrose's son W.W.Bemrose in 1889.

[Gibson, Hon H., *A Case of Fine China* (Derby 1993) 15-76.]

LLOYD, Kevin Reardon (1949-1998)

Kevin Lloyd was an actor, mainly specializing in television, who acquired much celebrity as a character called Alfred ('Tosh') Lines in ITVs long-running saga called *The Bill*. The programme itself was intended as a weekly policier to fill a prime-time slot, but after a short time its quirky individuality earned it a considerable following, and it was turned, to all intents and purposes, into a 'soap'. Lloyd's character, rarely out of his light coloured Macintosh – hence, presumably, the soubriquet – was ubiquitous, endearing and apt, and it earned him an enormous following, especially in his native city, where he was persuaded to involve himself with a large number of charities and voluntary activities. Lloyd had been in The Bill for almost ten years at the time of his summary dismissal for alcoholism in late April 1998. He refused to countenance living in London, and the pressure of work, voluntary activities and constant long-distance commuting seem to have led to his affliction, as a result of which he died on 2nd May, 1998.

Kevin Reardon Lloyd was of Welsh stock, but was born in Alvaston 28th March, 1949, elder son of Sgt. Aled Ellis (Taft) Lloyd, Derby Borough Constabulary, who was tragically killed in a car crash en route to answering a bogus 999 call, and his wife Agnes. The grandfather was also a policeman, in the RIC, but was killed by the IRA in The Troubles of the early 1920s. Kevin Lloyd was educated at Wyndham Street Junior School and at Bemrose School before being articled to one of the partners of Messrs. Taylor, Simpson & Mosley, solicitors, of St Mary's Gate; a career in the legal profession beckoned. However, he soon resolved to become an actor and went on to train at East 15 School of Drama, London, making his debut in *The Importance of Being Earnest* in 1973. The same year he appeared in *What the Butler Saw* (where he met his wife) thereafter working with the Royal Shakespeare Company and at the Bristol Old Vic, combining this with appearances in *Z Cars*, *Coronation Street*, *Auf Wiedersehen Pet* and *Minder* on TV. He subsequently made over 400 appearances in *The Bill*.

He married in 1973, Lesley, daughter of Bernard Upson, and they lived at Stockbrook

House, Duffield, where they had four sons: Mark, James, Henry and Edward, and three daughters, of whom the eldest, Sophie, and youngest, Poppy, survive. In September 1991 they also adopted a Rumanian orphan, Eleanora Rahela Varga, Rumania being one of Kevin Lloyd's 'causes'. Lloyd parted from his wife in 1996, setting up in Ashbourne with Rita Hudson. His brother, Terry, of Cuddington, Bucks, has worked as an ITN war correspondent, and by his wife Lynne has a son, Oliver, and a daughter, Chelsey. Kevin Lloyd is unique amongst those chronicled in these pages in having been the subject of the television programme *This is Your Life*, in March, 1992.

(Derby Evening Telegraph 13/3/1989;2714/ 1996; 4 & 8/5198; Derby Express, 10/10/1991; 5/3/92;7/4 & 4/5/98; Derbyshire Now! 4/92 34-36)

LOATES, Thomas (1867-1909)

Tom Loates was one of three brothers who were all highly-successful jockeys. One, Charles, seems never to have won a classic but the other, Sam, won seven between 1884 and 1900 and was champion jockey with 160 winners in 1899, including the 1884 and 1885 Derbys, the former with a dramatic dead heat on Harvester and the latter on Sir Visto. Tom was probably the most celebrated of the three, riding for most of his career for the Duke of Portland. In 1889 he won the Derby on Donovan, repeating the achievement in 1893 on Isinglass, on which he won the St Leger the same year – his best, in fact, for he came home on Isinglass in the 2,000 Guineas as well – a classic he also won three years later on St Frusquin. Also in 1893 he won the 1,000 Guineas on Siffleuse.

Tom Loates was the seventh child and third son of Archibald Loates (b.1822), sometime landlord of the Oddfellows' Arms, King Street who, on 26th July 1845 married at St Werburgh's, Louisa, daughter of Samuel Cooper, a labourer. Archibald, named after his grandfather – also a labourer – was the third son of Charles Loates of York Street, a shoemaker. Tom was born on 6th October 1867, Samuel two years before and Charles, who was one of the first jockeys in the UK to adopt the US style of riding – short leathers, forward seat, etc. – was the youngest. Their nephew, Sam Heapy (son of Samuel Job Heapy, a Midland Railway telegraph clerk who had married the brothers' sister Sarah Ann in 1875) was also a jockey, going on to become the premier jockey and later a trainer in Belgium.

Tom rode his first winner in 1883 when attached to Joseph Cannon's stable, then weighing a remarkable four stone. He was champion jockey with 167 winners in 1889 and a year later with 147 wins but, with Sam, he was refused a licence by the Jockey Club in the following season. In 1893, however, he came back as champion with 222 victories, the highest total since Fred Archer. Of the three, only Charles married and had issue – two children, Charles Archibald and Mabel – Sam dying in 1932 and Tom at Brighton on 28th September 1909, both unmarried. Sam left £74,000, the highest of any of his profession up to that time. As a group, 1885 was the memorable year: all three finished in the Derby – Sam winning, Charles 7th on Chibiadus and Tom 10th on Raconteur.

[Local records; DET 4/6/1980; family members.]

LOMBE, John (c.1693-1722)

Half brother of SIR THOMAS LOMBE (q.v.) John Lombe was the pro-active partner in the founding of the Derby silk mill. He was born at Norwich, probably in 1693, son of Henry Lombe and his second wife, a Miss Wilmot, possibly a Derby woman. He was probably apprenticed to Sir Thomas Lombe, who subsequently encouraged him to visit Italy and make himself familiar with the processes of silk throwing. He was described as 'One whose head is extremely well turned for the mechanics.' Hutton added that he was 'a man of spirit, a good draughts-man and an excellent mechanic.' John returned from Italy with at least two workmen to assist in setting up the new factory, which was brilliantly engineered by GEORGE SOROCOLD (q.v.) who oversaw the erection of much of the machinery in the Moot Hall, where it was tested, to plans sent in advance before Lombe had even returned in 1717, before being installed later in the new building.

Unfortunately, the Piedmontese were so

England, his half brother JOHN *(q.v.)* acting as his agent. He was the eldest son of Henry Lombe, a Norwich worsted weaver and was born there 5th September 1685, being, with his brother, orphaned in 1695. The family was an old Norfolk one, for long involved with the cloth trade. In the early part of Queen Anne's reign Lombe was in London, apprenticed to Samuel Totton, a mercer, gained his Freedom of the City, and eventually became established as a merchant. In 1718 he obtained a patent for the silk machinery his brother was covertly copying in Italy, although he took pains to obfuscate the details in order to hinder potential imitators once the patent ran out. Ironically, the process had already been published, as early as 1607 at Padua, by V.Zonca, a copy of whose treatise was in Oxford's Bodleian Library all the time – unbeknown to the Lombes or, it seems, anyone else!

The Derby Mill was begun from as early as 1715 on an island on the west side of the Derwent adjacent to a previous, unsuccessful, silk mill built about 1702 by Thomas Cotchett, a retired Mickleover attorney. It was completed in 1719 and eventually became a prosperous concern. It was taken over by several owners, rebuilt after a fire in 1826 and in 1890 the southern element, the Doubling Shop collapsed. The remainder was extensively re-constructed after a fire in 1910, two years after silk production had given way to the business of F.W.HAMPSHIRE *(q.v.)*. It now contains Derby's Industrial Museum, opened in 1974, under a lease from the electricity undertaking which expires in 2006.

Lombe's patent expired in 1732, but he was given a £14,000 lump sum in compensation by Parliament rather than an extension, although he had made more than £80,000 from the enterprise by that date, a figure he mendaciously witheld. A condition of his original patent was that models of his machines were to be deposited in a public place.

Lombe was an Alderman of Bassishaw Ward, London (unlike his brother, he eschewed living in Derby) and was Sheriff in 1727, being knighted on 8th July that year, when he attended court to present a congratulatory address from

enraged by John's success in stealing their processes that they despatched a woman to Derby to gain his confidence and administer a slow poison which finally killed him on 16th November 1722. His funeral at All Saints' was held in great pomp, thousands of people attending, and he was buried in a mausoleum erected at the south end of an island in the Derwent opposite his house by the Silk Mill, which he had previously landscaped with topiary. Unfortunately it was largely washed away in a flood before the end of the century.

Lombe's share of the Mill passed to his cousin William, who was, it seems, a depressive and shot himself, Sir Thomas then inheriting his share. Lombe was unmarried.

[Hutton, W., *History of Derby* (1791) 196, and see below.]

LOMBE, Sir Thomas (1685-1739)

Sir Thomas Lombe was the prime mover of the introduction of silk throwing machinery into the City to George II, on his accession. He married Elizabeth Turner and had two daughters, Hannah and Mary Turner Lombe. He died 3rd February 1739 at his home in Devonshire Square, London leaving a fortune estimated at £120,000. His widow died 18th November 1753. Mary Turner married on 24th April 1749 James Maitland, Earl of Lauderdale and Hannah married in 1740 Sir Robert Clifton Bt, MP for East Retford.

[New DNB; Hutton *loc.cit.*; *Gentleman's Magazine* IX (1739) 47; Defoe, D., *op.cit.* III. 38.]

LONGLAND, Sir Jack (1905-1993)

A most notable former Director of Education for Derbyshire, Sir Jack Longland was also an influential government advisor on educational and other matters and had an international reputation as an alpinst and mountaineer, serving as President of the Alpine Club 1974-76, of the British Mountaineering Council and of the Cambridge University Mountaineering Club. He also wrote numerous articles on mountaineering for a number of books and journals. He had joined Cambridge University Mountaineering Club as an undergraduate (at Jesus College) in his second year, 1925, combining this with excelling at a variety of other sports (he was later four times regional champion at pole vault). He later said that as "these traditional games began to recede into the background as I got older... mountains became more important." The crowning moment of his career was his inclusion in the 1933 Everest expedition, when he was one of the party which successfully reached the North Col at 27,000 feet. Needless to say, as Derbyshire Education Director, he founded the mountain training centre at White Hall north of Buxton and the youth training centre at Lea Green. In the early 1960s the Robbins Report re-fired thoughts about the establishment of a university in Derbyshire; Longland thought that it was worth trying to get one established, but doubted whether Derbyshire had a claim, being already surrounded by Leicester, Manchester, Sheffield and Nottingham Universities; 30 years later he

was to see one established the year before his death on 4th December 1993.

John Laurence Longland was born on 26th June 1905, son of Rev. Ernest Henry Longland of Cambridge (d.1956) and Emily Rose, youngest daughter of Sir James Henry Clifden Crockett, of Dallingham Lodge, Northamptonshire, and educated at King's School, Worcester before proceeding to Cambridge. On graduation he spent two years at Magdalene and a year at the University of Königsberg before becoming a lecturer at the University of Durham. Whilst there he met and in 1934 married Margaret Lowrey daughter of Arthur Harrison of Durham, an organ builder, (and granddaughter of an Archdeacon of Northumberland), by whom he had two sons and two daughters.

From 1940 to 1942 Longland was Deputy Education Officer for Hertfordshire, moving to Dorset thereafter for nearly seven years as Co-education Officer before being appointed to Derbyshire in the latter year, serving until 1970. During this time (1966-69) he served with distinction on the Royal Commission on Local Government, and from 1970 to 1974 was Vice-

Chairman of the Sports Council. He was knighted in 1970. He was also a distinguished and influential broadcaster, having been first interviewed on the wireless on his return from Everest in 1933. He was a man blessed with an easy manner, a quick wit and a 'voice that serves well his extraordinary command of words'.
[*Who's Who* (1978) 1491; DLC 7/1964; *Daily Telegraph* obit. 7/12/1993.]

LUCE, Maj. Gen. Sir Richard, KCMG, CB, FRCS, FSA (1867-1952)

Richard Luce was not originally a Derby man. He came from Wiltshire, son of Col. Charles Luce of Haccombe, Wilts, by Mary, daughter of H. Visger and his ancestry included many who rose to high rank in the Army or Navy. Educated at Clifton College and Christ's College, Cambridge, where he took a first in the Natural Science Tripos, he trained as a surgeon to 1893 at Guy's Hospital. His first appointment outside Guy's was at York, and it was an early marriage that obliged him to seek a more substantial appointment which he found in Derby. It was, in fact, a partnership in a 'club' practise for working class patients (who valued him highly, apparently) but this led concurrently to surgical work at the then newly opened Royal Infirmary. In addition, he held appointments at Ripley and Wirksworth cottage hospitals and the Derby Children's Hospital.

It is not surprising that, in view of his military antecedents, Richard Luce became active in the Territorial Army and in due time became a very distinguished part-time soldier, receiving the Volunteer Decoration.

When World War One broke out he joined the RAMC, fought at Gallipoli, and in 1917 was nominated Director of Medical Services in the Middle East, promoted to Major-General. As a result of all this he was created successively, Commander of the Bath, Commander of the Order of St Michael and St George, and finally in 1919, Knight Commander of that same Order.

After the war he returned to his medical work in Derby but this time as a private consultant at

his house at 42 Friar Gate, which his father had purchased for him on his marriage in 1897, and which he occupied until 1925.

Luce was modest man and a popular figure in social and political circles in the town. Shortly before the 1924 General Election, one of the two prospective Conservative candidates resigned, and at the last minute Luce, never a particularly political man, accepted the invitation to stand in his place.

At that time Derby was a two-member Borough Constituency and the result of the election was most interesting. J.H.THOMAS *(q.v.)* retained his seat for Labour but Sir Richard Luce pushed the other Labour candidate, ALD. W.R.RAYNES *(q.v.)*, into third place, though by fewer than 300 votes, while his fellow Conservative, Mrs Hulse, finished fourth. There can be no doubt that Sir Richard's reputation both as a soldier and a surgeon, and perhaps most particularly, his long practise among the working men of Derby and their families did much to earn him his seat in the House of Commons.

So, not far off his sixtieth year, Sir Richard Luce added to his other professions of scholar, surgeon and soldier, that of the politician. But he was never to be promoted to office; he was, in fact, the perfect constituency MP, assiduous in dealing with problems of the people of Derby.

In 1929, Will Raynes took his revenge and wrested the seat from Sir Richard with 12,000 votes to spare. Shortly afterwards Sir Richard retired to Romsey where he took an active part in the life of the town, becoming Mayor in 1935-36. In his retirement he wrote two scholarly works: one on the Benedictine Monastery at Malmesbury, the town of his birth, and the other, on the history of Romsey and its Abbey, where he was eventually laid to rest on 22nd February 1952 at the age of 85.

Sir Richard Luce's great-nephew, also a Richard, – grandson of Luce's elder brother Adml. John Luce (1870-1932) and then Minister of the Arts – came to Derby in 1989 visiting Pickford's House museum and the house next door where his great uncle lived and practised for nearly 30 years. In 1991, he too was knighted, so becoming the second Sir Richard Luce to sit in the House of Commons.

[Derby Civic Society *Newsletter* No. 61 (Spring 1992); *Times* 23/2/1952; DA 1/2/1929; Craven (1987) 71.]

MAC DERMOTT, Lt. Col. Niall, CBE, QC (1915-1996)

Niall Mac Dermott, who died in February 1996 aged 79, was from 1962 to 1970 Labour MP for Derby North. He had previously sat from 1957 to 1959 for Lewisham North (where he was defeated by Chris Chataway) and the sudden death of Gp. Capt. WILCOCK *(q.v.)*, who had been elected with LORD NÖEL-BAKER *(q.v.)* in the Labour land-slide of 1945, afforded him an opportunity to return to the House. However, his Parliamentary career came suddenly to an end in 1970 with his resignation to take up the general secretaryship of the International Commission of Jurists. By the time he retired in 1990 he had been decorated by

several foreign governments as well as receiving a well-deserved CBE the following year for services to International Justice.

It was undoubtedly Mac Dermott's absolute commitment to justice, human rights and the role of law which had drawn him towards the Labour party which he joined in 1956. Yet in himself and his career he embodied much that the 'Old' Labour of those days held in greatest contempt: he was an aristocrat, the product of an

élite education, and a former senior intelligence officer. The latter arose from War Service in the Intelligence Corps (in which he rose to Lieutenant Colonel) some of his time being actively engaged in espionage, latterly as a GSO l i/c counter intelligence, 21 Army Group, from the Normandy Beaches to Hamburg. Latterly he used his forensic skills (for he was a barrister who went on to take silk in 1963) to track down and interrogate senior Nazis, including Goebbels. For this work he was gazetted OBE (Military).

His family background was extremely distin-guished, and in the context of his chosen politi-cal creed, had much to commend it. His father, Henry, a Dublin barrister, was the lapsed third son of the Catholic Hugh Hyacinth O'Rorke Mac Dermott, The Mac Dermott (ie Clan

Chief), Prince of Coolavin and Moylurgh PC, QC, DL, JP, who served as Irish Attorney General from 1892. The family seat is Coolavin, Monasteraden Co. Sligo, and The Mac Dermott was (and his successor is) descended in the male line from Murrynach Mullathan a 7th century King of Connaught. His descendant Maolrona Mòr was 1st Prince of Moylurgh and Coolavin in the later 10th century, and although the family lands were reduced from a principality to an estate under the hateful Cromwell and extinguished altogether by William III, Coolavin was re-purchased by the family after the Catholic Emancipation Act had made such a move possible. Indeed the Mac Dermotts were one of the few mediatized Irish Princely families not to join the Flight of the Wild Geese, and furthermore, the MP's great-great-grandfather was one of the leading lights of the United Irishmen in the 18th century.

Niall Mac Dermott was born in 1915 and educated at Rugby; thereafter he followed reading modern languages at Corpus Christi (Cambridge) and law at Balliol (Oxford). He went on to marry, in 1940, Violet Maxwell, a member of another old Irish family, in this case an Ascendancy one. However, despite the birth of their son, John, they divorced in 1965. This was due to his long *affaire* with a Soviet-Italian language student, Ludmila Benevento, whom he married in 1966 when he was Harold Wilson's First Secretary to the Treasury. Unfortunately, although Mac Dermott had warned Wilson about these events (and had been given no reason to fear any repercussions), MI5 took a different view, and for a week interrogated the hapless Mrs Mac Dermott. The result was that MI5 was not happy with her, and Wilson, ever paranoid over intelligence matters, changed his tune in 1967, whereupon Mac Dermott, by now Minister of Planning, felt in an exceedingly equivocal position and resigned his ministry; it was only with great difficulty that he was persuaded not to resign Derby North prematurely and force a bye-election at a time of electoral unpopularity as well.

He thereafter became (from 1972-74) Recorder of Newark and from 1973 to 1986

Chairman of the Geneva Special Committee for Human Rights. He was an exceptionally competent advocate, his patrician manner being allied to a quicksilver intelligence and a Circeronian belief in moving those whom he addressed instead of combatting them. His commitment to Justice in the wider sense made him a concientious MP as well as the most distinguished Irishman – in all senses – ever connected with Derby.

[Derby Civic Society *Newsletter* 69 (Summer 1996); Burke's *Irish Family Records* (1976) 755-7.]

MADELEY, Rev. Edward (1778-1827)

Edward Madeley was a Swedenborgian pastor who built up the reputation and congregation of the New Jerusalem Chapel, London Road. Almost as soon as it had been built in 1802 however, a breakaway faction started a rival congregation in King Street, but the town was hardly ready for two groups of such a radical sect. Madeley took over in 1819 and by his death 25th November 1827 had re-united the congregation at the same time instilling a spirituality which had previously lapsed somewhat.

Edward Madeley was the third and youngest son of Thomas Madeley of Yoxall (Staffordshire), farmer, by Elizabeth Shipton. The family were previously 200 years at Doveridge and were a younger branch of the Tudor Madeleys of Denstone Hall (Staffordshire). James, the eldest brother, continued the family farm, but the next brother, Thomas set up as a silk manufacturer in Cavendish Street, Derby later at Little City, where he built some of the worst artisans' housing in the Borough for his workers. He was a founder of the New Jerusalem Church in 1802. Edward, born 1778 at Yoxall, was apprenticed to the silk trade and from around 1800 worked in Derby at Dawes's tape mill. It was partly the grinding social conditions of some of his brother's workforce that persuaded him to become a pastor and he was ordained 12th August 1818. A fine terracotta bust of him in the style of George Cocker is still in the New Church, Littleover.

Madeley died at his house on Burton Road.

By his wife, Sarah, he had three sons, of whom one was Ald. Thomas Madeley (1804-72) who eventually inherited his uncle's silk mills and was Mayor of Derby (1853-54). Another, also Edward (1828-54), was a prominent Swedenborgian minister as well; a daughter married a son of Edward Clulow, the Derby railway stationer.

[*Modern Mayors of Derby* 1. (1909) 12; Printed pamphlets at the New Church Library, Littleover; Tachella, *op.cit.*; Yoxall and Doveridge Parish Registers; Hunter, J., *FMG.* III, 1021.]

MANSFIELD, Isaac (c.1670-1740)

Mansfield was a *stuccadore* – an ornamental plaster worker – of national reputation; he was the architect James Gibbs' favourite English-born craftsman in this sphere, and his surviving work has a crispness and verve to it which is not always apparent in contemporary work of this kind. Amongst his commissions were ornamental plasterwork at Houghton (Norfolk), Castle Howard (Yorks, 1710), St George's, Hanover Square (London, 1712-24), St John's, Westminster (1714-38), St George, Bloomsbury (1720-30), Burlington House, Picadilly (1720-21), Chicheley Hall (Bucks, 1721), Langleys (Essex, 1721), Christchurch, Spitalfields (1723-29), Goodwood (Sussex, 1725), Blenheim (Oxon, 1725), the Senate House, Cambridge (1725), Claremont (Surrey, 1730) and Kew (Surrey, 1730). Amongst the architects who commissioned him, apart from Gibbs, were Lord Burlington, Francis Smith of Warwick, Vanburgh, Hawksmoor, Thomas Archer and William Kent.

He lived alternately in London (Henrietta Street, close, to Gibbs's house) and York, being made a freeman of the latter – possibly through the good offices of Lord Burlington – on 4th October 1704. He was successful enough to be chosen Sheriff of York 1728-29. He was the only son of another fine *stuccadore* Samuel Mansfield of Derby (1633-98) who was a partner of Richard Huss (whose brother Henry was an architect closely associated with some of the projects of GEORGE SOROCOLD (*q.v.*) including designs for the Silk Mill) and who worked at Sudbury Hall (1672-75) and Chatsworth (1694). His will (dated 8/10/1697) cuts Isaac off with a shilling but leaves 'cottages near to St Mary's Gate' to his wife Hannah (née Towle) and six daughters. Samuel was the great-grandson of Edward Mansfield of Derby (d.1593).

Isaac was born about 1670 and was probably apprenticed to his father, working by 1697. He died, bankrupt, in London 4th January 1740, when his obituary described him as 'plaisterer… to his Majesties Palaces and likewise plaisterer to HRH the Prince of Wales.' He left a son Isaac.

[Beard, G., *Craftsmen and Interior Decoration in England 1660-1820* (London, 2nd edition 1986) 141, 172, 270. *Daily Post* 4/1/1740; Derby registers.]

MANSFIELD, Richard (1857-1907)

Richard Mansfield was an extremely accomplished actor who later turned author and impresario, promoting plays, operettas and performances all over Europe and a great deal in America, latterly being domiciled in New York the better able to promote shows over there.

Mansfield was the eldest son of William Mansfield, a Derby wine merchant who later went to London. Himself an amateur musician and theatre enthusiast, he married an international diva, Erminia Rüdersdorff of Berlin. It was in Heligoland that Richard was born 24th May 1857 but he was brought up with his mother in Berlin, his father having died in 1861 when he was four. Until he was 12 he travelled the world with her, greedily imbibing the life. In January 1869, however, he was sent to Derby School, being joined by his brother Henry in the September. He left in 1872, studied for the Indian Civil Service, then went to art school, thereafter devoting himself to acting, drawing large houses when he returned to Derby 10th December 1888 to play at the Grand Theatre. He led his own company specialising in Comic Opera and Shakespeare. He died in New York 30th August 1907, leaving a wife, Beatrice Cameron, an exleading lady. His brother Henry was an equally talented musician who studied in Italy, and made his career in Germany.

[Tachella, *op.cit.* 34, 77, 78; *Who Was Who* (1897-1915) 345-46; *Who Was Who in America,* 1. 774.]

MASON, John (1794-1847)

A carpenter (later architect) and a junior member of the dynasty which produced a famous Derby paint-making concern, he was the only son of John Mason (1771-1832), being baptized at St Peters 30th March 1794. Somewhere around 1828 he built London Terrace, an elegant row of five three storey residences on London Road, having previously served as a clerk of works to Francis Goodwin at the County Gaol (1826-27) and under Habershon at the Guildhall (1828), both at Derby. At the fomer he designed and added bastions following the 1831 Reform Riot. Mason's great grandmother was a great aunt of KIRK BOOTT *(q.v.)* the elder.

In 1836 he designed the Liversage Almshouses, also on London Road, in Jacobethan style, and it was in the same year that he was appointed Surveyor of Bridges for the southern half of Derbyshire, in which capacity he served up to his death almost 11 years later. In 1838 he built Christ Church, Hulland and a year later, Holy Trinity, Tansley. Another church was the rebuilding of the medieval St Mary the Virgin, Boulton (1840). He also built three houses in Green Lane, the church at Appleby Magna (Leics), the Union Workhouse, Osmaston Road (1839) and was in charge of the culverting of Markeaton Brook at Derby to form Victoria Street (1837-38 at a cost of £1,400). He died at Littleover in 1847.

[Pevsner, 293 and n. 339; Glover (1829) II.469, 479, 608; Quarter Sessions Records; DM.30/1/1828; 17/4/1839; 22/3 & 5/7/1839; 22/3 & 5/7/1843; 4/12/1844.]

MAWE, John (1766-1829)

John Mawe was a minerologist, geologist and traveller whose reputation, like that of JOHN WHITEHURST FRS *(q.v.),* is much neglected despite his importance. As a traveller, especially in Brazil, he gave an eye-witness account of life and topography in South America when it was hardly known in Europe outside Portugal; as a mineral dealer he made much diverse and obscure material available for study by himself and chiefly by others. He was also a confident carver.

Mawe was born in Iron Gate, Derby, in 1766 younger son of Samuel Mawe (1735-83) a baker, both in Queen Street and at Stanley, a few miles away. His grandfather, John, was a dissenter and button maker who died in 1763. His mother was Elizabeth Massey of Leeds, who married his father at All Saints' on 25th May 1759: in the register the witness is JOHN WHITEHURST *(q.v.)* and the entry is preceded by that of George Whitehurst, the philosopher's brother and followed by that of RICHARD BROWN *(q.v.),* which sequence encapsulates his social circle impressively. Elizabeth died in 1776 and Samuel remarried Fawnia Beighton (d.1822). From about 1777 or '78 to 1793 Mawe became a merchant marine officer and it could well be that youthful acquaintance with Whitehurst and Brown combined with visits to many exotic corners of the globe fostered his own interests in minerals and natural history. He was certainly collecting minerals before he left the sea in 1793 to become a partner with Richard Brown, forming the firm of Brown & Son and Mawe of Derby and London, Mawe seeing to the London end, including the showroom shared until 1798 with WILLIAM DUESBURY II *(q.v.).* To cement the arrangement he married, at St Pauls', Covent Garden 1st November 1794, Sarah (1767-1846) Brown's elder daughter.

Mawe dealt with a rich variety of clients, eventually coming into contact with the Spanish Royal Family (then in exile), and had already connections in a number of European capitals. In 1800 he had toured Scotland seeking specimens for sale and in 1802 published *The Mineralogy of Derbyshire* in which we learn that, when not in London he resided at Castleton. The same year he went to France and in 1804 set off for South America, leading to his publishing *Travels in Brazil* (1812); he wrote five other books 1813-25. He died in 1829 and there is an elegant monument to him at Castleton Church. He left a daughter Sarah Anne, who married Tatlow Tissington, grandson of ANTHONY TISSINGTON FRS *(q.v.)*. A John Mawe who in 1832 married at St Alkmund's, Derby Mary, daughter of Richard Brown (IV) could be an otherwise unattested son, or a grandson of Mawe's elder brother Samuel, who had continued his father's trade as a baker.

[DNB; Torrens, H., *John Mawe* (Keele 1990); Britton, J. & Brayley, E.W., *The Beauties' of England and Wales'* (1802) III.]

MESSERVY, Sir Godfrey (1924-1995)

Godfrey Messervy was chairman and chief executive of the motor component manufacturers Lucas Industries. He was a hard-working practical engineer who placed much emphasis on long term product development and in doing so, secured his 120-year-old company's future, modernising it thoroughly in the process.

Sir Roney Godfrey Collumbell Messervy was born in Derby 17th November 1924, his father, Roney Forshaw Messervy – a garage proprietor's son – being an engineer at Rolls Royce. His mother, Bertha Crosby Collumbell, belonged to an old dynasty of Derby tailors, ultimately descended from a cadet branch of the Columbells (sic) an ancient gentry family of Darley Dale.

Messervy went to Oundle and in 1943 enlisted in the Royal Engineers, obtaining a commission the following year. Thereupon he joined 1st Airbourne Division, after Arnhem taking part in the liberation of Norway and then serving in Palestine in 1947. Thereafter he went to Cambridge, joining Lucas in 1949, becoming general manager 20 years later. He joined the Board in 1971 and was executive Chairman 1980-87. He was also Chairman of Costains and Asda, President of the Society of Motor Manufacturers and Traders, The Birmingham Chamber of Commerce and was Vice-President of the Engineering Employers Federation. He

was knighted in 1986 and later retired to farm in Warwickshire. In 1952 he married Susan Patricia Gertrude, daughter of Reginald Arthur Nunn, DSO, DSC, RNVR, and died in August 1995 leaving a son and two daughters.

[Debrett, *op.cit.* (1990) 1257; *Daily Telegraph* 8/1995.]

MONEYPENNY, George (1738-1807)

George Moneypenny was a highly accomplished carver and sculptor who first appears in Derby in 1766 when his daughter Anne was baptised at St Werburgh's Church (she later married, in 1805, Edward Hollingshead of St Peter's Parish). His elder son William's birth is not registered in Derby, suggesting that his father was previously working elsewhere. Moneypenny's presence was owed either to his having met JOSEPH PICKFORD *(q.v.)* whilst the latter was still working for his uncle Joseph in London prior to 1760, coming to Derby with him as carver, or to his having been recruited by Robert Adam to work at Kedleston. Certainly he was at work there later carving the *paterae* on the boathouse, and subsequently worked under Pickford there 1776-82.

In either case, from *c.*1766 he and Pickford seem to have worked in tandem, probably at St Helen's House, Derby (1767), Wirksworth Moot Hall (1772), Ashford Hall (*c.*1776) and the Edensor Inn (1779-81). He was in charge of the sale of Pickford's stock on Nuns' Green after the architect's death in 1782 and thereafter seems to have carved fireplaces for others, eg. for Thomas Gardner, for Samuel Wyatt at Egginton (1782) and funerary monuments on his own account for many of Pickford's contemporaries in a very refined neo-classical style, many sporting urns with snake handles first seen on the entrance frieze at Ashford Hall.

The recently discovered original drawing of Joseph Wright's monument, at St Alkmunds, Derby (1797), is a classic, doubtless in his own hand. Moneypenny was also an artist and an engraver, illustrating the *History of Derby* by WILLIAM HUTTON *(q.v.,* 1791) with 17 plates, an east prospect and a map, although it has to be said that engraving was evidently not his forte. His wife Mary died in August 1803 and he died 25 November 1807, leaving two sons and a daughter. The younger son, George, was born in 1768 and trained as an architect after an apprenticeship to his father, possibly with Joseph Bonomi (1739-1808), with whom he was certainly associated in 1793. No Derby buildings by him have yet been identified, but his first known project was Leicester Gaol (1790-92), into which, ironically, he was thrown for debt, having run into financial difficulties as a result of working on it! He later practised in London, dying in 1830.

[Saunders, E.J., *Joseph Pickford of Derby,* (Stroud 1993) 71, 122, 128-29, 140, 147-59, 173-74; Colvin, *op.cit,* 660-61; DM. & 26/11/1807.]

MOORE, Henry (1776-1848)

Henry Moore was a largely unrecognised but extremely competent topographical painter, engraver and etcher, author of local guide books from 1818 and the inventor of a process of engraving onto black marble, for which he received a silver medal from the Society of Arts. His painting of *Derby From Little Chester* (1802) is a classic and was much copied by chinapainters and engravers.

Moore was baptised at St Peter's, Derby on 10th September 1776, son of Thomas, a non-conformist Stockinger, and Alice his wife. Further back in time, the family produced two brothers, Thomas (1629-74) and Henry (1622-91) both pewterers, and the former was Henry's great-grandfather. Henry the pewterer is also notable as having issued a ½d token in 1668.

From 1793, Moore was working at the Spar Works of RICHARD BROWN *(q.v.)* in King Street, this being the same year that JOHN MAWE *(q.v.)* joined Brown; Moore indeed must have been closely aquainted with him. In what capacity he worked is not clear, but he may have been employed copying designs for the factory to make. It was here that he evolved his system for etching onto Ashford Black Marble (and other spars) and a superb fireplace with an etched

tablet is in the Derby Judges' Lodgings (1811) and is highly likely to be an early example of his work in this medium. His system was later adopted with some fervour by the marble workers of Matlock and the Peak District later in the 19th century.

After he left Brown's works he set up as a drawing master and published a lengthy series of Derbyshire tourist guides. He died in 1848, leaving an only daughter.

[Robinson, *op.cit.* 53; information from Mrs W.C.Cooper (MS letter at Derby Museum of 1925); Parish registers.]

MORESBY, Adml. Sir Fairfax, RN, GCB (1787-1877)

Sir Fairfax Moresby was a dashing naval boat commander who distinguished himself during the war against Napoleon clearing parts of the Mediterranean of French privateers and pirates. He also performed heroic and sterling service at the Seige of Trieste, being made Knight of the Order of Maria Theresa, a Commander of the Order of the Bath (CB) and received a sword of honour from the merchants of Malta. After the war he spent several years as Captain of the Frigate *HMS Menai,* suppressing the slave trade off the W. African coast and those of S. Arabia. So successful was he that, at the request of Wilberforce (the intimate friend of THOMAS GISBORNE *q.v.*), his posting was extended by a year, until June 1823. In 1849 he was promoted Rear Admiral, serving in 1850-53 as Commander-in-Chief Pacific Fleet, resulting in his promotion to Vice-Admiral (1856) and Admiral in 1862; in 1870 he was made Admiral of the Fleet.

Fairfax Moresby was a member of a Derby family and the third generation to be so named. Charles Moresby had come to Derby early in the 18th century, having married Elizabeth, daughter of Francis Stevenson of Unstone Hall, and their sons were John, of Unstone, Shelley Moresby, a Sheffield apothecary and Fairfax, later a Derby physician who was apprenticed to HENRY FRANCEYS *(q.v.)* 5th July 1742. His son, Fairfax

(1753-1824) had a successful career as a puisne judge in India (on the recommendation of JOHN WHITEHURST *(q.v.)* to Matthew Boulton in 1777) retiring to Riber Hall in 1786, and who later settled at Stowe House, Lichfield (Staffordshire), and ultimately Exmouth (Devon). Sir Fairfax himself was born at Riber Hall in 1787, his mother being Mary, daughter of Joseph Rotten of Duffield. He entered the navy as a midshipman in 1799 on *HMS London*. His first command was *HMS Eclair* followed by the brig *HMS Wizard* in 1811.

He married Maria Eliza Louisa, youngest daughter of John Williams of Bakewell, and was made DCL (Oxford) 1854 and Grand Cross of the Bath 28th March 1865. He died at his home, Bronwylfa, Exmouth 21st January 1877 leaving two sons, one of whom was Cdr. Matthew Fortescue Moresby, also a succesful naval officer, whose son Fairfax (born 1861) was the fifth generation to be so named. The other was Vice-Admiral John Moresby, RN. whose eldest son, Cdr. Fairfax Moresby RN was lost when *HMS Sappho* went down in the Bass Strait in 1858. [DNB; Tachella, *op.cit.,* First Supplement 1760-70 (Derby 1903) 16; Walford, E., *County Families* (1863) 711; Craven (1996) 215; Kelly, *Handbook* (1911) 1200.]

MOULT, Edward Walker (1926-1986)

Ted Moult was one of Derby and Derbyshire's (indeed the Nation's) best-loved characters from the 1960s onwards. A chance application to appear on a quiz programme from Norwich called *What Do You Know?* (from which he was promptly eliminated in the first round) brought him almost unlimited appearances, his natural dry humour and drollery achieving an unrivalled empathy with the viewers. He was offered a place on *Ask Me Another*, followed by *What's My Line?* and from then on his cheerful countenance was a regular morale booster on national television. Later on he made a series of near-legendary Everest Double Glazing advertisements ('All right, Reg, turn 'er on').

Part of Moult's appeal was that he was a

farmer, which rather embellished his image, or perhaps encouraged him to conform to a certain stereotype carried in the average urban viewer's mind. Nevertheless, farmer he was, having cultivated the 260 acres of The Scaddows, Ticknall, from 1958 after a tenancy at Sinfin and some years learning his trade on farms in Nottinghamshire (where he started), Quarndon and Mickleover. Throughout his life, broadcasting, however well-known it made him, always came second to agriculture.

Yet the Moults had no previous connection with agriculture whatever. Edward Walker Moult was born in Derby on 4th February 1926, son of a draper, Reginald Arthur Moult and Elsie May Walker (1893-1982) his wife. The Moults were a dynasty of drapers; indeed, William, son of John Moult of Osmaston Street (as Osmaston Road was then called), set up as such around 1800. He died in 1813 and his son William was also a draper whose own elder son William Thomas Moult (d.1908) was a draper and tailor of Osmaston Road, as well. He had five sons, of whom Ted Moult's father, Reginald, was the youngest. The elder two, William Henry (1877-1950), and Alfred Edward, were both Derby

Aldermen, the latter serving as Mayor 1932-33. The third brother, Francis (1881-1940), 'broke the mould' and instead of becoming a draper was a solicitor whose firm still exists, and who married Caroline Moore, a descendant of ELIAS DE ALLESTREY *(q.v.)*. Reginald, though, stuck to men's outfitting.

Moult was educated at Derby School from 1937, working on local farms in his holidays, inspired by his maternal grandfather, a cattle dealer and butcher. He left to take his first job on the land at 15 in 1941. He died, tragically by his own hand, 3rd September 1986 at home, leaving a wife, Maria, three sons and three daughters. His eldest son, William Joseph, has followed him into the media, in his case on a full-time basis.
[DLC 5/1966, 30; *Modern Mayors of Derby* (1937) II.; *Who's Who In Derbyshire* (1934) 123; Obit, DET. 4/9/1986.]

MOZLEY, Anne (1809-1891)

The Mozleys were a family of printers from Gainsborough (Lincs) and their story parallels that of the Bemroses in many ways. Henry Mozley (1773-1845) was the third generation of the family in the trade at Gainsborough, although the family claimed to have originated at Conisburgh (Yorks). He moved his business to Derby in 1815 and in 1828 purchased The Friary as his residence. On Christmas Day 1800 he had married Jane (d.1867) daughter of Thomas Brambles of Burlington and they had a large and talented family of six sons and five daughters. The elder two sons, Henry (1801-57) and John (1805-72) continued the printing and publishing firm, the former also serving as Mayor of Derby 1847-48, and was a solicitor and coroner before taking his own life at the Friary in 1857. The third son, Thomas (1806-93) was, with his brother J.B.MOZLEY *(q.v.)* a founder of the Oxford movement and the author of *Reminiscences* (1885) which includes vignettes of the son of JOSEPH PICKFORD *(q.v.)*, and of C.S.HOPE *(q.v.)*. His wife, Harriet Elizabeth (d.1852) was sister to Cardinal Newman.

Anne, born at Gainsborough 17th September

1809, was the second daughter and fifth child of the elder Henry. She was educated at home, taking over as housekeeper to her brother Thomas and devoted herself to literature, publishing her first volume, *Passages from the Poets* in 1837. She produced two other volumes of poetry in 1843 and 1845, and from 1847 reviewed books for the *Christian Remembrancer*, writing later for *Bentley's Quarterly* as well. It was in 1859 that she gave Eliot's *Adam Bede* its best review in the latter publication. From 1861 to 1877 she contributed to the *Saturday Review,* collecting her pieces in two volumes called *Essays on Social Subjects.* In 1865 she also wrote for *Blackwood's Magazine.* Her mother died in 1867, whereupon she lived at Barrow-on-Trent, later returning to Derby. She also edited the letters of her brother James *(q.v.)* and those of Cardinal Newman. She died at 158, Uttoxeter New Road, unmarried, 27th June 1891.
[DNB; Tilley, J., MS Pedigree in Derby Local Studies Library, Box 57/M.]

MOZLEY, Rev. Prof. James Bowling, DD, (1813-1878)

Dr James Mozley was professor of Divinity at Oxford from 1871 and had been a co-founder of the Oxford Movement in the 1840s, with his brother Thomas, Dr Pusey, Keble and John Henry Newman, later his brother-in-law. To promote their cause he took over the editorship of the *Christian Remembrancer* (to which his sister ANNE *(q.v.)* contributed) only laying down this office in 1855 after a change of heart following the Gotham case. Thereafter he adumbrated his modified view in *On the Augustinian Doctrine of Pre-destination* (1855), *On the Primitive Doctrine of Baptismal Regeneration* (1856) and in *A Review of the Baptismal Controversy* (1862). Besides these he wrote numerous other works and articles. He was described as 'after Mr Newman, the most forcible and impressive of the Oxford writers… a mind of great and rare power,' and as having 'sweetness, modesty, affectionateness, and generosity,' these qualities hidden, apparently, behind an impassive exterior.

Most of Mozley's achievements, however, came late to him. He was born at Derby 15th September 1813 and was educated at Grantham Grammar School (where he was unhappy) and Oriel College, Oxford, where the friends of his elder brother Thomas began to influence him. He took a poor degree, however, and failed to gain a fellowship; he was MA (1838) BD (1846) but did not attain his DD until 1871. In 1847 Mozley took an active part in returning W.E.Gladstone to parliament as the University's MP, and on becoming Prime Minister in 1868, Gladstone made Mozley a Canon of Westminster (1869), a preferment exchanged with the Oxford divinity professorship two years later. His lecturing style was said to have been wooden and dull, but the content, without fail, was excellent.

He married in 1856, Aurelia (d.1872), daughter of Professor James A.Ogle, and was also rector of Old Shoreham, Sussex, where he died, without leaving issue, on 4th January 1878 after a long illness.

[DNB, and as previous article.]

MUNDY, Francis Nöel Clarke, JP, DL. (1739-1815)

F.N.C.Mundy was a pivotal figure in the development of Derby's 'intellectual revolution' of the later 18th century, being a powerful whig patron of the arts and sciences, exercising a benevolent influence from his seat at Markeston Hall which he much improved through the services of JOSEPH PICKFORD, WILLIAM EMES and JOHN WHITEHURST (q.v.). He was a friend of ERASMUS DARWIN (q.v.) and Anna Seward, the so-called 'Swan of Lichfield' and poet, and was sufficiently talented to write an epic poem *Needwood Forest* (1776) which drew a characteristic riposte called *Address to the Swilcar Oak* from Darwin. He was at the centre of a circle which embraced the Poles of Radburne and the Burdetts, but which at the same time did not bar such as Darwin and Whitehurst from his functions, as might have been expected in those days of rigid social distinctions. Rev. W.B.Stevens,

headmaster of Repton and tutor to one of Mundy's Burdett nephews, was also a regular visitor to Markeston along with Rev. Henry Peach, a kinsman of Whitehurst's. Stevens records that Mundy was known as 'French' and his second wife, Elizabeth (daughter of Sir Robert Burdett 4th Bt. of Foremark) as 'The Duchess' because of her grand ways. 'He was always oracular,' Stevens wrote, 'a man of petrifying pride.' Consequently he was not always tolerant of the Lunar Society grandees, for he lacked the schoolboyish humour of Whitehurst, Brooke Boothby, Thomas Day and R.L.Edgeworth, writing of the latter, 'a man eccentric, talkative to a tiresome degree.' Nevertheless his interests were wide for we find him in 1790 being taken to visit the Derbyshire geologist White Watson by Darwin and WILLIAM STRUTT (q.v.) whom he also befriended. He also employed his kinsman RICHARD LEAPER (q.v.) to build a villa on his estate in 1809-12. For nearly 50 years he presided over the local Bench, and is commemorated by a bust by Sir Francis Chantrey in the Shire Hall.

Francis Nöel Clarke Mundy was born at the family's Leicestershire seat, Osbaston Hall in 1739, son of Wrightson Mundy (1715-62) and Anne his wife, daughter of Sir Francis Burdett of Foremark Hall, Bt. Of his sisters, Elizabeth married 7th Earl Ferrers (nephew of EARL FERRERS, q.v.), Mary married Nicholas Boys (later Nicholas) who lived on the estate at Bowbridge House (which he rebuilt) and Millicent married Richard French of Abbott's Hill House, Derby. He went up to New College Oxford in 1757, undertook a Grand Tour, where he honed his artistic tastes, but cut this short on his father's death in 1762.

His father had replaced the uncomfortable Tudor house at Markeaton with one to designs by JAMES DENSTONE (q.v.) in 1755, so rather than live at Osbaston he and his first wife Elizabeth Ayrton moved back to Markeaton, which house and estate he set about improving. He served as High Sheriff in 1772, and had been, with five hunting friends, painted by JOSEPH WRIGHT (q.v.) ten years before. In old age, he was painted again, by R.R.Reinagle (1809) with

his grandson, William (1801-77). He died at Markeaton 23rd October 1815 leaving two sons, Francis Mundy MP (1771-1837) his successor, and Charles Godfrey (d.1838) of Burton Hall, (Leics) ancestor of the Massingberd-Mundys of Ormsby.

[Egerton, J., *Wright of Derby* (London 1990) 39-40; Nicholson, *op.cit.* 212-3; Craven (1996) 46, 55, 74, 79, 82, 90, 120, 185, 217; Burke, *Landed Gentry* (1952) 1742-3.]

MUNDY, Admiral Sir George (1805-1885)

Sir George Mundy was a notable naval commander who was a grandson of Admiral Lord Rodney, a fact he never quite forgot, fastidiously observing old-fashioned naval etiquette, wielding a dash of eccentricity and a harbouring certain pomposity of manner. He was C-in-C West Indies 1867-69 and subsequently of Portsmouth, retiring 1877 as Admiral of the Fleet. In some ways his career followed hard on the footsteps of FAIRFAX MORESBY *(q.v.)*; they even com-

manded *HMS Eclair* in succession in the 1820s.

George Rodney Mundy was born 19th April 1806, second son of Gen. Godrey Basil Mundy (author of a *Life of Lord Rodney*) and his wife Hon Sarah Brydges Rodney, daughter of the famous commander. Of his three brothers, two were Major Generals and one a Colonel; his sister Rosamund married 1st Lord Tredegar. His father was second son of Edward Miller Mundy MP of Shipley Hall, a notable Whig potentate and Derbyshire MP 1784 to 1822, who had a house in Derby. The family were a junior (but more numerous and opulent) branch of the Mundys of Markeaton Hall. In 1818 George entered the Royal Naval College at Portsmouth, passing out with his class medal and two years seniority in December 1819, later serving on the *Eclair* 1826-27 as Lieutenant. He subsequently distinguished himself in Borneo with Rajah Brooke suppressing pirates, at Palermo during the Italian Revolution, and in Syria. He was made Rear-Admiral in 1857, CB in 1859, KCB in 1862 and GCB in 1877. He was made Vice-Admiral 1867

and an Admiral two years later. He died unmarried 23rd December 1884.
[DNB; Burke, *Landed Gentry* (1952) 1840-41.]

MUNDY, Sir John (d.1538)

Elder son of Sir John Mundy of Checkendon, Oxon, Lord Mayor of London in 1495, by Isabel, daughter of Alderman John Pipes of London. He was a citizen and goldsmith of London. In 1522 he served as Lord Mayor of London, having in 1516 purchased from Lord Audley the estates of Markeaton, Mackworth and Allestree. The family had also an ancient Derbyshire descent. He married, first, Mary (or Margaret) and had a daughter who married sucvcessively Ald. Nicholas Jennings of London, Lord Edmund Howard (third son of the 2nd Duke of Norfolk, whose sister Catherine, by his first wife Joyce Culpepper, married (1540) King Henry VIII.) and thirdly Henry Mannox. Sir John Mundy himself mar-

ried, secondly, Juliana, daughter of William Browne, Lord Mayor of London 1507 and 1513 (ancestor of the Brownes of Stretton-en-le-Field, once in Derbyshire), and had six sons and four daughters, the eldest of the former being Vincent Mundy, ancestor of both the preceding *(q.v.)* and also a goldsmith. John Mundy was responsible for rebuilding Markeaton Hall – previously the seat of the Touchets, Lords Audley *(q.v.)* – *c.*1519 in the form of an early High House, and he greatly improved and expanded the estate. His second son, Thomas, was last Prior of Bodmin (Cornwall) before the Dissolution and John, the youngest son, also settled in Cornwall at Rialaton in 1546, founding a line there. Vincent was also an MP for Derby and died 27th May 1538.
[V. Derbys. 1569, 1611; Nichols, J., *History of Leicestershire* (1804) IV 525; Burke, *loc. cit.*]

MUNDY, Col. Sir Robert, KCMG (1813-1892)

Sir Robert Miller Mundy was the youngest brother of Godfrey, father of SIR GEORGE MUNDY *(q.v.)* and was born at Shipley Hall to Edward Miller Mundy MP (d.1822) in 1813. His mother was Edward's third wife, Catherine (d.1847) daughter of Adml. Sir Isaac Coffyn RN, MP, and widow of Richard Barwell of Stanstead Park (Sussex).

He entered Woolwich as a cadet in 1828 becoming a Lieutenant RA in 1833. He retired in 1846 as a Major, spent some time in the country and then offered his services to the Sultan of Turkey on the outbreak of the Crimean War, becoming a Lt. Col. in the Osmanli Horse Artillery until 1856, receiving the Order of the Mejidjieh (3rd class). In 1863 he was appointed Lieutenant Governor of Grenada holding several governorships in the British West Indies over the following decade. Finally, from 1874-77 he was Governor of the Honduras. He was made CMG in 1874 and KCMG in 1877 before retiring to Hollybank, Emsworth, Hants., where he died on 22nd March 1892.

He married on 16th October 1841, Isabelle Leybourne (d.1906) youngest daughter of Gen. E.W.L. Popham, of Littlecote House, Wilts., and had a son, Sub. Lt. Robert Leybourne Mundy RN (killed in the Ashanti War, 17th February 1874) and no less than 12 daughters. The 11th daughter, Rose, married in 1890 (her cousin) Admiral Godfrey Mundy eldest son of Maj. Gen. Pierrepont Mundy of Castle, Townshend, County Cork, younger brother of SIr GEORGE MUNDY *(q.v.)*.

[Sources: as previous entries.]

NAJEEB, Mohommed (1947-1991)

Mohommed Najeeb was a youthful and energetic son of a family which settled in Derby from Pakistan. His greatest achievement was to be the driving force behind the founding, building and completion of the Derby mosque on Rosehill Street. The mobilization of resources, the unifying of disparate factions and opposing aspirations posed a daunting task and the opening of the building (erected to designs by Graham Weston) was a considerable triumph.

Najeeb was born in India in 1947, and received a sound education. In Derby he was the proprietor of a successful travel agency and was a prime mover in the establishment of the Pakistan Community Centre in 1983. In 1989 and 1991 he stood unsuccessfully as a Tory candidate for election to the City Council, but died in September 1991, leaving a wife Nasim Akhtar and eight children. He lived in Madeley Street.

[DET *obit.* 9/1991.]

NEEDHAM, Joshua (1689-1735)

Derby in the early 18th century seems to have been full of craftsmen of the very highest abilities, and especially *stuccodori*, as witness ISAAC MANSFIELD *(q.v.)* and Abraham Denstone. Joshua Needham was another, whose abilities as both artist and craftsman were easily on a par with those of Mansfield, although he led a life more geared to working as part of the team of fine craftsmen assembled in the second decade of the 18th Century by the architect and builder Francis Smith of Warwick. Much is known of this élite group because in 1724 Smith attached a lead plaque (since, regrettably, lost) to the Hall at Sutton Scarsdale, his *chef d'oeuvre,* naming every man: an unique tribute.

Needham's presence may be inferred at a number of projects undertaken by Smith, no doubt including All Saints', Derby (now the Cathedral) where the Baroque plaster work is of a high order. Those places where he can be proved to have worked however include Chicheley Hall (Bucks, 1721), Sutton Scarsdale, Ditchley (Oxon) and The Guildhall, Worcester (1725; BAKEWELL *(q.v.)*, who almost certainly knew Needham, supplied the exuberant ironwork). The quality of the plasterwork to be seen in these buildings – especially Chicheley and Sutton Scarsdale (now a shell, but a full record survives including two rooms in the USA) – places Needham amongst the very best of his age.

Joshua Needham was baptized at All Saints' Derby 16th August 1689, eldest of the five sons of Joseph (grandson of Francis Needham), 'plaisterer' (b. 1663) and was no doubt apprenticed to him. He lived in St Alkmund's parish, probably in Bridge Gate, and married there 25th June 1715 Hannah Brookhouse, a member of an old and distinguished family of Derby merchants and tradesmen. He died in 1735 and was buried in St Alkmund's on 26th November leaving Hannah (who outlived him 34 years), three sons and four daughters. One son pre-deceased him in 1717, but Charles (b.1725) went on to become a plaisterer and William, made a freeman in September 1755, was a shoemaker who left two daughters.

[Beard, *op.cit.* 273; local records.]

NICHOLS, Col. Sir Edward H., TD (1911-1992)

Derby has had many town clerks over the last almost 400 years, but few have gone on to more than local fame. Such was not the case with Sir Edward Nichols who served at Borough from 1949 to 1953. He had first come to Derby in 1936 from Mansfield as Assistant Solicitor, being appointed deputy Town Clerk in 1940. He held the same post briefly in Leicester 1948-49 before returning to Derby as Town Clerk. He was also Honorary Lieutenant Colonel RA during the war years. He left Derby after 17 years to become Town Clerk of the City of London, a position which said much for his reputation. He retired in 1974 having been knighted in 1972.

Edward Henry Nichols was born 27 September 1911, only son of Henry James Nichols of Mansfield (Notts) and Agnes Annie his wife. He was educated at Queen Elizabeth's Grammar School there and Selwyn College Cambridge (BA, LLB) and was articled to the Town Clerk at Mansfield on coming down. In 1941 he married Gwendoline Hetty, daughter of Robert Elgar of Leeds. From 1953 they lived, with their son, at Esher and later at Claygate (Surrey). Nichols received the TD for his territorial army work in Derby, and was a knight of a number of foreign orders, including the Order of the North Star (Sweden). In 1974 he was made Honorary D. Litt, City University (London). He died in September 1992.

[Debrett, *op.cit.* 1350; *Who's Who* (1978) 1804.]

NIGHTINGALE, Florence, OM (1820-1910)

Florence Nightingale was one of the great heroines of the 19th century, who made her name singlehandedly (and against much official irritation and obstruction) trying to improve conditions for wounded and ill soldiers in the Crimea, to which end she established a military hospital at Scutari. Her lamp-lit tours of inspection lived long in the memories of her inmates and was disseminated by them to the media of the day who dubbed her the 'Lady of The Lamp', and she was lionised on her return. Most of the remainder of her life must have seemed like an anticlimax after the horrors of Scutari and she divided her time between living up to the demands of her celebrity and giving sound advice to those who sought it.

One who sought her advice was DR WILLIAM OGLE *(q.v.)*, the reformist physician who was appointed to the Derbyshire General Infirmary in 1860. Due to the (then unsuspected) flaws in the system of ventilation at the Infirmary, put in by WILLIAM STRUTT and CHARLES SYLVESTER *(q.q.v.)*, the mortality rate amongst patients was unacceptably high. He opened a lengthy correspondence with Florence which resulted in a complete rebuild of the Infirmary on lines suggested by her, with the addition of a new wing, plus chapel, kitchen, laundry, mortuary and operating theatre. All was designed by H.I.STEVENS *(q.v.)*, the wing named after Miss Nightingale and the whole was opened by Lord Vernon 12 November 1869. Hence, outside the new (1891-97) DRI was placed, in due course, her statue by Countess v. Gleichen.

Whilst this incident refers to Derby particularly, it is largely typical of the quite unremunerated consultative work she was, in retirement, constantly called upon to carry out, and her appointment, when it came in 1907, to the Order of Merit was long overdue. She was also made a DGStJ. and granted the freedom of the City of London 1908.

Florence Nightingale was born 12 May 1820 the younger daughter and coheiress of William Edward Shore of Lea Hurst, and Embley Park

(Hants) (1794-1874), a scion of an opulent banking family of Sheffield and Norton and of old Derbyshire descent. His father, William Shore of Tapton (1752-1822) was a fourth son and had married Mary, daughter and heir of George Evans of Cromford Bridge Hall (a cousin of THOMAS EVANS, *q.v.*). Her mother, in turn, was Anne, sister and heiress of the lead mine proprietor Peter Nightingale the younger of Lea Hall and Rock House, Cromford. On his death in 1803 his estates and enormous wealth passed to W.E.Shore, Florence's father, who in 1815 took the surname of Nightingale *in lieu* of Shore by Royal Sign Manual. Her mother was Frances, daughter of William Smith MP of Parandon, Essex, whose brother, Samuel, had married Florence's aunt, Mary Shore. It was their son William Shore Smith who ultimately inherited from Florence's father.

Florence, greatly against her genteel family's wishes, decided to take up nursing (then a very uncertain science) training with the Protestant Sisters of Mercy at Kaiserwerth am Rhein and, with the outbreak of war in the Crimea went thence, largely at her own expense, with a group of nurses. After the Battle of Inkerman she was forced to care for over 10,000 wounded soldiers, finding in the process, that more were dying from disease and insanitary conditions than from wounds. It was her determination to fight for improved conditions and her gift for administration that won her extensive public support at home. She returned with a testimonial fund of £50,000, founding nursing colleges in the London hospitals (the first being at St Thomas's, 1866), and inspiring that built opposite the DGI in London Road, Derby by Ogle. In due course, her system of nursing gained currency worldwide. She died at her London home in South Street W1, unmarried, 13th August 1910. Her sister, Parthenope, Lady Verney, had also died without issue a decade before.

[Burke, *Landed Gentry* (1937) 1685; Hunter, J., FMG, 1.142-3; Derby Local Studies Library Local MS575; *Derbyshire Miscellany* Pt.9 No.5 (Spring 1982) and Pt. 11 No.4 (Autumn 1987); Unpublished MS by Dr V.M.Leveaux, *passim*.]

NOEL-BAKER, Lord, see BAKER

OAKES, James, JP DL (1816-1868)

The Oakes family went, over a 50 year period, from selling beer to selling oil. James Oakes of Riddings, Somercotes, was a landed proprietor whose grandfather had purchased the estate for its potential mineral wealth, having amassed a fortune as an attorney in Derby. In 1847 in his New Deeps mine there occurred a flow of thick black oil from beds of shale. Oakes informed his brother-in-law Lyon Playfair (later 1st Lord Playfair, PC, GCB, FRS), whose friend James Young refined the crude oil into petroleum, producing 30 tons per month a year later. Although Young transferred his operations to Scotland some years later, the oil shale continued to be profitably exploited until 1885. Oakes takes credit for identifying the seepage (at first considered merely a hindrance to the profitable extraction of coal) and exploiting it. His income from coal mining and his iron works, however, made his oil earnings look like small beer; nevertheless it was a British First.

James Oakes was born at Derby on 11th March 1816, eldest of three sons and three daughters of James Oakes (1788-1845) and Sarah, daughter of Alderman Thomas Haden of Derby, which made Oakes, senior, brother-in-law to KIRK BOOTT (*q.v.*). The father was grandson of Benjamin Oakes (1712-66) for many years Landlord of the Nag's Head Inn, St Peter's Street, Derby. He was fifth in descent from James son of Thomas Oakes of Derby, living 1568/76. Benjamin's son James, of London Road, attorney, was Mayor of Derby 1819-20 and bought the Riddings estate in 1818 building the elegant house a year later.

James Oakes eschewed university and entered his father's business, taking it over on his death in 1845. On 30th July 1846 he married Marian, a daughter of William Milnes of Stubben Edge Hall. He died 31st July 1868 without leaving issue, the estate and industrial concerns passing to his brothers Thomas Haden Oakes (1819-

1902) and Charles Henry Oakes (1825-1906). [Burke, *Landed Gentry* (1952) 1912; Nixon *op.cit.* 76, 218; DET 21/10/1997.]

OGLE, Dr William (1824-1905)

William Ogle was an ardent medical reformer who, as physician, later consulting physician, to the Derbyshire General Infirmary from 1860 to 1891 was instrumental in bringing about the Derbyshire Royal Infirmary, the foundation stone of which was laid by Queen Victoria shortly before Ogle's retirement. On appointment to the DGI, 27th August 1860, Ogle found much that was wrong with the institution, and he shortly thereafter after engaged upon a correspondence with FLORENCE NIGHTINGALE *(q.v.)* concerning its improvement as well as the basis on which nursing standards could be enhanced. As a result, it was realised that the heating system pioneered by WILLIAM STRUTT & CHARLES SYLVESTER *(q.q.v.)* was actually contributing to the spread of disease, and that the hospital was lacking vital facilities not dreamed of in Strutt's time. The result was the comprehensive rebuilding of the edifice in 1868-70 by H.I.STEVENS *(q.v.)*, although the resulting facilities were never really more than a stop-gap dependent upon the complete replacement of the building from 1891 on a pavilion plan designed by Young & Hall of London. Ogle also founded the Derbyshire Nursing Institution opposite and a sanitary institution as well.

William Ogle was born in January 1824, son of a vicar of Skirbeck (Lincs) of an old Northumbrian family, being educated at Rugby under Dr Arnold before going up to St Catherine's, Cambridge where he qualified MA and MD going on to be a fellow of his college. He also studied at Edinburgh before beginning his career at the Rotunda, Dublin and from 1853 St George's, London. He married at Bradford in 1860 Margaret Lambert and lived at The Elms, Five Lamps, where they brought up three sons – John Bertram (b.1863, killed in a railway accident 1892), Rev. Hugh Lambert (b.1865), later curate of Bermondsey, and Philip Henry Douglas (b.1875).

Ogle was the first medical writer to use the

term 'immunity' in the medical sense, was a keen evangelical, a supporter of the YMCA and founder in 1862 of the Derby Medical Society which still uses his armorial bearings. He was doctrinaire, pedantic, tactless despite his integrity and a little humourless. 'His devotion to his chosen causes was inspired both by professional enthusiasm and by evangelical zeal.' He was elected FRCP in 1868, opened his school for nurses on 24th June 1860 and the Nightingale Wing of the DGI (also by Stevens) in December 1872. His innovations were much emulated elsewhere, however, and it is this aspect of his career which elevates him from a purely local eminence. He died at The Elms on 16th May 1905.

[Hubble, D., *William Ogle of Derby and Florence Nightingale* in *Medical History* III.3. (7/1959); information courtesy Dr V.M.Leveaux.]

OSBORNE, Ritter Dr Jacob (1808-1851)

Jacob Osborne was a distinguished physician in Prague whose contribution to the improvements in medical practice of his day marked him as an innovator. He was also the physician who was required to attend the Emperor whenever he should visit the Bohemian capital. For this he was made a Knight of the Order of Franz Josef.

Osborne was the son of Isaac Osborne of Georgswalder and Bohrîc (Bohemia) merchant in the wool trade (1780-1823) himself born at Field House, Spondon to Isaac Osborne, a London merchant of an old Spondon family. The elder Isaac was seventh in descent from William Osborne of Alvaston, yeoman (d.1586). He was also a Director of the Bank of England and purchased the Spondon house. Dr. Jacob's father was partner with his elder brother, Jacob, of Basinghall St (London) and in 1820 he married Carolina v. Salm of Schlukenau (1787-1830) and the elder son Joseph (1806-34) settled at Spondon on the family estate. However, on Joseph's early death without issue (his bride was HERBERT SPENCER'S *(q.v.)* relative Elizabeth Antill Jacob inherited the estate and the family business, the financial stability and responsibility determining him to marry, the following year, Elizabeth daughter of Dr Johann Grosse of Prague (1815-98) by whom he had three sons and three daughters. He involved himself extensively in Prague municipal affairs and in 1845 moved to 79 Brenntengasse, but died during a holiday with his family at Nizza 8th April 1851. His elder son Wilhelm Karl Jacob (1838-1925) sold all the Spondon property to Frederick Arkwright in 1869 and, despite marrying a Welsh woman, Isabelle Thomas, remained in Bohemia (Czech Republic) with his siblings.
[Information from Archpriest Basil Osborne; Parish Records; information from Michael G.Osborne.]

OTTER, AVM. Victor Charles, OBE (1914-1996)

Air Vice-Marshall Victor Charles Otter was an aeronautical engineer of considerable distinction whose career fell entirely within the armed services, culminating in a period when he was project director in charge of testing and evaluating the Hawker P1154/1127 VSTOL fighters which

eventually developed as the Harrier; it was to a large extent due to Otter's expertise and experience that the Harrier achieved the unqualified success it did.

Victor Charles Otter was born 9th February 1914, son of Robert Otter and his wife Annie and was educated at Weymouth Grammar school, entering the RAF as an apprentice in 1929, graduating to flying duties six years later. He commanded the engineering branch from 1940 and research and development 1942-47 before serving 18 months as Air Attaché at HM Embassy Budapest. From 1956-59 he was Chief Engineering Officer, Bomber Command, before being given the VSTOL prototypes assignment.

Otter, whose great relaxation was gliding, was made OBE (1945) and CBE (1967). He was also FRAeS, FIMechE. and MBIM, ending his career as Air Officer (Engineering) Air Support Command 1966-69, retiring with his wife, Iris Louise Dykes (who survived him and whom he had married in 1943) to Keats Avenue, Littleover where he died without issue 5th May 1996.
[*Who's Who* (1978) 1856; DET. 8/5/1996.]

PARKER, Rt. Hon Sir Thomas, 1st Earl of Macclesfield (1666-1732)

One accusation which has dogged government of late has been that of 'sleaze'. Now, despite that, our country is probably one which has the least corrupt system of government in the world, yet it was not always so. Although Britain led the way in Europe as a functioning democracy, it was once governed by a system of controlled corruption; a form of pragmatism evolved by Crown and Parliament in the face of rampant human nature encouraged in the hot-house atmosphere of the Court of Charles II.

Thus the 18th Century was an era which was no stranger to sleaze. Nevertheless, one former Derby MP yet managed to emerge as a master of it. This man was Lord Macclesfield, who was born Thomas Parker at Leek, Staffordshire, 23rd July 1666, son of a local attorney of a distin-

guished North East Derbyshire family. He was educated at Newport, Shropshire and subsequently at Derby School, from whence he went up to Trinity College, Cambridge in 1683.

In fact, Parker did not take his degree, but in February 1684 became a student at the Inner Temple, being called to the bar in May 1691. He then joined the Midland Circuit where his natural eloquence earned him the soubriquet 'The silver-tongued counsel'. William Hutton averred that *before* being called to the bar Parker had lived 'in Bridge Gate at the foot of the Bridge in the house next to the Three Crowns'. As the Huttons lived nearby and the event was within the memory of his grandfather we can take the fact of Parker's residence there as certain; however, the period was probably *after* Parker joined the Midland Circuit. It is worth bearing in mind that the senior branch of Parker's family had a town house in Friar Gate, which probably influenced his choice of residence.

In 1703 Parker was appointed Recorder of Derby in succession to SIR SIMON DEGGE (*q.v.*) who had held office since the end of the Civil War – 42 years! His Staffordshire connections were undoubtedly a major element in this. Further, in May 1705, he succeeded Thomas Stanhope of Elvaston as one of Derby's two MPs, with Lord James Cavendish, a younger son of the Duke of Devonshire. Both sat as Whigs, and it is a reflection of the times that Derby was then a very Tory town in a period of Tory dominance in government. Unfortunately for the Tories, the Whig burgesses of Derby rigged the polls as of right. In July 1705 Parker was knighted at Windsor and subsequently made his reputation in the prosecution of Rev. Henry Sacheverel whose radical Assize Sermon in Derby (later repeated in the Capital) presaged the coming storm of Jacobite rebellions. As a result of his success against Sacheverel and thanks to the patronage of the Duke of Somerset, Sir Thomas was made Lord Chief Justice in March 1710. He became Privy Councillor, and resigned his seat and Recordership at Derby. His successor in the former was the Tory Sir Richard Pye Bt. of Hoon Hall, and

in the latter the Whig William FitzHerbert of Tissington.

In 1711 the Tory premier, Lord Harley, recognising Parker's gifts as an advocate, offered him the Woolsack, but he gained much credit by refusing, but his time came – as he perhaps had appreciated – when Queen Anne died. He swiftly won the new monarch's favour, being created Lord Macclesfield in 1716 and receiving a pension of £2,000 p.a. In 1718 he accepted the Lord Chancellorship at last, being rewarded with the Earldom of Macclesfield (with remainder to his daughter, Lady Heathcote and her heirs male) in 1721. Shortly afterwards he repeated his success against Sacheverel by prosecuting Bishop Atterbury and his associates (including a direct forebear of the writer) for hatching a Jacobite plot. However in May 1725 Macclesfield unexpectedly resigned and within a fortnight had been impeached for corruption – 'enormous abuses'. He was accused of bribery, sale of offices, the appointment of spivs to offices of influence and the abuse of 'the statues of the Realm', ie the law. He was found guilty and was fined a colossal £30,000, being held in the Tower for six weeks pending discharge of the debt. He was forced to retire to private life at his seat, Shirburn Castle (Oxon), where his descendants live to this day. He had been elected FRS in 1713 and was prominent in retirement in encouraging young scientists and was a pallbearer at the funeral of Sir Isaac Newton in 1727. He also founded a Grammar School at Leek, and at his death on 28th April 1732 he left, by his wife, Janet Carrier of Wirksworth, a son, Viscount Parker, who succeeded as second Earl, and a daughter; Brig. Andrew Parker Bowles is a direct descendant of the former.

By working the corrupt system of his times too hard, Macclesfield succeeded in exposing himself as a grasping manipulator. Nevertheless, as a lawyer and orator he was very gifted and eloquent, and he appears to have been remembered with affection in Derby, where his sister lived on with her husband Leonard Fosbrooke. He was the epitome of his age: talent sullied by excess. [Hutton, *op.cit.*, 284-290; DNB; Craven (1987) 80-81.]

PARNELL, Reginald (1911-1964)

Reg Parnell was one of a group of motor racing drivers who achieved increasing success in the years following the Second World War, being an older contemporary of such men as Mike Hawthorne, Stirling Moss and Roy Salvadori. He had a number of Grand Prix victories to his name and finished a notable third in an Alfa Romeo at the Grand Prix de L'Europe at Silverstone 13th May 1950, the first ever World Championship race. By 1958 he was manager of the Aston Martin Grand Prix team, and retired in the early 1960s.

Reginald Parnell was the son of W.Parnell of Sunnyside, Alfreton Road, Derby, proprietor of the Standard Garage Co., Alfreton Road, a calling which, in common with many aspiring racing drivers those days, enabled his son to embark on this expensive and hazardous career. His mother was Alice. He had two other brothers (one of whom carried on the garage) and a sister, also Alice, Landlady of the White Horse, Morledge

and wife of George Baker who once ran the Royal Standard. Their daughter Doreen married Leonard Harfield, proprietor of the Promenade Hotel, Blackpool, and grandson of Herbert Harfield who is credited with the creation (in conjunction with the Borough Council and William Barron and Sons) of the lake and landscaping in Alvaston Park.

Parnell, whose career began in club racing in the 1930s, lived for a time at Etwall Hall before retiring to Wallfield House, Findern, where he died in January 1964, leaving a son, Timothy (b.1933) whose career in motor sport has been as notable: he was manager of the BRM F1 team 1966-73, leaving in 1975 to become a Director of the Mallory and Oulton Park Circuits. Now a farmer near Littleover, he has two sons, Michael (b.1971) and Richard (b.1973). Reg Parnell was a greatly liked figure in motor racing, and his early death in 1964 after retirement was tragic indeed.

[DET. 21/12/1966; DLC 4-5/64; Information courtesy Mrs E.Richardson.]

Reginald Parnell

PEARCE, Rt. Rev. Ald. Edmund Courtenay JP (1870-1935)

Dr Pearce was the first Diocesan Bishop of Derby after the creation of the Diocese in 1927, and did much to lay its foundations both spiritually and administratively. He was the only (so far) armigerous bishop of Derby, and his arms were carved above the entrance of the former Bateman seat of Breadsall Hill Top (designed by H.I.STEVENS, *q.v.*) which he acquired as the first bishop's palace. Pearce, apart from being a notable academic was one of the last ecclesiastics with a serious role in local government (c.f. Rev. C.S.HOPE), having served as Mayor of Cambridge 1917-18 and at the time of appointment to Derby was Chairman of Cambridgeshire County Council.

Edmund Courtenay Pearce was the younger son of James Pearce of Savile Row, London, and was born 17th December 1870, being educated at Christ's Hospital (where he was later for a time Almoner) from whence he proceeded to Corpus Christi, Cambridge (BA 1892, MA 1896, later DD and Ph.D). After ordination he was appointed assistant curate of St James', Muswell Hill (London) 1899-1900 and then from 1900 to 1906 vicar of St Benedict, Cambridge. He was appointed a Fellow of his college in 1895 and was Dean from 1901-14, when he was made Master, a position he held until he came to Derby in 1927. He was also University Vice-Chancellor in 1921-24, all of which achievements emphasise his organisational skills for which his appointment in 1927 made him so suitable. He had been elected a Cambridge Councillor in 1915 and for Cambridgeshire four years later, becoming a alderman of the latter in 1923. He was appointed to the bench in 1919 and was made Hon Ph.D (Athens) in 1924. He died at Derby in 1935 leaving, by his wife, Fanny Constance, daughter of Alfred Lyon of Middlecote (Devonshire) whom he married in 1899, a son Edmund James, born 1903.

[*Who Was Who,* Vol.III 1056; *Who's Who in Derbyshire* (1934) 132-33.]

PETTY, Ald. Mrs Elizabeth, JP (1875-1947)

Mrs Petty was notable for being the first woman to be Mayor of Derby, serving in 1936-37. She was first elected to the Council for Dale ward in 1922, having already served nine years as a member of the Board of Guardians. She was made Alderman in 1938.

Elizabeth Merryweather was born in 1875, the daughter of Henry Merryweather, of Norwood House, Southwell (Notts) JP, a notable horticulturalist and nurseryman who lived to a great age. She married Frank Swinbourne Petty of Manchester (d.1937) whose work brought the couple to Derby in September 1909, and they lived at 25, Mount Carmel Street. Ald. Mrs Petty

died in January 1947. Her heirs were the sons of her brother Alfred George Merryweather of Brinkley House, Southwell.
[DET. 23/10/1936; 9/11/1936; Local Studies, Tilley/P.]

PHILLIPS, Edward (1817-1881)

Edward Phillips was, with William Litherland *(q.v.)* the co-founder of the Royal Crown Derby factory in Derby in 1875-78, and was a member of a dynasty of china dealers reaching back to George Phillips of London (d.1675) a glass seller and Delftware dealer. He was Crown Derby's first Managing Director and took a strikingly successful leading role in the marketing of the new factory's products as well as in the production.

Phillips was the elder son of Jacob Phillips of Harley Street, London who had begun his career at Stoke on Trent and Hanley, where Edward

seems to have been born. His younger brother, Jonathan, had migrated to Canada by 1881; his two sisters, May June and Elizabeth Owen, never married. His uncle, another Jonathan, was a china dealer of 358/9 Oxford Street, London, whose father George had been a supplier to WILLIAM DUESBURY *(q.v.)*. The Edward Phillips who was a china painter at Derby in 1772 was probably a kinsman.

Phillips was trained by his father and worked at Hanley 1855-62 and thereafter at Worcester to 1875 when he moved to 64 Osmaston Road, Derby (later at 102) to begin the setting up of the factory. He died unmarried 15th December 1881, his heirs and executors being his two cousins William and George, Jonathan's sons, who were then still running the family retailing business in Oxford Street.
[Gibson, Hon H., *A Case of Fine China* (Derby 1993) 7-8, 10ff, 83-85.]

PICKERING, Rev. John, MA. (1706-1790)

John Pickering was one of the largely unsung group of Derby intellectuals who found themselves at the cutting edge of the more cerebral underpinning of the Industrial Revolution. He was a parish priest – one of a dynasty of vicars of Mackworth under the patronage of the Mundys of Markeaton – who served in succession to his father from 1731-90. He was also a mathematician and amateur astronomer, and a friend of EARL FERRERS *(q.v.)* and JOHN WHITE-HURST *(q.v.)* with whom he was one of the few known members of the first Derby Philosophical Society which appears to have flourished during the 1760s and 1770s, despite the later claim by his friend ERASMUS DARWIN *(q.v.)* to have founded this body in 1783. It is as mathematician and astronomer that he appears in his portrait by JOSEPH WRIGHT *(q.v.)* painted in *c*.1777/80.

Pickering was born at Mackworth second son of Rev. John Pickering and Anne his wife, in 1706, and was educated at Derby School, under the inspired headmastership of Rev. Anthony Blackwall, whose daughter Mary (b.1709) he married, in his own church, 20th September

1733. He was thus cousin to Rev. Thomas Blackwall, who played in musical soirées with JOSEPH WRIGHT, CHARLES HOPE and P.P.BURDETT (*q.q.v.*) all of whom he knew well. His mother-in-law's first husband was Rev. Thomas Cantrell, also an ex-head of Derby School and cousin of HENRY CANTRELL (*q.v.*). There are records of Pickerings as tenants, agents and almoners of the Mundys going back to the 16th century. John had an elder brother, William and a sister, Anne, Mrs William Harwood. He proceeded to Jesus College, Cambridge (BA 1727, MA 1731), being appointed to Mackworth by Wrightson Mundy in 1731, the year of his ordination. For six years (1768-73) he was tutor at St Helen's to REV. THOMAS GISBORNE (*q.v.*) to whose intellectual brilliance he must surely have contributed. He also lectured and gave demonstrations in science locally and indeed, can be viewed as a candidate for the philospher in Wright's 'Orrery'. Such was Gisborne's affection for him that he had Wright paint a copy of his portrait for him shortly after his death on 17th December 1790.

By his wife he had two children; William (1740-1802), believed to have been a founder member of Darwin's (revised) Philosophical Society, and who succeeded his father as vicar at Mackworth, and John, who also took holy orders. William's son George was the last of the family to be vicar of Mackworth.

[Tachella, *op.cit.*, 12; Nicholls, *Leicestershire* IV.509; Nicholson *op.cit.* I. 131, 134; Egerton, *op.cit.* No.148.]

PICKFORD, Joseph (1734-1782)

A son of William Pickford, mason, of Ashow, (Warw.) and his second wife Mary, Joseph was baptised at Ashow 6 October 1734. The Pickfords were a family of builders ultimately from Badger, Salop, who had forged close links with Smiths of Warwick. Orphaned at seven, Joseph went to London to live and serve successively as apprentice and as assistant to his uncle, Joseph Pickford of Hyde Park Corner, one of the leading builders of his day, and young Joseph worked with him at

Horse Guards, Cambridge University Library and at Holkham, Norfolk (for the Cokes), bringing him into direct contact with the first generation Palladians John Vardy and William Kent.

He came to Derby as Clerk of Works and later executant architect at Foremarke Hall, (1759-61) during which period he quoted Matthew Boulton for building Soho Hall, the first of many strong links with members of the Lunar Society. In 1761 he was employed, again by the Cokes, this time at Longford Hall, which he Georgianised and built a large, very fine stable block. Here he married Mary Wilkins, daughter of Wenman Coke's agent. In 1763-64 he built the Derby Assembly Rooms to the designs of WASHINGTON SHIRLEY, 5th EARL FERRERS (*q.v.*) before setting up independently in Derby where he worked with great success for the remainder of his life.

He was a friend of JOSEPH WRIGHT, ARA, PETER PEREZ BURDETT and JOHN WHITEHURST, FRS, (*q.q.v.*) building houses for both the latter and being painted by the former. He was, like most of his friends, a London

Freemason and in 1781 was made a member of the Corporation of Derby. At his unexpected death 13th July 1782 he left two sons, Thomas, who died aged 21 in June 1790 and Rev. Joseph (d.1844) latterly incumbent of Little Eaton and Quarndon, both of whom were painted as children by Wright.

Pickford's *oeuvre* may well be more extensive than is now understood; nevertheless, in a short life he achieved much, including the epoch-making application of Palladianism to an industrial building in the Etruria Works, Burslem for Josiah Wedgwood (1767-70), and St Helen's, Derby, possibly the finest Palladian townhouse surviving between London and York. He designed at least three townhouses in Ashbourne, one in Wirksworth, and several in Derby. His country houses included designs for a new house at Calke (1764); Hams Hall (Warw., 1764) and Ashford Hall (*c*.1776). He also designed St Mary's Church, Birmingham, an octagonal composition (1772) and acted as clerk of works at Kedleston 1775-82 in succession to JAMES DENSTONE (*q.v.*), almost certainly as a result of a reasonably close acquaintanceship with ROBERT ADAM going back to the 1760s. This influence made him a Neo-classicist at heart, but more often than not the Whiggish tastes of most of his clients led to his having to cloak his buildings in Palladian garb, Neo-classicism being relegated more to the detail. His effect in Derby was to raise dramatically the standards of architecture generally. His only assistant known was THOMAS GARDNER of Uttoxeter; although GEORGE MONEYPENNY II (*q.v.*) may well have been, and WILLIAM STRUTT (*q.v.*), too, may have acquired his architectural skills with Pickford.

[Saunders, E.J., *Joseph Pickford* (1993) *passim;* Craven, M., *John Whitehurst* (Mayfield, 1996) 61-68.]

PIGOT, Dr John Hollis (d.1794)

Dr Pigot is notable as the founder of the Tyrian Freemasonic Lodge in Derby 26th March 1785, of which he was first Master and as the man who re-established Freemasonry in Derby. This was after a gap of eight years, the previous Lodge, No.104 (The Virgin's Inn) having been founded 14th September 1732, but which later folded and was disbanded. The Tyrian Lodge (No. 468, later No. 253) met at the Tiger Inn, Cornmarket where the Derby Society of Musicians also met (perhaps no coincidence), and Pigot rapidly built up its membership and its reputation.

John Hollis Pigot was the son of Rev. John Pigot, vicar of Epperstone (Notts) by Bridget, daughter of William Becher of Southwell (Notts). His father died young and he was bought up by his mother under the guidance of his grandfather Hollis Pigot, vicar of Doncaster (d.1762). John Pigot, his great-grandfather had a small estate at Congleton (Cheshire) and was also of Southwell where the family had strong connections. It was no accident that later at least five Southwell grandees were early members of the Tyrian Lodge. J.H.Pigot's uncle William (1729-82) was one of the earlier sitters to JOSEPH WRIGHT (*q.v.*) at Doncaster.

Pigot came to Derby to practise as a physician in 1781 and later lived next door to Wright's friend Dr Beridge on Full Street but, like his father, he died young on 3rd August 1794. In 1781 he had married his cousin Margaret, daughter of Richard Becher of Southwell, by whom he had three sons and a daughter, the latter being Elizabeth (1783-1886) a poet, author and friend of Byron. The eldest son Dr John Pigot (1785-1871) was later an Alderman of Nottingham, whose second wife was a kinswoman of JOHN FLAMSTEED (*q.v.*); his brother Capt. Richard Pigott RN fought as a midshipman under Nelson at the Nile.

[Craven (1988) 111; Craven (1996) 170; Hunter, FMG. III. 1025-26; Boyes, M., *Love Without Wings* (Derby 1988), *Passim*; DNB.]

PIKE, Eliza Maria (1832-1905)

Miss Pike was the founder and proprietor of the *Derby Daily Telegraph* and its formidable editor from 1879. By perseverance and guile she was able to build the paper up until, after her death, the title eventually absorbed all its rivals, today appearing as the *Derby Evening Telegraph*, part of the Northcliffe group.

Eliza Maria Pike was the daughter of Walter Pike (1790-1859) and Elizabeth Ratcliffe and was born 21st April 1832 being baptised at Victoria Street Chapel.

Her aptitude for newspapers was in her blood, as she was involved with her father and uncle, John Beard Pike, founders (with their father William, a bookseller, printer and stationer) at 39 Cornmarket of the reformist *Derby and Chesterfield Reporter* in 1823. Walter edited it until 1843. In a sense the *Telegraph* (a daily) grew out of the *Reporter* (a weekly) and was also published initially from 39 Cornmarket; both papers were published together for many years until Miss Pike's successors closed the *Reporter* down in 1931 almost a year after the *Telegraph* (as E.M.Pike Ltd) had bought and closed the *Derby Mercury* (see S.DREWRY, *q.v.*). A year later, the *Telegraph* also took over the *Derby Daily Express* (since revived as a weekly 'admag'). E.M.Pike died at the Cedars, Kedleston Road, on 7th December 1905, unmarried.

[Derby Local Studies Library, Tilley/P.]

PIKE, Rev. J.G.D. (1784-1854)

Reverend John Pike was in many ways the creator of the Baptist congregation in Derby, increasing attendances, preaching inspiringly at all times and having a felicitous aptitude for pastoral work, deriving from a strong, humourous and benevolent character. He was General Baptist minister in Derby for over 44 years and strove mightily (but ultimately unsuccessfully) to unite the General Baptists with the Particular Baptists of the area. He was the first secretary of the General Baptist Foreign Mission from its foundation and secretary of the Derby and Derbyshire Bible Society. He also wrote 18 published works, some sermons, but a preponderance of pastorally inclined works in 'small portable volumes'. He was passionately fond of Derby and at his death left an unpublished MS of a History of Derby with Messrs. W. & G. Wilkins, his publishers.

John Gregory Deodatus Pike was born 6th April 1784 at Edmonton, Middlesex, son of Rev. Dr Pike, minister there; his mother was a descendant of Oliver Cromwell. He was the elder of two sons. He received from his father a 'good classical education' before being sent as an assistant teacher to a Baptist seminary. Later he studied at the Dissenting College at Wymondley, where by chance he met Rev. John Deacon who introduced him to the congregation of the Brook Street Chapel in Derby (then barely a decade old) in 1809 where there was a vacancy for a pastor. In July 1810 he was duly appointed, and it is a testimony to the power of his preaching that shortly afterwards money had to be raised for the insertion of a gallery into the building to accommodate the increased numbers. In 1814 he added the adjoining schoolrooms. This trend continuing, he obtained St Mary's Gate House from Samuel Evans of Darley Abbey for £4,000 and it was rebuilt internally to designs by J.Fenton of Chelmsford and opened for worship on 18th May 1842, with seating for 1,200.

He lived first in Full Street, but later in more

modest surroundings in Parker Street. He married on 22nd June 1811, Sarah, daughter of James and Joyce Sandars (James was a descendant of Col. THOMAS SANDERS (sic, *q.v.*), whose sister later married Pike's brother Washington, a Derby lace manufacturer. He died – as did ERASMUS DARWIN *(q.v.)* – at his desk in the act of writing to a friend, 4th September 1854 and was interred in Uttoxeter Road Cemetery under a colossal monument by J.B.ROBINSON *(q.v.)* recently listed grade II. A memorial parian bust of him by John Whitaker was sold widely after his death. He left four sons and two daughters, of whom the elder three sons all became Baptist Ministers, at Leicester, Bourne (Lincs), and Derby. The youngest, Josiah Gregory, worked as a silk broker. A grandson, Edward Carey Pike (son of James, the elder son) was also a Baptist minister at Clapton (London).

[*General Baptist Magazine Repository and Missionary Observer*', I (NS), II/1854 No.11 489-98; DM. 6/9/1854; *Derby Miscellany*, X/II pt.4 (Autumn 1993) 91; DET 19/1/1998.]

PLANCHÉ, Andrew (1728-1805)

Planché is notable insofar as he was the first man to produce porcelain in Derby, and was a co-founder, subsequently, of the China Factory on Nottingham Road c.1750 with WILLIAM DUESBURY *(q.v.)*. Shortly after finishing his apprenticeship with Edward Mounteney of Foster Lane (London) he appears to have come to Derby acquiring, it is said, a disused clay pipe kiln in Lodge Lane. Here he made small decorative objects, especially animals and some figures. The quality of these was exceptional, and before long the opportunity to expand caused him to be brought together with Duesbury probably through the initiative of the financier JOHN HEATH *(q.v.)*, the result being the setting up of the China Factory. It was not until 1756 that this arrangement was formalised as a working partnership, a deed to which Planché, Heath and Duesbury were parties being drawn up in that year. Yet after that, and the baptism of Planché's youngest son William, at St Alkmund's on 3rd

July that year, his name is absent from the factory's annals. It would appear that the natural talent Planché embodied was not matched by business acumen and that he was shortly thereafter elbowed aside and left Derby, obliged to seek pastures new. Nevertheless, high hopes must have been entertained for Planché's original venture for he was assisted in setting up by an illegitimate son of Louis-Henri de Bourbon, Prince de Condé, a member of the French Royal Family who had been himself closely associated with the Chantilly pottery from 1735. The son went to Hengoed Gobowen (Salop) in the later 1750s, where a disillusioned Planché followed him.

André Planché was born 14th March 1728 and baptised at the Hugenot Chapel, London on 24th of that month. He was the son of Paul Planché, Hugenot refugee and London coffee merchant, by his first wife Marie Anne Fournier, probably close kin to the Louis Fournier who was a potter at Chantilly in 1752. He had two other brothers, of whom the youngest Jacques (James, 1734-1816) was a watchmaker, and a sister. After his apprenticeship, he anglicised his name to Andrew and married at St Pancras (London) 22nd September 1747 Sarah (1723-1800) daughter of Thomas Stone. They had five sons: Andrew, Paul, Edmund, James (died an infant) and William. Even in Derby, his gallic charm must have been considerable, for in March 1756, a natural son (born to him by Margaret Burroughs) was christened at St Alkmund's on the 4th. This second James, however, also died young.

In later life Planché settled in Bath where he interested himself in the theatre and where in 1800 he re-married Catherine (1739-1813) a dyer. Some of his sons, indeed, took the surname Floor (as an English translation of Planché) and he died at 25 Stall Street, Bath, 6th January 1805. The antiquary, J.R.Planché FSA (1796-1880) Somerset Herald and playwright, was a cousin once removed.

[Jewitt, L.L., *Ceramic Art of Great Britain* (London 1883) 334-35; Bradley, G. & Anderson, J., *Derby Porcelain 1750-98* (London 1990) 28.]

PLIMSOLL, Samuel, MP (1824-1898)

Although Plimsoll was an MP for the Borough for 12 years, there is little in Derby that commemorates his name. To most people, of course, the name recalls the famous 'Plimsoll Line' – a circle intersected with a horizontal line (rather like the London Underground logo) painted on the hulls of cargo ships throughout the world as a safety measure. It marks the point beyond which it is unsafe to load the vessel in certain conditions. The item of footwear known as the plimsoll is said to derive its name from the resemblance of the sole to the 'load-line' device.

Of Hugenot descent, the Plimsoll family came from Bristol where he was born, the fourth son, 10th February 1824. His father Thomas was an excise officer and this necessitated many moves about the country before they finally settled in Sheffield in 1838. His mother was Priscilla, daughter of Josias Willing of Plymstock (Devon). In 1844, Samuel found himself the family breadwinner at the age of 20 following the sudden death of his father. He was then working in the brewery industry but his real ambition was to enter the then thriving coal trade. He succeeded in this and in due course was instrumental in extending the dropping and transfer of coal near its market in the London suburbs, where he is celebrated, in Finsbury Park, near to the railway line, in an eponymous public house. However, he was regarded as a young upstart and obstacles were thrown in his way, whereupon the resourceful young Plimsoll resolved his problems by 'marrying well', in 1858 to Eliza Ann (d.1882) daughter of Hugh Railton of Sheffield, ironfounder, which opened many doors to him, both social and commercial, as did his work as the local secretary co-ordinating the input of Sheffield's manufacturers to the Great Exhibition of 1851, which brought him into local prominence.

It opened political doors too. He stood as a radical for a Derby seat in 1865. At that time Derby had as bad a reputation as many other such seats for political corruption. Plimsoll lavished money freely in his attempt to win it, but in spite of this (or perhaps because of it) the voters elected his Tory opponent. But once again Plimsoll's tenacity saw him through for he continued to nurse the constituency and was successful in the election of 1868. Having achieved his ambitions both in commerce and in politics, he then cast about for a 'cause', something that would make his name. He found it in the dire state of merchant shipping. However, many of Britain's merchant vessels were small sailing ships capable of taking only 100 tons or so of cargo.

There were few laws or regulations to cover this state of affairs and unscrupulous owners could not only overload their ships but also send them to sea, however old and unseaworthy. His attention had already been drawn to the scandal of what he called 'floating coffins' from his work in the coal trade. Plimsoll had a practical turn of mind and invented a new system for loading coal onto ships, so he was able to see the conditions and the problems at first hand.

In 1873, he published *Our Merchant Seamen* which drew attention to the problems; and in the same year he addressed the Trades Union Congress. A Royal Commission on the state of Britain's merchant fleet was set up in 1874 and was quickly followed by Acts of Parliament in 1875 and 1876 to improve the safety of British shipping and the life of its sailors.

Plimsoll retained his seat in Derby until he retired in 1880 to make way for SIR WILLIAM HARCOURT *(q.v.)* then Home Secretary and later Chancellor of the Exchequer. Having failed to secure nominations for seats in Liverpool (1880) and in Sheffield (1885) the Parliamentary aspirations of the 'sailors' Friend' were at an end. Retirement for Plimsoll meant a hive of activity. His wife died, and he remarried Harriet Frankish, daughter of Joseph Armitage Wade JP of Hull, who bore him a surviving son, Samuel Richard Cobden Plimsoll, and two daughters. In 1889 he was elected first President of the newly formed National Amalgamated Sailors and Firemen's Union. He continued to support the cause of seamen – and railwaymen too – right until his death in Folkstone 3rd June 1898 at the age of 74. Needless to say, his gravestone features a circle crossed by a horizontal line: the Plimsoll Load Line.

[DNB; Jeffery Tillett; Ancient Monument Soc. *Transactions* XLI (1997) 70.]

POPE, Ronald (1920-1997)

Ronald Pope was a lecturer in Art at the colleges in both Derby and Nottingham and a notable sculptor with a national following. He was a specialist in the human figure although some of his work

was largely abstract; his favourite medium was undoubtedly metal although he also did some work in timber as well. It is possible to see the influence of both Giacometti and Brancusi in his mature work although in neither case could he be labelled derivative. He also did a number of architectural commissions, including 'Family of Man' (1964) for the foyer of Derby Museum (which has a fine collection of his works), and St Catherine for Sir Basil Spence's Church in Sheffield.

Ronald Pope was born in Gloucestershire in August 1920, and gained a BSc (Engineering) which took him to Rolls Royce as an engineer in the 1940s. From 1943 he was at Derby College of

Art as a student, proceeding to the Slade School of Fine Art in London 1946-48, where he studied ceramics under Herbert Mathews, gaining his Diploma in 1948. He lived for some time in Derby before renting the romantic retreat at Knowle Hill (Ticknall). He later moved to Melbourne where he died in 1997 on 14th May.

[Notes at Derby Museum, Art Dept; DET 16/5/1997.]

POUNTAIN, Ronald Dennis (Denny Dennis) (1913-1993)

Denny Dennis – the name he assumed in 1933 when his musical career began to blossom – was a notable, polished and very talented jazz singer in both Britain and the United States from the 1930s; in his day he would have been labelled a 'crooner' although he himself would have reminded people that his commitment to jazz was his first love, over the often more lucrative dance band work which is always associated with

more famous crooners like Sinatra and Crosby, with both of whom Dennis worked. He also sang with all the major orchestras of the day both before and after World War Two.

Ronald Dennis Pountain was the second son of a Derby carpenter and was born 1st November 1913 at 20 West Avenue. After an elementary education he became an apprentice electrician at Derby railway works, performing locally and gradually building up both reputation and contacts. His elder brother, Eric, was also a dance band singer as well as a fine saxophonist, going on to make a career in London as Barry Gray in 1937. He was killed in World War Two.

Dennis eventually retired to Kirkby-in-Furness (Cumbria) where he died the day after his 80th birthday, 1993, leaving a son. His first wife was Betty Fay, from whom he was divorced in 1945; he remarried Joan Armitage, from whom he was also divorced in 1981.
[DET. 17/11/93.]

PRICE, John (1795-1859)

John Price was son of the carpenter John Price of Derby (d.1816) and followed him into that calling at premises in the Market Place. By 1823 he was of Cornmarket 'cabinet maker, appraiser and auctioneer' although a few years later he was also offering 'architectual planning, estimating, surveying and appraising' at Lowndes Yard, Market Place. In 1833 he was merely 'architect and surveyor' at 7 Rotton Row although he was teaching architecture as well. He married Elizabeth (d.1871) daughter of James Pimm of Green Street, and they had four sons, the youngest of whom was the photographer Joseph Wheeldon Price (1830-90). Another son, William, a Littleover farmer, married the daughter of Derby artist George Mellor. He died at Littleover in 1859. He was a fertile inventor, and amongst his devices was a cast-iron window sill for casements opening inward to prevent rain from beating in, and a self-regulating digester for cooking meat.

His Derbyshire buildings include a labourer's cottage for the Osmaston Hall estate, Lea Green, Lea (a substantial Jacobethan Country House), a design for the Derby and Derbyshire Bank, Cornmarket, Derby (all before 1839); Churchdale Hall, Ashford; Haddon House, Bakewell (both c.1840); alterations and improvements to Alvaston Hall (c.1840) and a very sensitive rebuilding of the Jacobean House, Wardwick, Derby, to allow the pitching of Becket Street in 1853. He also recorded this important building in a series of beautifully executed plans and elevations before starting work.
[Drawings, Derby Museum; *Architecture East Midlands* 3-4/1979 p.35; *Derbyshire Life*; *Mechanics Institute Exhibition Catalogue* 1839 nos. 130/3, 5/4, 19/4 & 22/4; *Derby Mercury* 16/1/1817, 5/3/1823, 28/12/1825, 16/11/1833, 15/7/1840; Deeds to house in Green Street, Private Collection; information from Malcolm Burrows.]

RAPHAEL, Sir H.Herbert, Bt. MP (1859-1924)

Sir Herbert Raphael lived from 1906 to his death in 1924 at Allestree Hall, a tenancy he obtained from the Gisbornes in order to fulfil his obligations as Liberal MP for South Derbyshire. He was elected in the landslide of 1906 and lost his seat at the 'coupon' election of 1918. He was appointed a JP on arrival in Derbyshire in 1905 and during the war was appointed temporary Major, King's Royal Rifle Corps 1915-17 when he was made honorary Major, a post he held until 1924.

Raphael had no previous links with Derby or Derbyshire whatsoever; like SAMUEL PLIMSOLL *(q.v.)* before him he was a 'carpetbagging' MP. He was born in 1859, second son of Henry Lewis Raphael of London (d.1898) a member of a prominent Jewish banking family, by Henrietta his wife. He trained as a barrister at the Inner Temple (1883) and in 1884 married Rosalie, only daughter of G.F.Costar of Shanklin, IOW. He was in 1908 appointed a Trustee of the National Portrait Gallery. In 1911 he was created a baronet but died in 1924 without leaving issue when the title became extinct.

[Fox-Davies, AC., *Armorial Families* (1910) 1344; Kelly, *Handbook* (1924) 1268.]

RAWLINSON, James (1769-1848)

The Rawlinsons over three generations were a talented family, and James was in many ways the most eminent, being a painter of some distinction, specialising in portraits in oils. Although, like the much more famous JOSEPH WRIGHT *(q.v.)*, he mainly remained in Derby, and later – after the death of his father – at the family home Belle View, Matlock Bath, he painted many eminent contemporaries, including ERASMUS DARWIN *(q.v.)* – whom he also painted after Wright's later portrait – George Washington, Archibald Douglas, WILLIAM STRUTT *(q.v.)* and several of his family and circle. He also executed the stained glass Venetian window which once graced the east end of All Saints', Derby.

Rawlinson was born in 1769, son of George Rawlinson of Matlock Bath (1734-1823), an unsung but highly competent architect who designed Lady Glenorchy's Chapel at Cromford and many of the elegant houses in Matlock Bath, and of his wife Anna. According to a label on the back of a self-portrait of the artist George Romney (sold at Christie's 8/6/1995), he was a pupil of that artist. He set up in Derby around 1790, moving to Matlock Bath in 1823, where he died 25th July 1848 being interred in All Saints', Derby. By his wife (who died 28th June the previous year) he had a daughter, Eliza, an accomplished landscape painter. She accompanied her father on a tour through Italy in 1829 where her work won her the membership and the diploma of the Royal Acadamy of Artists at Lucca 'as a testimony of her talent'.

[Glover, S., *Peak Guide* (Derby 1830) 123; DM. 5/11/1823; 30/6/1847; 2/8/1848; Local MS 3202 83.]

RAYNER, Louise (1832-1924).

Louise Rayner was a member of the numerous progeny of the Derbyshire (and London) artist

Samuel Rayner (1806-79) an architectural draughtsman, lithographer, author, publisher and art dealer. He was also a skilled engraver on Black Marble using the technique invented by HENRY MOORE *(q.v.)*. Samuel's elder brother John was also an artist, as were seven of Samuel's three sons and six daughters, a hotbed of talent fostered by the consistent impecuniousness of their father. Of them all, Louise's was the most precocious talent, and her limpid watercolours do far more than merely record the topography, both urban and rural, from which she drew her inspiration.

Louisa Ingram Rayner was born at Matlock Bath 21st June 1832, third daughter of Samuel, and his wife Ann Manser (also an artist; 1802-90). The family were originally from Colnbrook (Bucks), and Louise (as she was always known) was brought up in Derby before the family moved to London in the 1840s. At this period, Samuel was partner to Robert Moseley, spar manufacturer, carver and gilder of Cornmarket, Derby, 1836-43. She no doubt learned her art there and later with her parents. She died unmarried 8th October 1924. Of her siblings the artists included Derby-born Richard Manser Rayner (1843-1908) – two of whose children were also professional artists, Arthur (1878-1961) and Ada (1881-1919) – Ann (called Nancy; 1826-55, OWS), Rhoda (Rose; 1828-1921), Frances, Mrs Copinger (1834-c.1880), Margaret (1837-1920) and Grace (b.1841). Frances' son Ernest Edward Copinger (1871-1900) was also an artist of some attainment.

[Wallis, J., *et al*, *The Rayners, a Family of Artists*, Derby (1996) Exhibition catalogue; information courtesy Dr J.Measham.]

RAYNES, Alderman William Robert, JP (1871-1966)

He was invariably referred to as 'Raynes of Derby' but Will Raynes was not, in fact, a Derbeian, for he was born in Chasetown (Staffs) 26th January 1871 son of Heanor-born blacksmith Henry Eley Raynes and Phoebe, a south London girl. The family moved to Wilmorton (9 Archer Street) in 1883 and William Robert attended Wilmorton School. He later worked as a newsboy, then at Fletcher's Lace Mill and as a printer with the Co-op before moving to Nottingham as a Trades Union official, 1897-1900. In the latter year he returned to set up as Master Printer, a business he finally relinquished in 1915 to become Secretary and Organiser of the Derby Labour Party, when he lived at 13 Commerce Street.

He was elected to the Council (as one of the first Labour intake) for Osmaston Ward in 1911 after seven attempts (starting in 1903). In 1921-22 he was first Labour Mayor and in 1925 the first Alderman from the party; he capped this by being the first Labour man to receive the Honourary Freedom of the Borough, an honour his successors regrettably no longer bestow. His first bid to be elected to Parliament for Derby was in 1922, but he was beaten by CHARLES

ROBERTS *(q.v.)* suceeding on the second attempt in 1923, only to lose to SIR RICHARD LUCE *(q.v.)* a year later. In 1929 he was again returned but, refusing to join National Labour in 1931, he was once more defeated, this time by W.A.REID *(q.v.)*. His only Parliamentary role was as Chairman of a Committee set up to examine the feasability of a Humber Bridge. In 1930 he concluded it was not possible; it took almost 50 years for engineering to develop techniques that challenged this finding.

His true strength was in local government, and he oversaw many vital Derby projects, including the first Direct Labour Organisation, Derby's power station (although perhaps insensitively sited!), the 1932 Flood Prevention Scheme (based on the one devised by HERBERT SPENCER *(q.v.)* in 1850 and rejected in his lifetime) and the Ring

Road, part of which was named Raynesway after him. He married Alice Elizabeth (1869-1957) daughter of Thomas Foster of Heanor, and latterly they lived in Empress Road. He died – still an Alderman – 30th January 1966. His brother, Rev. Ernest C.Raynes of Chellaston (1887-1984) was a Methodist minister who founded Raynes Methodist Church, Steubeville, Ohio, USA, of whose sons one, Roger, became a Methodist minister as well as is his own son Philip, whilst the younger, Peter, stood as a Liberal Candidate at Farnham (Surrey) in 1979 – Heaven knows what his distinguished uncle would have thought of that!

[*Modern Mayors of Derby* (1937) 11. 45-46; *Who's Who in Derbyshire* (1934) 142; DET. 9/8/1988; Hodgkin, A., *Wilmorton* (1996) 45.]

REDHEAD, Henry, see Yorke

REID, William Allan (1865-1952)

W.A.Reid was a Derby solicitor swept into Parliament in the National Government landslide of 1931 in the Conservative interest, defeating Will Raynes *(q.v.)*. He held no ministerial posts and served until he retired at the 1945 election when Gp. Capt. WILCOCK *(q.v.)* won his seat.

William Allan Reid was of Scots stock, born at Derby 11th October 1865, a son of John Reid of Ockbrook House, a civil engineer and Midland Railway gas manager to 1900. His mother, Agnes, was a daughter of Alan Roberts. After a private education, Reid qualified as a solicitor in 1895, practising from Bank Chambers, Iron Gate, part of the firm established by Sir CLEMENT BOWRING *(q.v.)*, then Walmesley, Reid and Bowring. He was Chairman of Derby Children's Hospital 1920-31, and a Carlton Club member. On 14th February 1917 he married Ethel Walker (d. 6th June 1943), widow of Dr Henry Boam (close kinsman to Aldermen Henry and Cornelius Boam, both Mayors of Derby), daughter of W.Walker Smith of Derby and heiress of her brother C.A.Walker-Smith of Ockbrook. They lived at Allerton Mount, Duffield Road, but

there was no issue, although Ald. E.W.H.Reid, Mayor in 1979 is a kinsman. He died in 1952.

[Stenson, M. & Lees, S., *Who's Who of British Members of Parliament* (Brighton 1979); *Who's Who in Derbyshire* (1934) 143.]

RICE, Joan (1930-1997)

Joan Rice was one of the Rank Corporation's film starlets of the 1950s, her best remembered role being as Maid Marion in Disney's 1952 *Robin Hood* opposite Richard Todd. However, despite a number of similar roles, the big breakthrough in films ever eluded her and she forsook the cinema in the 1960s to spend seven years in provincial repertory, which she much enjoyed, and which, in turn, more suited her talents. She appeared in 11 films between 1950 and 1961 making a brief comeback in 1970 in *The Horror of Frankenstein*. After retirement she worked as an estate agent in Maidenhead.

Joan Rice was born in Derby 3rd February 1930, one of four sisters. Her father was imprisoned for child abuse and she spent eight years in a convent orphanage in Nottingham. After a brief spell in service she went to London with half-a-crown (12½p) in her purse and took work as a 'nippy' (waitress) in Lyon's Corner House at £3 per week. In 1949 she won her employers' 'Miss Nippy' contest, which afforded her an introduction to the theatrical agent Joan Reese who obtained a screen test for her. Her first substantial role was in *Blackmailed* with Dirk Bogarde and Mai Zetterling in 1950.

She married in 1953 David Green, son of US comic Harry Green, by whom they had a son, but they divorced in 1964. Twenty years later she re-married former *Daily Sketch* journalist Ken McKenzie, who survives her. She died in 1997.

[*Daily Telegraph*, Obituary.]

RICHARDSON, Arthur Walker (1907-1983)

Arthur Richardson was a member of a long-established family of curriers, later also leather merchants, originating at Horsley Woodhouse in the 17th century. His grandfather William Milward Richardson was a Director of the Derby Gas, Light and Coke Company, in the affairs of all of which concerns (except the latter, nationalised after World War Two) Arthur also took a keen interest. A Derbyshire cricketer 1928-36, he was captain during the latter season when they won the County Championship..

Arthur Walker Richardson was born at Abbott's Hill House, Derby, second son of William Henry Richardson (1872-1932) who in 1926 sold the house (hard by the tannery from which the family's fortunes stemmed) for re-development and moved to the Leylands (see RICHARD LEAPER *q.v.*). His older brother, Ven. John Farquhar Richardson (1904-91) was a much-loved Archdeacon of Derby 1952-73 and father of two Anglican parsons. Richardson died at his house, Quarndon Hill on 29th July 1983, and one of his sons, George William Richardson, also played cricket for Derbyshire 1958-65, as has Alastair of the next generation, from 1991.
[DET; Local Studies, Tilley/R.]

RIVERS, Pte. Jacob, VC (1881-1915)

Jacob Rivers was born on the 17th November 1881 at Court 12, Bridge Gate, Derby and was one of three sons born to George Rivers, labourer, and his wife Adeline Holmes, whom he married at St Michael's 4th February 1876. His family were poor, Jacob's father having died at the early age of 41, leaving his mother to bring the children up on her own. As soon as they were old enough, the brothers left home and on 3rd June 1898, at the age of 18, Jacob enlisted in the Royal Scots Fusiliers. He served in India for seven years before being discharged to the reserve on 3rd June 1907, where he served for a further five years. On leaving the army he found employment as a labourer on the ballast trains for the Midland Railway at Derby where he worked until the outbreak of World War One. On 18th August 1914, Jacob re-enlisted into the army, this time joining the Sherwood Foresters (Notting-

hamshire and Derbyshire) Regiment. He was posted to the 1st Battalion and, because of his previous military training, was sent to France with one of the first drafts. Jacob Rivers saw much heavy fighting with the Regiment and it was at Neuve Chapelle on 12th March 1915, that Jacob Rivers was to win his Victoria Cross, bombarding with grenades a large number of Germans outflanking a company of his battalion, sacrificing his life, but causing the enemy troops to retire, thus saving the threatened company. He was gazetted VC 28th April 1915, but his body was never recovered due to the heavy fighting at the time and he has no known grave. His name, however, is commemorated on the La Tourt Memorial, France.

Jacob's Victoria Cross was presented to his mother by King George V at Buckingham Palace on 29th November 1916. So proud were the people of Derby at the award of the Victoria Cross to Jacob that on 23rd March 1923 they made his mother an Honorary Freeman, an honour she shared with Earl Haig and the Duke of

Devonshire. Mrs Rivers died on 1st March 1937 and was buried in the Nottingham Road Cemetery, Derby, were a memorial to Jacob now stands. His nephew, son of his sister Elizabeth, was living in the 1960s and his great-nephew is Victor Benson, a local schoolmaster.

[DET. 9/3/1994; Parish registers; McCrery, op.cit., 36-37.]

RIVETT, Thomas, MP, JP, DL (1713-1763)

Thomas Rivett was a co-founder, with JOHN HEATH (q.v.) and the potter William Butts, of the Cockpit Hill pottery about 1750, which concern produced some very refined earthenware products until it closed in 1780 as a result of Heath's bankruptcy the year before. No doubt, had Rivett survived by that date he would have helped it through the crisis, but his sons evidently felt less affinity with the venture. He was also a considerable landowner, having a seat at Mappleton Manor, land at Blore and being Lord of Calton, Staffordshire. He was also Whig MP for Derby 1748 to 1754 and a successful maltster.

Thomas Rivett was born at Derby, being baptised at All Saints' 12th August 1713, elder son of Alderman Thomas Rivett, maltster (1679-1724) of Derby and Blore, which estate he purchased in 1718. The elder Rivett had also served as Mayor of Derby in 1715-16. His mother was Elizabeth, daughter of Humphrey Eaton of Derby (d.1746), who provided lodgings for the Duke of Perth during the 'Forty Five; a great uncle of the father, John Rivett, fought as a Colonel for the Royalist cause in the civil war, whilst his brother, Thomas (1606-60) sweated away under SIR JOHN GELL (q.v.) in Derby as a Blacksmith, later a maltster. Our Thomas, however, was educated at Derby and the Inner Temple, being called to the bar in 1739.

Rivett was also a Derby Alderman, serving as Mayor 1761-62 and was appointed a Deputy Lieutenant during the crisis of anticipation in autumn 1745 when PRINCE CHARLES EDWARD STUART (q.v.) was drawing closer to Derbyshire. He married in April 1749 Anne Maria daughter of Rev. Charles Sibley (d.1740), rector of Blore, whose uncle George Gretton

(father-in-law of JOHN WHITEHURST (q.v.)), had preceded him there, and they lived on the Morledge, possibly at Cockpit Hill House. He died at Bath 6th April 1763 and was buried at All Saints' seven days later; his will was proved 10th May 1763. He had four sons and five daughters. The eldest son Rev. Thomas Rivett was rector of Maresfield (Sussex); the fourth, James, was father of SIR JAMES RIVETT-CARNAC (q.v.), and Elizabeth Catherine, the second daughter, married Gen. John Carnac, but had no issue, leaving her brother James as her husband's heir.

[Local records; Information from Messrs. Howard Usher and David Swinscoe; Burke, Peerage (1970) 484 – where the descent for the family is erroneously adduced from the Rivetts of Suffolk.]

RIVETT-CARNAC, Sir James, Bt, MP (1784-1846)

Sir James Rivett-Carnac was a prominent member of the Honourable East India Company, then one of the most powerful non-governmental organisations in the world, later twice becoming its Chairman, in 1836-37, a rare honour. He also served 1838-41 as governor of Bombay, being raised to a baronetcy 12th March 1836. He was MP for Sandwich as a Whig 1837-38 but resigned his seat to take up his post in Bombay.

James Rivett was born in Derby 11th of November 1784, son of James Rivett HEICS (1759-1804) second son of THOMAS RIVETT (q.v.). In 1801 his father, as heir of his uncle by marriage, Gen. John Carnac MP (1716-1800) a former Commander-in-Chief of Bengal, assumed the surname and arms of Rivett-Carnac. His mother was Henrietta, daughter and coheiress of James Fisher of Great Yarmouth (Norfolk) and he was the eldest of three sons and four daughters. James entered the service of the Honourable East India Company in 1801 becoming an officer of the Madras Native Infantry, but his father, being assistant governor of Bombay, obtained for him the post of ADC to the governor there. He was later Resident in the

Principality of Baroda, and spent many years campaigning against (and largely suppressing) the native practise of infanticide in Gujerat and elsewhere. He retired as a Major in 1822 being appointed a Director of the Company five years later. He was a man who tackled everything with great zeal, letter writing included: his correspondents included his friends the Duke of Wellington, Lord Melbourne, and Marquess Wellesley for whom he had obtained a pension of £20,000 from the East India Company on his retirement.

He married Anne Marie, daughter of William Richards of Penglais (Cardigan) and died at his seat near Lymington (Hants) 4th January 1846 leaving three sons. The elder, John, suceeded him as 2nd baronet, and William, the second, was also in the East India Company's service as a Judge in Bengal, in the Civil Service of which state the third son, Charles, also served.
[Burke, *Peerage* (1970) 484-86; DNB.]

RIVETT-CARNAC, Vice-Adml. James, CBE, CB, DSC, DL (1891-1970)

Admiral James Rivett-Carnac was a notable Captain of the Battleship *HMS Rodney* 1941-43 and was later Vice-Admiral Commanding the British Fleet during the final operations against the Japanese in 1945 and continued *en post* until 1947 when he retired.

A descendant of SIR JAMES RIVETT-CARNAC (*q.v.*), James Rivett-Carnac was the second son of Rev. Sir Clenell George Rivett-Carnac 6th Bt, by Emma, daughter of Rev. George Crabbe and was born in 1891. He was educated at Britannia Royal Naval College, and served from 1917. He was Commodore, New Zealand Division 1938-39. He was made CBE and CB as well as winning the DSC. In retirement he was Chairman of the Thringoe (Suffolk) RDC 1958-61. He died 7th October 1970 leaving two sons, of whom the younger, Rev. Sir Thomas Nicholas Rivett-Cranac (b.1927) succeeded his elder brother George as 8th baronet in 1972.
[Sources: as previous; *Who Was Who*.]

ROBERTS, Ald. Charles Henry JP (1865-1959)

Although his father bore the same names as Lady Thatcher's, the similarity between these two politicians ends there! Unlike the former Prime Minister, Roberts was a Liberal and perennial backbencher. His Parliamentary career began when he contested Wednesbury (Staffs) in 1895 and Osgold Cross (Yorks) four years later, before being elected for Lincoln in 1906 at the second attempt. He served during World War One as Under Secretary for India (1914-15), Comptroller of the Household (1915-16) and Chairman of Lloyd-George's National Health Insurance Joint Committee. He lost his seat at the 'coupon' election of 1918 and was returned as a Liberal for Derby in succession to Alderman Green (*q.v.*) in November 1922 only to lose again to WILL RAYNES (*q.v.*) 13 months later. Thereafter he retired to Naworth Castle (the home of his wife, Lady Cecilia Howard, (d.1947) second daughter of 9th Earl of Carlisle) and joined the Cumberland County Council, becoming Chairman 1938-58 and Deputy Chairman of the Cumberland Quarter Sessions.

Roberts was the son of Rev. Alfred Roberts, vicar of Tidebrook, Sussex, and was born 22nd August 1865, being educated at Marlborough and Balliol (Oxon). He became a fellow of Exeter College in 1889 and a tutor at Balliol as well as a Commissioner in Lunacy. By his wife, whom he married on 7th April 1891, he left a son and two daughters when he died 25th June 1959, having led his County Council to the age of 93! His London address was 10 Holland Park later the home of 1st Viscount Stansgate and thus of Tony Benn, MP for Chesterfield. He also lived at Bracklands, Hindhead, Surrey.
[*Who Was Who*; Stenton and Lees *loc.cit.*; Lodge's *Peerage* (1911) 423.]

ROBERTSON, George (1777-1833)

George Robertson was one of a select coterie of china painters employed by the China Factory who can be claimed as amongst the very best. His particular speciality was in the painting of landscapes, at which he excelled.

He was born, probably in London, son of another George Robertson, a minor artist of Scots descent in 1777 and came to Derby in *c.*1796/7 to work for DUESBURY *(q.v.)* and MICHAEL KEAN *(q.v.)*. A year later he married Anne, daughter of another exceptional china artist, JOHN YATES *(q.v.)* at St Alkmund's on 15th April. His wife's sister later married John Wallis, coach proprietor and landlord of the New Inn, making him kin to JOSEPH WRIGHT and KIRK BOOTT *(q.v.)*. After leaving Derby around 1820 he went into a decline and died in Nottingham Asylum 8th January 1833. He left a son, James, born March 1799.
[Local records; Jewitt, *op.cit* 345.]

ROBINSON, Joseph Barlow (1821-1883)

A highly successful and prolific sculptor and carver, J.B.Robinson was probably the best in the Victorian period in the Derby area. He was born at South Wingfield, 'son of a stone mason from Belper' who was probably Edward Robinson of New Road, Belper, 1835, but who died when Joseph was young, leaving him to be bought up by his grandfather, Joseph, at South Wingfield. Another Edward Robinson of Belper, brick manufacturer (1862) may have been a brother.

Robinson was apprenticed to a mason in London and worked extensively on the Palace of Westminster, leaving to set up a works on London Road, Derby in 1851. From 1860 to about 1873 he had a showroom on Derwent Street East, but he moved his works to Parliament Street thereafter. He lived on Uttoxeter New Road, where his garden, extant as late as 1970, was crowded with architectural carvings and statuary. He worked extensively with H.I.STEVENS, and carried out country house and church commissions throughout the region, his last work being the second staircase and other embellishments at Locko Park (1883). Three of his more spectacular funerary monuments in Uttoxeter Road Cemetery were recently listed.

He also wrote an eccentric collection of jottings in large format called *Derbyshire Gatherings* engagingly illustrated by himself and published locally in 1866. He married Christina, daughter of Lord Oxford's agent at Eyewood (Herefordshire) where he was then at work restoring a ceiling, and at his death 18th January 1883 left a son Joseph (b.1859) and a daughter, Elizabeth Christine (b. 1853).
[Information courtesy James Darwin Esq; Derby Local Studies Library Tilley/R.]

ROBINSON, Philip (1914-1997)

Philip Robinson was joint managing director of the Royal Crown Derby Company from 1953 to 1959, when he became Chairman, guiding a rather old-fashioned firm through the difficult post-war years and getting it to thrive during the 1960s. He left in 1963 deciding to conduct research independently into new techniques in the pottery industry. He therefore joined the board of the Abbeydale Bone China Company, Duffield, a firm he had helped set up in 1961, as production director with additional responsibility for sales and design. He retired from this firm in 1974.

Phillip I.Robinson was born in 1914, son of Harold T.Robinson of Cauldon (Staffordshire) who purchased Royal Crown Derby in 1929 and

who served as the Company's chairman until his death in 1953. An uncle, J.A.Robinson was director there from 1929 as well. In 1930 he was office boy at Ridgeway's Bedford Works in Hanley, but advanced himself rapidly becoming Professor of Free Fine Art at Worcester College of Art 1938-39, and in 1940 he went to Royal Crown Derby as a designer, succeeding his father as joint managing director in 1953. He was a JP (1954) and Treasurer of Derby Conservative Association 1946-52. He had laid the foundation stone of Baker Street United Reform Church, Crewton in July 1935; he was able to attend the 50th anniversary in 1995. He died in January 1997, leaving, by his wife Dorothy, a son, John (b.1956), a daughter, Ann, and seven grandchildren.

[DET. 27/1/1997; *Derby Express* 12/7/1995; Twitchett,J., *Royal Crown Derby* (London 1976) 45f.]

ROE, Sir Thomas, 1st Lord (1832-1923)

Tommy Roe was something of a fixture in the Derby firmament for over 64 years. A Liberal in politics with a keen interest in education and welfare, he represented Derby in Parliament from 1883 to 1895 and from 1895 until 1917. During that time most of Roe's more effective work was done in committee, for as a speaker he was not noted for eloquence, becoming known as 'Tommy Ditto' from his habit of endorsing the oratorical flights of fellow Liberals by leaping to his feet and saying "And I say ditto to that!" Roe was elected a councillor for Castle ward in 1858, aged 26, and in 1867-68 served the first of three terms as Mayor, his other terms being 1896-97 and 1910-11, the longest span between the first and last Mayoralties recorded in Derby – 44 years.

Roe was for many years a trustee of the British School, Orchard Street (founded by WILLIAM STRUTT, *q.v.*) and a founder member of the Derby School Board from 1871, later becoming its Chairman. He was also a member of the Litchurch Local Board (and its second Chairman); was for 28 years a churchwarden of St Peter's, a member of the Board of Guardians

and a Liversage Charity Trustee, as well as serving on a number of other local charities and concerns. He was also a great supporter of the work of the various Friendly Societies.

Roe was born 13th July 1832, eldest son of Alderman Thomas Roe (1805-79) himself Mayor of Derby 1863-64, of a Ravenstone family. His mother was Deborah, daughter of Absalom Oakley, a Derby gardener and although of very humble beginnings, Roe *père* built up a prosperous timber business into which young Thomas was apprenticed at 14, becoming a partner in 1854. The ramifications of the dynasty were such

that a good number of local families, nearly all artisans, were related to the Roes, and Sir Thomas to his credit never lost touch with them despite the dizzy heights to which he rose, a characteristic he shared with LORD GODBER *(q.v.)*. Roe, who lived at Litchurch House (and later at Grove Villa, Osmaston Road) married very late, in 1903, Emily (d.1909) daughter of MATTHEW KIRTLEY *(q.v.)* and there were no children. His brother Charles Fox Roe FRSA (1844-1908) was a London barrister; one sister, Sarah married

REUBEN EASTWOOD *(q.v.)*, the other, Eliza, married to Alderman James Newbold (Mayor 1887) and served as Roe's Mayoress on all three occasions. All of his mother's brothers worked for the family sawmill which, however, ended in a disastrous fire during Roe's second Mayoralty. Octavius Oakley, the artist also was a cousin (see A.O.DEACON, *q.v.*).

Roe was knighted for political services in 1894 and received the Honorary Freedom of the Borough in 1909 in recognition of 50 years continuous service. He was raised to the peerage by Lloyd George in 1917 as 1st Lord Roe of Derby, but the title became extinct on his death 7th June 1923.

[MMD. I. 24-26, 91-92; II. 28-29; Tilley/R.; Parish Registers; MIs Uttoxeter Road Cemetery; Briscoe.]

ROE, Dr William Robert (1843-1920)

Dr Roe was the founder and first headmaster of the Derby Deaf and Dumb Institution, (later the Royal School for the Deaf) in 1874. His success in educating children with learning handicaps was outstanding and he was a great believer in physical education as well. His pupils, despite their disabilities, managed to win the National Physical Recreation Society's All England Challenge Shield early in the school's history. It is a measure of his success both as educator and fund raiser that he managed, by 1894, to obtain both Royal patronage (1890) and to erect a colossal purpose-built complex in Friar Gate to designs by R.Ernest Ryley. The building was lavishly decorated by carved 'Jacobethan' ornamentation specifically executed by deaf craftsmen. He also wrote *Our Deaf and Dumb* and *Anecdotes and Incidents of the Deaf and Dumb* both of which sold largely. He was also an active Freemason at the Arboretum Lodge, a company director, governor of several local institutions and Chairman of Friar Gate Ward Conservative Association.

William Robert Roe was born at Heanor 25 March 1848, son of William Roe of Heanor and Derby, joiner and cabinet maker, and was edu-

cated at Belper School. In 1893 he received an Hon PhD. from an American University in recognition of his work. Ryley also designed a Fine Arts and Crafts House for him in 1895, The Red House, Belper Road, where he died in 1920.

He had three sons, of whom the youngest, Kenneth John (b.1897) served in World War One (as Lt., 13th Bn. Sherwood Foresters) and the second, William Carey Roe (b.1886) succeeded his father as principal of the Royal School for the Deaf.

[Briscoe, *op.cit.* 350; *Who's Who in Derbyshire* (1934) 149; Tachella, *op.cit.* 155.]

ROLLS, Capt. Hon. Charles Stewart, FRGS. (1877-1910)

Charles Stewart Rolls was the youngest son of a Monmouthshire industrialist and landowner John Allan Rolls MP, created in 1892 1st Lord Llangattock. He was born at the family's London home on 23 August 1877 and educated at Eton and Trinity College, Cambrige (BA 1895, MA

1902). He then studied engineering at Crewe Loco Works and also obtained a merchant marine 3rd engineers' certificate. He bought his first car in 1895 (a 3½hp Peugeot) – the fourth Englishman to own one. He joined the RAC in 1897. From 1900 he was active in motor reliability trials and races, and formed C.S.Rolls Ltd. in London with Claude Johnson, the intention being to manufacture cars, although only selling was done until he encountered HENRY ROYCE (q.v.) and his 1904 prototype. Their resulting partnership is history.

In 1903 he had become a Captain in the Motor Volunteer Corps, and gradually became more interested in flying, meeting Wilbur Wright at Le Mans in 1908, one of whose aeroplanes he duly acquired, soon becoming an expert aviator. In June 1910 he made the first double crossing of the Channel, but was killed flying at Bournemouth on 12th July that year, unmarried – the first Englishman to be killed flying an aeroplane. His father died in 1912 and with the death of his eldest brother in the trenches in October 1916, the family title became extinct. Like his freind and collaborator, Henry Royce – whom he tried hard (but in his lifetime unsuccessfully) to persuade to make aero engines to the same standard as the firm's cars – he never lived in Derby, and his statue graces the Market Place of his native Monmouth. In the firm he helped found at Derby, though, his name endures, for all that locals invariably refer to it as 'Royce's'.
[DNB; Burke, *Peerage* (1931) 1509.]

ROSTRON, Joe (1910-1993)

Joe Rostron was, from 1929 to 1934 a remarkable and successful professional boxer winning 120 out of 133 bouts. On his retirement he came to Derby, serving as the landlord of, successively, *The Woodlark,* Bridge Street; the *Old Angel,* Cornmarket, and the *Post Office Hotel,* Victoria Street, retiring from the latter after its transformation into the *Spotted Horse* in 1963 (it is now called *Lloyd's,* but surely should be named after its most notable host?).

Joseph Rostron was born in Heywood, Lancs, in 1910 and was educated at a local elementary school, where he acquired his aptitude for boxing, honing his skills at bouts in local clubs and booths. He died in Derby 12th December 1993. By his wife, Vera, who predeceased him, he left a daughter Jean Anne, wife of Keith Morris of Derby.
[DET. 14/12/1993.]

ROYCE, Sir Henry, 1st Bt, OBE (1863-1933)

Henry Royce was an engineer of incomparable talent, which ability, combined with a high degree of perfectionism, led to the evolution of 'the finest car in the world'. The first prototype, built as a result of the engineer Royce's disgust at a Deauville he had bought the previous year, emerged in 1904 and so caught the imagination of the London dealer Hon C.S.ROLLS (q.v.) in its quietness and perfection that he arranged to take Royce's entire output and to sell the cars as Rolls-Royces. A formal partnership resulted in 1906 and in 1907 the new firm moved from Manchester's Cooke Street (where Royce had originally set up in 1884 making electrical equipment) to Nightingale Road, Derby, where cars were built until 1939. At the same time Royce restricted the possible range of cars he would produce, his motto being 'organise and specialise'. The single model was the peerless Silver Ghost (1907) which was made for some 20 years. Thereafter, for a brief period, the firm did make several models; the Phantom 1, the 20/25hp and the 25/30hp. In 1931 Royce took over Bentley motors, and transformed the latter two models into the 3½ litre and 4¼ litre 'silent Sports Cars'.

The partnership with Rolls brought aviation into the equation, Rolls being a pioneer aviator. He early urged the production of an aero engine of similar reliability into the car. Royce resisted until the pressures of World War One forced his hand, posthumously proving Charles Rolls right; this was to be the future of the company. The result of Royce's war effort was the award in 1918 of an OBE. Later, his decision to supply Supermarine with an engine to challenge for the Schneider Trophy (which the combination of airframe and engine in the Supermarine S6 and S6B won in 1929 and 1931, setting a new air speed record of 408mph) laid the foundation for the future 'Merlin' engine, prototype designs for

which he oversaw before his death in 1933. And it is said that the Merlin won the (second) War.

Frederick Henry Royce was born in Rutland on 27th March 1863. It has always been accepted, until recently, that his father was James Royce of Alwalton Mills in that county (1830-1873), but his great-nephew, Peter, has established that he was the son of James's father, Henry William Royce of South Luffenham Flour Mills (b.1803) by a servant, and that James and his wife, Mary, third daughter of Benjamin King of Edwins Hall, Woodham Ferrers, Essex, thereupon adopted him as their own to obfuscate the true situation and avoid a scandal. James and Mary also had a son (the grandfather of Peter Royce who himself joined Rolls-Royce in Derby as an aero engineer in 1948, married and has five children) and three daughters. H.W.Royce was himself son of Henry Royce of Wing, Rutland. Unfortunately, Henry's adoptive father died suddenly in 1873, and within a year or two he had to find work. Later, through the generosity of an aunt, he was able to embark upon an engineering apprenticeship at the Great Northern Railway's loco works at Doncaster, but his aunt could no longer support him and he had to work in a factory instead. In 1882 he became a tester in a London electrical factory and attended night classes. He founded his own firm in Cooke Strreet, Manchester with A.E.Claremont in 1884, as F.H.Royce and Co. (from 1894 Royce Ltd).

Henry Royce married 16th May 1893 Minnie Grace (d.1936) daughter of Alfred Punt of London and they later lived at West Wittering (Sussex), but never in Derby; they had no issue. He was given a baronetcy 26th June 1930 becoming Sir Henry Royce, Bt. of Seaton, Rutland, his ancestors back at least to his great-grandfather having being natives of that county. He was also a member of the Institutes of Mechanical Engineers, Electrical Engineers and Aeronautical Engineers. After the Schneider Cup success it was said of him that, 'Mr Royce is not a man who prides himself upon inventing things. He likes to perfect things already in existence' a precept which applied equally well to Royce's protégé LORD HIVES (q.v.) and his development of Whittle's jet engine from 1944.

A statue of Royce by Derwent Wood RA was erected in Derby, but no permanent site was ever found for it, and the timid City Fathers, instead of giving it real prominence, handed it over to the Company to erect in front of their new offices at Sinfin, inside which was already a bust of him by William MacMillan.

[DNB; Burke, *Peerage* (1931) 2046; DLC 2/1970; DET, 2 & 6/4/1998.]

RUBBRA, Arthur Alexander, CBE FRAeS (1903-1982)

Arthur Rubbra was another of the talented engineers who worked at Rolls-Royce in the formative years of British Aviation, being Technical Director 1954-66, Chief Technical Adviser from 1966 and consultant two years later. He was also a director of British Space Development, an advisor on Fuel and Power at the Ministry of Power, and a governor of Manchester College of Technology.

Arthur Alexander Rubbra was the younger of two highly talented sons of Edmund James Rubbra of Northampton (d.1947); his elder brother was the composer Prof. Edmund Rubbra, and both were made CBE in the same honours list in 1960. Arthur was educated at Northampton School and gained his BSc at Bristol University. In 1925 he joined Rolls-Royce in Derby in the Experimental Department, later

becoming assistant chief designer and chief designer 1940-44, thereafter assistant (1944-51) and deputy Chief Engineer (1951-54). He was a fellow of the Royal Aeronautical Society.

In 1930 he married Lilian Agnes, daughter of Samuel Webster of Derby, and they lived at 100 Belper Road, where he died in 1982, leaving a son, Colin D.Rubbra and a granddaughter.

[Kelly, *Handbook* (1970) 1707; DET.]

ST HELENS, LORD, see FITZHERBERT

SANDERS, Col. (Sir) Thomas, MP (1610-1695)

Thomas Sanders was a leading figure locally during the Civil War and an ardent opponent of SIR JOHN GELL *(q.v.)* for all that they fought on the same side. Partly their differences were personal, partly because Sanders was an Independent (by far the more fanatical religious element on the Parliamentary Side), whilst Gell was a Presbyterian, and partly because, having garrisoned Burton upon Trent for Gell in April 1643 with 200 infantry, 60 dragoons and a gun, he switched allegiance to Col. Haughton, the Parliamentary commander in Staffordshire, at a crucial time for Derby, when Gell was desperate for the return of his troops. Nevertheless, that October Sanders was elected to the Derbyshire County Committee, largely full of Gell's relatives and supporters, and proceeded to dominate it with his own sympathisers. Later he used his pull as a county landed gentleman to raise several troops of horse, also placing his own supporters in them as officers.

He and Gell really fell out over Gell's brother's candidacy for Parliament in the Recruiter election of September 1645, designed to 'top up' the Commons after the depredations of deaths and purges of Royalists. Although Thomas Gell was elected, it was by rigging the vote, and it took nearly 18 months for the Committee of Privileges to confirm the result. Gell said of Sanders (a man of high moral courage and a formidable opponent, like many fanatics), that he 'had rather fight with Major Sanders than with any Cavalier in England' and that he would 'have his pennyworth out of him'. Subsequently, Gell was impeached and removed from his charge at Derby through Sanders' intriguing; the latter however, went on to be a Colonel in the New Model Army and to hold a Cromwellian Knighthood (not recognised after the Restoration). He fought at Worcester (1653) and with Cromwell in Scotland before losing his commission for being too radical in 1654, only to be reinstated in 1659 in time to help put down Booth's rising. His failure to suppress a riot in favour of a Restoration in Derby was his last act in the saga.

Thomas Sanders was the eldest of nine sons (and three daughters) of Collingwood Sanders (1578-1653) of Cauldwell Hall, and Ireton Parva (near Kedleston). His great-grandfather had acquired Lullington by marriage; previously the family were of Charlewood and Sanderstead, Surrey. His mother was Elizabeth, daughter and heiress of the Presbyterian Edmund Sleigh of Derby and Little Ireton (which he had bought from Gen. Lord Ireton earlier). He was born at his grandfather Sleigh's house in Derby 19th August 1610 and proceeded to Derby School

(c.1620) and Repton; however he did not go to University. When Civil War broke out he was commissioned by Gell as a Captain in his Regiment. After the war he escaped persecution (despite his extremist views) and retired to his estates, where he died, full of years, in 1695. He married Elizabeth, daughter of Henry Goring of Kingston (Staffordshire) and had six sons and two daughters. His eldest son and heir, Samuel, predeceased him leaving, by his second wife, a grand-daughter and heiress who brought Cauldwell Hall to her husband John Mortimer. Samuel's son John (by his third marriage) was of Parkfields, Mackworth, ancestor of the Derby branch of the family, of which Alderman John Sandars (*sic*) was mayor 1839-40, and of many others.

[Visitation of Derby 1662-63; Stone, *op.cit.* 38, 44, 57, 63, 66-70, 78-79, 112; Tachella, *op.cit.* 2.]

Du SAUTOY, S/Ldr. Peter Francis, CBE (1912-1995)

Peter du Sautoy was for five years Chairman of Faber Music Ltd., and Faber (Publishers) 1971-76 as well as a member of the Board of Yale University Press and on the executive committee of the International Publishers' Association. He was also President, *Groupe des Editeurs de Livres de la CEE* and a Council member of the Aldeburgh (Suffolk) Festival from 1976. He was a notable music lover and a key figure in the world of music publishing.

Peter Francis du Sautoy was born 19th February 1912, elder son of Col. Edward Frank du Sautoy OBE (1885-1964) of Warren Hill (Staffordshire) and Eardisland (Herefords.) by his wife, Mabel Emmeline Annie, daughter of W.H.Howse of Handsworth (Birmingham). His grandfather, George (1859-1927), was a Derby brick manufacturer whose own father Edward (1820-74) had been a prominent Derby builder and contractor. The family stem from Jacques du Sautoy, sieur de Melk (Alsace) whose descendant Lt. Pierre Francois du Sautoy was a French naval officer captured by *HMS Lion* off Guinea in 1755.

He settled on parole in Laverstoke (Hants) and his children (by a succession of three English wives) became Protestants. Edward du Sautoy (the builder) was Lt. du Sautoy's great-grandson.

Peter du Sautoy was educated at Uppingham, where he was a Foundation Scholar, and Wadham College, Oxford (MA). He went thence to the Dept of Printed Books, British Museum, in 1935 and a year or so later to be assistant education officer at Oxford, leaving to take a Commission in the RAF in 1940, rising to the rank of Squadron Leader. He joined Faber & Faber in 1946, becoming a director shortly thereafter. He was appointed CBE in 1964.

Du Sautoy married 18th December 1937 Phillis Mary (Mollie) daughter of Sir. Francis Floud KCB, KCSI, KCMG and lived at Aldeburgh. He died 17th July 1995, leaving two sons, Bernard and Stephen, and seven grandchildren. Cllr. George Martin du Sautoy of Derby (b.1941) is his nephew.

[*Who's Who* (1978) 720; Burke, *Landed Gentry* (1952) 722-23; Debrett, *Handbook* (1992) 508; Information courtesy G.M. du Sautoy, Esq.]

SHAW, Lt. Gen. Rt. Hon Sir Frederick, PC, KCB (1861-1942)

General Sir Frederick Shaw, Director of Home defence at the War Office 1915-16, was made Chief of the General Staff by Lloyd George in 1916, serving until the end of hostilities in Europe whereupon he was handed the most poisoned chalice of all: C-in-C Ireland, still seething after 18 month's of rebellion. He was promoted to Lt. General in 1919 and struggled manfully to bring Ireland to order, but retired in 1920 without having achieved stability. For the following decade he was Honorary Colonel of the Gloucestershire regiment.

Frederick Charles Shaw was the second son of John Shaw JP (1826-1906) land agent, of 34, St Mary's Gate and Normanton House, by his wife Mary Jane, daughter of Joseph Cantrell of Ashby-de-la-Zouch (Leics). Mrs Shaw's mother was Anna Maria (1798-1887) a daughter of JOHN

WHITEHURST II *(q.v.)* and her sister Maud (1837-1913) married Joseph Shaw (1827-1906) a Derby solicitor and an uncle of Frederick. The Shaws had ultimately come to Derby from Rosliston. Frederick was born 31st July 1861 at Regent Terrace, Derby and was educated at Repton 1874-78. He was commissioned into the 2nd Bn. 45/95th (Sherwood Foresters') Regiment in 1881 serving in the Egyptian expedition in the following year, and he served in South Africa 1899-1902. He was later also Governor of Kandia, in Crete. In 1913 he was appointed to command 9th Infantry Brigade and in 1915 took command of 29th and 13th Divisions before going to the War Office. He was appointed KCB in 1917 and a Privy Councillor (Ireland) in 1918. He was also holder of the Legion d'Honneur, the White Eagle (Serbia) and Wen Hu (China). He married in October 1890 Florence Edith (d.1918) daughter of Rev. Canon John Denton of Ashby and latterly they lived at Baronwyke, Chichester (Sussex). He died 6th January 1942 leaving a daughter, Phyllis, Mrs Alfred Howell Evans-Gwynne, who, in her turn, left two daughters.

[Kelly, *Handbook* (1939) 1649; Information from Michael Shaw, Esq; Briscoe, *op. cit.* 309, 352.]

SHAW, Sir John, KCMG. (1894-1982)

Sir John Shaw led a distinguised career as a colonial official and diplomat, culminating with his appointmaont as Governor and C-in-C of Trinidad and Tobago in 1947. He had previously served as Chief Secretary of Palestine 1943-46, (acting High Commissioner 1945) his deft handling of the delicate sensibilities in the region securing him a knighthood in the latter year. He was made KCMG on his appointment to Trinidad.

John Valentine Wistar Shaw was the only son of John Shaw of Derby (1860-1923) and Alstonefield Manor who was land agent to the extensive Harpur-Crewe estates. John senior was also the elder brother of SIR FREDERICK SHAW

(q.v.); there was one other brother, W.H.C.Shaw and two sisters. J.V.W.Shaw's third name was derived from the surname of his mother, Emma Wistar, his father's first wife. He had a sister too, Violet Alderson Shaw. He was educated at Repton before serving with the Royal Engineers 1914-19 in France and Palestine, where he was mentioned in dispatches. He then opted for the Colonial Service, his first posting, in 1921, being to the Gold Coast (1921-35) followed by five more years in Palestine, a region on which he rapidly became a notable expert. In 1940 he spent three years as Colonial Secretary, Cyprus, which resulted in a second mention in despatches and, in 1942, a CMG.

He retired in 1950, living at Winchelsea (Sussex) with his wife, Josephine Mary, daughter of Joseph Simpson of Horsehay (Salop), whom he had married in 1926. He died in 1982 leaving two sons, Michael and John Jeremy, the latter liv-

ing with his family in Aukland (NZ) and the former at Winchelsea.

[*Who's Who* (1978) 22-23; Information from Michael Shaw Esq.]

SHIRLEY, Admiral Sir Washington, KG, FRS, 5th Earl Ferrers (1727-1778)

Lord Ferrers was a man of exceptional gifts: naval architect, astronomer (he was made FRS for his observation in 1760 of the transit of Venus), and Vice-Admiral RN; he was also in 1775 an honorary exhibitor at the Royal Academy. In 1760, the execution of his brother Laurence, 4th Lord Ferrers, for the murder of his steward, cut short his promising naval career, but this quickly turned him to develop his architectural talents. He immediately began a wholesale rebuilding of the family seat at Staunton Harold, employing the young William Henderson of Loughborough to oversee the work. In 1763 he designed (on behalf of a committee of Gentlemen and Noblemen of the County, of which he was a member) the Derby Assembly Rooms, this time employing JOSEPH PICKFORD *(q.v.)* as executant architect. The interiors, however, were finished a decade later to the designs of Robert and James Adam, of whom the former remarked of Ferrers' designs: 'I imagine there must be a good deal of difficulty to manage it (the decoration) cleverly, however I never saw a room so awkward that something good could be made of it.'

Ferrers was born 26th May 1722 second son of Hon. Laurence Shirley by his wife Anne, daughter of Sir Walter Clarges, Bt. His father was youngest son of Sir Robert Shirley, Bt, 1st Earl Ferrers and a descendant in the female line of ROBERT FERRERS, EARL OF DERBY *(q.v.)*. He entered the Navy at an early age, being appointed 2nd Lieutenant five years later. He was promoted post Captain 19th April 1746, but came off the active list in 1760 when he succeeded. Nevertheless, he was made Rear Admiral of the White 31st March 1775 and Vice-Admiral of the Blue on 7th December following. He was further promoted Vice-Admiral of the White 19th January 1778.

His influence was far reaching and benign; his astronomical activities drew in P.P.BURDETT *(q.v.)* and James Ferguson; his building activities greatly benefited Pickford and his patronage of JOSEPH WRIGHT *(q.v.)* from whom he commissioned *The Orrery* had far reaching consequences for the development of British art. He married Anne, daughter of John Elliot of Plymouth (d.1791) but had no issue on his death on 2nd October 1778 at Chartley Hall (Staffordshire) – the ruined castle in the park of which twice inspired Wright to insert it into his landscapes. He was succeeded as 6th Earl by a nephew.

[DNB, Saunders, *op.cit* 59-63; Burke, *Peerage* (1970) 998-1001.]

SHORE, Jane (d.1527)

Jane became mistress to Edward IV in about 1473 or 1474, and she exerted a considerable influence over the king. She combined with noteworthy physical charms a ready wit, a gift of repartee, could read and write (a considerable attainment in those days) and knew instinctively when to keep her mouth shut. Further, Sir Thomas More claimed that her influence on her monarch was entirely benign; that she never spoke against anyone and that she frequently 'put in a good word' for those out of favour stands greatly to her credit.

Until 1972 even her identity was in doubt, but it is now possible to identify her as Elizabeth (not Jane, surely only a soubriquet) daughter of John Lambert, a London mercer of great fortune and Amy Marshall, his wife. At some date before 1474 she married William Shore (d.1494) a Derby-born mercer based in London, Middleburg (Zeeland), and Derby, whose first wife, the sister of John Agard of Foston, had died. Elizabeth, as we must call her, petitioned the Pope for a divorce from Shore, on grounds of frigidity and impotence, in 1476 and this appears to have succeeded, for Shore seems subsequently to have gone abroad for eight or ten years. The effect was, of course, to declare him impotent and to deny him any further opportunity for marriage. He died without issue in 1494, although cousins continued his family line in Derby (see below). Shore's ex-wife's troubles began on the death of Edward IV in 1483. She transferred her affections to the Marquess of Dorset, but was briefly imprisoned for adultery and later paraded through the city as a harlot. However, she survived to re-marry the King's solicitor Thomas Lynam (it is not clear if the marriage actually took place, however), but she is believed to have died in relative poverty early in 1527, without having had any known issue. In her old age she was befriended by Sir Thomas More.

[DNB; DAJ. CVI (1986) 130-31; Craven (1988) 45.]

SHORE, Sir John, MD (1616-1680)

Sir John Shore was a Restoration courtier and physician who was knighted at Whitehall 6th January 1667 by Charles II, to whom he had acted as medical adviser on behalf of Nell Gwyn, amongst others. Shore was a protégé of the 1st Duke of Newcastle and Shore's Derby residence, indeed, was Newcastle House on the north side of the Market Place on which, in 1670, the then Dr Shore paid tax on a considerable 18 hearths.

A distant relative of the husband of JANE SHORE *(q.v.)* Sir John Shore was born in 1616 at Snitterton Hall, eldest of four sons of John Shore of that place (which his Grandfather, John, purchased in 1596 and who died in 1639) by Mary Burgess, an Edwinstowe (Notts) heiress. A Thomas Shore was Bailiff of Derby 1385/6 and MP for the Borough in 1397 and 1411; his son was probably the Sir John Shore who appears in the 1433 list of Derbyshire Gentlemen whom the Lords Teignmouth *(q.v.)* claimed as an ancestor. Shore is thought to have been educated at Derby School from whence he proceeded to Christs' College Cambridge taking his MD in 1656. His first wife was Dorothy, daughter of John Harpur of Breadsall, the widow of Sir John FitzHerbert of Norbury. She died, apparently without issue, 16th March 1666. He remarried Sarah (d.1727) daughter of John Chambers of Derby (kin to THOMAS CHAMBERS *(q.v.)*) and had two sons and two (in some sources four) daughters. The elder son, baptised at All Saints', Derby 20th

November 1693 (d.1741) was of London and, by Sarah, daughter of Abraham Wilner of Barking, Essex was ancestor of SIR JOHN SHORE, 1ST LORD TEIGNMOUTH *(q.v.)*.

[Visitation 1662; Foster's *Peerage* (1881) 50-51; Burke, *Peerage* (1970) 2616-17.]

SHORE, Sir John, Bt. 1st Lord Teignmouth, PC (1751-1834)

Lord Teignmouth was a member of the Supreme Council of Bengal 1786-89 and Governor-General of India from 1792-97, being created a baronet 2nd October 1792, this despite Shore having been (in Edmund Burke's opinion) tainted by an involvement in the affairs of Warren Hastings. His period in office was marked by a quietetude arising from his pursuit of an 'unambitious and equitable' policy, largely dictated by the wishes of Parliament and the East India Company. Generally, he was more keen to extend trade than the territories of the Company's domains. The negative side of this was to allow the French to build up their strength and the Mahratta Princes to harry Hyderabad. The resulting military lull also encouraged Tippoo Sultan to expand his forces. However he

successfully brought about a change in the succession in Oudh at great personal risk, with widely praised results. On laying down office he was raised to the Peerage of Ireland as 1st Lord Teignmouth of Teignmouth, Devon, 24th October 1797, taking his title from his home, whence he had moved on marrying, 14th February 1786, Charlotte (d. 13th July 1834) daughter and heir of James Cornish of that place.

John Shore was born in St James', London, 8th October 1751 elder son of Thomas Shore (1710-59) of Heathcote near Hartington (from which John took the title of his baronetcy) and Melton, Suffolk, only son of John Shore of London, himself the elder son of SIR JOHN SHORE (q.v.). His younger brother, Rev. Thomas William Shore was vicar of Sandal (Yorks) and Ollerton (Devon) and left descendants. John was educated at Harrow where he was a contemporary of R.B.Sheridan and 1st Marquess of Hastings. After a book-keeping course at Hoxton he entered the East India Company's service, being appointed to the Secret Political Department in 1769. He became an expert in oriental languages.

After his retirement as Governor General he was in 1807 appointed a member of the East India Company's Board of Control, and was simultaneously appointed to the Privy Council. He never took his seat in the Irish Parliament, and later turned to religion, becoming first President of the British and Foreign Bible Society. He died at his London house 14th February 1834 – his wedding anniversary – and was buried in Marylebone Parish Church. He was succeeded by the eldest of his three sons, Charles John, with the death in 1981 of whose great-grandson, Sir Frederick Maxwell Anthony Shore, 7th Lord Teignmouth, the titles became extinct. Lord Macaulay, a friend, said of Teignmouth, that, 'of his integrity, humanity and honour it is impossible to speak too lightly.' [DNB; Burke, loc.cit.]

SIMMONDS, Thomas Charles (d.1912)

Thomas Simmonds was the virtual founder (with A.O.DEACON, q.v.) of the Derby School of Art and its first principal. From 1871 to 1889 he was also drawing master at Derby School, his son Thomas Charles acting as his deputy 1886-89 before succeeding him. Simmonds was a great supporter of the Arts and Crafts Movement; his last house, Ravenshoe, 272 Burton Road, was probably designed by himself and built by C.E.Humphries in the latter's favourite white brick c.1876. It was full of closely designed individual details, all hand made to the highest standards, even down to window latches, door furniture, carved ornament and so on, much of it quite possibly executed by his more talented pupils. Conversion of the house after his son moved out into a Synagogue preserved much of this only for it all to be swept away when the building was tastelessly gutted by the Walbrook Housing Association in 1986.

Simmonds' career began in Cheltenham and in 1881-85 he was head of Glasgow Art School. He left two sons, Thomas – also and artist and teacher (who continued his father's Atelier of Art at Ravenshoe) and Douglas (b.1886.) as well as a daughter, Minnie Evelyn Constance, who in 1895 married Frederick Edward (1863-1901) third son of WILLIAM BEMROSE II (q.v.) by whom she had two sons, Eric and Cyril. T.C.Simmonds was made Hon ARCA (Lond) in 1903 and died in 1912.
[Tachella, op.cit., xvi, xvii, 143; Derbyshire Red Book (1913) 264; DM. 16/8/1912.]

SIMPSON, Sir George Clarke, KCB, CBE (1878-1965)

Sir George Simpson was a polar explorer who went with Capt. Scott to the Antartic on his ill-fated 1912 expedition and an important pioneer of modern meteorology, serving as Director of the Meteorological Office 1920-38 and President of the British Meteorological Society 1940-42. His presence on the 1910-12 British Antarctic expedition was through his work as Scientific Assistant at the British Meteorological Office (1905-06), at the Indian Meteorological Department (1906-10) and his lecturing at the

University of Manchester. He was also a friend of Lt. H.R.Bowers (who later perished with Scott) who prophetically wrote to him as the Pole party set out, 'I regard the chances of Captain Scott's success as practically certain. But one cannot legislate against catastrophe – that is in the hands of God alone…'

George Clarke Simpson was born over his father's hardware shop at 44 East Street, Derby on 2nd September 1878 second of three sons, and third of seven children. His father was Alderman Arthur Simpson JP (1851-1917) Mayor of Derby 1907-08; his mother was Alice Lambton (1853-1937) daughter of T.W.Clarke of Sutton Bridge, Lincs. The family was an old Derby one, Ald. Simpson being 5th in descent from Isaac Simpson, living 1730. Three of his brothers formed a brush manufacturing business in Birmingham, one, George, being father of Rev. Prof. David Capell Simpson, professor of the Interpretation of Holy Scripture at Oxford. George was brought up at the later family home at Lambton Villa, 69, Wilson Street.

'Sunny Jim' Simpson was educated at the Diocesan School, Friar Gate, did a few years as a Sunday School teacher before entering Owen's College Manchester, going on to the University of Göttingen. He became a fellow of the University of Manchester in 1901 becoming D.Sc, and being elected FRS in 1915. He was appointed CBE in 1919, CB in 1926 and was promoted KCB in 1935. He was also holder of an honorary LLD. (Aberdeen).

He married on 23rd September 1914 Dorothy, daughter of Cecil Stephen of Sydney NSW and they lived in London where they had three sons and a daughter. The eldest son, Scott Simpson (1915-81) was named after Simpson's friend Capt. Scott (Lady Scott was his godmother); he was later professor of geology at Exeter University. Scott Simpson's own grandson, Scott Hurrell Simpson is a Ministry of Defence metallurgist and former international canoeist. Sir George's nephew by marriage was the late A.R. (Nick) Carter MBE (1914-96) for long an ornament of the Derby Shakespeare Society. Sir George died in 1965.

[DET. 7/12/1984; *Who's Who* (1961) 2788; Information courtesy late Mary Carter, and Mr Michael Simpson.]

SMITH, John Raphael (1751-1812)

J.R.Smith was a superb mezzotint engraver and print publisher, producing over 300 prints and employing the young Thomas Girtin and J.M.W.Turner to colour them. He was also a portraitist in pastels and an occasional miniaturist of some distinction. He only occasionally painted in oils, usually of genre subjects, two of which, *The Moralist* (1786) and *The Widow's Tale* (1783) have recently been acquired by Derby Museum.

He owed his singularly appropriate middle name to his father, the Derby landscape artist, Thomas Smith (d.1767), who had christened his elder brother Thomas Coreggio. The latter was reared an artist, but was less successful that John Raphael, resorting to advertising in the *Derby Mercury*, 18th March 1768, his services for 'Coach, sign and house painting, oil and bur-

nished guilding... etc.'. Thomas died in September 1811. There was a third brother, Charles Leonardo born in 1756, but who appears to have died young, and a sister, Catherine Felicia who was born in 1760 and who married at Duffield in June 1790, James Alexander Wright of Chapel-en-le-Frith. Their mother's name was Hannah and the family lived in a largish house on Bridge Gate.

John Raphael was baptised at St Alkmund's on 25th May 1751, and after an elementary education was apprenticed to Thomas Sale, a prominent linen draper and close friend of JOSEPH WRIGHT *(q.v.)*, which may suggest a connection between Wright and the elder Smith. Two years later, however, at the death of his father at Bristol, he went to London to continue shopwork before engraving his first mezzotint in 1769, becoming Engraver to the Prince of Wales in 1784. He copied works by Wright (over 20), Zoffany, Ramsay and Romney and exhibited at the Royal Academy between 1779 and 1805. He also painted – in oils – an extremely fine portrait of the Derbyshire radical Sir Francis Burdett, Bt MP, of Foremarke in 1799.

He had more or less retired by 1802 when he moved to Sheffield where he produced some small pastel studies and encouraged the youmg Derbyshire-born Francis Chantrey, going on to settle in Doncaster in 1809, where he died on 2nd March 1812. He married twice, leaving by his first wife a daughter, Emma and a son named, in the family tradition, John Rubens Smith (1775-1847). Emma was also an artist of talent by 1808 (when she was 21) and her brother was a successful painter and engraver who emigrated to the USA in 1809, dying in New York aged 72 on 21st August 1847.

[Local records; Notes in Derby Museum's Art Dept.; Waterhouse, E., *Dictionary of Eighteenth Century British Painters* (Woodbridge, 1981) 353; DM 18/9/1767; DLC 2/1973.]

SMITH, Sir John (1828-1897)

'Brassy Smith's' has for generations been the name associated with a large brass and white-

metal foundry on Cotton Lane which only closed in 1996. It was established by Sir John Smith on Traffic Street in the 1850s, supplying components to the Midland Railway, but it prospered exceedingly and moved to Cotton Lane some 25 years later, becoming a Limited Liability Company with nationwide connections and contracts. These went well beyond the field of railway engineering, encompassing heavy engineering and household appliances as well as very fine quality domestic work (including gilt bronze) like door escutcheons, balustrades, lamps etc. Indeed Sir John's elegant Regency House on Duffield Road (enlarged by him in the 1880s) boasted an exceptional range of such objects all, unfortunately, swept away by its demolition in 1991.

John 'Brassy' Smith was the son of George Smith, a Derby man, but was born at Ashby-de-la-Zouch (Leics) where his parents were then living, although he was educated in Derby. He was a self-made man according to himself, but George was, in fact, a small scale brassfounder (supplier of such things as clock components) and after an apprenticeship in the trade he transformed the business in Traffic Street to good effect.

He was elected a councillor for Bridge Ward in 1862, transferring to Derwent Ward in 1887, and was an excellent committee man. He became Mayor in 1872-73 an alderman and JP, and presided over the Royal Visit of the Prince of Wales in December 1872 with great panache, being rewarded with a Knighthood in the Golden Jubilee honours of 1887. A liberal, he was also a prominent freemason and patron of Derby School. Smith married twice, his second wife being the daughter of John Snow of Southampton who died 3rd September 1898, some nine months after Sir John, who died at Parkfield's House on 10th December 1897 without issue. His heir was his nephew Cllr. Albert Ottewell, who continued the foundry with as much success as his uncle.

[MMD. 1. 34, 36.]

SOAR, Rebecca, Mrs Oswald Crompton (1895-1947)

Rebecca Crompton (as she is usually known) was one of the country's leading exponents of the art of embroidery and indeed, did much to take it from the drawing room and into the art gallery. She was a Board of Education Inspector from 1930 and a lecturer in art (and especially embroidery and textile design) at both the Royal College of Art and the Victoria and Albert Museum.

Rebecca Soar was the second of four daughters of William Soar, a Midland Railway official of an old-established Derby family, and was born 7th August 1895. She also had a brother, Harry, born two years before her. Rebecca was educated (as one of the first intake) at Parkfields Cedars Girls' Grammar School and from 1913-16 at Derby School of Art. In 1917 she obtained a post as an art teacher at Northampton, moving to Croydon (Surrey) School of Art in 1923 where she taught for 12 years. In 1922 she met and later married Oswald Crompton RMS, ARCA, also a

lecturer and artist at Northampton, who was later Principal of Croydon Art School. They later lived at Ealing. Their only child, Phyllida, died aged eight in 1930. Mrs Crompton died 25th August 1947; her neice Rebecca Dorman (daughter of her sister Phyllis, later Mrs Speakman) having been named after her.

[Local Studies Library, various records; notes accompanying an exhibition at Pickford's House, Derby, 1995.]

SOROCOLD, George (1668-1738)

George Sorocold was one of several unsung heroes of Derby, being primarily a hydraulic engineer of great talent who is most famous locally for installing Derby's first piped water supply. This was achieved in 1691-93 by using a patent wheel which rose and fell without loss of efficiency with the height of the river. The water was raised by a screw to a tank behind St Michael's Church from whence it was piped (through four miles of bored out elm piping) to a number of public outlets in the town. In falling from the holding tank to pipe the water drove a device for boring out fresh wooden pipes (and which was later adapted by him to grind flints) which effectively made the system self-financing. He installed 18 similar schemes in other UK towns and cities including two in London. He went on to develop hydraulic works of a similar nature for gentlemen's parks, notably at Sprotborough (Yorks), Melbourne and Calke. He also developed the work of Sir Cornelius Vermuyden (1595-1677) in draining lead and coal mines and indeed, may have been trained by one of Sir Cornelius' assistants. He seems to have worked closely with Thomas Savery (with Newcomen, a pioneer of the 'fire-engine', or atmospheric engine) who spoke highly of his friend.

Sorocold was of Lancastrian minor gentry stock, although his grandfather bought land in Egginton parish and his father James (1627-75) seems to have lived there and in Derby, where George was born in 1668. He was probably brought up by Elizabeth, his mother, after his father's death, and may have served an apprenticeship with Vermuyden's assistants at Wirksworth. His earliest work was a water supply at Macclesfield 1685-87 and the re-casting and hanging the 10 bells at All Saints', Derby in 1687; soon afterwards he installed a Carillon there too. His pumps were installed at mines as far apart as Sheldon (Derbys) – owned by JOHN FLAMSTEED *(q.v.)* – and Alloa (Scotland).

He worked on river improvements, on the Derwent Navigation (1702, implemented 1721), the Lea (Middlesex), Lower Aire (Yorks) and the Cam. He advocated using locks with low falls in preference to few locks with falls of over 4 or 5 feet. He also seems to have been involved in the building of Rotherhithe Docks (London) and, with Thomas Steer, received the Freedom of Liverpool for building the first wet dock there in 1708.

His greatest work was in the engineering and building of the Derby Silk Mill for JOHN and SIR THOMAS LOMBE *(q.v.)*, 1718-21. Although some statements suggest a misfortune befell him before 1717 – 'the ingenious, unfortunate mathematician' – he was later recorded as falling into the Silk Mill Water Wheel and emerging unharmed by Daniel Defoe (1727). His family's surrender of the Derby Waterworks lease in 1738 suggests he died about then, although when and where exactly has so far eluded research.

He married at All Saints' 7th December 1684, Mary, sister of Ald. HENRY FRANCEYS *(q.v.)* and they had 13 children by 1702, of whom four are known. His wife died in 1728. He was also a gifted cartographer, as the maps he drew for presentation to Parliament of his various river improvement schemes are of outstanding quality. He may also have known JOHN WHITEHURST FRS *(q.v.)* whose own interest in hydraulics is otherwise difficult to account for. It is also possible that he installed an atmospheric engine at the Derby Silk Mill *c.*1727/32. His influence as an intellectual bridge between Flamsteed and the circle of Whitehurst may have been crucial, but requires further research.

[DAJ. LVII (1936.) 43-93; Jenkins, R., *George Sorocold, a chapter in the History of Public Water Supply* (Cambridge, 1936.) 149-53; Newcomen Society, *Transactions* XXIX (1953-55) 39; Defoe, D., *A Tour Throughout the Whole Island of Great Britain* (London 1727) III.38 & (1748); Craven, (1996) 14-18.]

SPENCER, Herbert (1820-1903)

Herbert Spencer was arguably the greatest philosopher of his age and the originator of the modern science of sociology which emerged in his *First Principles of Sociology* (1876, 3 vols.). He also wrote extensively on science and the application of knowledge, on ethics and, in a divergent and individual way, on psychology. He was never a great reader of the works of others (he said that he 'threw down' Kant after reading a few pages, on the grounds that he didn't agree with him) and his own writings were at the same time limited by this lack of background, but full of fresh insights as a result of his thought being unfettered by those of others. He believed (as did ERASMUS DARWIN *(q.v.)*, by whom he was indirectly influenced) in the unity of all science and that the basic processes in all the realms of being are essentially identical. He also sought to draw out a relationship between biology and sociology which led him to embrace the theories of Erasmus Darwin's grandson Charles.

By evolution Spencer meant the processes of increasing differentiation and integration which he believed could be discerned in all the aspects of the universe, and that in this sense evolution is much more apparent in human social aggregates than in the field of organic nature.

Spencer not only introduced the concept of 'structural functionalism' but also laid the foundations for a cybernetic analysis of social phenomena, in addition to developing ideas which, in a crude form, underlie most contemporary thinking about 'development' and 'resistance to change'. In his early work *Education* (1861) he suggested that children should be trained not by traditional discipline and learning methods but by being given the greatest possible amount of freedom, sentiments rapidly going out of fashion today. In stark contrast, in *Man Versus the State*

Herbert Spencer

(1884) he advocated the greatest possible diminution in the interference of government in peoples' lives, a trend also currently going into eclipse.

Herbert Spencer was born in a house (later shortsightedly destroyed by the City fathers of Derby) in Exeter Street 27th April 1820, the only surviving child of (William) George Spencer (1790-1866) and Harriet, daughter and heiress of John Holmes, of Brailsford and Derby, a plumber and glazier who had once been an apprentice of and assistant to JOHN CHATTERTON FRS *(q.v.)*.

The family had been Kirk Ireton yeomen since the later 16th century, and his grandfather, Matthew (1762-1827), had come to Derby where he established a school at 4 Green Lane. He was a Wesleyan whose parents had been amongst John Wesley's earliest local followers, and believed in offering an education which did not neglect science and the arts, coming increasingly under the influence of Erasmus Darwin, whose own beliefs closely matched this pattern, and whose second family (by the former Mrs Pole) received their primary education under Spencer. Indeed the school roll bears the names of many in Darwin's circle, including the younger Whitehursts, Emeses, Strutts and Davises. Spencer's father, eldest of four (surviving) sons and a daughter, continued the school and was also secretary of Darwin's Derby Philosophical Society under the younger JOHN CHATTERTON (q.v.).

Spencer's upbringing, later at 8 Wilmot Street (also demolished) was neglected by his father (to whom, nevertheless, he was devoted) and he shone only at science and mathematics at school although his father greatly encouraged his interests in these fields. In 1833 he went to his uncle, Rev. Thomas Spencer (1796-1853), incumbent of Hinton Charterhouse and a leading radical, for some three years before embarking on a career as a civil engineer engaged in railway construction. It was at this period, having witnessed the disastrous Derby flood of 1st April 1842, that he evolved an ambitious scheme to prevent a recurrence involving sluices on the Markeaton Brook and a movable barrier south of the Borough on the Derwent, which he offered (without success) to the City Fathers. Ironically, it was adopted almost unaltered after the equally serious inundation of 22nd May 1932, nearly 30 years after his death at Brighton, unmarried, on 8th December 1903.

Also in his youthful period he came to identify himself with the Chartist movement, anti-corn law legislation, with the issues of slavery, and Universal Suffrage, becoming honorary secretary of the Derby branch of the Chartist movement. In 1848 he was appointed sub-editor of *The Economist*, a post that enabled him to build up his acquaintanceships in London. At this time he became very close to Mary Ann Evans (George Eliot) 'the most admirable woman I ever met' whom he ultimately did not marry as 'the absence of personal beauty restrained the growth of his affection'! He was also, from about 1854-55, beset with a series of nervous breakdowns which plagued the remainder of his life and made writing difficult. Nevertheless, from the later 1860s his work and fame suddenly blossomed and his financial worries began to wane. In character, he was highly likeable, but 'beset with the certainty of his own rectitude', which at times hampered his relationships. He also consistantly declined the honours which from the 1880s were showered upon him; he also became obsessively pacifist with advancing age. Only in his last years would he allow his portrait to be painted, although RICHARD KEENE (q.v.) photographed him as a young man.

His uncle Henry, (1792-1834) a Macclesfield and Derby lace manufacturer, married Elizabeth, daughter of William Antill of Spondon whose grandson William Antill Spencer was one of his heirs. The issue of another uncle, John, an attorney, migrated to California where their posterity remain.

[DNB; *Autobiography* (2 vols. London 1904); Derby Local Studies library, various records.]

SPRY, Constance, OBE (1886-1960)

Constance Spry was perhaps the first person to promote the arrangement of flowers to an art form, henceforward to be studied and taken seriously. Her totally fresh approach to all aspects of flowers – leaves, branches and fruits – for decorative purposes established her with a reputation worldwide which she enhanced by writing, lecturing, broadcasting and opening a shop in London. Becoming rapidly a *sine que non* at Royal and Society functions, her expertise became much sought after, the weddings of the Duke of Gloucester, Princess Elizabeth (now HM The Queen) and at the coronation in 1953 being the apogee of her career and resulted in the OBE in the latter year.

Constance Fletcher was born in Wilson Street, Derby on 5th December 1886, only daughter – with five sons – of George Fletcher, a former Midland Railway clerk who had become head of Derby Technical School in the 1890s. Her mother was Henrietta Maria Clark. The family later moved to Dublin where her father was appointed assistant secretary to the Irish Department of Agriculture. She was educated at Alexandra School and College, Dublin and her facility with blooms became evident at an early age. However, she devoted herself to the care of children in South Ireland under the Marchioness of Aberdeen, but with the outbreak of World War One she was appointed head of Women's Staff at the Dept of Aircraft Construction, Ministry of Munitions. After the war, she became principal of the London County Council Day Continuation school in Homerton. In the 1930s she started a school of floristry and flower decoration, and this developed a cookery element and later was established at Winkfield Place (Berks) as an academy teaching young people all aspects of efficient home management; in a sense the first 'finishing school'.

Spry (her *nom-de-plume*) wrote 12 books on her subject, designed vases, carpet patterns, encouraged the flower club movement and lectured in most of the English-speaking world. She died unmarried, at Winkfield on 3rd January 1960.

[DNB; Coxhead, E., *Constance Spry* (London, 1975).]

STANLEY Rt. Hon Sir Albert, 1st Lord Ashfield, MP, PC (1874-1948)

Lord Ashfield was that rare thing, a Derbeian expert on railways who was unconnected with the Midland Railway. In fact, his earlier years were spent in America, and it was American railway management practices he was schooled in, mainly metropolitan (today's urban rapid transit systems), his first major post being from 1895-1907 General Manager of American Electric Railways in Detroit and New Jersey. In 1907 he

was appointed General Manager of the Metropolitan District railway in London, running successively the Underground Group (1912-14, 1919-33) the London Passenger Transport Board (1933-47) and becoming a member of the nationalised British Transport Commission in 1948.

Albert Henry Knattriess was born in New Normanton 8th November 1874, son of Henry Knattriess (d.1932), coach painter, of immigrant stock, and Elizabeth (d.1925) daughter of George Twigg of Derby. When Albert was about six, the family migrated to Detroit (USA) and two years later his father adopted the surname of Stanley in lieu of Knattriess. Two relatives, Clement and Frederick Knattriess, who respectively established a pork butchery in Abbey Street and a provision dealership in Derby Street, chose to remain in Derby. After an effortless passage through the American public educational system, Albert Stanley chose railway administration as his career. On 5th December 1904, he married Grace Lowrey, daughter of Edward L. Woodruff of Detroit.

During World War One Stanley was appointed Director General of Mechanical Transport and was elected to Parliament as a Conservative for Ashton-under-Lyne in 1916 serving as President of the Board of Trade under Lloyd George until he resigned his seat in 1920 to take up a peerage (of 9th January) as 1st Lord Ashfield of Southwell. He had been made a Privy Councillor in 1916 and Knighted two years earlier. He was also a director of ICI and the Midland Bank and lived at Sunningdale (Berks). He died 4th November 1948 leaving two daughters, Marion Woodruff (who was four times married and left issue by her third husband R.A. Hubbard) and Grace Lowrey, latterly Mrs H.J. Buckmaster.

[DNB; Burke, *Peerage* (1931) 229.]

STENSON, John (1747-1817)

John Stenson was Derby's first barometer and scientific instrument maker, a genuine eccentric, tenor, musician and 'A most punctual and upright man' whose chief relaxation was all-year-round bathing in the River Derwent. He also made saccharometers, hygrometers, thermometers and 'electrical pistols', advertising his services in the *Derby Mercury* in stanzas of amusing doggerel which, taken with his reputation for musicianship – which surely brought him into contact with CHARLES DENBY, JOSEPH WRIGHT and P.P.BURDETT *(q.q.v.)* – may have been merely the lyrics of songs of his own devising.

John Stenson was born in St Werburgh's parish and baptised at that church 6th March 1747, elder son of Joseph Stenson (1718-99), a stockiner and May Brown of Findern. The grandfather, Thomas, was a framework-knitter from Foremark who died in All Saints' parish in 1751. Joseph had two brothers, Thomas (1706-75) also a stockiner (whose own son became a bookseller) and John (1713-80) a hosier. Young John would seem to have been apprenticed a weatherglass maker to none other than JOHN WHITEHURST FRS *(q.v.)* probably 1761-68, for he is the only maker who used Whitehurst's patent 0-60 scale on his barometers in lieu of the more usual 28-31 inches. There are eight endearingly wayward advertisements for his services in the *Derby Mercury* by 1792 and others later. The name of his wife has not emerged, but his son, a musician, was proposed as the successor of Charles Denby as organist of All Saints' in December 1792 but was unsuccessful. He died at home in Bag Lane (East Street) in February 1817. [Craven (1996) 108-112; Local parish registers; *Derby Mercury* 27/6/1782, etc. to 5/7/1792, 27/12/1792; Poll Books.]

STEVENS, Henry Isaac, FRIBA (1806-1873)

Second son of Isaac Nehemiah Stevens of Pimlico (London, later of Ockbrook) Steward to Derbyshire landowner Lord Chesterfield (1776-1856), Henry was grandson of James Stevens. his mother was Elizabeth Young who married Isaac Nehemiah at St George's, Hanover Square, 18th March 1799. The third son, Nehemiah Edward

Stevens (1814-79) was also an architect but neither lived nor practised in Derbyshire. Henry was baptised 15th November 1806 at St George's, Hanover Square, and was probably trained at Bretby, under William Martin, Lord Chesterfield's Agent and also an Architect, where the family seem to have had close connections. He also probably studied in the office of Sir Jeffrey Wyatville, who designed Bretby Castle with Martin, and he married Martin's daughter, Anne, at Repton (7/8/1832) settling and beginning work at Hartshorne, also on Lord Chesterfield's estate. They had four children (John Henry, 1833-37; Richard Howe, 1841-42; Jane, 1835-50 and Emily, b.1838) of whom only the youngest outlived her parents, dying unmarried 28th April 1895. By 1841 they were living in Derby (3 The Terrace, London Road) with an office in the Cornmarket. Stevens was Churchwarden of All Saints' 1842-43 but by 1852 the family was living at Mackworth. About 1865 he built himself the Hollies, 20 Pear Tree Road, and by this time he had transferred his office to 45 Friar Gate, to which he added a jokey brick porch in neo-Norman style. He served as a Tory Councillor 1862-64 and 1866-69, and his will is dated 18th November 1872. He died at home 30th April 1873, his wife moving to Quarndon where she lived until she died at 82 on 21st February 1884. He was FRIBA by 1851.

Stevens was Derby's foremost and most accomplished Victorian architect, with an extensive ecclesiastical practice. He was an assured practitioner of gothic revival, although his secular work was largely Jacobethan. Nevertheless, on the rare occasions he was able to build in classical styles, he showed a deft touch, as with the Neo-Grec 93 Friar Gate (*c.*1842), the improvements at Calke Abbey (1842), Full Street, Derby, Baths (1856) and the Congregational Chapel, London Road, Derby, of 1843-45. His parish churches ranged from St James, Shardlow (1837-38) – which he later claimed he could never pass by but felt obliged to avert his eyes – to SS Philip and James, Atlow of 1873-74, taking in other notable examples at Stapenhill (1838), St Martin, Osmaston-by-Ashbourne (1845); St Alkmund,

Derby (1846), and 34 others. He also built numerous parsonages and schools including several in Derby of which one survives in Friar Gate. Other Derbyshire public buildings included Shardlow Workhouse (1837); the demolished Derby Savings Bank, Friar Gate (1839-40), and the branch at Ashbourne (1843), Ironville Mechanics' Institute (1848), two large extensions to the Derbyshire General Infirmary (1850 and 1867), the Diocesan Training College, Derby (1851), the Temperance Hall nearby (1853), Derby's new market complex and hotel (1852-61), the Melbourne Athenaeum (1853), a brewery at Burton (1854-55), Nottingham Road Cemetery, Derby (1854-55) and Ashby Market Hall (Leics, 1856-57).

He designed a number of shops in Derby and a great variety of domestic work, including villas – much like his parsonages – and some country houses. Most, like Breadsall Hill Top (1867) were relatively modest in scale; his greatest was the vast Osmaston Manor of 1846-49 for Francis Wright. This included Lodges, ancilliary and garden buildings, and most of a new village nearby including a new church; a noble and exciting ensemble marred since 1964 by the destruction of the house itself.

Stevens was joined in partnership by F.J.Robinson in 1864 who had joined him as a pupil from 1859. They also had a London office from 1856 to c.1862 which might suggest that some work undertaken in the London area may yet come to light.

[Askey, Mark, unpublished thesis 1994; local Census returns; *Derby Mercury* 2/5/1838, 26/2/1840, 20/5/1840; Jacques, A.S., *History of Melbourne* (Derby 1933) 90-91; Swift, J., *History of Hazlewood* (Derby 1931) etc.]

STEVENS, Henry (1856-1934)

Henry Stevens is famous as the inventor of that quintessentially American delicacy the hot dog, but ironically was born and bred in Derby. Despite the essential nature of the hot dog, Stevens was a successful American potato merchant and entrepreneur.

Harold Mosley Stevens was born in Litchurch, Derby in 1856, eldest of three sons; their father was probably James Stevens of Regent Street, Litchurch, Midland Railway Locomotive foreman at Derby and later at St Pancras. The younger brother was James Erasmus Stevens (b.1864), later of Rotherham (Yorks). Harold went to the USA in 1890 and, after suffering some vicissitudes, made a fortune printing baseball score cards and selling them at games. It was also at baseball matches that an accident of convenience over decorum obliged him to obtain a snack by placing a sausage in a bun. Once invented, however, Stevens did not fail to capitalise upon it, and his licensed vendors of hot dogs soon became fixtures on the corners of American city streets. He died in the USA on 2nd May 1934, leaving, by his wife Mary (who was from Doncaster), two sons, Francis Claud and Harold A.Stevens (1879-1961) who continued the business, and a daughter, Anne.

[*New York Herald Tribune* 4/5/1934; Derbyshire Family History Society *Branch News* 62 (6/1992) 14, 73 (6/1993) 37; DET. 16/11/1961.]

STRUTT, Rt. Hon Edward, 1st Lord Belper, FRS (1801-1880)

Edward Strutt was the scion of a most notable Derbyshire family, and the only son of WILLIAM STRUTT FRS *(q.v.)* of St Helen's House, Derby. He was the eldest grandson of the cotton pioneer JEDEDIAH STRUTT *(q.v.)* and was born in Derby 26th October 1801, his mother being Barbara, the daughter of THOMAS EVANS *(q.v.)* of Darley Abbey, financier and cotton manufacturer.

Edward's father was for over 30 years Chairman of the Derby Improvement Commission, inventor, architect, radical and educational pioneer. He was a protegé of Erasmus Darwin and thus carried into the 19th century the radical ethos and scientific enquiry of the Lunar Society.

The son embodied many of his father's virtues but combined them with political acumen and a more national vision. He was educated in the scientific tradition at Manchester College, York, before going up to Trinity, Cambridge, where he was President of the Union. He graduated BA in 1823 and MA three years later. He then went to Lincoln's Inn, transferring to the Inner Temple in 1825 but was never called to the bar. In London he was befriended by his father's friend, the philosophical radical, Jeremy Bentham and also by James and John Stuart Mill, thus strengthening his radical credentials. In 1830 – the year of his father's death – he returned to Derby, taking up residence in the family town house St Helen's – much improved in its 'Domestic Economy' by his father – and entered Parliament as one of the Derby MPs, whereupon he swiftly established himself at the forefront of the radical wing of the Liberal Party, becoming Chief Commissioner for Railways 1846-48.

However, both he and his colleague, the Staffordshire grandee Hon. Frederick Leveson – Gower, were disqualified at Derby in the election of 1847 due to their agents (unbeknown to either of the candidates) having accepted bribes. However, he returned to Parliament in 1851 for Arundel, which seat he exchanged for Nottingham a year later. He then took up residence on the family estate at Kingston-upon-Soar (Notts) upon which he built the present Hall. He retained the seat until 1856 when he was elevated to the peerage as first Lord Belper. His only government post was as Chancellor for the Duchy of Lancaster 1852-54. He became an authority on free trade, law reform and (of course) education.

His honours were numerous: he was High Sheriff for Nottinghamshire in 1850, elected FRS in 1860 (and became FGS and FZS later), an Honorary LLD (Cambridge) in 1862, Lord Lieutenant of Nottinghamshire in 1864 and President of University College, London 1871.

He married in March 1837 Amelia Harriet, daughter of Dr William Otter, another educational reformer and a notable Bishop of Chichester, the union producing eight children. His four daughters became respectively Lady Le Marchant, Mrs Kenelm Digby, Mrs Henry Gale

(later Mrs Henry Handford) and Mrs George Murray Smith. The eldest son, William, died young; his youngest, Frederick, was another brilliant man who served as Mayor of Derby in 1902-03. He died at his London home, 75, Eaton Square on 30th June 1880, being succeeded by his second son, Henry. Although never active in the Strutts' commercial enterprises, he remained a partner, and was responsible for the development for residential purposes of the park of his Derby House at St Helen's – hence Strutt's Park – with its streets named after members of the family and places associated with it. His contribution to the development of UK radical (non-socialist) politics was considerable, transforming the Liberal party during his lifetime.
[DNB; Burke *Peerage* (1970).]

STRUTT, Jedidiah (1726-1797)

Jedidiah Strutt was, with Sir Richard Arkwright and THOMAS EVANS (*q.v.*) one of the great pioneers of the cotton spinning industry in Derbyshire and an improver of the stocking frame invented by William Lee more than a century before. With his first partner, William Woollatt – the Findern and Derby hosier who became Strutt's brother-in-law – he took out two patents (no.722 of 19/4/1758 and no.734 of 10/1/1759) for 'a machine furnished with a set of turning needles to be fixed as a stocking frame for making turned ribbed stockings' which could be switched from ribbed to plain work as needed. They set up to manufacture the Derby Patent Rib in Derby in 1760 and quickly prospered. In 1768, mainly due to a 'cash-flow problem' Arkwright and Samuel Need joined the partnership, Strutt seeing more of a future for the former's spinning frame than his Nottingham bankers, the Wrights. Strutt suggested some amendments to Arkwright's device which was finally patented on 3rd July 1769, and a works was established at Cromford with another at Belper. The partnership was dissolved in 1782, when Arkwright retained the Mills at Cromford and Strutt those at Belper and Derby. He also established a calico mill in Derby (designed by his ingenious son

WILLIAM STRUTT *(q.v.)* according to his 'fire-proof' principles) and a silk mill (turning out the less refined 'tram' thread) in the Morledge. Also, on 19th July 1770 with his brother Joseph (1724-94) – ancestor of the Birmingham dynasty of Chamberlain – took out patent No. 964 for a machine 'for roasting boiling and baking, consisting of a portable firestove, an airjack and a meatscreen' which sounds as if it owes something to JOHN WHITEHURST'S *(q.v.)* patent roasting apparatus, and was improved upon by Strutt's son William.

Jedidiah was the second of the three sons of William Strutt of Newton Old Hall, Blackwell, yeoman, of a family that had been in the parish since at least 1670, but which also had links with Essex, maintained, obliquely, by Jedidiah's brother Joseph, after his move to open a mill at Rickmansworth (Herts). Another member of the family was an early clockmaker at Newton, which might explain the brothers' talent with their roasting apparatus. His mother was Martha, daughter of Joseph Statham of Hazlewood, and the youngest brother was William (1730-1800). Jedidiah was born at Newton Old Hall in 1726 and in 1740 articled to Ralph Massey, a Findern Wheelwright, taking a hand with the family farm from 1747. He married Elizabeth Woollatt in the same year that he collaborated with her brother over the stocking frame. A Unitarian, he was instrumental in taking over the Friar Gate Presbyterian chapel, Derby, for that sect and establishing the Unitarian Chapel at Belper. He lived at Thorntree House, No. 1 St Peter's Street, Derby, until about 1780 when he let his third son Joseph Strutt (1765-1844) occupy it, moving to Exeter House – rebuilt by THOMAS CHAMBERS (q.v.) – where he died after a long illness on 6th May 1797. He was painted (like his former partner Arkwright) by JOSEPH WRIGHT (q.v.). He had three sons WILLIAM (q.v.), George Benson, of Belper (1761-1841) and Joseph (1761-1844), who later gave Derby its Arboretum, Britain's first public park in 1840. [DNB; Burke, *Peerage, loc.cit.*; local records; Derby Local Studies Library MS 8022 f.212; Burke, *Landed Gentry* (1898) II. 1421.]

STRUTT, William, FRS (1756-1830)

William Strutt, the eldest son of JEDIDIAH SJRUTT (q.v.), was virtual ruler of Derby from 1792 to 1829, the years in which he chaired the various Improvement Commissions, set up by Acts of Parliament from 1792 (second Nuns' Green Act) to enable a group of powerful local men to raise rates and revenue in ways which the

Corporation of Derby, hamstrung by a series of ancient Royal Charters, could not, and apply such monies to the improvement of the streets, buildings and infrastructure of the Borough. In this capacity he oversaw the provision of a new bridge over the Derwent (1789-94, by Thomas Harrison of Chester), seven new bridges over the Markeaton Brook (designed by himself), repairing and lighting the main streets, the opening up of land to industry, laying of roads and erection of houses on Nuns' Green, a tract of land lying north of Friar Gate and south-west of Kedleston Road, as well as numerous other works: a Borough Gaol, County Gaol and the total reform of the watch, cutting personnel almost in half through the judicious use of the watchman's clock which he claimed to have invented himself, with help from his mentor ERASMUS DARWIN (q.v.); the former belief that this device was invented by JOHN WHITEHURST FRS (q.v.) is not untenable, given Darwin's involvement. It was made by the great horologer's nephew and successor.

Connected to these improvements, although not done under the Commissioners' aegis, was the promotion of the Derby Canal (1796) in which Strutt played a major role, and the erection of the Derbyshire General Infirmary (1806-10) which Strutt oversaw, helped finance and, with the architect Samuel Brown and engineer CHARLES SYLVESTER (q.v.) designed. It contained devices for heating, ventilation and sanitation which were attributed to Strutt and himself by Sylvester but which clearly owe much to John Whitehurst's work at Clumber Park (1774-76) and St Thomas's Hospital, London (1778).

Strutt, indeed, was, throughout his life, credited with being a prolific inventor – of fireproof mills (at Derby and later at Belper), the epicyclic clock (echoes of Whitehurst, and James Watt's sun and planet gear for steam engines) and domestic hot water heating systems as installed (with his father's roasters) at his home, from 1803 St Helen's, sold to him by REV. THOMAS GISBORNE (q.v.). He also invented a patent range – also shades of Whitehurst – made by Harrison's Foundry, and called the Derby Range, and he was a considerable architect designing, apart from the Markeaton Brook bridges, his own house in Nuns' Green, Friar Gate House (*c*.1791), and family houses: Milford House, Green Hall, Belper and Bridge Hill House of which only the first survives. He also designed the family mills at Belper and other subsidiary structures.

Always radical, the Strutts were a very close family, and remained on friendly terms with surviving Lunar Society members like Darwin, Wedgwood (a co-promoter of the 1792 Nuns' Green Act), Matthew Boulton and R.L. Edgeworth who visited him at St Helen's with his novelist daughter Maria, as did the poet Tom Moore. Moore's visit coincided with one from Robert Owen, whose relentless earnestness successfully turned William against socialism. He was also a friend of the educator Joseph Lancaster (forming a Lancastrian School in Orchard Street in 1812) and Jeremy Bentham. His concern for the family's workforce was extensive even by modern standards and he was probably responsible for the specification for the firm's housing, as at Long Row, Belper and elsewhere.

William Strutt was born at Newton Old Hall 20th July 1756 and educated at the Dissenting Academy at Findern, where his mother's family had roots, and later with Mr Wilkinson at Nottingham. He was apprenticed to his father at 14, and took responsibilities of a weighty kind from a few years later. The family were zealous for self-improvement and William and his youngest brother Joseph spent long hours reading and imbibing knowledge from others, among them, of course, Erasmus Darwin; on 26th June 1817 he was elected FRS without even having sought the honour. He was a burgess of Derby at 23 in 1779 and was a founder member of the Derby Philosophical Society, succeeding Darwin as president in 1802. His fruitful encouragement of others, especially KIRK BOOTT (*q.v.*) was also a notable feature of his benevolent nature. Despite huge wealth, he was also frugal without being thought mean.

He married on 12th January 1793, Barbara,

daughter of THOMAS EVANS (*q.v.*), whose brothers William and Walter successively married his elder sister, Elizabeth; the younger sister married Samuel Fox of Osmaston Hall, Derby. They had a son, LORD BELPER (*q.v.*) and five daughters, all of whom died unmarried. He himself died on 30th December, 1830, Maria Edgeworth writing of him 'as the ingenious, indefatigable and benevolent Mr William Strutt'. Derby may have lost a dictator after a 'reign' of over 40 years, but one whose humanity and moral principles were such as to mark him as the City's only benevolent despot. His achievements still adorn Derby, despite the depredations of modern development.

[DNB; Hacker, C.L., *William Strutt of Derby* in DAJ. LXXX (1960) 49-70; DM. 2/1/1831, etc.]

STUART, HRH Prince Charles Edward, KG (1720-1788)

Prince Charles Edward Stuart, or Bonnie Prince Charlie, entered Derby, en route to London to claim his father's throne, about three pm on the afternoon of 4th December 1745, with something approaching 7,500 troops and a thousand or so others. Immediately beforehand the town crier had proclaimed his father, HRH Prince James Edward Stuart, as King James III of England and VIII of Scotland. One enthusiastic witness of these events was REV. HENRY CANTRELL (*q.v.*); less enthusiastic was the Whig 'Equity' Wright, who took his family, including JOSEPH WRIGHT (*q.v.*), across the Trent to Repton.

Once installed in the town, Prince Charles Edward took up residence in Exeter House, owned by Lord Exeter, son-in-law of THOMAS CHAMBERS (*q.v.*). An advance party seized Swarkestone Bridge, but the remainder settled in their billets remarkably harmoniously. The following day, whilst his men were gathering horses and exacting financial contributions, the Prince attended a (Protestant) service in All Saints' before visiting several local gentlemen to drum up support for his cause – all without effect. On

George and *de jure* James III and VIII and Clementina, daughter of Prince James Sobieski, granddaughter of John III, King of Poland (1674-96). As son and heir of James II and VII, Charles's father was legitimate cliamant to the thrones of England, Scotland, (France) and Ireland, the so-called Glorious Revolution having placed Mary II, James II's daughter (by his first, morganatic, marriage) on the throne, with her ambitious Protestant husband William III.

Charles Edward had a shaky education, successively in the hands of Jesuits, Protestant tutors and various military officers yet, although some aspects of his knowledge were patchy, he was a good linguist, musician and appreciator of the arts. At 15 he served with distinction in the seige of Gaeta under the Duke of Liria. His natural courage, dignity and intelligence put fresh heart into the Jacobite cause and in 1745 he placed himself at the head of what turned out to be the last attempt to restore the kingdoms to their legitimate rulers, quickly taking control of all Scotland (bar Edinburgh Castle's garrison which was effectively contained), and doing so under a manifesto which, in its promise of freedom of Religion and various other liberal measures, was very revolutionary for its time.

The story of the 'Forty Five' rebellion is well known, as is its tragic end at Culloden in April 1746, the flight of the prince, and the retribution meted out to the Highlands by the forces of the unpopular Government of George II. Hindsight has led some to blame Prince Charles Edward – Bonnie Prince Charlie – for this, but the heaping of ignominy is an inevitable consequence of failure, and that failure was by no means Charles' fault. Conversely, hindsight also tells us that he indeed came close to success, with the monarch in London making preparations for flight and cabinet ministers making covert overtures to the insurgent leaders.

Derby was the pivotal locale in all this, and as such the history of Europe hung in the balance upon the events unfolding in and around the Borough on 5th December 1745. Consequently, the erection of a fine equestrian statue in Derby to mark the 250th anniversary of the Attempt was

his return an acrimonious meeting of his privy council took place in Exeter House, at which the Prince and the Duke of Perth were the only ones keen to press on to London, whilst Lord George Murray and the other Chiefs believed a withdrawal north of the Scots border was essential. With hindsight, it is possible to see that Lord George, prompted by disinformation from two captured 'spies' (actually government 'plants'), was being unduly cautious. However, on the night of 5th, Lord George won the day. After a well-attended evening *levée* in the Moot Hall (at which prophetically, Charles' Royal Standard was knocked over in the crush and broken) that night, the Jacobite forces began to withdraw long before first light the following morning. As far as Derby was concerned it was the end of two days at the very crucible of history, for the decision to return to Scotland was a fateful one, leading to inevitable disaster. Charles's judgement to press on had been fundamentally sound.

Charles Edward Louis Philip Casimir Stuart was born in Rome 31st December 1720 elder son and heir of James Edward Stuart, Chevalier de St entirely fitting, and exists through the vision of some, the munificence of its private donor and in spite of the antipathy of the City Council. Nevertheless, Bonnie Prince Charlie, whose later conversion to Protestantism and physical and emotional decline stemmed in part from the failure of the enterprise (and which today would no doubt be ameliorated by 'Counselling') is a figure of first importance in 18th century European history and one whose links with Derby are inescapable and indissoluble. Of the 'Forty Five, Dr Johnson later remarked that it 'was a noble attempt'. He died, broken, alcoholic and dissipated on 31st January 1788, leaving a natural daughter (by Clementine Walkinshaw, Countess of Alberstroff), Lady Charlotte Stuart (1753-1789). [DNB; Eardley-Simpson, L,. *Derby and the Forty-five* (London 1955); Craven (1988) 74-82.]

SULLEY, Arthur Lindsay (1906-1994)

Arthur Sulley was a distinguished Olympic oarsman, winning a silver medal for Britain in 1928; he also coxed the Cambridge crew in the boat races of 1928 and 1929. He was in his working

life Managing Director and Chairman (1965-75) of James Smith and Co., Drewry Lane, the uniform manufacturers, a firm he was with for 45 years.

Arthur Lindsay Sulley was born 7th November 1906 and educated at public school and Cambridge. Latterly he and his wife Marjorie (died September 1995, and for many years chair-

man of the Derby bench) lived on Burley Lane, Quarndon. He died the day before his 88th birthday, 1994, leaving three sons and five granddaughters. One son, James S.Sulley was also cox of the Cambridge crew, in 1958.
[DET. 7&16/11/1994; 11/1/1975; 50/9/1993; DA 28/2/1958.]

SUTHERLAND, Graham Vivian, OM, RA (1905-1980)

Graham Sutherland was a distinguished artist with his own gallery at Picton Castle (Pembs) from 1976 who shot to fame with his startlingly organic 'Christ in Majesty' tapestry hung in the new Coventry Cathedral in 1962. From 1952 12 retrospective exhibitions of his work were held in Europe and America; his first exhibition of portraiture was held at the National Portrait Gallery in 1977, and he is represented in the permanent collections of nine European and American Galleries. He was made OM in 1960.

Graham Vivian Sutherland was born in London on 24th August 1905, elder of two sons of George Humphreys Vivian Sutherland, a barrister of Derby and later London, and Elsie, daughter of James Foster of Tooting (Surrey). George was himself elder son of Councillor George Sutherland FRGS (1845-99) first headmaster of St Andrew's School, Litchurch, and Catherine, daughter of Charles Humphreys, the architect and builder who created Arboretum Square, where both Sutherland and Humphreys lived. An uncle of Graham's was Maj. Francis Hubert ('Budge') Sutherland of the LMS at Derby and an ex-Sherwood Forester later described as 'an important member of the Railway Aristocracy'.

It was 'Budge' who persuaded Graham to take an apprenticeship at the Derby railway works after his period at Epsom College. However, railway engineering soon palled and Sutherland obtained a place to study art at Goldsmiths' College.

He lived for most of his career in London, but later retired to Menton (France). In 1922 he married Kathleen Frances Barry (1906-91), but there was no issue at his death in 1980. Graham Sutherland's brother, Dr Carol Humphries Vivian Sutherland (1908-86) was perhaps the most distinguished numismatist of his era and keeper of the Heberden Room at the Ashmolean; his wife Monica la Fontaine, Mrs R.W.Porter, (daughter of Rev. C.M.McAnally) was a descendant of the french author La Fontaine and an historian and journalist.

[Tachella, *op.cit.,* 118; *Who's Who* (1978) 2581-82; *Times,* 16/5/1986.]

SYLVESTER, Charles (1774-1828)

Sylvester was a self-taught engineer whose career began with his invention of the process of galvanising corrodable metals by coating them in zinc about 1802. He met WILLIAM STRUTT *(q.v.)* in 1807 whilst lecturing, and the two struck up a most fruitful and long lasting friendship, beginning with Sylvester working for Strutt as an engineer at Belper and Derby from then until 1820. In this time, Sylvester developed a central heating boiler (called the Derby Hot Air Stove) which was installed in Strutt's Derbyshire General Infirmary, hot air being ducted into wards in a system clearly based on WHITEHURST'S *(q.v.)* work at St Thomas's Hospital in 1778. In the long term it is notable that he omitted to fit cleaning ports, which resulted in the system breaking down, with very unhealthy results in the 1860s. Also inspired by Whitehurst and other Lunar Society ideas, Sylvester and Strutt built many other Domestic innovations into the Infirmary, all published in 1819 in the former's book *The Philosophy of Domestic Economy.* He also undertook analysis of the waters of the Chalybeate Spring at Bakewell and designed the first hot baths at Buxton in The Crescent in 1818 for the Duke of Devonshire.

Sylvester was born in 1774, the son of Joseph Sylvester of Norton, Derbys (now part of Sheffield) a nailor and scythesmith and his first wife Sarah Mills (d.1777) whom he married at Rotherham 5th March 1767. They had three other children and a further 11 (including a son,

Joshua) were born to Joseph by his second wife Rebecca Berry. Sylvester had no formal education but taught himself to write, science and other disciplines whilst working as a plated wire drawer's apprentice in Sheffield *c.*1790-93.

In 1820 he left Derby and went to 60 Great Russell Street, London, to set up his own company, specialising in heating, ventilation and domestic engineering, which quickly achieved success. 1824 saw him appointed to a committee of the Liverpool and Manchester Railway to report on George Stephenson's plans for the line. He died in London January 1828 leaving a son and successor, John Sylvester (1799-1852) and two daughters. The son expanded the firm, exhibited successfully at the Great Exhibition and left it to his brother-in-law, Thomas Creswick who sold it to Sylvester's old managing clerk, Samuel Egan Rosser. It is now Rosser and Russell plc. of London. A bust of him by his friend Sir Francis Chantrey is in Derby Museum.

[Leslie, J.M., *Rosser and Russell: The First 200*

years (London 1974); Langham, M. & Wells, C., *Buxton, a Pictorial History* (Chichester 1993) 4; Sylvester, C., *The Philosophy of Domestic Economy* (London 1819).]

TAYLOR, Helen Louise (b.1850)

Miss Taylor is notable as the only female pupil ever to have graced the dour benches of Derby School prior to its so-called 'comprehensivisation' in the later part of the present century. She was a poet and author of mildly moralistic stories for the young, something in the manner of JANE JERRAM *(q.v.)*. She wrote *Manor House Exhibition* (1883), *Out of the Way* (1883), *Little Christian's Pilgrimage* (1888), *The Sunday Pleasure Book* and *Christiana* (1890), *Hymns For Church Festivals* (1892) and contributed to numerous magazines.

Helen Louise Taylor was born 20th January 1850 at the family home, 284 Uttoxeter New Road. She was the only daughter of George Taylor, proprietor of the Nun's Street Mill, where he was a silk goods manufacturer, until made bankrupt in 1856. Her mother, Julia Towle of Borrowash, married George at Ockbrook 9th January 1849. Helen had two brothers, George William Taylor FZS, natural historian and author, and Edward Ernest Taylor (1856-1927) a schoolmaster who shared the Uttoxeter New Road house with Helen for most of their lives.

It is quite unclear how Miss Taylor came to be admitted to Derby School, except that she went there in September 1858 aged 8 years and two years later won second prize for English History and Scripture History – ultimately the main planks for much of her writing. She died unmarried.

[Tachella, *op.cit.* 50; DM. 17/1/1849 & 2/1/1856.]

THOMAS, Rt. Hon James Henry, PC, MP, JP (1874-1949)

'Jimmy' Thomas was elected one of the MPs for Derby in January 1910 in succession to Richard Bell, in the Labour interest, and held it until his

resignation in May 1936, over 26 years. At the time of his election he was President of the NUR, and served as General Secretary 1918-24 and 1925-31. In the first Labour government (1924) he was Secretary of State for the Colonies, and in the second of Ramsay Macdonald's administrations was Lord Privy Seal (June 1929-June 1930) and Secretary of State for the Dominions until the dissolution in August 1931. He was pragmatist enough to support Macdonald's National Government that year, and sufficiently convinced of his stand to forfeit the support of many of his friends in the mainstream Labour movement who would have no truck with the turn events took that summer.

Accordingly he was re-elected as National Labour MP in 1931, resuming his Cabinet seat for the Colonies until May 1936 when he caused a budget leak and was obliged to resign.

Thomas was born in Newport (Mon) 3rd October 1874 and, after an elementary school education, joined the Great Western Railway, becoming a member of the Union (later the NUR) in which he became active. He was later based at Swindon (GWR HQ) and sat as a local councillor there before winning the Derby seat. In 1898 he married Agnes Hill of Newport, and they had three sons and two daughters.

He was made Privy Councillor in 1917, Hon LLD (Cantab) 1920 and Hon DCL (Oxon) 1926 and lived at 12 Thurlow Road, Dulwich, where he served as a JP (Kent). In 1920 he was President of the International Federation of Trades Unions for five years and served as TUC President the same year. He seems to have been trying to build bridges between himself and the Labour Party in 1936, for his budget leak was to Labour and might have been an attempt to rebuild his credibility, as the Party's strength was growing after the humiliating defeat by the National Government in 1931. He was defeated at the 1936 election by PHILIP NOEL-BAKER (q.v.) the Labour candidate at Derby, and died at Dulwich 21st January 1949.
[Stenton, *Members of Parliament,* vol.III 352; Who Was Who 1941-1950 (vol IV 195) 1143.]

THOMPSON, Eric (1927-1996)

Eric Thompson was a member of the British Olympic cycling team during two Olympiads, those at Melbourne (1960) and Rome (1964), and was a major contender in the sport until he retired in 1966. He later worked as an insurance official moving from Derby to Woodhouse Eaves (Leics), on his appointment as head of Prudential's Loughborough district, where he died 23rd May 1996.

He was born in Derby in 1927, oldest of four sons (there were also two daughters) of Mr Thompson of Brayfield Avenue – he was either Alfred William or John Henry Thompson, the latter working as a firefighter in 1935. He took up competitive cycling as a teenager, he also won the tandem title with David Handley in 1961.
[DET 25 & 29/5/1996; 30/6/1989; 5/12/1966 DA. 18/8/1961]

TIMMS, Ven. George (1910-1997)

The Venerable George Timms was a prominent liturgist, hymn writer and administrator in the Church of England who made notable contributions to the *New English Hymnal* and the *Alternative Service Book*. A leading expert in liturgy, he was by no means opposed to change, but his revisions were subject to two fervently held convictions: that the traditions of Anglican worship be adhered to in spirit and practice and that the new services should be theologically correct and impressive in themselves; to this end he was able to deploy a strong visual sense and an acute sensitivity to language. Timms was also appalled by the tawdriness of many of the hymns ansd prayers that became current in the 1960s and in attempting to do much better finished by writing fourteen new hymns for the NEH published in 1986, and regarded as the best contemporary hymn book. For the ASB he contributed the 73 collects required modelled on traditional form and each displaying theological insight and economy of language; few are more than four lines long.

George Boorne Timms was born at Highwood, Burton Road, Derby (now the Victoria Park Hotel) 4th October 1904, son of accountant, John Timms, who was himself probably the son of Samuel Timms of High Street, Litchurch, an hydraulic engineer with the Litchurch Local Board. He was educated at Derby School and St Edmund Hall, Oxford, going on to the monastic college at Mirfield, Yorks, being ordained in 1935. Two high church curacies indicated his allegiance to the Catholic wing of the Church, and from 1938 to 1954 he was Secretary of the Anglican Society, and from 1944 he was Oxford Diocesan Inspector of Schools. In 1949 he became Priest Vicar and Sacrist of Southwark Cathedral and in 1952 became vicar of St Mary, Primrose Hill (London). Here he became known for the beauty and dignity of his services adding responsibilty for St Paul's, Hampstead in 1957, becoming Rural Dean of Hampstead two years later. He was elected to the Church Assembly in 1955.

In 1964 Timms was appointed Director of Ordination Training for London, Examining Chaplain to the Bishop and Prebendary of St Paul's Cathedral, taking on the parish responsi-bilities of St Andrew, Holborn and he was appointed Archdeacon of Hackney in 1971. From 1965-69 he was a member of the ill-fated Anglican-Methodist Unity Commision, and many years later was awarded a Papal medal for services to Christian Unity. He wrote two books: a defence of Cranmer's liturgy in 1946 and *A Manual for Holy Week* in 1967. He retired to Kent in 1981 and died unmarried on 19th November 1997.

[*Daily Telegraph* obit., 20/11/1997; *The Derbeian*; Kelly's *Directory*, 1908.]

TISSINGTON, Anthony, FRS (1705-1776)

Anthony Tissington is an obscure figure in many ways, but was the proprietor of a very prosperous mining company which owned coal, copper and lead mines not only in Derbyshire but in Yorkshirc, Durham and Scotland. His partners were his brother George, a mineral agent at Winster and his son-in-law John Tatlow of Codnor. A deed of 14th July 1774 itemizes the firm's profit over 17 years as an ernormous £29,400; JOHN WHITEHURST *(q.v.),* a close friend of Tissington's from at least the 1730s, owned 1/48th of the firm. It was probably Tissington who was instrumental in drawing the attention of DARWIN, Whitehurst and Boulton to Blue John stone. Tissington had an enquiring mind and wrote a number of papers on mining matters and geology, being elected a Fellow of the Royal Society in 1767. He lived in Derby for most of his career, at a house in Irongate (probably almost opposite Whitehurst) but moved to Swanwick Hall in the 1760s where his friend Benjamin Franklin stayed with him.

Anthony Tissington was born in 1705, a member of a yeoman family of Brassington traceable from the early 16th century, but his immediate ancestor was Godfrey Tissington of Carsington. Godfrey's second son Anthony (b.1603) was the first of three men of this name of whom the third, of Darley Dale, married Mary Ragge in 1704 and was the mining entrepreneur's father. He himself married at Darley Dale on 16th March 1730 Sarah Wall, a member of a prominent local family from Cowley with lead mining interests – possibly the impetus behind Anthony's subsequent activities. They had two sons and a daughter: The eldest son was Anthony Tissington (1732-1815) who married three times and carried on his father's business until he sold up and retired in 1795. His brother George Buxton Tissington was a mineralogist of Matlock and their sister Mary married John Tatlow of Codnor (d.1763) a partner of her father. Their son John married a daughter of JOHN MAWE *(q.v.).* Anthony Tissington died in 1776.

[Craven (1996), 42, 75-76, 88-89, 93-95, 223; Derby Local Studies Library Box 57/T and *Derbyshire Worthies* VII.96.]

TOMASIUK, Irene (1953-1996)

Irene Tomasiuk was the first woman news sub editor in Fleet Street, being so appointed by the *Daily Telegraph* in the mid-1980s. She later became responsible for the court and social pages, 'combining an eye for page make-up with an ability to quickly spot small errors'. She was known as a sympathetic, and when necessary a forceful professional. Her competence under pressure won over her colleagues in a male-oriented sector of the newspaper world aided by her taste for a pint of Guiness after the hurly-burly of a day's work. She was also a tireless collector of unwanted or discarded books from the newspaper's offices which she would sell to raise money for charity. Her early death ended a newspaper career of much promise.

Irene Tomasiuk was the daughter of a Polish refugee who had settled in Derby after World War Two and had become a railwayman. She was born in Derby on 12th February 1953 and was educated at Homelands Grammar School in Normanton, going on to study politics at the University of Warwick. She then trained with Mirror Group Newspapers at Cardiff, worked briefly as a sub-editor on the *Daily Mirror* at Manchester before becoming a freelance moving to the Manchester office of the *Daily Telegraph* in 1978. She died 27th October 1996 of meningitis, leaving a son, Nicholas, born in 1993.
[*Daily Telegraph*, 28/10/1996.]

TOUCHET, Sir James, 7th Lord Audley KB (c.1465-1497)

Lord Audley, the ancient seat of whose family was at Markeaton, was notable as having been the most highly placed leader of the Cornish rebellion of 1497, at the head of which he placed himself at Wells (Somerset). His motives for so doing are unclear, except that he appears to have accumulated a crushing burden of debt, probably through his accompanying Henry VII to France in 1492. The rising itself, ostensibly a reaction to a punitive tax levied upon the realm as a result of a war against the Scots sparked by Perkin Warbeck's rebellion, was probably the result of manipulation by Yorkist elements, for Henry's tax was not, in fact, designed to fall at all heavily on the poorer elements of society. As Audley's grandfather had lost his life at the Battle of Blore Heath (Salop.) on the Lancastrian side, a Yorkist motive seems

less likely for Audley's participation although his father was a minister of Edward IV's; desperation the more probable motive. The rebel forces, led by Lord Audley were defeated by Lord Oxford near Blackheath 17th June 1497 and Audley was captured, tried, convicted, sentenced to death and executed two weeks later.

Hon James Touchet was born in 1465 at Markeaton, son of JOHN TOUCHET, 6th LORD AUDLEY (*q.v.*) by his wife, Anne, daughter and heiress of Sir Thomas Itchingham (who remarried John Rogers, dying in 1498). The family's progenitor Goscelin (Joscelyn) de Touchet had been sub-tenant of Hugh d'Avranches, Earl of Chester in the Manors of Markeaton, Mackworth and Allestree in 1086, and the family were closely related to HUGH and WAKELIN DE DERBY (*q.q.v.*). Goscelin's descendant in the 11th generation, Sir John Touchet of Markeaton (killed at La Rochelle 1371) married Hon Joan Audley, daughter and heiress of James Audley, 4th Lord Audley of Heleigh (Cheshire) on whose decease in 1386 their grandson John was summoned to Parliament as a Baron in his own name and their great grandson as (6th) Lord Audley.

James was invested KB by the Prince of Wales in 1475 and succeeded his father in 1492, the year he accompanied Henry VII to France and may have begun his spiral of debt. He married, firstly, Hon Joan Bourchier, daughter of Fulk, Lord FitzWarine, by whom he had a son, John. He remarried Margaret, daughter of Richard Dayrell of Willington Dayrell (Bucks) by Margaret, Countess of Stafford, a daughter of the Duke of Somerset, thus making him a kinsman of the Royal House.

After his death and attainder, his son was restored in blood and honour in 1512, but sold his Derbyshire estates to SIR JOHN MUNDY (*q.v.*) in 1516. His great-grandson, George Touchet, 9th Lord Audley, went to Ireland, was wounded at the Battle of Kingsale (24 Dec 1601) and was summoned to the Irish Parliament in 1614, being created two years later Lord Audley of Orier, Co. Armagh and Earl of Castlehaven. He was grandfather of JAMES TOUCHET, 3rd Earl of Castlehaven (*q.v.*).

[DNB; GEC *Complete Peerage* (1889) 1, 197-202; II.180-182; Burke, J., *Extinct and Dormant Peerages* (London 1883) 535, 623; Statham, S.P.H., in DAJ. XLVIII (1926) 95-96.]

TOUCHET, Rt. Hon. Gen. James, 3rd Earl of Castlehaven (d.1684)

Lord Castlehaven was a notable Irish cavalry commander, who became caught up in the Irish rising of 1641 and went on to command a section of the rebel forces when his (at that time undoubted) loyalty to the government was questioned. He enjoyed considerable success and also was invaluable in aiding the passage of Royalist Irish troops from Wexford to England to help the king, with whose cause his own side in Ireland had ultimately become attached.

When the Royalist cause in Ireland was lost, he left for the continent, fighting under Prince Rupert at the Battle of Landrecies, but returned with the Marquess of Ormonde, his old Commander, to Ireland in 1648. In the January following he was appointed General of the Horse campaigning with some success until the Royal and Confederate cause was near collapse. He was then constituted C-in-C of Munster and Co. Clare where again he met with some favourable results in clashes with the Derbyshire-born Gen. Henry Ireton but was forced again to retire to France on 10th April 1652.

Hon James Touchet was the eldest son and heir of Mervyn, 2nd Earl of Castlehaven and his first wife Elizabeth, daughter and heiress of Alderman Benedict Barnham of London, and was born, probably in Ireland, about 1617. His father, however, was executed for a series of unspeakable crimes (including bestiality, sodomy and rape, the latter including that of his second wife Anne, Lady Chandos, a daughter of the Earl of Derby) on Tower Hill 14th May 1631 – the second of this notable Derby family to die in this ignominious manner (cf. JAMES TOUCHET, 7th Lord Audley). This disaster resulted in the attainder of his English barony of Audley, although not (for technical reasons) of his Irish Peerages. James had married at 14, Elizabeth Bridges, daughter of his father's second wife by her first husband Grey, 5th Lord Chandos of Sudeley, who had been subjected to rape by her mother's lover Fulwar Skipwith at the age of 12. This, and the total neglect he received in childhood, led him to 'shop' his father to the Crown, with the unfortunate result that the attainder passed against his father deprived him of his family property. He was, however, created Lord Audley of Hely (*sic*) in 1633 (confirmed by Act of Parliament in 1678) re-granted his seat at Maddentown Co. Kildare and he decided to become a professional soldier, serving on the contintent to 1638 and returning when the prospect of war at home became a reality.

After going into exile in 1652 he was appointed Major General of the Irish Contingents in the Spanish Service, fighting a series of successful engagements in the French civil war. On his return to England in 1660, he found all his remaining property lost and received a grant of wastes in various counties through which, by judicious exploitation, he was able to rebuild his fortunes. He also received an Irish pension and later fought against the Dutch 1667-68, for the Spanish at Maastricht in 1676 and Mons in 1678. He retired in 1680 and wrote his memoirs. He died at Kilcash, Co. Tipperary (his sister's house) 11th October 1684 without leaving issue. He was succeeded by his brother Mervyn as 4th Earl of Castlehaven, 14th Lord Audley. The Earldom became extinct on the death of John, 8th Earl of Castlehaven in 1777, although the barony of Audley (with those of Touchet of Markeaton and Martin) continues.
[DNB; sources as preceding article.]

TOUCHET, Rt. Hon. John, PC, KG, 6th Lord Audley (*c*.1430-1491)

John, Lord Audley was Lord Treasurer of England from 1484-85 and a Privy Councillor from 1471. Thus, during the crucial final 18 months of Richard III's short and troubled reign he weilded great influence and his financial advice played a large part in the king's subsequent conduct of events.

John Touchet was the son and heir of James, 5th Lord Audley, of Markeaton and Mackworth by his first wife, Hon Margaret Roos, daughter of William, Lord Roos. His father had been a notable and largely successful commander in the Hundred Years' War but was killed during the Wars of the Roses 23rd September 1459 at the battle of Blore Heath (Salop). Young John was summoned as 6th Lord Audley – which peerage seems to include those of Martin (inherited by his Audley forbears) and Touchet of Markeaton (as his grandfather had been summoned 21st Decembter 1405) – and went with Edward IV to Calais in 1460 where he was taken prisoner by the French. In 1471, he was not only made PC but given joint command of the Army, venturing to Brittany in 1475.

After Henry VII's victory at Bosworth, his career went into eclipse and he retired to his seat Markeaton Hall, dying 26th September (or December) 1491. He married Anne, daughter and heir of Sir Thomas Itchingham, and he left, amongst others, a son and heir JAMES TOUCHET (7th) LORD AUDLEY *(q.v.)*. [Sources as previous articles.]

TOWNSEND, Ernest (1880-1944)

Ernest Townsend was probably, after JOSEPH WRIGHT *(q.v.)*, Derby's finest artist, although, like Wright, he eschewed life in London and returned to his native place to paint, specialising in portraiture, although he also produced a series of very fine topographical scenes, encouraged by the local philanthropist and patron Alfred Goodey. He also did a large number of flower paintings, many undertaken as 'thank you' presents or gifts, for friends at Christmas or on Birthdays. His unrealised potential was summed up by the critic of a national newspaper who came to the 1989 retrospective exhibition at Derby Museum and remarked that, had Townsend stayed in London as a young man he would have been famous as Opie or Sargent 'instead of wasting

his talents on provincial mayors and freemasons'!

Ernest Townsend was born in 1880, youngest of the five children of James Townsend, a coachbuilder with Holmes (later Sanderson & Holmes) London Road, Royal Warrant holders. His mother died in 1888, leaving him to be brought up by his elder sister, Florence. After an elementary education he was articled to James Wright, architect of Derby in 1894, whose junior partner, Thomas Harrison Thorpe spotted his facility with a paintbrush and encouraged him to nurture his talents. He had already in 1898 been awarded a medal by the National Department of Arts and Sciences and in the same year was elected a member of the Derby Sketching Club. He thereupon attended the Derby Art School under T.C.SIMMONDS *(q.v.)*, whom he later painted, leaving for Heatherley's School of Fine Art, Chelsea and from there he gained a place in the Royal Academy Schools in 1902. Here he won two silver medals, the Landseer scholarship for figure painting and the Creswick prize, with a painting 'Willows and Weeds' now in Derby

Museum. His tutors included Sargent, Sir George Calusen and Sir Lawrence Alma-Tadema, and he made the acquaintanceship there of Aubrey Beardsley, Alfred Munnings, Augustus John and Laura Knight. He left London in 1907, however, just as the UK *avant-garde* was developing, but leaving most of the movement's precepts behind him. He was ever a very private person, wanting to paint; London's artistic social life did not suit him. He did, however, travel in France and The Netherlands before settling in Otter Street and marrying, in 1912, Elsie Doris, daughter of Peter Campbell of Balaclava Road, a sketching club stalwart and an artist employed at Bemrose's. He later moved to a studio and house at 31, Full Street, where his sons David (d.1997) and Bruce were born.

Townsend's portraits included J.H.THOMAS *(q.v.)*, LORD ROE *(q.v.)*, Winston Churchill, George VI, SIR HENRY BEMROSE *(q.v.)* and SIR FRANCIS LEY *(q.v.)*. He also painted municipal worthies in towns in Yorkshire, Lancashire and all over the Midlands, his output being prodigious. He also painted a lively frieze for the Whitehall Cinema, St Peter's Street, and during World War Two worked extensively camouflaging potential targets, including Rolls-Royce works. He died in January 1944.
[DET. 10/3/1976; Derby Museum Catalogues, Retrospective Exhibitions 1989 and 1994; *Who's Who In Art* (1934) 402-03.]

TUTBURY, Thomas de (c.1300-1370)

Thomas de Tutbury represented Derby in Parliament more times than any other single person during the medieval period, serving eight times between 1328 and 1361. He was also a burgess and was Bailiff of Derby in 1352-53. Although little more is known about him, it is clear from this record that he must have been a figure of considerable consequence locally if not further afield. He seems to have owed his position to a connection with the powerful dynasty of HUGH DE DERBY *(q.v.)* and is one of the few members of it to have survived the Black Death, serving continuously through the crisis of the

late 1340s. Indeed, he probably – as so many others who came through the pestilence unscathed – managed to amass a great deal of additional property at knock-down prices. His death is recorded in 1370.

The first member of the family in Derby would appear to have been William de Tutbury who was involved in property transactions there in the period 1270/86, and married, Emma, widow of John Le Palmer (also known as John de London) a burgess of Derby and of London and a wealthy merchant who was also the great-great-grandson of Hugh the Dean; Palmer died without issue around 1282. The family, whose name suggests an ultimate origin across the Dove at Tutbury had held land at Winshill two generations before, and members witnessed deeds concerning land at both Ashbourne and Hollington. The first on record is Gode of Tutbury living *c.*1130/50. Ferhun de Tutbury, MP for Derby in 1327-28, almost certainly the son of William and Emma, and Thomas was either his younger brother or his son. He was also the man, in all probability, who witnessed a deed concerning land at Horsley in 1360, all of which suggests that the family were old retainers of the Ferrers, Earls of Derby, who had switched their allegiance to the (Royal) Earls of Lancaster and Derby after the fall of the Ferrers in 1268.

Another witness of the Horsley transaction was William de Tutbury, probably Thomas' son (or brother) who was granted lands at Egginton the year before. The Chaplain, Richard de Tutbury, who quitclaimed lands 'lately held' by William, was clearly William's heir and probably therefore his son. Thereafter the family vanish from record.
[Jeayes, *op.cit.* (1906) 55, 975, 981, 1176/77, 1340, 1455,2610; *Darley Cartulary*, A. 1xviii and A.1xix; Simpson, *op.cit.* III. 756-58.]

UNWIN, Capt. Edward W, VC, CB, CMG (1864-1950)

Caplain E.W.Unwin VC was a naval officer who won the VC in an heroic action off the

Dardenelles in 1915, in which campaign he was also previously mentioned in despatches. He had earlier served with distinction in the punitive naval expedition to Benin in 1897. He was principal naval transport officer, Eastern Mediterranean 1918-19 and he retired with the rank of Captain RN in 1920. In retirement at Forest Lodge, Hythe (Hants) he became a distinguished yachtsman holding the cup of the best cruise for three successive years in succession.

Edward Wilberforce Unwin was born 17th March 1864, son of Capt. Edward Wilberforce Unwin MA (b.1818), himself second son of Rev. Edward Unwin of Highfield, Derby (1767-1847) vicar of St Werburgh's 1809-47 and a great antagonist of Rev. CHARLES STEAD HOPE (q.v.). He was also of Wootton Lodge, near Ashbourne, as was the elder E.W.Unwin, and the family long retained property in Derby. James Unwin, the Vicar of St Werburgh's father, was originally from Great Baddow (Essex) and had married the heiress of the Wheelers of Wootton. Unwin married twice: firstly to Henrietta Jane Carnac, by whom he had no issue, and secondly in 1897 to Evelyn, daughter of Maj Gen William Dobree Carey of Guernsey. They had two sons and two daughters.

Unwin, who entered the Navy after taking his degree (MA),was made CMG in 1916 and CB in 1919. He was a member of the Hampshire bench and a DL (Hants) from 1929. He died 19th April 1950.
[*Who Was Who* (1941-50) 1176; Kelly (1935); Local Studies, Tilley/U.]

WADE, Sir Willoughby Francis, FRCP, (1827-1906)

Sir Willoughby Wade was President of the British Medical Association in 1893 and consulting physician to the Birmingham General Hospital. He was Professor of the Practice of Physical and Clinical Medicine at Queen's College and a prolific medical author, knighted in 1896.

Willoughby Francis Wade was one of five sons of Rev. Edward Michael Wade (1792-1867) first vicar of St George (later Holy Trinity) Derby from 1837 to 1867, by the daughter of Mr Justice Fox, an Irish judge. Wade's grandfather, Robert, was from County Meath: his Aunt married Derby Councillor and businessman Thomas Battersby. W.F.Wade was brought up in Derby, but educated at Rugby going on to Trinity College, Dublin (BA 1849, MB 1851, Hon MD 1896) and became a member (1859) and Fellow (1871) of the Royal College of Physicians in London. He spent most of his working life, however, attached in various capacities to the Birmingham General Hospital. He married, in 1880, Augusta Frances, daughter of Sir John Power, 2nd Bt. (his cousin) but died at his home in Florence 28th May 1906, leaving no issue. A cousin was the diplomat Sir Thomas Francis Wade (1818-95) later Professor of Chinese at Cambridge.
[Debrett, *Knightage* (1905) 882-83; Burke, *Irish Family Records* (1976) 1172-73; DNB.]

WAKEFIELD, Sir Charles, 1st Viscount, GCVO (1859-1941)

Lord Wakefield was Lord Mayor of London in 1915 and was a self-made multi-millionaire who acquired his fortune importing and refining oil through his firm C.C.Wakefield Ltd., which he started in Liverpool. His honours and benefactions, including sponsorship of Sir Alan Cobham's flight to Australia and back of 1926 and the world water speed record holders Miss England I, II and III, take up more than one entire column in his *Who's Who* entry. One of his chief interests was aviation and the aviation industry which he zealously supported and he was appointed to the board of numerous related companies where his considerable experience and expertise, were much prized.

Charles Cheers Wakefield was born in Derby in 1859, son of John Wakefield (1825-90) a Liverpool customs officer who had been born in Derby to Thomas Wakefield (1800-60) later of Normanton Road, of a family which came ultimately from Chester. His mother was Mary, daughter of William Cheers of Manchester and he was the fourth and youngest son. He was educated at the Liverpool Institute and he married 17th February 1888 Sarah Frances, daughter of John Graham, who in due course was made a Dame of the Venerable order of St John, of which order he, too, became a Knight of Justice. He was knighted 26th June 1908, and made a baronet 16th February 1917. He was raised to the peerage as Lord Wakefield of Hythe (Kent, where he had a seat) 20 January 1930, being raised to a Viscountcy as Viscount Wakefield in 1934. He was made GCVO in 1936, and held six orders, awarded by various other nations. He was Sheriff of London 1907-08, Hon LLD, Hon FRAeS and many other honours He died without leaving issue at Hythe 15th January 1941 when his honours became extinct.

[DNB; *Who Was Who* (1941-1950)1189-90; Burke, *Peerage* (1931) 2396.]

WARD, James, RA (1769-1859)

James Ward was a prolific and, in his day, considered a very fine painter of animal subjects, but he began as a skilled mezzotint engraver. His output was consistent and his robustness of nature came through strongly in his pictures, especially in large set pieces such as his epic *Allegory of Waterloo* of 1817, done for the Royal Institution.

Ward was born in London on 23rd October 1769 and worked for a time under JOHN RAPHAEL SMITH *(q.v.)* but was afterwards apprenticed to his own elder brother, William (1766-1826), another ex-pupil of Smith who later married the sister of George Morland RA (who himself married their sister Anne). He later followed Smith as painter and mezzotinter to the Prince of Wales and exhibited over 400 paintings at the Royal Academy, to which he was elected in 1811.

He married his second wife at All Saints', Derby in 1827: Charlotte, daughter of George Fritche of Derby (sister of CHRISTOPHER FRITCHE *q.v.*) and resided in the town until 1830 when he moved to Cheshunt (Herts), where he died on 23rd November 1859. His son, George Raphael Ward (1798-1878), was a distin-

guished engraver whose daughter Henrietta married the unrelated Edward Mathew Ward (1816-79) also an artist of note.

[DNB: Parish records; Glover's *Directory of Derby* (1827).]

WARWICK, John Alfred (1821-1896)

Warwick was a signalling and telegraphic engineer who did much to improve safety on the Midland Railway (for which company he worked in Derby from 1851) through his ingenuity and foresight. He ultimately rose to become superintendent of signals and telegraphs, which gave him the scope to let his innovative abilities have full rein. His other claim to fame was his long-standing friendship and collaboration with RICHARD KEENE *(q.v.)*. They seem to have been together on Keene's earliest photographic forays, and a number of Keene's prints and stereos bear his name. Indeed, so many of

Keene's views have Keene in them that the presumption is that Warwick actually took a great many of them. If so, he must take much of the credit for the quality of Keene's earlier work.

John Alfred Warwick was born at Manchester on 15th September 1821 although he was brought up at Rotherham, where his father Thomas Oliver Warwick MD (originally from Cheshire) had earlier founded the infirmary; his mother was called Mary. He was an only son, but he had three sisters of whom the eldest, Rebecca Wylde Warwick (Mrs H.Ames, d.1895) was a professor of music at Liverpool. In 1853 Warwick married Elizabeth Kate Hudson of Ilkeston, and they had two sons (one died young) and seven daughters, a burgeoning family, which caused them to move from 53 Mount Street, Derby, to Brook Cottage, Ockbrook (now Ockbrook Lodge). Warwick died there 17th September 1896. Gertrude (1865-1953), the fourth daughter, married 6th August 1892 the Moravian Bishop at Ockbrook, Arthur Stanley Ward; their daughter Greta Sanderson was a distinguished artist.

The son, also John Alfred, himself had a son, John Francis Warwick MBE (1905-96) of Church Street, Alvaston as well as three daughters, one of whom Gertrude Ethel (1891-1961) became wife of 1st LORD HIVES *(q.v.)*. J.F. (Jack) Warwick was for 50 years a Rolls Royce employee, mainly as a development engineer, being closely involved with work on the 'R' engine of 1929 and its development, the Merlin. He married and had a daughter.

[Birks, *op.cit.* 1-24, information from the late Mrs B.Armstead; DET. 9/10/1996; family papers.]

WAST(E), Joan (1532-1555)

Queen Mary's reign saw the execution, on grounds of religion, of Derby's celebrated 'martyr', Joan Wast, by burning. As this appears to have been the only instance of an adherent of the sort of Protestantism advocated under the reign of Edward VI being martyred in Derby (unlike some other centres), her case has become famous. Doubly so, insofar as Joan was handicapped by blindness.

The elder daughter of William Wast, barber and ropemaker of All Saints' and himself a younger brother of Thomas Wast, an opulent tradesman, Joan was born blind in 1532 and, as

so often with handicapped people, reached maturity finding in the church 'a very present help in time of trouble'. This introduction to the hope which the church can bring took place under Edward VI and the vernacular Bible and Prayer Book. When Queen Mary caused the re-adoption of Catholic rites, Joan must have been hit hard, much in the same way as Church of England members have been affected in recent years by the unilateral imposition of the Alternative Service Book and by the calling into question of traditional beliefs by go-ahead Bishops. She adopted a conservative and vocal stance, especially over the doctrine of the tran-substantiation, and being blind, was in some ways insensitive to the advantages of tact. Eventually, she was arrested on the orders of the Diocesan Bishop by the reluctant bailiffs, Richard Moore and William Bainbrigge, and brought before the Bishop and her chief accuser, a hard-line Catholic, Dr Anthony Draycot, Diocesan Chancellor. A stubborness born out of a belief in her own rectitude, combined with the ruthless determination of Draycot not to allow his own Bishop to temporise with her, led to her condemnation and a writ of *De Haeretico Comburendo* was served. On 1 August 1555, the unfortunate girl was made to listen to a vitupera-tive and unforgiving sermon from Draycot before being taken to Windmill Pit on the north side of Mill Hill Lane and burned. She is said to have died with considerable dignity.
[Craven (1988) 51-52; Simpson, *op.cit.* III, 662-670.]

WEBSTER, Moses (1792-1870)

Webster was a flower painter at Derby Porcelain Factory from *c.*1819 to 1825, whose productions were 'truthful and beautifully coloured' athough today they are said to have a 'somewhat dashed and faded appearance'. Nevertheless, he was undoubtedly the best of the later flower painters, his groups being carefully composed and done with zest and freedom of execution. He also occasionally painted birds. He left the Derby fac-tory in 1825 to pursue a career as a drawing mas-

ter which he did with considerable success, his style extending to include superb views of local seats and landscapes. He also drew on stone to create lithographs of his work for sale, engraved by L.Hague and Sr. Gauci. His pictures were nearly always in water colour or pencil.

Moses Webster was born at the house of his father, Robert Webster, in Becketwell Lane and was baptized at St Werburgh 16th October 1792. His mother, Elizabeth Bentley, had married his father at Duffield on 28th August 1785, and there was a younger brother, Robert (1805-81) later of 190 Parliament Street. The father's own father and grandfather were both called Robert, the first marrying Mary Jackson of Shottle at Duffield in 1733.

Moses was apprenticed at an early age at the Derby China Factory before moving first to London and then to Worcester, and at the latter city studied from 1814-16 at a private art school. Webster's fondness for including roses in his flower groups at Worcester prompted a colleague to pen the lines:

If Moses composes
His posies of roses,
Of sweeter he can't then compose;
No flower else that grows,
Can compare with the rose;
If you doubt it consult your own nose!

His drawing from memory of the Derby china factory is the only depiction of the complex (apart from one or two fragmentary architect's elevations) considered at all reliable, and he did it in old age along with a sketch plan of the layout. He died, apparently unmarried, at Derby on 20th October 1870.
[Parish records; Haslem, *op.cit.* 116-117.]

WESTON, Rev. Walter, FRGS (1861-1940)

Walter Weston was a notable missionary priest described as the 'Father of modern Alpinism' most of whose career was spent in Japan. Whilst there he developed a deep love of the mountains of the interior of the main islands which he explored, recording geographical, geological and botanical phenomena, and also taking a series of

very fine photographs of the scenery, flora and fauna, as well as townscapes and a graphic record of the 1905 earthquake. A direct result of these activities was his love of mountaineering, and his career he adapted to accommodate this. He became a pioneer Japanese alpinist and his memory is much revered in both Japan and Italy, where he also climbed a great deal.

Walter Weston was born at Mileash House, Darley Abbey, on Christmas Day 1861, sixth of the eight sons of Cllr. John Weston (d.1878) an elastic webbing manufacturer whose firm, Weston and Thompson, had a mill in Parliament Street. His mother was Emma Britland, who married on Christmas Eve 1849. His grandfather, another John, was also a Derby man. Walter, like his brothers, was educated at Derby School before going on to Clare College, Cambridge, BA (1883) MA (1887), where he was a noted footballer. He was prepared for ordination at Ridley College, Cambridge and was appointed British Chaplain at Kohè (Japan) in 1888. He returned to the UK in 1895 as curate of Christ Church, Wimbledon, later again going back to the SPG mission Yokohama (1902-05); then, after five years as vicar of Ewell (Surrey) he once again

returned to Japan as British Chaplain. His first book was *Mountaineering and Exploring in the Japanese Alps* (1896); he also wrote *The Playground of the Far East* (1918) and he was elected a Fellow of the Royal Geographical Society on the strength of it. In 1937 the Emperor of Japan made him a Knight of the Order of the Sacred Teasure. Weston married in 1902, Frances Emily (d.1937) daughter of SIR FRANCIS FOX *(q.v.)* and died without issue on 27 March 1940.

[Tachella, *op.cit.* 96; *Oddfellows' Companion to Derby* (1892) 233; Derbyshire Family History Society *Branch News* LXII (6/1992) 13; *Who Was Who* (1927-40); Marianni, F., *Walter Weston, L'incanto del Giappone* (Turin, 1995).]

WHEELDON, Mrs Alice (1867-1919)

Alice Wheeldon was a left-wing revolutionary, suffragist and militant pacifist who became notorious as the prime mover behind a plot to assassinate the Prime Minister, Lloyd George, and Arthur Henderson in 1917. Looked at in the cold light of day, the scheme hardly seemed to hold water, but she involved several members of her own family in it, with (for them) disastrous results. The method chosen was poison, and the direct motive was the treatment meted out to her son, who was a Great War conscientious objector. She conspired with her two daughters Hettie (an Ilkeston schoolteacher) and Alice, with Alice's husband, a Portsmouth chemist, Alfred Mason, who was to procure the poison (curare) to be delivered via an airgun pellet. Elaborate preparations were made, but on 29th January 1917 all four were arrested. Their trial was held over four and a half days in March that year, F.E.Smith (later Earl of Birkenhead) leading for the prosecution. Although the charge was tantamount to treason, Mrs Wheeldon evaded the supreme penalty, receiving ten years; Mason got seven, his wife five; Hetty was acquitted. Recently released state papers, however, suggest strongly that Mrs Wheeldon was encouraged in her plans by an *agent provocateur* from MI5, although she does not appear to have needed too much enticement. The theory that the family were framed from start to finish, however, fails to hold up.

Wheeldon was a deserted wife who lived above a second-hand clothes shop in Pear Tree Road. She had four children: William, the picked-on conscientious objector, Nellie, Henrietta and Alice. The subsequent careers of the first two say everything about the extremism with which Alice Wheeldon had inculcated her family: William went to the USSR in 1919 and took citizenship; ironically he was liquidated by the CHEKA in 1927. Nellie married socialist leader Tom Bell whom she accompanied to the USSR. Hettie (d.1920) married Arthur MacManus of Glasgow, later first Chairman of the British Communist Party. Mrs Wheeldon herself continued in her beliefs (which included, as F.E.Smith lost no time in emphasising at the trial, a desire to kill the King as well) but died 20 February 1919.
[Craven (1988) 214; File at Derby Local Studies Library; DET 26 &27/12/1997.]

WHEELDON, William (1789-1847)

William Wheeldon was the nephew of the great WILLIAM BILLINGSLEY *(q.v.)* and one of a dis-

tinguished group of Derby China Factory flower painters which included his uncle and MOSES WEBSTER *(q.v.)*. As an apprentice he worked with Billingsley at Pinxton from January 1801, being further apprenticed to Michael Kean at Derby the following year, working there until 1823. In that year he succeeded to the proprietorship of a shop at 22 Bridge Gate, formerly his uncle's residence; he later became the landlord of the Nottingham Arms Inn nearby, whilst his brother, John, kept the Chesterfield Arms not far away on Nottingham Road. He also became a maltster, combining this with corn and flour dealing.

William Wheeldon was born in 1789 the second of five sons of William Wheeldon (b.1755) a stockiner, by Ann Rigley his wife, her sister Sarah later marrying William Billingsley. His elder brother John (b.1781) became a maltster and innkeeper, and his sons George, Edmund and John were also maltsters. William, senior, was the son of another stockiner John (1726-97), son of William. The china painter had three sons and a daughter, Mary, whose husband Samuel Fletcher had previously been married to Sarah Wallis, niece of JOSEPH WRIGHT *(q.v.)*. All the sons became maltsters, building the business up into a large and prosperous concern. The second son was Alderman George Wheeldon (1832-99) Mayor of Derby in 1873-74 who entertained the Prince and Princess of Wales during their visit to Derby and left a large family. Wheeldon died in 1847.
[Haslem, *op.cit.* 52,112; Poll Books; *Directories;* MMD.1.36.]

WHINYATES, Gen. Sir Edward, KCB, KH (1782-1865)

Sir Edward Whinyates was an extremely successful and dashing artillery commander who fought a particularly effective series of engagements in the Peninsular war and who commanded 2nd Rocket Troop at Waterloo where his fire power helped to break d'Erlon's Corps. He was later, from 1852, director general of artillery and commandant at Woolwich until 1856. He was also

Colonel Commandant of the RHA from 1864. His work in the army of occupation after Waterloo earned him a knighthood (of the Guelphic order) in 1823 and he was made CB in 1831. He was promoted to KCB on 18 May 1860.

Edward Charles Whinyates was born on 6th May 1782, third son of Maj. Thomas Whinyates (1755-1806) of Abbotsleigh, Devonshire by Catherine, fourth daughter of Sir Thomas Frankland 5th Bt, of Thirkelby (Yorks). Four of his five brothers were also military men – Rear Admiral Thomas (1778-1857), Capt. George Barrington RN (1783-1808), Maj. Gen. Frederick William (1793-1881) and Gen Francis Frankland (1796-1887), of whom only Frederick left issue. Edward was educated at Mr Newcombe's school, Hackney and RMA Woolwich from 1796, being commissioned second lieutenant RA on 1798, serving thereafter on the Helder and at Madeira. He later served in Jamaica and was present at Copenhagen.

Whinyates' family were from Chellaston, where they are traceable to Thomas Whinyards (*sic*) who died in 1567. His great-grandfather Charles Whinyates sold up Chellaston Manor and estate in 1726, but Edward's marriage in 1827 to Sarah Elizabeth, only daughter of Samuel Crompton of Woodend (Yorks), who had been Mayor of Derby in 1782 and 1788 (son of SAMUEL CROMPTON, *q.v.*), re-established the local connection. Unfortunately, she died aged 27 the following year and was interred in St Werburgh's, Derby, beneath a monument of great dignity of 1832 by Sir Francis Chantrey. There were no children and he never remarried, dying on Christmas Day, 1865 at Cheltenham.
[DNB; MI at St Werburgh's; parish records; Wolley, W., *History of Derbyshire* (n.d, *c.*1713), DRS edition, vol.V1 (1981) 48; Local Studies Library, Deeds 6492 & 6945.]

WHITAKER, John (*c.*1804-1874)

John Whitaker was the last member of a remarkable dynasty of China painters, gilders and modellers connected with the Derby Porcelain Factory, being a highly skilled figure modeller who rose to become superintendent of the figure makers (1830) and works foreman (1842), only leaving when the works were closed by ALD. THOMAS CLARKE (*q.v.*). He then worked as figure maker at Minton's at Stoke, but never susequently matched the quality of his work at Derby.

John Whitaker was probably born in 1804, as he was apprenticed to the Derby factory (presumably at 14) in 1818; his age at death in October 1874 is given as 67, but that is likely to be erroneous in view of the apprenticeship. His father, William, is described in local sources only as 'son of an apprentice of William Duesbury' and we know nothing about him. However, the grandfather, Richard (1760-88) was a Derby China modeller apprenticed in 1774 who, by Elizabeth Webster, had another son, John, a gilder, of Cross Lanes (Derby, now Macklin Street).

John worked at Derby until 1826 when he joined George Cocker in his china factory in Friar Gate. He married Anne, sister of John Stanesby, yet another Derby China painter, and left five sons and three daughters. John, the second son (1813-71), was a former Derby China employee who later became an important fabric designer in Manchester; Samuel, the fourth son (1818-99) was an accountant, a co-founder of the Derbyshire Building Society and served as Mayor of Derby 1886-87. The Whitaker family had previously been millers at Little Eaton.

John Whitaker married at St Alkmund's, 24 September 1821 Sarah Perry and died at Stoke-on-Trent in 1874. They had a daughter who later married Edwin Ottewell, a cousin of SIR JOHN SMITH (*q.v.*).
[Haslem, *op.cit.* l10, 162-63 167; parish registers; MMD.1 65-66; information from Mrs J.M.Morris, Crawley, Sussex.]

WHITAKER, Joseph (1813-1894)

Joseph Whitaker was a botanist who did important research in South Australia and later in Derbyshire. He was also a seedsman, florist, nurseryman and farmer whose contribution to horticulture (especially in collaboration with William Barron of Borrowash) was of considerable importance.

Joseph Whitaker was the son of Joseph Whitaker of Quarndon, labourer, and Sarah Clarke and he was baptised at Quarndon on 8th February 1813; he also had a sister, later Mrs Hughes. He was working as a gardener when his obvious horticultural and botanical flair was brought to the attention of Col GEORGE GAWLER *(q.v.)* probably through one of his Cox cousins. So impressed was Gawler that he took him to South Australia for the duration of his governorship 1838-40. He returned in April 1840 and wrote up much of his material for his patron before being appointed master of the new school at Breadsall in 1842, which post he continued in until about 1870, living at Manchester Terrace, Ashbourne Road, Derby. Thereafter he resigned, took a cottage on the Bloomfield estate at Ferriby Brook and began his career as a florist and seedsman in 1871. He was described as farmer a decade later and was churchwarden at Morley Church, where a monument commemorates his death at Breadsall, March 1894. His wife, Mary, by whom he had no issue, pre-deceased him by four years, aged 84. His heirs were his nephew Thomas Hughes, also formerly of Manchester Terrace, and Philip William Clarke, his mother's nephew. Another kinswomen was Susan, née Clarke, Mrs Josiah Huss, whose husband was a descendant of Henry Huss, architect to GEORGE SOROCOLD *(q.v.)*.

[Information courtesy N.J.Moyes, Esq; Will dated 27/11/1893 (DRO D96/1/87, p.436-47).]

WHITEHURST, John, FRS (1713-1788)

John Whitehurst lived in Derby from 1736 to 1780 and may be considered one of the foremost natural philosophers – today we would say scientists – of his age. His association, as a founder member of the Lunar Society of Birmingham, with ERASMUS DARWIN *(q.v.)*, Josiah Wedgwood, Matthew Boulton, James Watt, James Keir and their like formed the intellectual cockpit from which the burgeoning Industrial Revolution was guided to fruition. Whitehurst was by calling a clockmaker, and an extremely good one, with several innovations to his credit,

not least of which were the round dial, long-case clock, a thoroughgoing standardisation of parts and the manufacture of components to very high tolerances. He was also responsible for some outstanding clocks in association with his friends James Ferguson FRS, Matthew Boulton FRS and Benjamin Franklin FRS: notably the three wheel clock, tidal clock, sidereal and astronomical clocks. As an engineer, little was beyond him and he also made compasses, waywisers, timers for pottery kilns, pyrometers, precision timers and a device from which he intended to standarise measures of length, distance, volume and weight. His superb barometers used a scale of his own devising which presaged the millibar for measuring atmospheric pressure by over a century.

He was also active in hydraulics, 'domestic economy' – stoves, back boilers, roasting devices, central heating, flushing WCs, etc. – meteorology, steam engines, spinning machines and astronomy. Only his lifelong friend Darwin had a more fertile brain. His most important achievement however, was in geology. In 1763 he sent Franklin (an occasional visitor to his house in Derby) the outline of his theory on the origin and formation of the earth, at length published

in 1778 as *An Inquiry into the Original State and Formation of the Earth* the second edition of which (1786) included a section on the strata of Derbyshire. His material on vulcanology, fossils and the stratification of rocks enable him to be viewed as the father of modern geology. His work on strata much facilitated the prospecting and mining of minerals such as coal, lead and copper and he had a stake in the extractive operations of ANTHONY TISSINGTON *(q.v.)*. His championship of Blue John as an ornamental material was invaluable to Boulton and probably ensured the success of RICHARD BROWN *(q.v.)*. His knowledge of minerals was also of inestimable value to Josiah Wedgwood whose works owed as much to his ideas as to PICKFORD'S designs. His circle of friends, acquaintances and correspondents was international, and his portrait was painted twice by JOSEPH WRIGHT *(q.v.)*.

Whitehurst was born 10 April 1713, the eldest son of John Whitehurst, a Congleton (Cheshire) clockmaker, himself the fourth son of Egerton Whitehurst of Whitehurst, in Dilhorne (Staffordshire) where the family had farmed, hovering between the status of yeomen and gentlemen, for many generations. His interest in geology was fostered by his father in long walks in the Derbyshire Peak District. His education is said to have been rudimentary (but was certainly adequate) and was completed by apprenticeship to his father. Thereafter he visited Ireland and London (at least) before deciding to set up in Derby about 1736, gaining his freedom to trade as a burgess by presenting a turret clock to the Corporation for installation in the new (1731) Guildhall. His house in Iron Gate still stands, albeit altered by RICHARD KEENE *(q.v.)*, although in 1764 he moved to a house in Queen Street rebuilt for him by Pickford, which had once been the home of JOHN FLAMSTEED *(q.v.)* and was later that of Joseph Wright. He was Churchwarden of All Saints' (where he rebuilt the clock and carrillon) 1761-62 and on 9th January 1745, married Elizabeth (d.1784) daughter of Rev. George Gretton and aunt of GEORGE GRETTON *(q.v.)*. Their only child, James, died in infancy in January 1753.

The friendship and patronage of 2nd Duke of Newcastle (for whose new seat at Clumber Park, Notts, he had devised a system of plumbing far in advance of its time) obtained him the position of Stamper of the Money Weights at the Royal Mint under an Act of 1774. Although in the long term a sinecure, freeing him from the day-to-day supervision of his Derby clockworks, it involved quite a bit of initial work for which he made three precision coin balances. From this time too he lived increasingly at Bolt Court, Fleet Street, London, finally leaving Derby in 1780. He was free to publish *The Inquiry* and pursue his more esoteric inventions, dying in London 18th February 1788. He left his property and clock-making business to his nephew JOHN WHITEHURST II *(q.v.)*, son of his brother James who had succeeded to their father's firm in Congleton. George (1721-93) and William Whitehurst (d.1782), his younger brothers, had been successively works manager for John. Of his sisters, Mary married the clockmaker Joseph Finney of Liverpool; Anne was the mother of the artist William Hodges RA. Whitehurst was elected FRS in 1779, and belonged to a London Freemasonic Lodge by 1772, as well as several coffee house societies.
[Craven, M., *John Whitehurst* (Mayfield 1996) *passim*.]

WHITEHURST, John (II) (1761-1834)

John Whitehurst was the nephew and successor of his uncle JOHN WHITEHURST FRS *(q.v.)* being the fifth of seven sons of the latter's brother, James (1719-1800) and Elizabeth Corley (d.1805). He was born at Astbury (Cheshire) in December 1761 and was probably apprenticed to his father. Shortly thereafter he appears to have gone to Derby to run his uncle's works in succession to the philosopher's brother William who died in 1782.

He married at Derby, Jane Howard, on 22nd November 1785. In 1793 he sold his uncle's house in Queen Street, its next occupant being J0SEPH WRIGHT *(q.v.)*, and moved to 22, Iron Gate – next to his uncle's first Derby residence –

where later JOHN DAVIS and EDWIN HASLAM *(q.q.v.)* were to flourish. In December 1793 he was initiated into the Tyrian Freemasonic Lodge, a connection which drew him into the ambit of ERASMUS DARWIN and WILLIAM STRUTT, FRS *(q.q.v.)*. He, like his uncle, served as church-warden of All Saints' (in 1812-13) and was undoubtedly a Tory, for in 1831 the Reform Rioters smashed the windows of his house, at 1 Cherry Street, whence he had moved shortly before. Whitehurst's greatest achievement was to perfect and make practical the noctuary or watchman's clock, apparently invented about 1786 by Strutt and Darwin, but quite probably incorporating an idea of his uncle's, although the matter now seems to lie beyond proof. These clocks were of the highest utility for the security of large buildings and works and their introduction by Strutt into the rota of the Derby Watch enabled a reduction in personnel of 50 per cent to be made. Whitehurst continued to improve the design over his lifetime and his firm produced many hundreds during the remainder of its existence.

His clockmaking was less reliant on standardisation than his uncle's, and his output much more eclectic, although he persisted with several of his predecessor's standard types, including his superb angle barometers, before evolving his own highly characteristic stick variety. From 1809 he took into partnership his eldest son, JOHN *(q.v.)* and thenceforth until his death at Cherry Street in October, 1834, the firm's clocks were signed WHITEHURST & SON/DERBY and usually numbered.

He left three sons and four daughters. The second son, Charles Howard Whitehurst, QC (1796-1879) was an eminent advocate of the Middle Temple who was called to the bar on the 2nd August 1822 and made his name defending two strikebreakers on a charge of murder during the Derby Silk Trades' Lock-out of 1833-34. He took silk on 10th July 1844 and died unmarried at his home in Brixton on 13th March 1879. The other brother, William, became an Anglican clergyman who remained unmarried. Whitehurst's younger daughter Anna Maria married the

Ashby (Leics) surgeon, Joseph Cantrell; another, Elizabeth, married Thomas Cardale d'Ewes, also of Ashby.

[As preceding article.]

WHITEHURST, John (III) (1788-1855)

The third and last of the succession of eminent Derby clockmakers called John Whitehurst was famous for something he never, in the event, achieved: building the clock to go in the Tower of the Palace of Westminster. The specification, devised by Astronomer Royal Sir George Airy, was so demanding that only John Whitehurst and E.J.Dent of London tendered for it; Whitehurst's tender was chosen, but he died before work could start, and without him, Dent got the job by default.

John Whitehurst was the eldest son of JOHN WHITEHURST II *(q.v.)* and was born in Queen Street, Derby in February 1788. He was educated at Matthew George Spencer's academy and then apprenticed to his father whom he joined in partnership in 1809. He also followed his father into

the Tyrian Lodge of Freemasons by 1826, when he served as Provincial Grand Secretary, and he was churchwarden of St Alkmund's Church in 1845-46. He lived nearby, in North Parade.

He once again moved towards the standardisation of components for his clocks and specialised in intricately fitted wall-clocks which he adapted to fit into long (rather plain) cases, virtually superseding the standard long-case clock. Overall, production seems to have risen, including fine turret clocks, and he brought in relations from Cheshire and Staffordshire to help in the works at Derby, leading to the establishment of several minor branches of the family in Derby, descendants of which are with us still. In 1851 he had a workforce of 12, one of whom was John Smith – who left after a row with the foreman, Thomas Woodward, and set up on his own a firm which is still flourishing.

Whitehurst died, unmarried, at North Parade on 21st September 1855, 'a sound church man and a true Conservative'. Woodward took the works over, but his former employer's heir, his brother C.H.Whitehurst, QC, sold the firm as a going concern to the Roskells of Liverpool, who failed to capitalise on the reputation and goodwill of almost 120 years, and finally closed the works in 1862. Both Smith and the Woodwards claimed to be the firm's true successors (the latter made clocks in the same style for longer); the machinery was sold to Haycock of Ashbourne. [Sources as for two preceding articles.]

WILCOCK, Gp. Capt. C.A.B., OBE, AFC, FRAeS (1898-1962)

Group Captain Wilcock was one of those men who fought for King and Country during World War One and was disillusioned about the non-materialisation of the 'land fit for heroes' promised by Lloyd George; he consequently joined the Labour Party in 1921 and later the Fabian Society. He successfully stood against the intending successor to W.A.Reid in 1945 in tandem with Philip Noël-Baker. It was in his time that the 1948 Representation of the People Act

created two specific Derby constituencies, his seat becoming Derby North.

Clifford Arthur Bowman Wilcock was born in London 28th April 1898 and was educated at St Dunstan's, which he left to join the colours (in the London Scottish) before his 17th birthday. He later transferred to the Queen's Royal West Surreys, being wounded at the Second Battle of Ypres (1917). He later obtained a commission in the Royal Flying Corps, winning the AFC and stayed in the RAF after the close of hostilities. He served in Egypt 1921-23 with 208 Sqn. and later in Iraq. His *Curriculum Vitae* states that he studied engineering and went to Edinburgh University, and it is difficult to see when this was. Either he left the RAF in 1918/19 and rejoined after his degree in 1921 or he was released to do this around 1930 – a most unusual proceeding in those days (although commonplace today). He formed one of the first RAFVR squadrons in 1937 and retired from the RAF in 1938.

At the outbreak of war in 1939 Wilcock was recalled to the Air Ministry, receiving the OBE in 1944. He resigned in 1945 to stand for Derby. He served as Chairman of the Committee on Licensing, Recruitment and Training of Personnel for Civil Aviation. He was an underwriter at Lloyds, a director of several avaition companies (not then a stigma for MPs) as well as Mecca Ltd., a governor of Westminster Hospital and a Freeman of the City of London.

He lived in London at 78, Buckingham Gate, SW1 and died in a London hospital 14th January 1962 after a short illness, leaving a widow, three sons and three daughters, all of whom married. [*Who Was Who* 1961-70; *Times* 15/1/1962; DET. 15/1/1962.]

WILLOUGHBY, Percival (1596-1685)

Dr Percival Willoughby was a physician and one of the first people to specialise in gynaecology contributing, through his book, *Observations in Midwifery* (which, however, was not published until 1863!) much of the basis for modern practice in childbirth. He was no mere theorist, however, and had an extensive practice throughout the Midlands, frequently delivering babies himself, partly because no-one else was available (except relatives of the mother, or servants) and partly to train others.

Percival Willoughby was born in 1596, the third son of Sir Percival Willoughby MP, himself great-grandson of Sir Thomas, the third son of Sir Christopher Willoughby of Parham, a family which originated at Willoughby (Lincs.). His mother was of another, unrelated, family of Willoughby, having been one of the six daughters and co-heiresses of Sir Francis Willoughby of Wollaton Hall (Notts) for whom Robert Smythson built the surviving Elizabethan Prodigy House in the 1580s. The Willoughbys of Wollaton were descended from one Ralph Bugge of Nottingham and Bakewell, lead merchant, son of Ralph de Nottingham. Bugge's son was of Willoughby-on-the-Wolds (Notts), taking his new name from there. His son Richard purchased Wollaton before 1324. The Willoughbys of Risley were the senior branch of this family.

Strangely, in view of Percival Willoughby's future career, his parents obtained a writ against his father's pregnant mother that her posthumous pregnancy was genuine, for there was great unease amongst the five Willoughby co-heiresses of Wollaton that the late arrival of a son would deprive them of a share in a lucrative inheritance; thus, Dorothy (widow of Sir Francis) was confined and guarded until she gave birth – to a girl, to general relief.

Percival and his brothers were educated at Rugby and then at Eton, all three going on to Oxford, Percival to Trinity. He was then, in 1619, articled to Dr Frames van Otten for seven years to be taught 'Music, physick and Surgery… to use him like a son, maintain him like a gentleman and …teach him the secrets of Physick.' He ultimately is said to have taken his MD, marrying in 1631 Elizabeth (d.February 1667), daughter of Sir Francis Coke of Trusley. The family resided in Derby from the outset living in the rebuilt, eastward, portion of the late 15th century mansion in Tenant Street known as the Old Mayor's Parlour. They had two daughters and four sons. all of whom appear to have died unmarried,

except the daughters who became Helen, Mrs Hart and Dorothy, Mrs Burton (of Aldercar). On 20th February 1641, Willoughby was admitted LRCP, but the record fails to mention a doctorate; possibly he never completed his MD, although the initials appear on his graveslab in St Peter's Church, Derby.

Throughout his professional life, Willoughby kept a log of his cases, from which it is possible to work out that he was actually in practice from as early as 1624. In 1669 he wrote, 'Nigh 45 years have I practised in the Midwife's bed and in it, I humbly thank God for his assistance and help, I ever delivered all women to whom I was called Mrs (William) Allestry (Sic,q.v.) only excepted and my not delivering her was occasion'd by the straightness of the passages and the unusual ill conformation of the bones near adjoining the womb, with the hardness of the child's skull.'

In the 1650s he moved to Stafford and in 1656 to London 'for the better education of my children'. Nevertheless, by 1660 he had returned to Derby, having trained Helen, his elder daughter, as his nurse. She was later able to set up as a surgical midwife on her own account in Staffordshire and London. Even in old age Willoughby did not hesitate to travel as far as, for instance, Ridgeway (NE Derbyshire, almost on the edge of Sheffield) to attend a woman with a potentially difficult birth. By 1670, his youngest son was also acting as his assistant and the evidence suggests that he eventually took over, allowing Percival to retire. He died at his house in Derby and was buried in St Peter's (where his grave slab may still be seen) on 5th October 1685. Mrs Maria Willoughby, widow, who was buried at St Peter's on 19th October 1705 was probably an unrecorded second wife or daughter-in-law.

It is the best proof of Willoughby's greatness, apart from the techniques he pioneered which we now take for granted, that 'he could make all things simple and could recount them in simple language'. One of his chief causes was to banish the traditional midwives as doing more harm than good, replacing them with those trained in his own precepts. In 1646 at Twyford he found 'midwives, tormenting the woman' and a few years later he visited a 'whimsical, conceited woman with a scrimshaw midwife who nearly kill'd her'. Willoughby appears to have continuously saved life when others would have been prepared to leave for dead. It is worth noting, too, that the dissemination of Willoughby's methods during the 18th century was thanks to the medical teaching of Derbyshire-born Dr Thomas Denman (1733-1815) – father of Lord Chancellor Denman – who acquired the MS of Percival's Journal and was much struck by it, teaching therefrom and passing it on to his son-in-law, Sir Richard Croft, of Croft, 6th Bt, MD, through whose influence it was ultimately published.

[DAJ LIX (1937) 67-94; *ibid.*, XLVIII (1926) 29, 32; Burke, *Peerage* (1970) 1806-07.]

WILMOT, Sir Edward, Bt, FRS, MD (1693-1786)

Sir Edward Wilmot was Physician General to the Army, Physician in Ordinary to Queen Caroline, the Prince of Wales, George II and George III; his patients also included the Great and Good of his day, including the Duke of Newcastle and the Archbishop of Canterbury. He was rewarded with a baronetcy on 15th February 1759.

Edward Wilmot was born at Chaddesden Hall on 29th October 1693, elder of two sons of Robert Wilmot of Chaddesden by Joyce, daughter and ultimate co-heiress of William Sacheverell of Staunton (Leics). The family had been seated at Chaddesden since 1626 and Robert was the great-grandson of John Wilmot of Spondon, the founder of the family, who was said to have been a scion of the Wilmots of Sutton-on-Soar (Notts). Edward was educated at Derby School and St John's Cambridge (BA 1714, HA 1718, MD 1725) where he later was elected a Fellow. He was a member of the College of Physicians from 1725 and was elected FRS five years later. He practised in London and was appointed physician to St Thomas' Hospital (cf. TH0MAS GISBORNE), becoming Physician General in 1740.

He married Sarah Marsh, daughter of Richard

Meade, MD, his predecessor as Royal Physician to George II, and had a son and two daughters. His wife was painted by J0SEPH WRIGHT *(q.v.)*. He died at Heringstone (Dorset) on 21st November 1786 and was succeeded in his baronetcy by his son (Sir) Robert Meade Wilmot, 2nd Bt, (1731-93). His brother, Rev. Richard Wimot married the daughter of Simon Degge (see SIR SIMON DEGGE) and was ancestor of the Wilmot-Sitwells of Stainsby House, Smalley. [Burke, *Peerage* (1970) 2841; DNB.]

WILMOT, Col. Sir Henry, 5th Bt, VC, KCB, MP (1831-1901)

The great-great-grandson of SIR EDWARD WILMOT, 1st Bt. *(q.v.)*, Henry Wilmot was born at Chaddesden Hall on 3rd February 1831, second son of Sir Sacheverel Wilmot, Bt. (1801-72); his mother was Maria, daughter of Edward Miller Mundy MP of Shipley Hall, and there were three other sons and three daughters. Henry was educated at Rugby, following which, in 1849, he was commissioned into the 43rd Light Infantry transferring to the 2nd Bn. The Rifle Brigade two years later. He served in the Crimea, including the Sebastopol campaign.

In July, 1857 he was appointed Deputy Judge Advocate in India, and became swiftly involved with the supression of the Indian Mutiny. It was in heavy fighting in and around Lucknow on 11th March 1858 that Wilmot won the VC for saving the lives of four men – one wounded – facing a perilous situation and under constant fire from the enemy. The award was gazetted on 24th December that year. Wilmot later served in the second China War (1860-61), being Judge Advocate General to the expeditionary force. He retired with the rank of Major thereafter, returning to Chaddesden. He entered politics not long afterwards, being elected in the Conservative Interest for South Derbyshire in 1868, being re-elected in 1874 and 1880. The death of his elder brother without issue in 1872 saw him succeed as 5th Baronet along with the responsibilities of the large Chaddesden estate; he was made KCB in 1897.

Sir Henry, who became Colonel of his local TA unit in later life, died unmarried at his house in Bournemouth, 'Chaddesden', 7th April 1901, being succeeded by his nephew Sir Ralph Wilmot, later (1918) killed in action in World War One. Ralph's successor, pressed by death duties, sold the Chaddesden estate in 1924; the hall was demolished two years later.

[Burke, *Peerage* (1970) 2842; DNB; McCreery, *op.cit.* 18; Briscoe, *op.cit.* 387.]

WILMOT, Rt. Hon Sir John Eardley (1709-1792)

Sir John Eardley Wilmot was an exceedingly distinguished Chief Justice who served between 1766 and 1771 subsequently twice refusing the Lord Chancellorship and hence a peerage. He also presided over the celebrated case of the reformer John Wilkes versus Lord Halifax, and was notable for the equity of his judgements.

He was born 16th August 1709 at Derby, second son of Robert Wilmot of Osmaston Hall and Ursula, a daughter and co-heiress of Sir Samuel Marow of Berkswell Hall, Warwickshire, which estate Sir John ultimately inherited. His great-grandfather, Sir Nicholas Wilmot of Osmaston Hall, was a younger son of Robert, of Chaddesden, ancestor of SIR EDWARD and SIR HENRY WILMOT (*q.q.v.*). His grandmother was Elizabeth, daughter and heiress of Edward Eardley of Eardley (Staffordshire) from whom Sir John derived his middle name. He was educated at Derby School and then at Lichfield, where he was a contemporary of Dr Johnson and David Garrick. He went up to Trinity Hall, Cambridge, going on to the Inner Temple, being called to the Bar in 1732.

He declined to be a KC, the Sergeantship and a seat in Parliament but, in 1755, was appointed a Justice of the King's Bench Division and was, exceptionally, simultaneously knighted. He narrowly escaped death while sitting at Worcester in 1757 when a stack of chimneys fell through the court's roof, killing several people including at least one of the advocates.

Sir John married, in 1743, Sarah, daughter of THOMAS RIVETT MP (*q.v.*) and had a son, John and a daughter who married Sir Sampson Gideon, 1st Lord Eardley, Britain's first Jewish Peer. John Eardley Wilmot refused a baronetcy and twice turned down peerages but, in 1821, his grandson and heir, JOHN (*q.v.*), was raised to a baronetcy in recognition of Sir John's highly distinguished services. He died at Berkswell Hall on 5th February 1792.

[Simpson, *op.cit.* III 673-79; DNB.]

WILMOT, Sir John Eardley, 1st Bt, FRS (1783-1847)

Sir John Eardley-Wilmot was the homonymous grandson of SIR JOHN EARDLEY WILMOT (*q.v.*) and was a distinguished and pioneering botanist and author of *An Abridgement of Blackstone's Commentaries*' (London, 1822); he was also a diplomat whose career was blighted by his dismissal in 1846 as Lieutenant Governor of Van Diemen's Land through his 'supposed indifference to the morals of the convicts under his charge' – for Van Diemen's Land was then a penal colony. He had resigned his North Warwickshire Parliamentary seat to take up this post in 1843 with some reluctance (for he had held it 11 years) and he died in Van Diemen's Land after his dismissal whilst waiting (in an unhealthy climate to say the least) for a passage home.

John Eardley-Wilmot was born on 21st February 1783 the only son of John Eardley Wilmot of Berkswell Hall (Warw.) who in 1812, had assumed the additional surname and arms of Eardley (of Audley, Staffordshire).

His mother, Frances, daughter of Samuel Sainthill, was his father's first wife, and John was an only son among four daughters. His father (1750-1815) was MP for Tiverton (Devon) 1776-84 and for Coventry (1784-96) and an FRS, FSA and an author; his second wife was Sarah Haslam.

The younger Sir John was educated at Lincoln's Inn following Harrow, and he was called to the bar in 1806. He married, firstly, on 21st May 1808, Elizabeth Emma (d.1818) daughter of Dr Caleb Hillier Parry of Bath, by whom he had six sons and two daughters. On 30th August 1819 he remarried Elizabeth (d.1869) daughter of Sir Robert Chester of Bush Hall (Herts) a putative descendant of SIMON DE CHESTER (*q.v.*), and had two more sons. He was made DCL (Oxon.), FRS, FLS and on 23rd August 1821 was created a baronet, dying at Hobart Town, Van Diemen's Land 3rd February 1847, being succeeded by his eldest son, Sir John Eardley Wilmot (1810-92) as second baronet. His second son, Frederick Marow Wilmot (1812-77) was a Major-General RA and his fourth, Arthur Parry Wilmot, CB (1815-86) rose to the rank of Vice-Admiral, RN.

[Burke, *Peerage* (1970) 2843-45; DNB.]

WILMOT, Sir Robert, 1st Bt (1708-1772)

Sir Robert Wilmot was the elder brother of Sir JOHN EARDLEY WILMOT (*q.v.*) and was the most senior civil servant in Ireland for more than

30 years, being Secretary to 12 successive Lords Lieutenant; he was also Secrertary to the Duke of Devonshire when the latter served as Lord Chamberlain. He was created a baronet 15th September 1772, dying two months later on 14th November.

Robert Wilmot was born about 1708, being son and heir of Robert Wilmot of Osmaston Hall, Derby, by Ursula, daughter and co-heiress of Sir Samuel Marow, and a descendant of Edward III. Robert's grandfather was Sir Nicholas Wilmot, Sergeant-at-Law and deputy recorder of Nottingham, second son of Robert Wilmot of Chaddesden, on whom the Osmaston estate was settled. Sir Nicholas' son, Robert (MP for Derby 1689-96) had built the Hall at Osmaston in the latter year, probably to designs of Sir William Wilson.

There is no apparent record of Sir Robert Wilmot, the subject of this memoir, having been married, although he had a 'reputed' son, Robert, another, William, and a daughter, Elizabeth. On his father's death the former inherited his baronetcy under the terms of a special remainder, having in 1760 been obliged to seek a variation in the family arms, being granted Wilmot *with a bordure engrailed argent.* Sir Robert's grandson, Rt. Hon, Sir Robert Wilmot, 3rd Bt. (1784-1841) was governor and C-in-C Ceylon (Sri Lanka, 1831-37) a notable botanist and a prolific political pamphleteer, opposed to his neighbour, the radical MP Sir Francis Burdett. He married the heiress of the Hortons of Catton Hall, assuming their surname and arms additionally to his own by Royal Licence in 1823; his successor did likewise in 1871, and the family moved to Catton, letting Osmaston Hall to Samuel Fox. The title became extinct in 1931.

[Burke, *Peerage* (1862) 1138; Foster, J., *Baronetage* (1882) 664; DRO D3155.]

WILMOT, Sir Sainthill Eardley, KCIE (1852-1929)

Sainthill Eardley-Wilmot was a forester by training and by trade, holding successively the posts of

Inspector General of Indian Forests (1903-09) and Commissioner of the UK Forestry Development Commission (1910-19) in which latter capacity he paved the way for the establishment of the Forestry Commission under an Act of 1911. In India he had, with the blessing and encouragement of the Viceroy, his distant cousin Lord Curzon, established the Imperial Forest Research Institute at Dehra Dun in 1906, a foundation which later developed into the Forest Research Institute (FRI) – the largest of its kind in the world – opened in 1929 a few weeks before Wilmot's death. He also wrote profusely, starting with a series of Silvicultural papers chiefly dealing with the care of Indian trees. These were followed, in 1906, by *Notes on the Influence of Forests on the Storage and Regulation of the Water Supply* – an ecological text book well ahead of its time in its conservationist outlook. In 1910 he published *Forest Life and Sport in India* which was regarded as a classic, and two years later followed it with *The Life of a Tiger* and *The Life of an Elephant*. He was made CIE in 1908 and knighted as KCIE on retirement.

Sainthill Eardley-Wilmot was a grandson of SIR JOHN EARDLEY-WILMOT 1st Bt. *(q.v.)* his father Augustus Hillier Eardley-Wilmot (d.1892) having been born at Chaddesden Hall in 1818, the sixth son. He became a police magistrate at Hobart, Tasmania (Australia), where Sainthill was born on 17th July 1852, the third of a further six sons and two daughters; his mother was Matilda Jessie (d.1904), daughter of a Hobart banker, John Dunn.

The family returned to London in 1855 and Sainthill was educated at East Budleigh, Devon, and after a forestry training in Germany, joined the Indian Forest Service – in which he remained all his life, bar three years (1900-03) in Burma, which he disliked intensely. He married twice, in 1884 to Emma Elizabeth (d.1890) daughter of George Casey of Winterbourne St Leonard's (Dorset) by whom he had a daughter, Helen Jessie, MBE (1885-1963). He remarried in 1891 Mabel Boisragon, daughter of William Henry Winter of Tunbridge Wells (Kent) to whom a further daughter was born, Mabel Iris, Mrs

G.H.Dummett. Sir Sainthill died on 13th November 1929.
[DNB; Burke, *Peerage*, (1970) 2844.]

WOODIWISS, Ald. Sir Abraham JP (1828-1884)

Sir Abraham Woodiwiss was a multi-millionnaire and philanthropist who made his fortune as a railway contractor. Amongst the many lucrative contracts was his first – the Evesham (Worcestershire) bridge over the Severn – and, much later, that to construct the Ilkeston-Egginton Junction extension of the Great Northern Railway in 1875-76, for which

Woodiwiss turned to his friend and fellow Derby Councillor ANDREW HANDYSIDE *(q.v.)* to supply the bridges, notably that over the Derwent at Little Chester and the highly ornamental one over Friar Gate. He also used his fortune to embellish the Borough, buying up land alongside the Markeaton Brook west of St James' Bridge and covering it over in order to produce a sinuous street called The Strand, embellished with a fine sweep of Classical buildings designed by Giles and Brookhouse. He created the Strand Arcade in imitation of London's Burlington Arcade, the once exclusively gated Hartington Street (the houses mainly designed by George Henry Sheffield), funded the rebuilding of the Mechanics' Institute and gave land for an extension of the Arboretum. His influence and generosity was such that he, uniquely in the 19th century, served two terms in succession as Mayor of Derby, 1880-82, during the first of which he acted as the Borough's host to the Prince of Wales when he visited the Royal Agricultural Show on Osmaston Hall's park.

Abraham Woodiwiss was born at Belper on 2nd October 1828, son of George Woodiwiss of Duffield (1798-1866), fourth of seven sons, by a daughter of James Bunting. The family lived on Hopping Hill, George being a stone mason at a quarry on Holbrook Moor. The family had been previously at Bonsall, George being fifth in descent from Henry Woodiwiss (b.1640). Several relatives were subsequently employed by Abraham in his contracting firm including Samuel, his eldest brother. The latter's sons, John and Walter, and John's son, another Walter (1871-1948) all worked for Abraham and lived in Derby.

Woodiwiss received an elementary education before joining a railway construction firm, learning the business and frugally husbanding his slender resources before setting up on his own – minor contracts completed within time leading to more lucrative ones. Not long after starting up he took into partnership George Benton, trading thereafter as Benton & Woodiwiss. Locally, they also built the North Staffordshire Railway's line from Stoke-upon-Trent into Derby. He married at Duffield on 30th October 1848 Emma Newton, daughter of Newton Wright of Crich and they (in true Woodiwiss fashion) had seven sons and two daughters. His eldest son Abraham (1855-1912) was also twice Mayor of Derby serving in 1888 and 1901. In March 1866, Abraham, senior, settled in Derby and in 1875 was elected to a seat on the Litchurch Local Board, transferring to the Borough in 1878 as Councillor for Litchurch Ward when Derby absorbed the old Local Broard on being made a County Borough that year. He was appointed an alderman in 1881, being knighted in 1883. He purchased The Pastures, Littleover, dying there on 24th February 1884. His fifth son, George (1856-1906) was Mayor of Bath in 1897. A great-nephew, Samuel Henry Woodiwiss (1899-1989) was born in Derby (to Samuel, of Belper, (1860-1902), a son of Sir Abraham's eldest brother) and became a teacher but had also played for Derby County in goal before moving to Hereford United; he was later headmaster of a school at Winchester and was first principal of the Teacher Training College at Alsager (Cheshire), later retiring to Usk (Mon.)

[MMD.I.51-56; Higginson, M., *The Friar Gate Line* (Derby 1989) 20-22; *D. Telegraph* 18/5/1989; information from several kinsmen; Burke, *Landed Gentry* (1898) II. 1635; Craven (1988) 178-179.]

WRIGHT, Joseph, ARA (1734-1797)

Joseph Wright was one of the most important British painters of the Georgian Age, whose reputation, however, was for nearly two centuries undeservedly in eclipse, being written off as merely a talented provicial, simply because he huffily refused election to the Royal Academy and subsequently declined to live and work in London. Yet, as the man who immortalised in paint with great flair and honesty many of the intellectuals and creative men who – partly through the touchstone of the Lunar Society – fuelled the burgeoning industrial revolution, has a crucial place, not only in the history of art, but in that of his era. Wright also, in an incomparable

series of paintings of scientific subjects starting with *A Philosopher Lecturing Upon an Orrery* of 1765 (commissioned earlier by his patron EARL FERRERS *q.v.*), including *An Experiment with a Bird in the Air Pump* (1768) and *The Alchymist Discovering Phosphorus* (1771), captured the fascination and awe which the upsurge in interest in science and natural philosophy was beginning to engender generally. A further series of paintings of industrial subjects – iron forges, blacksmiths' shops, Arkwright's Mill and so forth – made the link firmly with the industrial revolution and brought his subject matter close to the contemporary concept of The Sublime.

Likewise, Wright's paintings of *Mount Vesuvius in Eruption* – linked firmly to the geological interests of JOHN WHITEHURST *(q.v.)* in a celebrated letter home to his brother Richard from Italy (which he visited 1774-75) – forms the starting point in a series revelling in the widening understanding of the natural world, especially as seen and understood by his friends Whitehurst and ERASMUS DARWIN *(q.v.)*. Views of Matlock High Tor – subject of a stratigraphical section in Whitehurst's *Inquiry* (1778) – studies of convoluted formations of rocks and other striking landscapes are clearly based on sites favoured

by Darwin and his friends. The aesthetically challenging painting *Rocks with Waterfall* (1772) for instance seems plainly to have been painted at Darwin's request to show a particular geological formation rather than a piece of classic scenery. Many of Wright's paintings also revolve around central or obscured sources of light and moonlit landscapes (and even moonlit portraits in the case of a pair of *Mr & Mrs William Hayley*), and scenes of people with inflated bladders seem to link directly to Whitehurst's treatise *On the Ventilation of Rooms, on Chimnies and Garden Stoves*, the first part of which contains a disquisition on the properties of heated air, citing prominently the use of bladders in related experiments.

Other paintings seem to highlight the potential conflict between the spiritual and the scientific (a problem also grappled with by Whitehurst in the first edition of his *Inquiry*), whilst he was constantly striving to perfect his landscape techniques, as in his late (1793) *Rydal Waterfall,* where he wrote to a friend about the subtle effects he was attempting to capture. All through this rich and varied *oeuvre* he continued to paint portraits – his bread and butter – not only of the luminaries of science but also of all sorts of local characters, from members of the Gentry to humbler folk, and also people from many other parts of the Midlands. Some classic double portraits or conversation pieces like those of *Mr & Mrs P.P.Burdett* (1765), *Mr & Mrs Thomas Coltman* (1772) and *Mr & Mrs d'Ewes Coke and their kinsman Daniel Parker Coke* (*c.*1781) are amongst the very finest such subjects of the era.

Joseph Wright was born at 28 Iron Gate, Derby (since demolished) on 3rd September 1734, third son of John Wright (1697-1767) one of the Borough's superior attorneys, and dubbed 'Equity' by his contemporaries due to his reputation for fair dealing. He served as Town Clerk of Derby 1756-65, being 'a good Whig', whose chief clients were the Gisbornes. The family was descended from Richard Wright of Seighford (Staffordshire) a yeoman living in 1496, and they had improved their lot through a succession of country parsons, including the artist's great-grandfather Rev. John Wright (1640-81), vicar of

Seighford and rector of Longford (Derbys), the latter preferment bringing the patronage of the Cokes, later shared with JOSEPH PICKFORD *(q.v.)* – a close friend of the artist's – as was that of Lord Ferrers. Wright's cousin was Dr Richard Wright FRS (1739-86) a London physician who married the heiress of Sir James Gray, 2nd Bt. of Denhill (Kent), and Equity Wright's second son also became a distinguished physician, and colleague of Erasmus Darwin's. Wright's mother was Hannah, daughter and heiress of another attorney, Edward Brookes (1664-1736) through whose family Wright became connected to the core of the oligarchy that controlled the Borough. The family were also connected, through the Gells of Wirksworth, with a whole network of local Gentry families.

Joseph Wright was educated at Derby School where he was a contemporary of ROBERT BAGE *(q.v.)* and the father of REV. CHARLES STEAD HOPE *(q.v.)*. His elder brothers John (1729-98), an attorney, and Richard (1730-1804), the doctor, were also there. In 1751 he went to study under Thomas Hudson in London for two years returning for two more years from 1756 and, it seems, he spent some time studying in the studio of Allan Ramsay as well. From about 1759 he commenced his career, painting the great and good of Derby and those of various other East Midland and Northern towns.

Wright married, covertly, at Ault Hucknall on 19th July 1773 Anne (Hannah), daughter of Joseph Swift of Staveley, a lead miner and part-time lead merchant whose brother John, a Matlock yeoman, had enacted a deed concerning property in Derby before 'Equity' Wright in March 1739. Thus, although the Wrights played the marriage down, (Joseph Swift's calling being thought a trifle *infra dig.* for an attorney's son) the families had been in contact for over 30 years. Anne's great-great-neice was the mother of the 19th century Derbyshire artist George Turner (1841-1910).

The Wrights left for Italy shortly after the wedding, Joseph only apprising his family of the marriage by letter once they had left. Their first child, Anna Romana, was born in Rome in 1774,

and there were two other daughters and two sons, John (1781-98) and Joseph (1786-1830), the latter being a missionary who settled in Nova Scotia and whose son, Dr Alfred Wright, was the last of Joseph's male posterity, dying in Edinburgh in 1907.

The Wrights lived from 1772 to 1793 at Old St Helen's House on a lease from William Fitzherbert, one of his patrons, and brother of LORD ST HELEN'S *(q.v.)*. Here Anne died in 1790, but in 1793 he moved into Whitehurst's former home at 27 Queen Street – also the childhood home of JOHN FLAMSTEED FRS *(q.v.)* – where the artist died on 29th August 1797, 'One of the most original, wide-ranging and consistently interesting 18th-century artists.'
[Nicholson, B., *Joseph Wright, Painter of Light*, 2 Vols. (London, 1968); Egerton, J., *et al*, *Wright of Derby* (London, 1990); Wallis, J., *Joseph Wright of Derby* (Derby, 1997); Bemrose, W., *Life and Works of Joseph Wright* (Derby, 1885) and Craven, (1996) *op.cit.* 53-70.]

WYLD, Frederick Henry (1900-1976)

Fred Wyld was an Olympic Bronze medallist in cycling, coming third in the 50km track event at the 1924 (Paris) Olympic Games. He won 14 national cycling championships, five in 1928 alone, and his active career as a sports cyclist lasted until 1930 when he joined the ranks of the Derby Borough Police Force, retiring in 1960. He had two brothers, Ralph (Arthur) and Percy, both of whom were also in the British National Cycling team for the 1928 Olympics, when the latter, too, won bronze.

Frederick Henry Wyld was born in Derby in June 1900, one of three brothers. Ralph opened a cycle shop at 61 Nottingham Road in 1927 (moving to No. 95 in 1933) and his son Ralph (Paul) Wyld continued the proprietorship of this locally well-known establishment until 1995. Percy was of 20 Kingsley Street in 1935, the Directory of this date adding an 'e' on to his surname but not to that of his siblings. Frederick Wyld lived at Dovedale, Valley Road, Littleover, and died in April 1976.

[DET 26/1/1995; Watson, S., *Mickleover and Littleover* (Derby, 1993) 70.]

YATES, Benjamin (c.1709-1778)

Benjamin Yates was a maker of ornamental wrought-ironwork, succeeding his mentor ROBERT BAKEWELL *(q.v.)* (whose foreman he was for many years) on the latter's death in 1752, subsequently moving the workshop from Oakes's Yard, St Peter's Street to Friar Gate, near St Werburgh's Church Yard. His skills were hardly less inferior to those of Bakewell, except that his best work was done in the Neo-Classical age, for example his superb screen and gates for Robert Adam at Kedleston Hall, which style left far less scope for the baroque and Rococo exuberance in bar, curl and repoussé work in which Bakewell had felt free to indulge. The consequent sparseness and severity of much of his output strikes the senses less, relying almost solely on quality of execution and impeccable proportion, which may perhaps explain why Yates's name is less well-known than it deserves to be.

Yates was probably born at Brentford, Middlesex, but his father was William Yates of Derby, born 1678. He was almost certainly also a gatemaker, and he was either away from Derby in 1710, the date of the first relevant Poll Book, or was not a burgess. He may have been working at Hampton Court at this time. The family, although an old one in Derby, going back to a William Yates of St Peter's Parish of 1600, do not seem to have been particularly prosperous, for William's grandfather, another William (1600-72) was taxed on but one hearth in 1670. Benjamin's grandfather was this William's fourth son, John (1642-81).

Benjamin seems to have been apprenticed in London (or served there as a journeyman) with the eminent smith Jean Montigny who had significantly worked with Tijou at Hampton Court and later on his own account at Canons, Middlesex, for the 1st Duke of Chandos; it was Montigny's workshop on the Edgeware Road that is said to have inspired the variations called *The Harmonious Blacksmith* by Handel, who

often played at Canons – and the composer was also drawn in old age at Hudson's studio by JOSEPH WRIGHT *(q.v.)*. In his will Montigny left Benjamin Yates and his sister £10 each; it seems to confirm therefore that their father was indeed also a smith, or possibly a gardener, working for some time in the metropolis on some major project like Hampton Court, and that his children were born nearby; several Yateses are recorded at Brentford. Benjamin married at St Alkmund's on 21st May 1730 Lydia Hodgkinson (d.1789) and probably entered Bakewell's *atelier* at about the same time. His death occurred in Friar Gate in February 1778 and he was buried at St Werburgh's on the 17th.

Yates was succeeded in his business by his eldest son, William (1731-1800), who was responsible for the beautifully proportioned gates at Darley Hall, Derby, among others. With William, however, the business ended, the craft, seemingly, with it, until revived by William Haslam *(q.v.* EDWIN HASLAM) more than a generation later, for of William's sons, David became a miller and William was a 'fireman for glazing and burning china' at the Derby China Factory. Benjamin and Lydia had four other sons, of whom Joseph became a gardener, probably working at Calke Abbey. There were also five daughters, one of whom, Lydia, married Thomas Kirk, a notable Derby cabinet maker.

[Information courtesy Edward Saunders; local parish registers & Poll Books.]

YORKE, Henry (1772-1813)

Henry Yorke was a revolutionary who claimed, with at least partial justification, to have taken part in three major political upheavals before he was 22: The American (he had to be under 10!), the French and in the Netherlands. In 1792 he propounded black emancipation, although his first pamphlet, published not long before, had adumbrated precisely the opposite! He then went to Paris 'madly in love with Liberty', witnessing Louis XVI's fateful appearance before The Convention, and he was a member of the British Club there before leaving, in a hurry, convinced that his arrest was imminent.

He returned to Britain via Holland and joined a radical club in Derby. In 1793 he was sent by its committee to Sheffield to assist a similar group, being arrested there after delivering himself of a rabble-rousing oration, and was convicted of sedition at York, being sentenced to two years in gaol, bound over for seven years and fined £100. He was not, in the event, released until 1798, during which time his opinions had moderated to some extent (thus establishing the efficacy of a prison sentence for some offenders at least!). He wrote letters to *The Star* under the *nom-de-plume* 'Alfred' or 'Galgaucus' and later became part-proprietor of the *True Briton,* revisiting France in 1802.

He was still sufficiently combative to have had to be restrained from fighting a duel with Sir Francis Burdett Bt. of Foremark, the radical MP, and in 1801 and 1811 issued synopses of lectures delivered in London on political and historical topics. His last undertaking – mainly done in order to provide some income – was to prepare a new, enlarged, edition of John Campbell's *Lives of British Admirals.*

Henry Yorke was born Henry Redhead in the West Indies in 1772, but was brought up from an early age in Little Eaton and Derby, where he lived for a time after his revolutionary travels. It may be that he had family connections in Little Eaton, otherwise the reasons for his choice of domicile are unclear, although these have so far evaded research. His education in not known, although it was of sufficient quality for him to have qualified as a barrister at the Inner Temple from 1801. About the time of his visit to France he assumed the surname of Yorke (which may, of course, have been a family one) and he was always subsequently so known.

His stint in gaol was not all bad, for whilst incarcerated in Dorchester Castle he met the daughter of Mr Andrews, the Keeper (governor), and in 1800 married her, leaving, at his death in Chelsea on 18th January 1813, four children. He was the author of several polemical works of which the best was probably *Thoughts on Civil Government* published in 1800.

[DNB.]

Index classified by callings

Most people mentioned in the main text were famous for more than one area of endeavour, e.g., Sir Francis Seymour Haden, who was knighted for his work as a surgeon, yet was more famous as an etcher. Therefore what follows has a slightly arbitary nature, in that I have classified everyone but once. Certain categories are also a lot more general than others.

Academics
Cooper, Sir William Mansfield (1903-1992) 59
Hobson, Ernest William (1856-1933) 116

Antiquaries
Bemrose, William II (1831-1908) 36
Cox, Rev. John Charles (1843-1919) 60
Degge, Simon (1694-1729) 70
Hope, Sir W.H. St John (1854-1919) 120

Architects
Aiton, Norah see Aiton, Sir John 15
Blore, Edward (1787-1879) 42
Currey, Percy Heylin (1864-1942) 65
Denstone, James (1724-1780) 71
Duesbury, Henry (1806-1872) 77
Eaton, George Morley (d.1940) 79
Finney, John (1729-1804) 84
Fryer, Edward (1852-1883) 96
Leaper, Richard (1759-1838) 130
Mason, John (1794-1847) 142
Moneypenny, George, II, (1768-1830) see Moneypenny, George (d.1807) 143
Pickford, Joseph (1734-1782) 160
Price, John (1795-1859) 166
Stevens, Henry Isaac (1806-1873) 192

Artists
Barber, Thomas (1771-1843) 27
Bassano, Francis (1675-1746) 29
Birchall, William Minshall (b.1884) 41
Boultbee, John (1753-1812) 44
Deacon, Augustus Oakley (1819-1899) 69
Foster, Edward (1762-1864) 91
Gadsby, William Hippon (1845-1925) 97
Gamble, John Curzon 97
Gresley, Cuthbert (1876-1963) 103
Gresley, Frank (1855-1930) 103
Gresley, Harold (1892-1969) 103
Gresley, James Stephen (1829-1908) 103
Haden, Sir Francis Seymour (1818-1910) 104
Legge, Phyllis Mary 131
Moore, Henry (1776-1848) 144
Rawlinson, James (1789-1848) 167
Rayner, Louise (1832-1924) 167
Rayner family see Louise Rayner 167
Smith, John Raphael (1751-1812) 185
Smith, Emma (b.1787) see Smith, John Raphael 186
Smith, John Rubens (1775-1847) see Smith, John Raphael 186
Smith, Thomas (d.1767) see Smith, John Raphael 185
Soar, Rebecca (1895-1947) 187
Spry, Constance (1886-1960) 190
Sutherland, Graham Vivian (1905-1980) 198
Townsend, Ernest (1880-1944) 206
Ward, James (1769-1859) 200
Wright, Joseph (1734-1797) 224

Astrologer
Allestrey, Richard (b.1577) 161

Astronomers
Cokayne, Rev. William (1717-1798) 57
Flamsteed, Rev. John (1646-1719) 88

Authors
Bage, Robert (1728-1801) 23
Irish, EIizabeth May (d.1992) 124
Jerram, Jane E. (c1810-1873) 126
Mozley, Anne (1809-1891) 146
Taylor, Helen Louise (b.1850) 201

Aviation (see also engineers, industrialists)
Jeffs, George James (1900-1996) 126

Rolls, Hon. Chartes Stuart (1877-1910) 175

Bankers
Crompton, Abraham (1648-1725) 61
Crompton, Samuel (*c*1712-1782) 62
Evans, Thomas (1723-1814) 82
Heath, John (1705-1782) 114

Botanists
Whitaker, Joseph (1813-1894) 214
Wilmot, Sir John Eardley, Bt. (1783-1847) 221

Brewers
Allsopp, Sir Henry, Lord Hindlip (1811-1887) 20
Bass, Michael Thomas (1799-1884) 28
Clarke, Thomas (1814-1877) 55

Cartographer
Burdett, Peter Perez (1734-1793) 48

Cavaliers
Allestrey, William (1598-1655) 17
Bate, Thomas (d.1643) 30
Firebrace, Sir Henry (1619-1691) 85
Touchet, James, Earl of Castlehaven
    (d.1684) 205

Ceramic Pioneers/Artists
Billingsley, William (1758-1828) 39
Bloor, Robert (1778-1846) 42
Duesbury, William I (1725-1786) 77
Duesbury, William II (1751-1796) 78
Edwards, William (b.1796) 80
Hancock, Sampson (1817-1895) 107
Holzendorff, Georg Count v. (b.1838) 119
Kean, Michael (*c*1760-1823) 128
Litherland, William (1803-1883) 133
Phillips, Edward (1817-1881) 159
Planche, Andrew (1728-1805)
Rivett, Thomas (1713-1763) 169
Webster, Moses (1792-1870) 211
Wheeldon, William (1789-1847) 213
Whitaker,John (*c*1804-1874) 214

Churchmen
Bingham, Rev. John (1607-1689) 40
Cantrell, Rev. Henry (1685-1773) 50
Chaddesden, Ralph de (d.1266) 52

Chaddesden, Henry de (d.1354) see Chaddesden,
    Ralph de 52
Cotton, Rev. John (1584-1652) 59
Derby, Hugh de (d. by 1179) 72
Fisher, Most Rev. Geoffrey Francis (1887-
    1972) 85
Gretton, Very Rev. George (*c*1755-1820) 104
Ham, Very Rev. Herbert (1869-1965) 105
Hodgson, Very Rev. Francis (1781-1852) 118
Hope, Rev. Charles Stead (1762-1841) 120
Mozley, Rev. Prof. James Bowling (1817-1878) 146
Pearce, Rt. Rev. Edmund Courtenay (1870-
    1935) 158
Richardson, Ven .John Farquhar (1904-1991)
    see Richardson, Arthur 170
Timms, Ven. George (1910-1997) 202

Civil Servants
Bateman, Sir A.E. (1844-1929) 31
Bateman, Edward Lewis (1834-1909) 31
Cox, Sir Christopher William Machell (1899-
    1982) 60
Wilmot, Sir Robert, Bt. (1708-1772) 222

Clock & Instrument Makers
Bregazzi, Samuel (1782-1841) 45
Davis, John (1810-1873) 68
Stenson, John (1747-1817) 191
Whitehurst, John II (1761-1834) 216
Whitehurst, John III (1788-1855) 217

Colonial Administrators
Gawlor, George (1795-1869) 97
Gisborne, Hon. William (1825-1898) 101
Mundy, Sir Robert (1813-1892) 149
Rivett-Carnac, Sir James, Bt (1784-1846) 171
Shaw, Sir John (1894-1982) 181
Shore, Sir John, Lord Teignmouth (1751-
    1834) 183

Community Leaders
Dhindsa, Nirmal Singh (1933-1996) 74
Najeeb, Mohommed (1947-1991) 150
Petty, Elizabeth (1875-1947) 158

Courtesan
Shore, Jane (d.1527) 182

Craftsmen

Bakewell, Robert (1682-1752) 26

Brown, Richard (1736-1816) 46

Chatterton, John I (1742-1800) 54

Denstone, Abraham (1687-1753) see Denstone, James 71

Emes, John (1763-1808) 81

Haslam, Edwin (1843-1913) 112

Haslam, William (1805-1878) see Haslam, Edwin 112

Mansfield, Isaac (*c*1670-1740) 141

Needham, Joshua (1689-1735) 150

Yates, Benjamin (*c*1709-1778) 227

Yates, William, see Yates, Benjamin 227

Criminal

Bullock, Noah (1644-1687) 47

Diplomats

Fitzherbert, Alleyne, Lord St. Helens (1753-1839) 87

Howe, Sir Robert George (1893-1981) 121

Dissenters

Madeley, Rev. Edward (1778-1827) 140

Pike, Rev. John Gregory Deodatus (1784-1854) 162

Eccentric

Eddowes. Michael (1903-1993) 80

Educators

Allestrey, Rev. Prof. Richard (1619-1681) 17

Bater, Rev. Alfred Brenchley (d.1933) 32

Fisher, Phyllis Anne (1913-1994) 86

Hawkins, Helen (1888-1985) 112

James, Eric John Francis, Lord James of Rusholme (1909-1992) 124

Roe, William Robert (1843-1920) 175

Simmonds, Thomas Charles (d.1912) 184

Engineers (Non-railway)

Bell, Sir John Ferguson (1856-1937) 33

Fox, Sir Charles (1810-1874) 93

Fox, Sir Charles Douglas (1840-1921) 93

Fox, Sir Francis (1844-1927) 93

Fox, James (1760-1835) 94

Handyside, Andrew (1805-1887) 107

Harvey-Bailey, Alec (1920-1997) 110

Harvey-Bailey, Robert W. (d.1986) see Harvey-Bailey, Alec 110

Hobson, Harold (1891-1973) 116

Holmes. Kenneth Soar (1912-1995) 119

Otter, Victor Charles (1914-1996) 154

Royce, Sir Frederick Henry Bt (1863-1933) 176

Rubbra, Arthur Alexander (1903-1982) 178

Sorocold, George (1668-1738) 186

Sylvester, Charles (1774-1828) 200

Warwick, John Francis (1905-1996), see Warwick, John Alfred 210

Entertainers

Moult, Edward Walker (1926-1986) 145

Pountain, Ronald Dennis (1913-1993) 165

Freemason

Pigot, John Hollis (d.1794) 161

Heroes

Hewitt, Henry Richardson (d.1912) 114

Nightingale, Florence (1820-1910) 151

Historian

Hutton, William 123

Industrialists

Aiton, Sir John (1864-1950) 14

Bemrose, Sir H.H. (1827-1911) 34

Bemrose, Sir Max (1904-1986) 35

Bemrose, Wiliam (1792-1880) 35

Bingham, Sir J.E., Bt. (1839-1915) 40

Boott, Kirk (1790-1837) 43

Chambers, Thomas (1660-1726) 52

Crompton, George (1823-1897) 62

Eastwood, Reuben (1833-1877) 79

Godber, Frederick, Lord Godber (1888-1976) 101

Hampshire, Frederick Wiliam (1863-1941) 106

Haslam, Sir Alfred Seale (1844-1927) 110

Hives, Ernest Walter, Lord Hives (1886-1965) 114

Ley, Sir Francis, Bt. (1846-1916) 131

Lombe, John (*c*1693-1722) 135

Lombe, Sir Thomas (1685-1739) 136

Messervy, Sir Godfrey (1924-1995) 143

Oakes, James (1816-1868) 152

Robinson, Philip (1914-1997) 173

Smith, Sir John (1828-1897) 186

Stanley, Sir Albert, Lord Ashfield (1874-1948) 191

Stevens, Henry (1856-1934) 193
Strutt, Jedediah (1726-1797) 194
Tissington, Anthony (1715-1776) 203
Wakefield, Charles Cheers, Viscount Wakefield
    (1859-1941) 208
Woodiwiss, Sir Abraham (1828-1884) 223

Journalists
Barker, Sir H.H. (1898-1989) 28
Hobson, Sir Oscar Rudolph (1886-1961) 117
Tomasiuk, Irene (1953-1996) 203

Landowners
Allestrey, Elias de (d.1270) 16
Bateman, Sir Hugh, Bt. (1756-1824) 31
Ferrers, Robert, Earl of Derby (d.1139) 84
Mundy, Francis Noel Clarke (1739-1815) 147

Landscaper
Emes, William (1729-1803) 81

Lawyers
Degge, Sir Simon (1612-1703) 70
Nichols, Col. Sir Edward H. (1911-1992) 150
Parker, Thomas, Earl of Macclesfield (1666-
    1732) 155
Wilmot Sir John Eardley (1709-1792) 221

Lords Mayor of London
Cokayne, Francis (1688-1767) 57
Mundy, Sir John (d.1538) 149

Martyr
Wast, Joan (1532-1555) 210

Medical Men
Bent, Thomas (1792-1859) 38
Browne, Sir Geroge Buckston (1850-1945) 47
Butter, William (1726-1805) 49
Chauncey, William (d.1736) 55
Gisborne, Thomas (c1733-1806) 99
Linacre, Rev. Thomas (c1460-1524) 133
Luce, Sir Richard (1867-1952) 138
Ogle, William (1824-1905) 153
Osborne, Ritter Jacob (1808-1851) 153
Shore, Sir John (1616-1680) 183
Wade, Sir Willoughby Francis (1827-1906)
    208

Willoughby, Percival (1596-1685) 218
Wilmot, Sir Edward, Bt. (1693-1786) 220

Military Men
Aethelwulf (d.871) 14
Bambrigge, Gen. Sir Philip (1786-1862) 24
Cokayne, Col. Thomas (1697-1749) 57
Gell, Col. Sir John, Bt. (1593-1671) 98
Lilly, Col. Harold Hutchinson (1888-1954) 132
Shaw, Lt. Gen. Sir Frederick (1861-1942) 180
Whinyates, Gen. Sir Edward (1782-1865) 213

Mintmaster
Derby, Walkelin de 72

Musicians
Bassano, Christopher (1679-1745) 29
Binge, Ronald (1910-1979) 40
Cummings, Maria 65
Denby, Charles (c1735-1793) 70
Denby, William (d.1771) see Denby, Charles 70
Downes, Ralph William (1904-1997) 75
Fletcher, Percy Eastman (1879-1932) 89
Fritche, George Christopher (1769-1835) 96
Hawkridge, Douglas (1907-1983) 113

Naval Commanders
Moresby, Adml. Sir Fairfax (1787-1877) 144
Mundy, Adml. Sir George (1805-1885) 148
Rivett-Carnac, Adml. James (1891-1970) 171

Parliamentarians
Alibon, Robert 16
Allestrey, William (1641-1699) 17
Archdale, Richard (1746-1824) 21
Bagnoid, John (1643-1698) 24
Baker, Philip J. Noel, Lord Noel-Baker (1889-
    1982) 25
Bell, Richard (1859-1930) 33
Bennet, Gervase (1611-1660) 37
Benson, Sir George (1889-1973) 38
Cavendish, Gen. Hon. Henry F.C. (1789-1873) 51
Chester, Simon de 55
Coke, Daniel Parker (1745-1825) 58
Collins, Sir William Job (1859-1946) 58
Crompton, Sir Samuel, Bt. (1785-1848) 63
Dalton, John (1610-1679) 66
Drage, Geoffrey (1860-1955) 76

Evans, Sir Thomas William, Bt. (1821-1892) 83
Flint, Abraham John (1903-1971) 91
Green, Albert (1874-1941) 102
Harcourt, Sir William Vernon (1823-1904) 108
Heyworth, Lawrence (1786-1872) 115
Howell, Charles Alfred (1905-1974) 122
Lightbown, Sir David (1932-1995) 133
Mac Dermott, Niall (1915-1996) 139
Plimsoll, Samuel (1824-1898) 164
Raphael, Sir H.Herbert, Bt. (1859-1924) 166
Raynes, William R. (1871-1966) 168
Reid, William Allan (1865-1952) 169
Roberts, Charles Henry (1865-1959) 172
Roe, Sir Thomas, Lord Roe (1832-1923) 174
Thomas, James H. (1874-1949) 201
Touchet, John, 6th Lord Audley (c1430-1498) 204
Tutbury, Thomas de 207
Wilcock, Clifford Arthur Bowman (1898-1962) 218

Philanthropist
Crowshaw, Richard (1561-1631) 64

Philosopher
Spencer, Herbert (1820-1903) 188

Photographic Pioneers
Abney, Sir William de Wivelslie (1843-1920) 13
Keene, Richard (1825-1894) 128

Poets
Allestrey, James (1654-1686) 16
Bancroft, Thomas (c1600-1658) 27
Gisborne, John (1770-1851) 100

Publishers
Drewry, Samuel (d.1765) 77
Hobson, William (1825-1897) 118
Pike, Eliza Maria (1832-1905) 161
Sautoy, Peter Francis du (1912-1995) 179

Radicals
Gisborne, Rev. Thomas (1758-1846) 100
Hallowes, Nathaniel (1582-c1670) 105
Sanders, Co. (Sir) Thomas (1610-1695) 178
Strutt, Edward, Lord Belper (1801-1880) 193
Yorke, Henry (1772-1813) 227

Railwaymen
Allport, Sir James J. (1811-1892) 19
Charles, Alexis Leon (1851-1926) 53
Clayton, Thomas Gething (b.1880) 56
Deeley, Richard Mountford (1855-1944) 69
Fowler, Sir Henry (1870-1938) 92
Jarvis, Ronald (1911-1994) 125
Johnson, Samuel Waite (1831-1912) 127
Kirtley, Matthew (1813-1873) 129
Warwick, John Alfred (1821-1896) 209

Rebels
Babington, Anthony (1561-1586) 22
Touchet, Sir James, 7th Lord Audley (c1465-1497) 204
Wheeldon, Alice (1867-1919) 212

Royalty
Aethelflaeda (d.918) 13
Stuart, HRH Prince Charles Edward (1720-1788) 197

Scientists
Bemrose, Henry Howe Arnold (1857-1939) 34
Darwin, Erasmus (1731-1802) 66
Hobson, Alfred Dennis (1901-1974) 116
Mawe, John (1766-1829) 142
Pickering, Rev. John (1706-1790) 159
Shirley, Washington, 5th Earl Ferrers (1727-1778) 182
Simpson, Sir George Clarke (1878-1965) 184
Strutt, William (1756-1830) 193
Whitehurst, John I (1713-1788) 215
Wilmot, Sir Sainthill Eardley (1852-1929) 222

Sculptors
Coffee, William John (1773-c1846) 56
Moneypenny, George (1738-1807) 144
Pope, Ronald (1920-1997) 165
Robinson, Joseph Barlow (1821-1883) 173

Socialite
D6cker, Norah, Lady (1905-1983) 74

Sportsmen
Bloomer, Steve (1874-1938) – Soccer 41
Carter, Horatio Stratton (1913-1994) – Soccer 50

Craven, Hugh Bertie (1862-1944) – Field 61
Crooks, Samuel Dickinson (1908-1981) –
  Soccer 63
Curgenven, William Grafton (1841-1910) –
  Cricket 65
Francis, Percy Olivant (d.1947) – Soccer 95
Hampshire, David Alan (1918-1990) – Motor
  racing (see Hampshire, F.W.) 106
Jobey, George (1886-1962) – Soccer 126
Loates, Thomas (1867-1909) – Racing 135
Loates, Samuel (d.1932) – Racing (see Loates,
  Thomas) 135
Loates, Charles – Racing (see, Loates, Thomas) 135
Longland, Sir Jack (1905-1993) – Climbing 137
Parnell, Reg (1911-1964) – Motor racing 157
Richardson, Arthur Walker (1907-1983) –
  Cricket 169
Rostron, Joseph (1910-1993) – Boxing 176
Sulley, Arthur Lindsay (1906-1994) – Rowing 199
Thompson, Eric (1927-1996) – Cycling 202
Weston, Rev. Walter (1861-1940) – Climbing 211
Wyld, Frederick Henry (1900-1976) – Cycling 226

Theatrical

Bennett, Joan Sterndale (1914-1996) 37
Dexter John (1926-1990) 73
Lloyd, Kevin (1949-1998) 134
Mansfield, Richard (1857-1907) 141
Rice, Joan (1930-1997) 169

Trades & Businessmen

Ann, Sir Edwin (1852-1913) 20
Bowring, Sir Charles Clement (1844-1907) 44
Bradshaw, Anthony 45
Chatterton, John 11 (1771-1857) 54
Crump, Thomas (1800-1870) 64
Doughty, Samuel (1626-1710) 75
Fletcher, Richard (d.1607) 90
Franceys, Henry (1692-1747) 94
Harrison, Thomas Cuthbert (1906-1986) 109

VC Winners

Hudson, Charles Edward (1892-1956) 122
Humpstone, Robert (1832-1884) 123
Rivers, Jacob (1881-1915) 170
Unwin, Edward W. (1864-1950) 267
Wilmot, Sir Henry, Bt. (1831-1901) 220

There are 340 main biographies in the book, with more than fifteen subsidiary ones.

Of the foregoing:
20 were peers (3 for life only)
13 were baronets
49 were knights
22 were women (with 2 other subsidiary lives)

The earliest life is that of Ealdorman Aethelwulf; the latest is Kevin Lloyd.